CONFESSIONS OF A
GREENPEACE DROPOUT

*The making of a
sensible environmentalist*

Patrick Moore

Beatty Street
Publishing Inc.

Also by Patrick Moore:
Trees are the Answer

Copyright © 2010 Patrick Moore - Revised and Updated, 2013
All Rights reserved.
Published by Beatty Street Publishing Inc.
Printed by Lightning Source

Library and Archives Canada Cataloguing in Publication

Moore, Patrick Albert, 1947-
          Confessions of a Greenpeace dropout : the making of a sensible environmentalist / Patrick Moore.

Includes bibliographical references and index.
ISBN 978-0-9864808-2-9

          1. Moore, Patrick Albert, 1947-. 2. Greenpeace Foundation.
3. Environmentalists--Canada--Biography. 4. Conservationists--
Canada--Biography. I. Title.

GE56.M67A3 2010   333.72092   C2010-906814-9

For ordering information contact:
Beatty Street Publishing Inc.
4068 West 32nd Avenue, Vancouver, B.C., Canada V6S 1Z6
Phone: (604) 222-3393
Internet: www.ecosense.me
E-mail: pmoore@ecosense.me

Book design by Pablo Mandel / CircularStudio.com

This book is dedicated to the environment and
its miracles of nature that provide food, shelter,
clothing, transportation, communication,
and the energy to power our world.

It is also a tribute to the people who work in fields
and forests, on the sea and underground,
in labs, factories and power plants, making
civilization a continuing reality.

May we all follow a path toward a
sustainable future on our beautiful Earth.

You can't expect anyone to believe everything you say, and you can't expect everyone to believe anything you say.

Here's what I believe.

—Patrick Moore

Acknowledgements

I would like to acknowledge the many teachers and mentors I have had the privilege to study under and to receive wisdom from over the years. These include Dr. Oscar Sziklai, Dr. Hamish Kimmins, Dr. Buzz (C.S.) Holling, Dr. Vladmir Krajina, Professor Alistair Lucas, Professor Michael Goldberg and Dr. David Suzuki, during my years at the University of British Columbia.

In more recent times I have enjoyed good counsel and knowledge from Bob Hunter, Jim Bohlen, Ben Metcalfe, Terry Simmons, Dr. James Lovelock, Stuart Lang, David Hatherton, and Stewart Brand.

I would also like to acknowledge the contribution of Tom Tevlin and Trevor Figueiredo, my partners in Greenspirit Strategies and Beatty Street Publishing, and of Dawn Sondergaard and Christine Tevlin, all of whom have spent many hours to help make this book a reality.

I want to thank Alex Avery for his assistance with the early stages of the project, and for suggesting the main title of the book.

Many thanks to Deborah Viets, who performed the final edit and taught me a thing or two about punctuation and style.

I am grateful for the unfailing support of Eileen Moore, my wife and partner for 40 years. She worked beside me in many early Greenpeace campaigns, raised our two fine boys, Jonathan and Nicholas, traveled with me to distant shores, and continues to work with me through thick and thin.

Contents

INTRODUCTION   *1*

CHAPTER I
First Principles   *13*

CHAPTER II
Our Present Predicament   *32*

CHAPTER III
Beginnings   *37*

CHAPTER IV
No Nukes Now!   *46*

CHAPTER V
Saving the Whales   *59*

CHAPTER VI
Baby Seals and Movie Stars   *73*

CHAPTER VII
Taking the Reins   *89*

CHAPTER VIII
Growing Pains   *102*

CHAPTER IX
Greenpeace Goes Global   *111*

CHAPTER X
Consensus and Sustainable Development Discovered   *121*

CHAPTER XI
Jailed Whales, Curtains of Death, Raising Fish, and Sinking Rainbows   *129*

CHAPTER XII
Greenpeace Sails Off the Deep End *139*

CHAPTER XIII
Round Tables and Square Pegs *163*

CHAPTER XIV
Trees Are The Answer *187*

CHAPTER XV
Energy to Power Our World *202*

CHAPTER XVI
Food, Nutrition, and Genetic Science *273*

CHAPTER XVII
Biodiversity, Endangered Species, and Extinction *301*

CHAPTER XVIII
Chemicals Are Us *319*

CHAPTER XIX
Population Is Us *335*

CHAPTER XX
Sustainable Mining *339*

CHAPTER XXI
Climate of Fear *342*

CHAPTER XXII
Charting a Sensible Course to a Sustainable Future *387*

INDEX *390*

Introduction

The Third World War will be the war to save the environment.
— U Thant, Secretary-General of the United Nations, 1969

You could call me a Greenpeace dropout, but that is not an entirely accurate description of how or why I left the organization 15 years after I helped create it. I'd like to think Greenpeace left me, rather than the other way around, but that too is not entirely correct.

The truth is Greenpeace and I underwent divergent evolutions. I became a sensible environmentalist; Greenpeace became increasingly senseless as it adopted an agenda that is antiscience, antibusiness, and downright antihuman.

This is the story of our transformations.

The last half of the 20th century was marked by a revulsion for war and a new awareness of the environment. Beatniks, hippies, eco-freaks, and greens in their turn fashioned a new philosophy that embraced peace and ecology as the overarching principles of a civilized world. Spurred by more than 30 years of ever-present fear that global nuclear holocaust would wipe out humanity and much of the living world, we led a new war—a war to save the earth. I've had the good fortune to be a general in that war.

My boot camp had no screaming sergeant or rifle drills. Still, the sense of duty and purpose of mission we had at the beginning was as acute as any assault on a common enemy. We campaigned against the bomb-makers, whale-killers, polluters, and anyone else who threatened civilization or the environment. In the process we won the hearts and minds of people around the world. We were Greenpeace.

I joined Greenpeace before it was even called by that name. The Don't Make a Wave Committee was meeting weekly in the basement of the Unitarian church in Vancouver.

In April 1971 I saw a small article in the *Vancouver Sun* about a group planning to sail a boat from Vancouver across the North Pacific to protest U.S. hydrogen bomb testing in Alaska. I immediately realized this was something real I could do, way beyond taking ecology classes and studying at a desk. I wrote the organizers and was invited to join the weekly meetings of the small group that would soon become Greenpeace.

The early days of Greenpeace were heady indeed. It was 1971 and the height of the hippy era. I was in a bitter battle to obtain my PhD in ecology at the University of British Columbia over the objections of a few industry-backed professors who had forced their way onto my thesis committee. I became radicalized and joined the group of antinuclear activists.

We realized all-out nuclear war would be the end of both civilization and the environment–hence the name we soon adopted, Greenpeace, as in "let it be a green peace." We chartered an old fishing boat to sail to ground zero to focus public attention on the nuclear tests. We believed the revolution should be a celebration. We sang protest songs, drank beer, smoked pot, and had a generally good time—even while being tossed about on the notoriously dangerous waters of the North Pacific.

We survived that first voyage, but we never made it to the test site. The U.S. Coast Guard cut us off at Akutan Harbor and made us turn back. However, our mission was a success because our protest was reported in the media across North America. As a result, thousands of people from Canada and the U.S. marched on border crossings across the continent on the day of the H-bomb test and shut the crossings down. Soon after, President Nixon cancelled the remaining tests in that series. We could hardly believe what our ragtag band of peaceniks had accomplished in just a few short months. We realized that a few people could change the world if they just got up and did something.

It was the beginning of a very wild ride.

High on the victory of vanquishing a world superpower, in early 1972 we repeated our "take it to ground zero" protests with France, which was still conducting atmospheric tests of atomic and hydrogen bombs on Mururoa, a small atoll in the South Pacific. France had refused to sign the 1963 treaty banning atmospheric testing signed by the Soviet Union, Great Britain, and the United States.

We found David McTaggart, a Canadian living in New Zealand who was willing to sail his small boat across the South Pacific, and the next protest was on. The first year the French Navy rammed a hole in the boat and forced it ashore. The second year they beat up our captain, an event secretly photographed by one of the crew. The beating catapulted the story to the front pages of French newspapers. Within the year France announced it would no longer conduct nuclear tests in the atmosphere.

In three years our little band of protesters had forced two superpowers to alter substantially their nuclear weapons testing programs. We proved again that a small group of dedicated people could effect real change at a global level. Nothing could stop us now. In 1975 we took on the challenge of saving the whales from extinction at the hands of huge factory whaling fleets. This campaign really put Greenpeace on the map and made us a worldwide icon. By the early 1980s we were confronting the annual slaughter of baby seals, opposing driftnet fisheries, protesting toxic waste dumping, blocking supertankers, and parachuting into nuclear reactor construction sites. Our campaigns were highly successful at changing opinions and energizing the public. Through the power of the media and the people, we were steadily influencing government policies and forcing industries to clean up their acts. We had achieved the support of the majority of people in the industrialized democracies.

By 1982 Greenpeace had grown into a full-fledged international movement with offices and staff around the world. We were bringing in $100 million a year in donations and half a dozen campaigns were occurring simultaneously.

During the early 1980s two things happened that altered my perspective on the direction in which environmentalism, in general, and Greenpeace, in particular, were heading. The first was my introduction to the concept of sustainable development at a global meeting of environmentalists. The second was the adoption of policies by my fellow Greenpeacers that I considered extremist and irrational. These two developments would set the stage for my transformation from a radical activist into a sensible environmentalist.

In 1982, the United Nations held a conference in Nairobi to celebrate the 10th anniversary of the first UN Environment Conference in Stockholm, which I had also attended. I was one of 85 environmental leaders from around the world who were invited to craft a statement of our collective goals for environmental protection. It quickly became apparent there were two nearly opposite perspectives in the room—the antidevelopment perspective of environmentalists from wealthy industrialized countries and the prodevelopment perspective of environmentalists from the poor developing countries.

As one developing country activist put it, taking a stand against development in his woefully poor country would get him laughed out of the room. It was hard to argue with his position. A well-fed person has many problems, a hungry person has but one. The same is true for development, or lack of it. We could see the tragic reality of poverty on the outskirts of our Kenyan host city. Those of us from industrialized countries recognized we had to be in favor of some kind of development, preferably the kind that didn't ruin the environment in the process. Thus the concept of sustainable development was born.

This was when I first fully realized there was another step beyond pure environmental activism. The real challenge was to figure out how to take the environmental values we had helped create and weave them into the social and economic fabric of our culture. This had to be done in ways that didn't undermine the economy and were socially acceptable. It was clearly a question of careful balance, not dogmatic adherence to a single principle.

I knew immediately that putting sustainable development into practice would be much more difficult than the protest campaigns we'd mounted over the past decade. It would require consensus and cooperation rather than confrontation and demonization. Greenpeace had no trouble with confrontation—hell, we'd made it an art form—but we had difficulty cooperating and making compromises. We were great at telling people what they should stop doing, but almost useless at helping people figure out what they should be doing instead.

It also seemed like the right time for me to make a change. I felt our primary task, raising mass public awareness of the importance of the environment, had been largely accomplished. By the early 1980s a majority of the public, at least in the Western democracies, agreed with us that the environment should be taken into account in all our activities. When most people agree with you it is probably time to stop beating them over the head and sit down with them to seek solutions to our environmental problems.

At the same time I chose to become less militant and more diplomatic, my Greenpeace colleagues became more extreme and intolerant of dissenting opinions from within.

In the early days we debated complex issues openly and often. It was a wonderful group to engage with in wide-ranging environmental policy discussions. The intellectual energy in the organization was infectious. We frequently disagreed about specific issues, yet our ultimate vision was largely shared. Importantly, we strove to be scientifically accurate. For years this had been the topic of many of our internal debates. I was the only Greenpeace activist with a PhD in ecology, and because I wouldn't allow exaggeration beyond reason I quickly earned the nickname "Dr. Truth." It wasn't always meant as a compliment. Despite my efforts, the movement abandoned science and logic somewhere in the mid-1980s, just as society was adopting the more reasonable items on our environmental agenda.

Ironically, this retreat from science and logic was partly a response to society's growing acceptance of environmental values. Some activists simply couldn't make the transition from confrontation to consensus; it was as if they needed a common enemy. When a majority of people decide they agree with all your reasonable ideas the only way you can remain confrontational and antiestablishment is to adopt ever more extreme positions, eventually abandoning science and logic altogether in favor of zero-tolerance policies.

The collapse of world communism and the fall of the Berlin Wall during the 1980s added to the trend toward extremism. The Cold War was over and the peace movement was largely disbanded. The peace movement had been mainly Western-based and anti-American in its leanings. Many of its members moved into the environmental movement, bringing with them their neo-Marxist, far-left agendas. To a considerable extent the environmental movement was hijacked by political and social activists who learned to use green language to cloak agendas that had more to do with anticapitalism and antiglobalization than with science or ecology. I remember visiting our Toronto office in 1985 and being surprised at how many of the new recruits were sporting army fatigues and red berets in support of the Sandinistas.

I don't blame them for seizing the opportunity. There was a lot of power in our movement and they saw how it could be turned to serve their agendas of revolutionary change and class struggle. But I differed with them because they were extremists who confused the issues and the public about the nature of our environment and our place in it. To this day they use the word *industry* as if it were a swear word. The same goes for *multinational, chemical, genetic, corporate, globalization,* and a host of other perfectly useful terms. Their propaganda campaign is aimed at promoting an ideology that I believe would be extremely damaging to both civilization and the environment.

Greenpeace had grown so large by the early 1980s that there was nothing one person could do to turn this tide. I put up a spirited debate on many issues at our council meetings, but when you are outvoted, that's democracy for you. There were a number of issues that gradually made it clear to me I was not in line with the politically correct thinking of the day.

One of the earliest manifestations of the extremism that developed in Greenpeace was its campaign to ban the element chlorine worldwide. It began innocently enough with campaigns against 2,4,5-T and dioxin, both rather objectionable substances that deserve to be restricted unless they are absolutely necessary. Both these chemicals happen to contain chlorine, and it wasn't long until this very important member of the periodic table of elements was dubbed the "devil's element" by the majority of representatives in our governing assembly. Even though I suggested banning entire elements was probably outside our jurisdiction, the hard-liners won the day.

It didn't matter that about 85 percent of our medicines are manufactured with chlorine chemistry, or that the addition of chlorine to drinking water represented the biggest advance in the history of public health. By 1991, four years after I left, Greenpeace had adopted a resolution calling for an end to "the use, export, and import of all organochlorines, elemental chlorine, and chlorinated oxidizing agents," stating, "There are no uses of chlorine which we regard as safe."[1] They might as well have called for a ban on living because it is not safe either. I knew I had made the right decision in parting ways, but it saddened me deeply that my Greenpeace had come to this. The "devil's element" is in fact the most important of all the elements for public health and medicine. This didn't matter to my colleagues, and for me it was proof enough that their fundamentalist position was antihuman in nature.

My growing interest in sustainable development had attracted me to aquaculture, the practice of farming the oceans rather than just hunting wild fish. Many fish stocks were badly overfished, and it was clear to me the best way to take the pressure off the wild stocks was to learn to farm them. We made this transition on the land 10,000 years ago with agriculture, and again with farming trees (silviculture) 250 years ago in Europe. I believed Greenpeace should adopt a policy of supporting sustainable aquaculture as a positive contribution to protecting the marine environment. Not only did this fall on deaf ears, a lot of my colleagues were actually hostile to the idea. I thought, If these people are against farming fish, what on earth are they in favor of?

Thus began a divergence of opinion about the way forward. I favored a balanced approach that recognized the necessity of factoring the needs of nearly seven billion people into the equation. I believed we could continue to provide the food, energy, and materials required for civilization while at the same time learning to reduce our negative impacts on the environment.

There is an unfortunate tendency among environmental activists to characterize the human species as a negative influence on the earth. We are likened to a malignant cancer that is spreading, threatening to destroy biodiversity, upsetting the balance of nature, causing the collapse of the global ecosystem. The great myth of the movement is that humans are not really part of nature, that we are somehow "unnatural" and apart from the "pure" natural world. For some reason this idea, like original sin, appeals to people who feel guilty about their existence. We are not worthy, they think.

How ironic that a central teaching of ecology is that humans are part of nature and inextricably connected to it along with all other forms of life. In this sense we are no different from a seagull or a starfish or a worm. But somehow the "deep ecologists" have managed to twist things to make us inferior even to worms, as if all other life forms are superior to us. I don't buy this philosophy of self-loathing.

Since I left Greenpeace, its members, and the majority of the movement, have adopted policy after policy that reflects their antihuman bias,

---

1. I. Amato, The Crusade Against Chlorine, Science, July 9, 1993: 152-154

CONFESSIONS OF A GREENPEACE DROPOUT

illustrates their rejection of science and technology, and actually increases the risk of harm to people and the environment. They oppose forestry even though it provides our most abundant renewable resource. They have zero tolerance for genetically modified food crops, even though this technology reduces pesticide use and improves nutrition for people who suffer from malnutrition. They continue to oppose nuclear energy, even though it is the best technology to replace fossil fuels and reduce greenhouse gas emissions. They campaign against hydroelectric projects despite the fact that hydro is by far the most abundant renewable source of electricity. And they support the vicious and misguided campaign against salmon farming, an industry that produces more than a million tons of heart-friendly food every year.

This divergence in opinion and policy is the result of a single difference of perspective. The extreme environmentalists see humans as the problem, an impediment to salvation, a blight on the landscape. Sensible environmentalists see humans as part of nature and as individuals who are capable of intelligent analysis and decision making and who can learn to integrate themselves into the web of life. The subject of forests and forestry offers a perfect example of this dichotomy.

Anti-forestry activists like those who belong to the Rainforest Action Network argue that we should minimize the number of trees we cut down and hence reduce the amount of wood we use. We are told this will "save" the forests. Indeed, in the absence of humans the forests would do just fine. But there isn't an absence of humans; there are nearly seven billion of us. We need materials to build our homes, offices, factories, and furniture, and we need farmland to produce food and fiber. It's not as if we can just stop eating or using resources, it's a matter of survival. If we decided to reduce our wood consumption, we would automatically increase our consumption of steel, concrete, and other nonrenewable resources. This would require a huge increase in energy consumption, largely from fossil fuels, to manufacture the steel and concrete, adding to air pollution and greenhouse gas emissions. So on balance, using less wood would result in increased damage to the environment.

Once we accept the existence of nearly seven billion people, the entire equation is altered. Now we want to maximize the use of renewable resources and keep as much land forested as possible. One of the best ways to do this is to use more wood sustainably. In fact, the more wood we use the more trees must be grown to supply the demand and the greater the economic incentive to keep land forested. This is a major reason North America has about the same area of forest today as it did 100 years ago; because we use so much wood, landowners plant trees and keep their land forested in order to supply the demand. It's not rocket science, but this fundamental economic relationship has managed to escape the attention of many activists, who automatically believe the way to save the forest is to reduce the use of wood.

There certainly are examples of unsustainable forest use, which results in the loss of forests. But these cases have virtually nothing to do with the forest industry and everything to do with poverty. In poor and underdeveloped countries where wood is the primary fuel for cooking and heating, forests have suffered badly. This is the case in many of the drier regions in the tropics, where fuel wood and charcoal production have denuded whole landscapes. Add to this the grazing pressure caused by goats, sheep, and cows and you have an unsustainable situation. In many of the tropical developing countries of Asia, Africa, and Latin America, the forests are shrinking as hundreds of millions of people cut a patch of forest to plant crops and graze animals just to grow enough food for their family. They don't have enough wealth to reforest land that is cut for fuel or timber, so the inevitable result is continued deforestation.

But outside of this context of extreme poverty, if people stopped using wood, there would be no incentive for private or public landowners to reforest their land. It would make more sense to get rid of the trees and plant corn, cotton, or soybeans, which are perfectly good crops that can pay the taxes and provide income for the landowners. It is really fortunate the demand for wood is high in North America, as it results in continually reforested landscapes.

It is regrettable that the public has been led to believe deforestation is caused by using wood to build our homes, package our goods, and provide paper for printing, packaging, and sanitation. The forest industries that provide wood for these purposes are, almost without exception, engaged in the practice of reforestation, the opposite of deforestation. In fact, more than 90 per cent of deforestation is caused by the conversion of forests to agriculture. The balance largely results from the unsustainable gathering of fuel wood and illegal logging that is followed by conversion to farming.

Clearly we can't solve this problem by banning agriculture or the use of wood for cooking and heating. Further on in the book we will analyze this issue more thoroughly, in particular, the role of intensive agriculture and forest management in conserving natural forests and biodiversity.

China, with its growing middle class, has established a larger area of new forest in the past 15 years than any other country. India, which is also growing wealthier, has doubled the forested area it had just 20 years ago. Why? Because the emerging middle class wants wood and paper and can afford it, so people have planted trees to provide it, thus increasing forest cover. No doubt government reforestation and conservation programs have also played a strong role in China's and India's increasing forest area, but these are contingent on there being enough wealth to support them. This is a win-win scenario for people and the environment, yet activists refuse to recognize this linkage between forest use and forest cover. This is just one example of how the environmental movement has lost its way, and of how it promotes policies that seem reasonable at first glance but are actually detrimental in the long run. Sustainability is all about the long run.

The main purpose of this book is to establish a new approach to environmentalism and to define sustainability as the key to achieving environmental goals. This requires embracing humans as a positive element in evolution rather than viewing us as some kind of mistake. The celebrated Canadian author Farley Mowat has described humans as a "fatally flawed species." This kind of pessimism may be politically correct today, but it is terribly self-defeating. Short of mass suicide there doesn't seem to be an appropriate response. I believe we should celebrate our existence and constantly put our minds toward making the world a better place for people and all the other species we share it with.

A lot of environmentalists are stuck in the 1970s and continue to promote a strain of leftish romanticism about idyllic rural village life powered by windmills and solar panels. They idealize poverty, seeing it as a noble way of life, and oppose all large developments. James Cameron, the multimillionaire producer of the most lucrative movie in history, *Avatar*, paints his face and joins the disaffected to protest a hydroelectric dam in the Amazon. Who needs lights and newfangled electric gadgets anyway? So what if hydroelectricity is by far the most important source of *renewable* electricity? These dreamers should look to the example of Stewart Brand, founder of the Whole Earth Catalogue and leader of the "back to the land" movement of the 1960s and 1970s. Today, in his wisdom, he supports nuclear energy, genetic engineering, and urbanization. He celebrates humanity for its creativity and industrious nature. He is not stuck in the 1970s and neither am I.

By the time you reach the end of this book, I hope you will have a new perspective on the important issues that define environmentalism today.

As you will see, I believe:

- We should be growing more trees and using more wood, not cutting fewer trees and using less wood as Greenpeace and its allies contend. Wood is the most important renewable material *and* energy resource.
- Those countries that have reserves of potential hydroelectric energy should build the dams required to deliver that energy. There is nothing wrong with creating more lakes in this world.
- Nuclear energy is essential for our future energy supply, especially if we wish to reduce our reliance on fossil fuels. It has proven to be clean, safe when compared to other technologies, reliable, and cost-effective
- Geothermal heat pumps, which too few people know about, are far

more important and cost-effective than either solar panels or windmills as a source of renewable energy. They should be required in all new buildings unless there is a good reason to use some other technology for heating, cooling, and making hot water.

- The most effective way to reduce our dependence on fossil fuels is to encourage the development of technologies that require less or no fossil fuels to operate. Electric cars, heat pumps, nuclear and hydroelectric energy, and biofuels are the answer, not cumbersome regulatory systems that stifle economic activity.
- Genetic science, including genetic engineering, will improve nutrition and end malnutrition, improve crop yields, reduce the environmental impact of farming, and make people and the environment healthier.
- Many activist campaigns designed to make us fear useful chemicals are based on misinformation and unwarranted fear.
- Aquaculture, including salmon and shrimp farming, will be one of our most important future sources of healthy food. It will also take pressure off depleted wild fish stocks and will employ millions of people productively.
- There is no cause for alarm about climate change. The climate is always changing. Some of the proposed "solutions" would be far worse than any imaginable consequence of global warming, which will likely be mostly positive. Cooling is what we should fear.
- Poverty is the worst environmental problem. Wealth and urbanization will stabilize the human population. Agriculture should be mechanized throughout the developing world. Disease and malnutrition can be largely eliminated by the application of modern technology. Health care, sanitation, literacy, and electrification should be provided to everyone.
- No whale or dolphin should be killed or captured anywhere, ever. This is one of my few religious beliefs. They are the only species on earth whose brains are larger than ours and it is impossible to kill or capture them humanely.
- The book is not meant to be an exhaustive treatment of the issues, nor is it a highly technical work. I have written it for a general audience interested in the wide range of current environmental issues. I have provided references where I think they might be useful for validation or further reading. All the website references can be accessed directly on the Internet by going to www.beattystreetpublishing.com

This is simply my story and my interpretation of the key elements of science and philosophy in the subjects of the environment and sustainability. In particular, I try to "connect the dots" among the main areas of concern: biodiversity, climate change, forests, energy, rivers, lakes and oceans, agriculture, chemicals, and population. This in turn leads to a radically different picture from the one provided by most activist groups today. It is a positive agenda that has the promise to lead to real solutions. This contrasts sharply with the doom-and-gloom predictions, food scares, and guilt trips that now pass for common fare in the media releases from Greenpeace and its allies.

In the following chapters I have done my best to weave the discussion of environmental issues into my 40-year journey as an ecologist and environmental activist. It begins with my early transition from an enthusiastic student of science into a radical environmental activist. After 15 years of campaigning around the world another transition occurred. I went from being a radical activist to a kind of environmental diplomat. As such I seek solutions rather than problems. For 28 years I have worked to define sustainability and to put it into practice, with the same fervor and enthusiasm I displayed during my 15 years in the environmental wars. I have had the good fortune to spend my entire career thinking about, discussing, and working on the wide range of issues that environmentalism embraces. I hope my effort to impart some of that history and thought will provide new insight into the relationship between ourselves and this beautiful earth we share.

CHAPTER 1

First Principles

Before beginning my story I want to clarify some terms. Many of the terms used to discuss environmental issues are confusing and mean different things to different people. It is not good enough to declare that something is *green* and *sustainable* or conversely *dirty* and *unsustainable*. The following sections describe as clearly as possible how I use these and other environmental terms as well as clarifying some fundamental concepts and principles in politics, science, and environmentalism. This is certainly not an exhaustive treatment of these concepts, but it will orient the reader to the way I view the world.

Sustainability Defined

It was five years after I first heard the term *sustainable development* in Nairobi, Kenya, in 1982 before it came into popular usage. In 1987 the UN World Commission on Environment and Development published *Our Common Future*, also called *The Brundtland Report* after Gro Harlem Brundtland, the former prime minister of Norway and chair of the Commission. The report called on the world's nations to adopt sustainable development as a philosophy that aims to balance environmental, social, and economic priorities and objectives. This document was widely quoted and millions of people learned of this new idea for environmentally acceptable development. The document contained the following, often quoted definition: "Sustainable development is development that meets the needs of the present without compromising the ability of future generations to meet their own needs."[2]

While I appreciate this definition it does not provide even a hint of how to achieve the stated objective. It says *what* but it doesn't say *how*. Over the years I have developed the following definition as a way of "operationalizing" the term: Sustainable development requires that we continue to obtain the food, energy, and materials necessary for our civilization, and perhaps even increase these resources in developing countries, while at the same time working to reduce our negative impacts on the environment through changes in our behavior (practices) and changes in our technologies.

Many activists will read this and say something like: "No way, man. The more people there are and the more resources they use, the more damage will be done to the environment." It is commonly believed that our ecological footprint can be measured directly from summing up the amount of resources we consume. This is one of the more dangerous myths in modern environmental thinking.

It is dangerous because it leads people, young people in particular, to give up any hope of saving the environment from an eventual collapse due to overpopulation and overconsumption. I recently spoke to a Grade 11 class at an inner-city school in the Bronx. During question period a young woman asked me matter-of-factly, "How many years will it be until the earth is dead?" She took it for granted that climate change would soon kill us all. This is the saddest thing about the extent to which apocalyptic predictions have taken root in the media, political forums, and among the general public. Many young people feel utterly bleak about their future.

It reminds me of the scene in the movie *Ghostbusters* where Rick Moranis, his body taken over by evil spirits, approaches a horse-drawn carriage near Central Park and confides to the horse that the end is near. As he careens down the street, he screams at the driver, "You will perish in flames!"

Not only is this sort of catastrophe theory dangerous and entirely self-defeating, it is simply not true. The earth has supported life for more than three billion years and is not about to become lifeless anytime soon. Note that leaves still burst out of their buds in spring, flower bulbs still come up in our gardens, birds return from their winter homes, and burrowing animals come out of hibernation.

More importantly, it *is* possible to continue to get the resources we need to survive while at the same time radically reducing our impact on the environment. Take a simple example; turn the light off when you leave

---

2. World Commission on Environment and Development, *Our Common Future* (Oxford: Oxford University Press, 1987).

the room you are in. This is a behavioral change, a change in practice, yet it can result in a huge difference in the amount of electricity the lightbulb uses. Then swap the incandescent lightbulb for a compact fluorescent bulb, a technological change, and now even when you are in the room with the light on you use less than 25 percent as much electricity as before. And the compact fluorescent bulb lasts up to five times as long, reducing materials use and replacement cost. These two actions—a change in practice and a change in technology— add up to a radical change in our environmental footprint. When light-emitting diodes (LEDs) become more common, it will take even less power to light our world.

This principle applies across the board to nearly everything we do in life. It applies to all the ways we obtain and use food, energy, and materials. In particular, at a personal level, it applies to our homes and our cars. For most people these two items are the largest consumers of both materials and energy, and we have considerable control over what sort of home and car we own.

I believe the best definition of *sustainable* has to do with constantly developing better practices and technologies that are in harmony with the environment rather than ones that cause damage to it. When we speak of sustainable forestry we mean doing it in a way that does not destroy biodiversity, includes reforestation, protects watercourses, etc. Sustainable agriculture means maintaining some natural areas in the landscape, preserving soil fertility, and minimizing deforestation through high-yield technology. The adjective *sustainable* can be used to describe most of the ways we get food, energy, and materials. The example of the lightbulb above could be called *sustainable illumination*.

The term *sustainability*, like many other words, is subject to overuse and misuse. But if we stick to the above broad definition I think it is the best term to describe a balanced approach that takes into account the real needs of people while working to maintain a healthy environment. This is not always simple. There are serious conflicts to deal with and sometimes mistakes will be made while attempting new approaches. But it only makes sense to work in this direction.

Balance is my favorite word. It represents an effort to find an agreement that satisfies everybody involved without causing undue hardship to anyone. While this may seem like a daunting task, unless you work to find common ground you will be condemned to endless conflict. Some people seem to thrive on conflict. Others are hopelessly pious and forgiving.

Amid the tumult of contemporary politics the best we can do is to seek the middle ground. Some may see this as selling out, but only the unthinking are that rigid in their views. The basis of progress is thinking, inquisitive people sharing thoughts and views and learning new ways to do old things. I am an optimist and I believe there are good reasons to feel this way, including the fact that the universe will continue to unfold in its glorious splendor.

I feel very optimistic because I have experienced so many situations where the outcome is a win-win-win for the environment, the community, and the economy. Here is a perfect example:

The Sacramento Valley in California was historically known as the Great Inland Sea. During the rainy season the banks of the Sacramento River and its tributaries would overflow, creating a temporary lake over an area of millions of acres. Since the arrival of agriculture the valley has been tamed by hundreds of levees and weirs, greatly reducing the frequency of flooding.

Of the millions of acres of farmland in the Sacramento Valley, more than 500,000 acres are used to grow rice, second only in the United States to Arkansas. Over the years, as the city of Sacramento grew larger, its citizens became increasingly annoyed with the rice farmers.

Farmers grow rice in fields that they flood in the spring, immediately after the seedlings are planted. Prior to harvest the fields are drained to allow access for harvesting equipment. After the harvest the traditional practice was to burn the stubble and leave the field an ash-covered barrens all winter. The ash provided a flush of nutrients for next year's crop. But half a million acres of burning stubble make a lot of smoke and soot. The air pollution filled the valley for weeks and the townsfolk were not amused.

It is not a simple matter to get farmers to change practices they have followed for thousands of years. But some farmers who realized their practices were unacceptable to their neighbors from an environmental perspective decided to take action. In the mid-1990s they were joined in a working committee by state environment and wildlife officials, local environmental groups, birdwatchers and bird scientists, and many others who wanted to find a solution to this problem. Within a few years there were over 100 people involved in the process. Partly due to the fact the committee was made up of diverse interests, it worked toward a solution that suited everyone.

Today the rice is still grown as usual in flooded fields that are drained prior to harvest. But the practice of burning the stubble has ended. Instead the fields are re-flooded and the stubble is left to decay in the water over the winter. This is an even more efficient way to recover the nutrients in the stubble. Today there is no air pollution, and the rice farmers are in the good graces of their neighbors. But the most amazing outcome is that the rice fields now provide wintering habitat for 14 species of shorebirds. Between 200,000 and 300,000 shorebirds and about three million ducks and geese make use of the rice fields, dabbling for bugs and worms in the rich sediment of the flooded fields.

In a brilliant stroke of fine-tuning, the farmers and their new friends realized that the legs of shorebird species range from short to long. For instance, sandpipers have short legs while avocets have long ones. So the farmers flood the various rice fields to different depths to accommodate shorebirds large, small, and in between.

The farmers still grow their crop and provide two million tons of staple food. Air pollution is a thing of the past and rather than a desolate burned landscape there is a thriving ecosystem with millions of birds feeding all winter. It's a win for the environment, a win for the community, and just as important a win for the farmers and their economy.

In September 2002 I was invited as the keynote speaker to a ceremony marking the designation of 550,000 acres of the Sacramento Valley's rice fields as a Shorebird Site of International Significance.[3] Many of the species that winter there pass from the Northern to the Southern Hemisphere annually. On that day I felt vindicated in my optimistic outlook for the future of human civilization and the global environment. The evolution of rice farming practices in the Sacramento Valley provides the definition of sustainability.

Renewable, Clean, Sustainable, and Green

We throw these four words around as if they were synonymous when they actually have distinct meanings.

Renewable is used to describe resources and energy supplies that have relatively short cycles of natural replenishment. Nearly all renewable resources are based on the sun's energy. These include biomass, hydroelectric energy, geothermal heat pumps, wind and solar energy, and the wood used for fuel, construction, and paper products. Trees, and the wood they produce, are the most abundant renewable material *and* energy resource. All our agricultural food crops as well as wild fish, game, and plants are renewable and based on solar energy.

The term *clean*, as in *clean technology*, is relatively new and simply refers to technology that does not pollute the environment. By this standard wind, solar, nuclear, and hydroelectric energy are all clean. But it is important to look at the full life cycle. All technologies have impacts on the environment. Bauxite ore must be mined to make aluminum for solar panels, cement must be produced for hydroelectric dams and nuclear plants, and factories must be built to produce liquid biofuels. So clean is a relative term meaning cleaner, much cleaner, we hope, than previous or alternative technologies.

Just because a resource is renewable doesn't mean it is clean. When wood is burned in an open fire it produces a lot of soot and volatile, toxic gases. Indoor smoke from fires for cooking and heating kills 1.5 million

---

3. Riceland Habitat, California Rice Commission, http://www.calrice.org/Environment/Wildlife/Shorebird+Habitat.htm

people annually, according to the World Health Organization.[4] Therefore renewable fuels such as wood, straw, and dung are the leading cause of death from air pollution.

Sustainability, originally called sustainable development, is a concept, not something fixed or absolute. Some have described it as a journey rather than a destination, as there is no final perfect state of sustainability. As we and our environment evolve we must adjust to changing circumstances. While it's nice to think there is some ideal state we could attain, sustainability is actually a perpetual work in progress.

Sustainability is a relative concept, depending on the time scale we consider. On one hand nothing is infinitely sustainable, even the sun will burn out (and evidently take the earth with it) billions of years from now. For practical purposes it makes sense to define sustainable in terms of human generations. It means getting away from just thinking about tomorrow or a few years from now and thinking 100, 200, even 500 years into the future.

And just because a resource is renewable doesn't mean it is sustainable. The vast herds of buffalo that roamed the plains were renewable but they were harvested at an unsustainable rate and nearly exterminated. More recently the Atlantic salmon and Atlantic cod have been severely overfished and have yet to recover. And sustainability is not only an environmental concept; it also includes economic and social factors. Solar voltaic panels use solar radiation, which in itself is highly sustainable. But at a cost of more than 50 cents per kilowatt-hour, 10 or more times the cost of conventional electricity sources, it is unlikely solar panels are economically sustainable, especially in developing countries.

In the same way that some things that are renewable are not necessarily sustainable, some nonrenewable resources are highly sustainable. Iron ore, which is used to make steel, is a classic example. Iron is nonrenewable, but there is so much of it in the earth's crust and it is so efficiently recycled that there is enough for at least tens of thousands of years, perhaps millions. Lead, zinc, copper, and coal are also very abundant and not likely to become scarce any time soon. Uranium and thorium, both of which can produce nuclear energy, are in sufficient supply to last thousands of years.

It is more important for a resource to be sustainable than it is to be renewable. And even renewable resources require nonrenewable resources to operate. Solar panels are made from aluminum, silicon, and gallium arsenide. Wind turbines require a lot of steel and concrete for their towers (about five times as much, per unit of energy produced, compared to a nuclear power plant).

---

4. Larry West, "Indoor Pollution from Cooking Fires Kills 1.5 Million People Annually," http://environment.about.com/od/pollution/a/stovepollution.htm

CONFESSIONS OF A GREENPEACE DROPOUT

Now we come to *green*, the most elusive and least precise of the four terms. Green is the most political term, as it tends to reflect personal biases and opinions as much as objective and measurable criteria. At its worst, green is a shameless marketing slogan, used to promote various products and services as environmentally friendly. Yet it is a useful term, a way of distinguishing relatively damaging technologies from ones that have less impact, if it is used objectively.

But green is very much in the eye of the beholder. We have green jobs, green energy, green buildings, Greenpeace and Greenspirit. Green includes renewable, sustainable, and clean. "Greens" believe in green attributes but disagree widely on what should be included in the category. Many Greens oppose hydroelectric energy even though it is the largest source of renewable electricity. Many Greens oppose nuclear energy even though it is sustainable and clean. And many Greens oppose or frown on forestry even though it provides our most abundant renewable energy and material resource. Solar panels and wind farms are considered green despite the fact that they are made with nonrenewable materials, some of which cause large greenhouse gas emissions when they are produced. Concrete is a prime example. I conclude that green is more of a political or marketing term than a scientific one and therefore refrain from using it when renewable, sustainable, or clean will do. If asked what green means to me, I would say it must pass the test of being sustainable and clean.

The term *greenwashing* has been adopted by environmentalists to describe communications, particularly from corporate interests, which they contend are misleading the public. There are plenty of good examples of corporate greenwashing. "Clean Coal" is my favorite case in point. But the characterization of solar panels as being green might also be questioned. How can a technology that costs 10 times as much as conventional electricity and that is made entirely of nonrenewable resources be green? How can windmills be green when they require five times as much steel and concrete per unit of power produced compared to nuclear plants and when they occupy vast areas of land? One might ask if the pot is not calling the kettle black in the war of words over what green really means.

Facts, Correlations, Causes, and Predictions

The headline screams:

"PHTHALATES LINKED TO ABNORMAL GENITALIA IN BABY BOYS."

First thought, What on earth is a phthalate? (The *ph* is silent and the first *a* is soft, so just say *thallate*.). Phthalates are a class of chemical used as softeners in vinyl (polyvinyl chloride, or PVC) products. Pure vinyl, such as the PVC pipe used for water lines, is rigid. Vinyl is unique in that it can absorb many other elements and compounds, giving it properties that cannot be attained in other plastics. Your credit cards are made of vinyl; they are not brittle because they contain a small amount of phthalate. Other flexible vinyl products include vinyl flooring, blood bags and vinyl tubing, vinyl upholstery, vinyl records, and insulation on wiring to name a few. Phthalates are one of the most tested chemicals we use and have been cleared of negative human health and environmental impacts by the highest authorities, unless you listen to the chemical-fear activists.

We will discuss this fear mongering in more detail in Chapter 18, which focuses on chemicals, but suffice it to say that there is a tidal wave of scary stories about phthalates in activist media releases and in the lifestyle sections of newspapers and magazines. Just search the Internet for "phthalates linked" and you will find they are linked to childhood obesity, autism, asthma, heart disease, and, of course, abnormal genitalia. So far they have not been linked to climate change!

I make this tongue-in-cheek reference to the term *linked* to introduce a discussion of the degree to which we *know* things. If we knew the answer, the above headline would have read, "Phthalates *cause* abnormal genitalia in boys." This highlights the difference between *causation* and *correlation*, one of the most important distinctions in science.

Causation is fairly straightforward. The moon causes the tides, lack of food causes hunger, and a combination of geography and rainfall causes rivers to run to the sea. Correlation is much more elusive. While correlation is a necessary property of causation, it does not prove causation by itself. For example, shark attacks and ice-cream consumption are highly correlated. In other words when shark attacks are highest, so is ice-cream consumption. And vice versa, when shark attacks are lowest, hardly any ice-cream is eaten. Can one conclude from this that ice-cream consumption *causes* shark attacks? Or that shark attacks *cause* ice-cream consumption? Of course not, they are each caused in part by a common factor, warm weather.

Correlation means two things appear to be related, possibly in a cause and effect relationship, even when they may not be. You walk under a ladder or a black cat crosses your path and then you have a bit of bad luck. That is a correlation, even if it is far-fetched. Correlation lies at the root of superstition and much of popular environmentalism. Some correlations are eventually proven to be causations. When they lack proof of causation, it becomes convenient for activists and journalists to imply that correlation equals causation. When they wish to make such implications, they fall back on the word linked. The use of this word seems to be justified by sparse evidence. Let's say that a certain chemical causes a statistically higher level of some abnormality in rats when administered at a very high dose rate. Activists and journalists will then imply that the chemical is linked to this same abnormality in humans, even though no human is ever exposed to such high levels of the chemical.

So when you read a headline or an introductory sentence that says one thing is linked to another, put on your thinking cap and question the assumption that one is actually caused by the other. Which brings us to *facts*.

We know facts are true. The earth revolves around the sun, one of the most important facts shown to be true, as demonstrated by Copernicus. Humans evolved from the apes, gravity pulls you toward the earth, sugar triggers the sweet receptors on the tongue, people fall in love: these are all facts. More mundanely, facts are observable phenomena that recur without failure. If, one day, gravity were not to work, its factualness would be in question. I'm not holding my breath.

It is fashionable in the politically correct world of postmodernist deconstructionism to claim objective facts do not exist. I reject this assumption. I agree that many things that were taken as facts in the past were actually cultural biases and had more to do with racial, sexual, and class discrimination than with scientifically verifiable truths. But in the realm of objective science there *are* facts, and I am one of them, as are you.

Then there are the problems of *misinformation* and *disinformation*. The former does not imply dishonest intentions whereas the latter does. Both involve spreading untruths and therefore result in people drawing inaccurate conclusions because they accept the information as the truth. Misinformation includes a statement such as "There is scientific proof that humans are the main cause of climate change." An example of disinformation might be "That scientist is in the pockets of industry" when there is no evidence that this is true.

And then we come to predictions, such as the following: "Scientists Predict Widespread Extinction by Global Warming."[5] People have been predicting the future since time immemorial. Even though they are not very good at it they keep trying. Some people actually think they know the future, as if they had a crystal ball. But they do not have a crystal ball; it is a mythical thing, found only in fantasy and science fiction. Still, this doesn't seem to deter them, especially when the prediction involves the end of civilization and the world as we know it.

"The end is nigh" has been cried from street corners for eons. The apocalypse is always just around that corner and people tend to believe this. Optimistic predictions are invariably greeted with disbelief while doom and gloom forecasts makes the news. We are a strange species: having developed the ability to consider the future, we tend to see the dark side even though we would obviously hope for a happy ending.

---

5. James Gorman, "Scientists Predict Widespread Extinction by Global Warming," *New York Times*, January 8, 2004, http://www.nytimes.com/2004/01/08/science/08CLIM.html

Of course there are some aspects of the future we can predict accurately: the tides, sunrise, our next birthday, and the movement of the planets. But most future events and circumstances cannot be predicted with certainty. There are simply too many variables, including the chaotic variable of chance. That's why people bet on horse races and boxing matches. That's why the weather report is wrong nearly as often as it is right, especially when it is for more than four or five days in the future. This kind of prediction is more like a wager; your odds of winning are better the more you know the horses, the boxers, and the meteorological conditions. But you will never get it right consistently.

The take-home message here is predictions are not the same as facts. We are constantly bombarded with predictions of future climate change, sea-level rise, floods, droughts, hurricanes, mass exodus of climate refugees, mass species extinction, and the end of civilization. These predictions are based largely on computer models, very complex computer models that purport to tell us what the climate (average weather) will be like in 50 or 100 years from now. The problem is that as complex as they are, the computer models are nowhere near as complex as the earth's climate system and all the variables involved, some of which we don't even understand. Frankly I wouldn't give two bits for these computer-based predictions. I give the modelers A for effort, but I would bet on the stock exchange or the outcome of the World Series long before I would bet on climate change.

As a first-year science major at the University of British Columbia I was lucky enough to enroll in a course offered by the English faculty, aimed at teaching critical thinking to science students. We took a copy of *Time* magazine and deconstructed it from cover to cover. The lesson I remember best is, never believe an article that has the words *may* or *might* in the first sentence. If you see a sentence with *may* in it, read it again but add *or may not* as in, "Chemical X may or may not cause cancer."

So whenever a statement is made by a politician, an activist, a journalist, or by me that purports to be a fact, take a closer look. Is it really a proven fact? Or is it a correlation masquerading as a causal relationship? Is it a proven causal relationship, such as "Light from the sun makes plants grow?" Or is it just a prediction of something to which we don't know the answer? Adopting this analytical approach will give you the power of critical thinking and make you a much more sensible environmentalist.

Philosophy, Religion, Politics, Dogma, Propaganda, and Science

You might think only a fool would attempt to discuss all the above terms in a few pages. I will leave you to be the judge.

Literally translated from Greek, philosophy means the love of knowledge and wisdom. In the strictest sense, then, there is no place for dishonesty or misinformation in one's philosophy of life. It is the pure expression of truth. But in the realm of ideas and opinions there are many shades of gray between black and white. The use of loaded words, their inflection and context, and the confusion of belief with proven fact create a minefield that is difficult to navigate. Add large doses of self-righteousness, fanaticism, and a willingness to use force and you have the turmoil of history as individuals, tribes, and nations come into conflict over control of people and resources. Leaders of all sides claim to speak for god or gods, higher principles of human nature, and superior genetic makeup as a justification for the raw furtherance of their interests.

Religion is largely based on beliefs that cannot be proven in the scientific sense. To justify these beliefs adherents often describe them as "self-evident," as if anyone could see it if only they would open their eyes. I grew up in a family of agnostics and my village had no church. My mother and father were very well read and kept up with current affairs. The views of my parents and my grandparents reflected a healthy mix of socialism and capitalism. This led to lively debate around the kitchen table and in the living room. I was fortunate to be exposed to a wide range of philosophies and political orientations at an early age. I rejected religion as superstition and embraced empiricism and science. At age eight I was writing illustrated essays about the planets and their orbital peculiarities.

The only exception to my secular family was my father's mother, Bernadette. She was a French-Canadian Catholic, who came from northern Ontario. She had converted to Christian Science after a traumatic childhood and had spent a lot of time pondering the mysteries of the spiritual side of life. I spent time with her in my early years and she explained to me the distinction between the world of the flesh and the world of the spirit. She found great comfort in the belief that there was a place with no pain. Although I retained my agnostic views, her influence gave me a feeling of something deeper. Perhaps it was okay to simply accept that the universe is in many ways unfathomable, that we are all very small in the contemplation of infinite space and time.

In my view, politics is the debate about what should happen next, and who's to blame for what happened before. There is always politics in religion but some cultures have decided, with mixed results, that there should be no religion in politics. The separation of church and state was apparently an English invention but soon spread to surrounding lands. But the Taliban and other sorts of radical Islam have not taken to this notion and thus has emerged one of the great divides in the world today. The rights of women, men, and children; the future of democracy; perhaps the prospect of peace in this world, all seem hinged on this divergence in philosophy and religion.

Politics largely adheres to left and right principles. The political left is primarily concerned with the needs of society as a whole, the common good, and the equality of individuals. The political right champions the rights of the individual, freedom, and private enterprise. On the far left lies communism, in which the state controls virtually everything, including industry, the media, and property. Modern socialism is center-left, allowing a large degree of individual freedom and private property but tending toward central control over redistribution of income, railroads, electrical generation, health care, and many other industries. Capitalism, on the right-center, favors private enterprise as the most efficient system to deliver goods and services and looks to individual competition as the driver of innovation and progress. On the far right, fascism is in many ways similar to communism. Both are forms of dictatorship. Fascism is usually characterized by the iron rule of an individual fanatic. Communism can be effectively dictated by an individual such as Kim Jong-un of North Korea, or by a committee, such as in the case of the People's Republic of China. It has been said that communism and fascism meet behind your back, a metaphor that points to how you can stretch your left and right arms back until they touch, so that you can't see how they may be plotting against you. Anarchism is the opposite of both communism and fascism in that it supports individual rights in nearly all aspects of political life. It is a bit fanciful in that it does not really recognize a role for government. Libertarianism is a more realistic form of anarchism in so far as it accepts sufficient central government to ensure peace and security but otherwise champions the free will of the individual.

I strongly believe that environmentalists should be centrist in their approach to politics. It is a great shame that the political left managed to hijack much of the environmental movement as it gained strength in the 1980s, casting the political right as "anti-environmental." Clearly there are examples of good environmental policies from both left and right perspectives. The left tends to support a regulatory approach while the right generally supports market-based policies. Both these approaches have merit and a combination of the two can often prove more effective than either approach alone. The task of a sensible environmentalist is to maintain a centrist position, taking the best ideas from both the right and left sides of the political spectrum. Let partisans on the left and right debate the issues from their perspectives: environmentalists must work to remain independent of party politics. Of course we all have our political orientations and that is natural. And politics is about much more than the environment. But we should try hard to prevent socialist or capitalist ideology from determining our positions on the environmental issues of the day. Common sense and pragmatism should prevail.

Dogma takes us into the world of frozen thought. For some reason many people stop learning at an early age. They believe they already know all that can be known, or at least all they want to know. Blind obedience, black and white interpretation, and zero tolerance of other people's ideas,

CONFESSIONS OF A GREENPEACE DROPOUT

even other people's honestly held opinions, even when those opinions are based on the best available information, these are the hallmarks of dogma. This is fertile ground for all manner of totalitarian regimes, despots and snake-oil salesmen. They often make a profit and gain power from the intolerance they embrace. And they would never admit they are dogmatic, which clearly means they are in denial.

Propaganda relies on loaded language and lies and perverts the truth. It serves dogma, racism, sexism, and ignorance of science. Hitler's infamous campaign against the Jews was based on associating them with negative words like *dirty*. Mugabe's dictatorship in Zimbabwe was fueled by the ridiculous assertion that England was trying to reassert its imperial power. Chinese authorities continue to deny the atrocity of Tiananmen Square. One of the principal tools of the propagandist is the association of negative or positive words with the subject of the deception. Greenpeace calls chlorine "the devil's element," PVC "the poison plastic," and nuclear energy "evil." Genetically modified foods are "Frankenfoods," "killer tomatoes," and "terminator seeds." Propaganda, along with the promotion of hate and violence, represents the dark side of communications.

Science is neither religion nor politics. But both misuse it with great abandon, and sometimes to great effect. Science has been with us since the earliest people discovered fire, stone tools, agriculture, bronze and steel. They didn't call it science then but it was the accumulation of knowledge that could be passed down through generations. Much of this knowledge took the form of advances in technology. The Chinese, the Egyptians, and the Mayans independently discovered truths about the universe. Then Copernicus discovered the earth was not the center of the universe and Galileo, to his peril, learned the sun did not revolve around the earth. Darwin completed the picture by proclaiming that humans were not the center of life and that they had descended from the apes. The horror of this revelation haunts creationists and fundamentalists to this day.

Science employs the empirical method to test hypotheses. A hypothesis is a statement that can be tested, such as "All dogs are brown." A sample of dogs is taken and it turns out they are not all brown. The hypothesis is disproved. Another hypothesis is "If I drop a rock from a height, it will fall to the ground." After thousands of replications the statement proves true in every case. The hypothesis is proved and soon becomes a theory, and ultimately a law, in this case a law of physics. A law is something that has never been disproved.

Science is not all powerful; it has its weaknesses. One of these is that you cannot prove a negative. For example, you can't prove UFOs do not exist. You could prove they do exist if you documented them sufficiently to be beyond doubt, like bringing one to the town square and displaying it for all to see. But in the absence of proving they do exist you can't prove they don't. This leads to a serious problem in the discussion over the safety of various chemicals, foods, and practices. Activists will commonly challenge government agencies and industry manufacturers to prove a certain chemical or product is not harmful. To most people this seems like a reasonable request. But it is impossible to accomplish through the scientific method. It is possible to prove a certain chemical is harmful and it is possible to prove a certain chemical is beneficial, but it is not possible to prove it is not harmful. That's because even if you do a million tests, and still see no evidence of harm, it is still possible you missed something or the test was not designed well enough.

Some problems in science are difficult to solve because there are too many variables and it is therefore not possible to determine a cause-effect relationship. Climate change is a classic example. So many variables affect the climate: the earth's wobbles, the sun's cycles, the many different greenhouse gases, human alteration of the environment, and other variables we may not even be aware of. This makes it nearly impossible to "prove" which of the variables has the largest impact. And then there is the fact that we have only one planet earth. It is impossible to do a statistical analysis with a sample of one.

The real strength of science is that it is based on two things: observable facts that can be repeated, and logic. There is no need for one-off miracles, mystics, or magic. And yet science is regularly abused by all manner of cunning politicians, zealous activists, proselytizers, and downright fakers. Our only defense against this abuse lies in our ability to think critically and to ask the right questions.

My main reason for the above discussion is to set the stage for a conversation about what *environment* and *environmentalist* really mean in today's language. Clearly the word environment simply refers to all things in our surroundings, but does it include us? This is an important question because if our goal is to "save the environment" it is essential to know if we, the humans, are included in the saving. Activists too often portray the situation as if the task is to save the environment *from* us, as if we were its enemy. I believe this is a self-defeating proposition. If we are the enemy, we might as well commit mass suicide. Some support this approach, unfortunately they aren't volunteering to go first. They tend to see themselves as the chosen ones, who are more enlightened than the teeming masses that are destroying the earth.

We are part of the environment and must therefore take responsibility for the task of harmonizing our existence with the other species on this planet. That doesn't mean we have to take a back seat or feel badly about the fact we eat other living things. That is our nature as much as it is the nature of every animal on earth. It is in our own self-interest to care about the totality of the environment, to learn to be good stewards of the planet, nurturing at the same time as consuming. This is our great challenge as we enter an age of unprecedented population levels and technological ability. A certain amount of humility should temper our dominant position in the food chain as we strive for a sustainable existence.

The term *environmentalism* came into popular usage in the 1960s, in conjunction with the prospect of nuclear holocaust and the societal revolution against war. Before then, someone who cared about nature was called either a naturalist or a conservationist, the latter implying an agenda to protect nature.

It is important to note the word environmentalism ends with *ism*, just like communism, socialism, capitalism, fascism, and anarchism. These words describe belief systems based on an adherence to a set of basic principles. Some people become "true believers" in one or another of these *isms*. They tend to become rigid in their beliefs and often resent other people who question them. Some people remain open minded and recognize that some of these *isms* have both positive and negative elements, often depending upon particular circumstances.

We have all experienced the peril of talking about politics and religion around the dinner table. They are on the one hand the most interesting of subjects and on the other the most difficult to discuss without conflict. Politics and religion lie at the root of most wars and civil strife. Yet they both speak to the very essence of our philosophies and our codes of conduct in daily life.

Throughout history there has been a competition between religious (spiritual) leaders and nonreligious (secular) leaders. In much of the world this has resulted in a formal separation of church and state, while in other countries religious leaders are the political leaders and in still others the political leaders have effectively eliminated the religious leaders.

The environmental movement has unfortunately become a hybrid in this regard. It is partly a political movement that aims to influence public policy, but it is also partly a religious movement in that many of its policies are based on beliefs rather than scientific facts. In addition the environmental movement seeks to gain support from religious leaders and individuals by appealing to their spiritual values. Environmentalism is to a large extent a populist movement that challenges established authority and appeals to the disenchanted, social revolutionaries, and idealists. "Pop environmentalism," like popular culture in general, tends to be shallow and sensational, moving from fad to fad. The pop environmentalists are generally self-assured, even smug in the belief they know the truth.

A classic example of pop environmentalism is the zero-tolerance position against the use of genetic modification to improve our food crops and medicines. There is absolutely no scientific basis for such a position yet it has taken root in many otherwise "sophisticated" countries with high standards of living and a well-educated public, such as Germany,

Britain, Austria, France, and New Zealand. Every major academy of science has endorsed the use of genetic enhancement as a way to improve nutrition and yield and to reduce the negative environmental impacts of agriculture. Nothing has been identified in the makeup of these improved crops that has the potential for negative effects. For nearly 15 years now, we have had the knowledge to eliminate malnutrition in the world, especially in the rice-eating cultures where nutrient deficiencies affect tens of millions of people. But groups like Greenpeace and the World Wildlife Fund have blocked these advances by promoting fear in the public and by supporting regulations that stifle research, development, and adoption of genetically modified crops. They are effectively condemning millions to suffering and death for the sake of a superstition. Surely this can't seriously be called environmentalism.

In a landmark speech before the Commonwealth Club in San Francisco in 2003, the late Dr. Michael Crichton said the environmental movement had become a religious movement. He observed, "Increasingly it seems facts aren't necessary, because the tenets of environmentalism are all about belief. It's about whether you are going to be a sinner, or saved. Whether you are going to be one of the people on the side of salvation, or on the side of doom. Whether you are going to be one of us, or one of them."

Dr. Crichton concluded, "Environmentalism needs to be absolutely based in objective and verifiable science, it needs to be rational, and it needs to be flexible. And it needs to be apolitical." In other words environmentalism should steer clear of both politics and religion. I agree with this analysis, but you have to dig deep in today's environmental dialogue to find much evidence of this approach. It leads me to conclude that we need to redefine environmentalism as a movement based on science and logic rather than belief and superstition. That is the challenge facing us all as we try to chart a course into a sustainable future. That is the challenge of becoming a sensible environmentalist.

A sensible environmentalist is dedicated to a definition of environmentalism based squarely on science and logic. This includes an objective appraisal of economics, such as recognizing that solar energy costs up to 10 times as much as conventional energy and that the sun doesn't shine at night. We must recognize we depend absolutely on the resources of the earth for our survival. The tendency of pop environmentalists to oppose every single mining development anywhere provides a clear example of abandonment of science and logic. We can't survive without mines because the minerals, metals, and fuels derived from them are absolutely essential. Have these people given up cell phones, laptops, and bicycles? Of course we must work to make our mines compatible with the sustainability of the environment. This means not poisoning the water and reclaiming the mined area when the mine is shut down. It means providing long-term benefits to local communities, such as education, training, and

CONFESSIONS OF A GREENPEACE DROPOUT

health care. These things are possible and indeed are being included in all modern mining developments. This is what sensible environmentalists believe in.

In the final analysis, environmentalism should be about learning how to extract the food, energy, and materials we need to survive while at the same time reducing our negative environmental impacts as we do so. That is the aspiration, the central spirit of sensible environmentalism. Not to despise ourselves but to use our intelligence to find win-win solutions to the pressing challenges we face today. I believe we can meet these challenges, and I will be the last one to sink into a doomsday funk. This is a big planet with a four-plus billion-year history. Life has survived and flourished for more than three billion of those years, an unfathomable scale of time. The evolution of life has continued through cataclysms far greater than we can imagine. It is not about to vanish anytime soon.

The "Precautionary Principle"

What kind of man would live where there is no daring? I don't believe in taking foolish chances, but nothing can be accomplished without taking any chance at all.
—Charles A. Lindbergh, American aviator

I have put "precautionary principle" in quotation marks above because it is not a principle. A principle is something you do as a rule, something you are not supposed to defy. If we actually followed something called the precautionary principle, we would never get out of bed in the morning for fear of the many risks involved in daily activity. We would certainly never voluntarily get into an automobile or cross a busy street. Yes, following such a doctrine sounds very high-minded and "principled" but it is simply not a very useful guide to daily life.

The precautionary principle stems from the idea that you don't need absolute proof of harm to ban a practice, chemical, or technology. So if one argues there is no proof that a certain chemical *does* cause harm, that is not sufficient. Activists will demand that the chemical's manufacturer prove it *does not* cause harm. This is a scientific impossibility so it's "Gotcha." Then the activists point to some unproven "link" between the chemical and an abnormality relating to sex organs or cancer, preferably both, the precautionary principle is invoked, and development is halted.

Greenpeace has been a leading advocate of the precautionary principle and has succeeded in having it enshrined in a number of international and national regulations. But a search of the Greenpeace International website does not reveal a very precise definition of what it thinks the principle is.[6]

---

6. Greenpeace International, "The Precautionary Principle," July 2, 2004, http://www.greenpeace.org/international/campaigns/

Greenpeace seems content to simply invoke the precautionary principle as if it is self-explanatory, when in fact there are many facets and angles to this idea. Is it enough simply to express the slightest doubt in order to stop producing new chemicals and technologies and grind everything to a halt? What degree of "uncertainty" is required before the principle kicks in? How does one measure "degree of uncertainty"? How are the benefits of doing something weighed against the risks of not doing it? Suppose you invent a genetically modified rice plant that can prevent blindness in 250,000 children each year, but Greenpeace says that planting the rice might pose a risk to the environment? Should Greenpeace have to prove the risk, or should it just have to blurt out "precautionary principle" to win the debate? And who is in charge of interpreting the precautionary principle on a case-by-case basis?

This is just the tip of the iceberg, but Greenpeace doesn't even want us to see the tip. It wants to be the final arbiter of all human activity. Many scholarly works have been written on the subject of the precautionary principle. For example, Indur Goklany has done a good job of explaining the concept in his book[7] and in his essays.[8]

A much more useful term is the *precautionary approach*. This is not a principle but rather a way of thinking and an attitude toward how we do things. It is the opposite of recklessness and requires every stone be turned in considering the safety of doing something new. In a simple sense it is a bit like safely crossing the road. We want to cross the road because we may find an opportunity on the other side. But we should always look both ways, make sure we have steady footing, and look both ways again before we set forth. We look, and the coast is clear, so off we go. Still it remains possible that, once we are halfway across the road, a jetliner or a thunderbolt may hurtle out of the sky and kill us. That is the unforeseen risk of crossing the road.

This example illustrates that there is no such thing as zero risk. The unexpected is always a possibility no matter how carefully we try to rule out risks. Some things remain unpredictable and can only be learned from experience, sometimes the hard way. This is perhaps the most important reason why the precautionary principle is an obstacle to progress rather than a safety feature. It can be used to block any activity at the whim of the enforcer. Strictly interpreted we would never be allowed to cross the road because we might be hit by lightning on the way to the other side. The so-called precautionary principle gives weight to the argument that nothing new should be attempted. This is no way to bring an end to war, poverty,

---

trade-and-the-environment/the-precautionary-principle

7. Indur M. Goklany, *The Precautionary Principle: A Critical Appraisal* (Washington, DC, Cato Institute, 2001).

8. Indur M. Goklany, "From Precautionary Principle to Risk-Risk Analysis," *Nature Biotechnology* 20 (November 2002), http://goklany.org/library/Nature%20Biotech%202002%20v20%20%201075.pdf

disease, famine, or suffering. It is a blueprint for stagnation and the status quo, yet to adopt a precautionary approach is reasonable.

Activists tend to look at only one side of the equation when it comes to risk. Take the example of adding chlorine to drinking water. Some argue that because chlorine can combine with organic matter in the water, there is a slight chance a carcinogenic substance may be produced. This might cause one death in a million people over their lifetimes. Why would we allow the possibility that someone might die if we add chlorine to drinking water? Because thousands will almost certainly die if we don't. Waterborne diseases like cholera can infect entire communities if the cholera bacteria gets into the water supply. As recently as 1991 there was a serious cholera outbreak in Peru that caused more than 250,000 people to become ill and that killed 1600. Lack of sanitation and insufficient chlorination of water supplies were the causes. Greenpeace has a policy to ban chlorine world-wide. This is an irresponsible position.

When applying the precautionary approach we must compare the risks and benefits of doing something with the risks and benefits of not doing that thing. This is not an exact science. Risks and uncertainties are difficult, sometimes impossible, to quantify. Therefore we need to take a reasoned approach, weighing all the factors on both sides and coming to an educated conclusion. It will always be necessary to make judgments on the relative merits of each case. But the last thing we should do is shackle ourselves to a principle that prevents action even when the benefits obviously outweigh the risks.

CHAPTER TWO

Our Present Predicament

Throughout the course of this book we will examine all the key environmental issues that make up the movement's agenda today. These include hot topics like genetic engineering, climate change, species extinction, and toxic waste. I will document the gradual extremism that has taken over the environmental movement that I helped launch, eventually compelling me to leave Greenpeace and make my own way down the environmental trail. And I will suggest sensible policy alternatives for a sustainable future.

I will discuss specific environmental issues, sometimes in detail. But the main point I will make is that environmentalism has gone off the rails and has become an apocalyptic religion that is self-defeating and demoralizing. If society is to tackle the very real and difficult challenges ahead, we must find and implement sensible and pragmatic solutions. Today's environmental movement, marked by intolerance and shrill tirades against capitalism and globalization, is simply not up to the job at hand. In fact, it has become a roadblock to meeting these challenges. In this chapter I will use the issues of climate change and energy production to show how the environmental movement has become disabled by its own ideology.

Every day we are bombarded with dire predictions of ecological collapse and social disintegration. We are told there is no time for debate; radical action is necessary now if we wish to avoid an apocalypse of biblical proportions. No one paints a negative picture better than Robert Kennedy Jr.:

Our generation faces the greatest moral and political crisis in human history. Will we take the steps necessary to avert catastrophic global warming or will we doom our children to a new Dark Ages in a world that is biologically and economically impoverished and defined by ever diminishing quality of life?...The scientific debate is over except among a few polluter-financed junk scientists and ideologically blinded flat Earthers.[9]

The question that might pop into a reader's mind: "Is this a load of sensationalist hogwash or is the world really coming to an end?" Some would say that the writer has an impressive pedigree, and an Ivy League education. His occupation as a senior lawyer with the Natural Resources Defense Council in Washington, D.C., gives him access to both what you know and who you know. At the very least he must be sincere in his fears, even if they are exaggerated, right?

Many scientists and nearly all environmental groups believe global warming is caused by burning fossil fuels such as coal, oil, and natural gas. Many other scientists believe the present global warming trend is a natural phenomenon similar to the other warming and cooling periods that have occurred throughout Earth's history. It is not possible to "scientifically prove" which opinion is correct because there are too many variables and we are talking about predicting the future, a difficult task for the simplest of issues. And climate change and global warming are anything but simple—this is one of the most complex and challenging areas in science today. As I stated earlier, we should remember that the crystal ball is actually a mythical object. And it is possible either or both positions are partly right; that there is a natural warming trend that is being accelerated by our fossil fuel emissions.

In later chapters we will explore the complexities of climate science and policy, but in this chapter I want to focus on the policy dilemma we face due to the environmental movement's positions on climate change and energy production. These positions have greatly influenced environmental and energy policies at national and international levels. To sum up the present predicament, most environmental groups oppose the continued use of fossil fuels, but they also oppose or ignore nearly all the available and affordable alternatives. They have adopted a policy framework on energy and climate change that is logically inconsistent, technically impossible, and entirely self-defeating.

Many environmentalists believe renewable wind energy can help displace fossil fuels and their greenhouse gas emissions. A large wind energy facility has been proposed for an offshore site near Martha's Vineyard at Cape Cod. Robert Kennedy Jr., with the help of his friends in Congress,

---

9. Robert Kennedy Jr., Facebook, April 27, 2005, http://www.facebook.com/group.php?gid=2204512237

is leading a campaign to defeat the proposal. He claims the location is inappropriate.[10] It is in fact an excellent location as the wind blows regularly; it is out of shipping lanes, and far enough from shore not to cause noise pollution.

How can someone who thinks the planet will self-destruct if we don't halt global warming be opposed to some windmills six miles from the shore? And even though Greenpeace claims to support wind energy it actively opposes another wind farm in the Western Isles of Scotland because it is "too big."[11] I don't think Greenpeace will stop global warming with small windmills.

This is the predicament we all find ourselves in today. Not so much that the world is coming to an end but in the words of the late Michael Crichton: "The greatest challenge facing mankind is the challenge of distinguishing reality from fantasy, truth from propaganda. Perceiving the truth has always been a challenge to mankind, but in the information age (or as I think of it, the disinformation age) it takes on a special urgency and importance."[12]

It all started with computers and the 1960s adage, "garbage in, garbage out." That was nothing compared with today's Internet frenzy. Just search the Internet for "mass extinction" and you will find we are in the midst of the apocalypse already, in case you hadn't noticed.[13] According to some authoritative-looking websites and ecology research groups, 50,000 species are going extinct every year and 100 years from now 50 percent of all species will be gone. Never mind that there isn't a shred of evidence to support such claims, it makes good grist for sensationalists, doomsday prophets, and CNN. Not coincidentally, it is good grist for milling up research grant renewals.

Of course much of this mass extinction is attributed to global warming, or climate change as it is more generally referred to. It is hard to find a problem that isn't linked to climate change these days. Again from Robert Kennedy Jr.:

Global warming could give us a future where erratic and chaotic weather, rising sea levels, and melting snowpack usher in an epic of drought, crop failure, famine, flood and mass extinctions—and the political instability that invariably accompanies dwindling resources. Millions of environmental refugees uprooted by these calamities will challenge the

10. Editorial, "Kennedy Picks the Wrong Side," New Bedford Standard-Times, August 21, 2005, http://archive.southcoasttoday.com/daily/08-05/08-21-05/kennedy.htm
11. BBC News, "Greenpeace Opposes Wind Farm Plan," April 6, 2005, http://news.bbc.co.uk/2/hi/uk_news/scotland/4415787.stm
12. Michael Crichton, "Remarks to the Commonwealth Club," San Francisco, September 15, 2003, http://www.monsanto.co.uk/news/ukshowlib.phtml?uid=7662
13. "The Current Mass Extinction," http://www.well.com/~davidu/extinction.html

existence of democracy, freedom, justice and human dignity in every corner of the globe.[14]

While Kennedy scales the heights of hyperbole, there are admittedly many reasonable people who believe human-caused global warming is a problem that needs to be addressed. Plenty of knowledgeable climatologists and scientists in related fields believe continued greenhouse gas emissions could pose a threat to climatic stability.

And there are, of course, knowledgeable and reasonable people who don't believe humans are causing the planet to heat up and rather that we're experiencing natural climate fluctuations. And there are people who believe even if we are causing global warming it may be beneficial, increasing growing seasons and reducing energy needs. The earth is actually relatively cool now compared to the many periods of warmer climate that occurred in the past.

So how do we, as a society, sort out the differing opinions, stances, and prescriptions to find a collective way forward when so many groups proclaim calamity at nearly every turn, while others proclaim no calamity at all?

First, we can look at the basic realities. Without accurate information on the current situation, it is hard to chart a sensible course for the future. This must be done scientifically, which means we must make decisions based on solid, credible information—not hype, dogma, or political agendas. Science is not a religion; it is the art of making accurate observations and interpretations of reality. From there we assess the various options and make pragmatic, sensible decisions.

We can all agree that humanity faces serious environmental challenges as we struggle to provide food, housing health care, clothing, transportation, and energy to the seven billion people who call Earth their home.

But the challenge is growing. The world's population is predicted to grow from 6.8 billion people in 2010 to 9.5 billion people sometime around the year 2050. Thankfully, population growth is already slowing, adding fewer people each year since 1997. Demographers expect the population will begin to decline slowly after we reach a peak of 9.5 billion. In addition to the sheer growth in numbers, in 2050 a larger percentage of the population (most, I hope) will be able to afford to be well fed, have access to medical care, own refrigerators, air conditioners, televisions, and will be able to afford to care about the environment more than they do today. This means instead of two billion people living modern lifestyles, there will be four to six billion, or two to three times more than today.

In a nutshell, this will double or perhaps triple the world's demand for food, minerals, forest products, and energy. That is the crux of the environ-

14. Robert Kennedy Jr., April 27, 2005, http://climatequotes.com/celebrities/robert-f-kennedy-jr/

mental challenge we face today: how do we double or triple food and energy production without fouling our garden and without converting the entire planet into food and fuel factories? How can wild nature survive in such a future?

There is no shortage of answers to this challenge. Sticking to the topic of energy and climate change, we're told to conserve energy, use more hydroelectric power, use more geothermal, use more wind, use more biofuels, use more solar, use tidal, use more nuclear, or simply increase fossil fuel consumption because man-made global warming is just a hoax anyway. All of these points of view may have a kernel of truth, but all are oversimplified prescriptions to very complex issues.

Today we face a wide divergence of opinions about whether or not the climate is warming, whether or not we are the primary culprit if it is warming, whether or not this will be good or bad, and what to do about it.

I do not deny that the climate has warmed; it has been doing so for more than 18,000 years—since the end of the last major glaciation, well before humans increased the concentration of CO_2 in the atmosphere. And I do not deny that we are part of the cause of the recent rise in carbon dioxide levels in the global atmosphere, primarily because we burn huge quantities of fossil fuels. I don't even deny we may be responsible for some of the present warming, but I do not believe we can be certain of this.

I know I've begun with some very large topics that require much more discussion. That will come later in the book. But for now my purpose is to demonstrate, by way of the climate change/energy issue, the divergence of opinion that forced me to make my own way in the environmental debate. I couldn't belong to an organization, or a movement, that demanded strict adherence to policies I thought deserved more debate, especially when there were logically inconsistent and contradictory positions taken on related issues. When environmentalism becomes an ideology or a religion, I'm out the door because I believe in continued open discussion of complex scientific issues about the future of civilization and the global environment. Simplistic, zero-tolerance, black-and-white positions are the enemy of sensible environmentalism. I believe in a more reasonable approach that provides practical solutions to real problems.

No doubt some of you are already groaning, while I hope others are cheering. My primary purpose is to stimulate thought and debate about some of the more interesting and important issues of our time. Of course for now my mind is made up about some of them, but I'd like to think I am open to new information and fresh arguments. That's all I ask of the reader, to bear with me through the story of my 40 years as an ecologist and environmental activist. During those years I've developed a vision for environmentalism in the 21st century. Allow me to share that vision with you.

CHAPTER THREE
Beginnings

My life began in the tiny fishing and logging village of Winter Harbour on the northwest tip of Vancouver Island, in the rain forest by the Pacific. My mother and father were the children of true pioneers, who had come to this remote place and learned to make a living from a tough wilderness. I grew up thinking 150 inches of rain a year was normal and that the ultimate freedom was a 12-foot wooden skiff with a two-horsepower outboard motor. There was no road to—or even in—Winter Harbour. I commuted with a few other children on my dad's small wooden tugboat to a one-room schoolhouse two miles away. It was a peaceful childhood, playing on the tide flats by the salmon-spawning streams in the rain forest.

The original Kwakiutl inhabitants of Winter Harbour called their village Cliena. They had survived by the beach for thousands of years on the abundant salmon, clams, and berries, and built their houses of cedar planks taken from the forest behind them. Over the years the people of Cliena were decimated by measles, smallpox, and other diseases introduced by early European settlers. (Many other aboriginal communities met a similar fate.) The village site had long been abandoned by the time my grandfather established his float camp in Winter Harbour in 1936, the few native survivors having relocated to the nearby community of Quatsino. I was born into this far-flung floating village on June 15, 1947.

The floating logging camp I was born into in Winter Harbour had about 50 residents. The family houses are on the right and the single men's cabins are on the left. This photo was taken in 1951.

The logging camp where I grew up was on floats made of old-growth trees cut along the shoreline. There were a dozen bunkhouses for the single men, a cookhouse, blacksmith shop, office, movie hall, and a half-dozen family houses. The fishing was best behind the cookhouse, where the flunky (the cook's assistant) threw the food scraps into the ocean (the "salt chuck" to us). Mothers worried their children would fall into the salt chuck and drown. A bulky kapok life jacket was mandatory dress outside the house. My first brush with death came at age four when I fell between two float-logs and became stuck facedown in the water between them. Luckily one of the loggers found me before I drowned.

There were no frills in the life of a West Coast logger in those early years. Four men bunked in each 12-by-24-foot shack, one to a corner, with a 45-gallon oil drum woodstove in the center, where rain soaked clothes were hung to dry. They worked six or seven days a week, getting up in the dark, working in the rain and wrestling in the mud to fix broken machinery. It was hard, relentless work, falling the huge trees, winching them down the mountain to the sea, where they could be boomed to the mill, all the while staying alert to avoid being slashed by a snapping cable or crushed by a run-away log. When the loggers were not working, there was nothing much to do back at the bunkhouse but play cards or listen to the radio. It was a lonely and sometimes miserable existence.

The early float camp era was ending during my boyhood. As the merchantable trees along the water's edge had all been harvested, my

CONFESSIONS OF A GREENPEACE DROPOUT

The float camp was moved ashore in 1954. This white house by the large spruce tree was my home until I was 14.

father, Bill Moore, obtained a lease in 1954 from the Kwakiutl to establish a permanent community on the original native village site. Roads were built to access timber farther up the valleys. Diesel-powered engines had replaced steam engines some years before, but it was the introduction of the motorized chainsaw, which replaced double-bitted axes and crosscut handsaws, that revolutionized logging. Productivity increased dramatically with this improvement in technology. Loggers and their families shared in the postwar boom in material culture and working-class affluence. It was a wonderful time to live in the rain forest.

I didn't know I lived in a rain forest; to us it was simply "the woods" and it rained a lot. When it rained for 30 days straight, we began to miss the sun. My playground and backyard was a recent clearcut across the road from our house. We didn't call it a clearcut because the word wasn't known; it was simply an opening or the "slash." The slash was a better place to play than the deep dark of the old-growth forest surrounding us. It was brighter and when the sun shone it was warmer and drier. The only other places where the sun came out were down on the dock and on the tide flats. In the clearing you could sit on a stump in the sun and all summer long the berries grew: first the salmonberries, then thimbleberries, then huckleberries, and finally the salal berries. They were all deliciously different and we shared them with birds, deer, and bears. As time went on, new trees came up and added year-round green to the logged area. The hemlocks, cedars, and firs that competed for sunlight eventually crowded

My dad, Bill Moore, worked alongside the other loggers six days a week, spending evenings and Sunday afternoon in the office tending to company affairs.

out the berry bushes. It was time to move on and to play in a more recent clearcut. From this experience I developed a very different impression of logging than one might gain from the popular press today.

Today I can walk through forests where my grandfather clearcut logged 60 and 70 years ago, and if it weren't for the presence of rotting, moss-covered stumps, you would never know the forests had once been cleared. The new forest is so lush and full of shrubs and ferns that all evidence of disturbance has disappeared. Bears, wolves, cougars, ravens, owls, eagles, and all the other forest-dwellers live there. The trees are straight and tall. Although they have not yet reached the great size of their predecessors, they form a dense and growing cover on land once cleared bare. The marvel of this renewal is that it took place entirely on its own, without the slightest help from human hands. There had been no thought given to reforestation or any other aspect of restoration. Nature has regenerated almost in spite of human disturbance and is rapidly returning to its original condition.

My dad was a big man who had inherited the logging camp at age 21 when his father, Albert, passed away. It was the beginning of World War II, the business was $40,000 in debt, a large sum at the time, and there were 60 grizzled loggers, all older than he was, and he had to be the boss. Dad worked day and night for 20 years before he could see any light at the end of the tunnel. In the woods dad could curse a blue streak while lines snapped and machines broke down. At home he was a well-read family man, who, although stern at times, would joke and play with us during

CONFESSIONS OF A GREENPEACE DROPOUT

My mom, Beverly, and my dad, Bill, about to go to "town" on a float plane, circa 1960. Our little village by the sea is in the background, the camp cookhouse is above.

his few hours away from work. He taught me about leadership and the fact that someone must take responsibility for making decisions, at home, in the workplace, and in government. He had a small business but he loomed large in his industry, becoming president of two industry associations, the BC Truckloggers Association and the Pacific Logging Congress. He cared about working people; he founded and chaired a number of initiatives in forestry education, worker safety, and loggers' sports. The saddest thing I've ever seen was his 10-year battle with Alzheimer's as it brought a proud man to his knees.

While dad taught me leadership, my mom, Beverly, taught me how to think. Also well read, she was the daughter of a hard-working West Coast salmon fishing family that struggled through the Great Depression. My granddad, Art, and his three brothers had pioneered the salmon fishing industry in Winter Harbour in the late 1930s. They were involved in the creation of the Kyuquot Fisherman's Co-op, an effort to get out from under the yoke of the big fish buyers who paid next to nothing for their hard labor. He and Granny Mary were Socialists of a peaceful nature. But like their Russian comrades they were atheists and rejected capitalism. This philosophy strongly influenced Mom, although her education and love of knowledge tempered her political fervor.

When I was 15 Mom introduced me to the great British philosopher, Bertrand Russell. While I found the first book she recommended, *Why I Am Not a Christian*, interesting, it was his writing in the social and scientific fields that really turned me on. I raced through *Authority and*

The view today from my cottage at Winter Harbour. When the sun shines it is one of the most beautiful places on earth. A local saying goes, "If you can't see the mountains, it's raining; if you can see the mountains, it's going to rain." Photo: Patrick Moore

the Individual, a treatise on the conflict between our rights as individuals and our obligations to the greater good of society. Then I discovered *Our Knowledge of the External World* and *Inquiry into Meaning and Truth*. I was fascinated by Russell's grasp of the scientific method but even more impressed with his critical thinking. Thus began my lifelong pursuit of knowledge in the sciences and my near obsession with thinking critically as a way of separating facts and logic from misinformation and propaganda.

In an era when classroom sex education didn't exist Mom taught me about the birds and the bees in a nice way. No doubt she was a big part of the reason there were no unwanted pregnancies in my younger years.

Around the same time I was sent off to boarding school in Vancouver, at age 14, the road came to Winter Harbour, 250 miles of bad gravel from the nearest pavement at Campbell River. We thought the road would bring new settlers to the village. Instead, it prompted an exodus. Today there are 11 full-time residents in my hometown, there were 75 before the road came in. I love it there.

My four years at St. George's private school in Vancouver were formative in a number of ways. I excelled in the arts and sciences and I made friends who I count as my best friends today. I found out I disliked contact sports, English rugby being the school's idea of how real men were made. Give me tennis or skiing over sports that require extreme body contact. So I failed as a jock even though I admired my fellow students who thought nothing of risking life and limb to get a ball across the line.

CONFESSIONS OF A GREENPEACE DROPOUT

After graduating from St. George's I enrolled in the Faculty of Science at the University of British Columbia in Vancouver in 1965, and soon developed a passion for the life sciences. During those years I really came to appreciate my home village in the wilderness. I had always been mechanically inclined: I was monkey-wrenching engines by the time I was eight and I built my first 12-foot plywood boat when I was 13. I imagined I would become an engineer or architect. Auspiciously, in retrospect, I nearly failed my first year at university after being at the top of my class throughout high school. It was a simple case of going a little wild after the imposed discipline of an English-style boarding school, but it meant I didn't qualify to enter the School of Engineering. Oscar Sziklai, a forestry professor-friend of my dad's, encouraged me to apply to the School of Forestry. Soon after I began to study trees and forests I realized I was even more fascinated by biology than by engineering or mechanics.

After excelling in first-year forestry I was given the opportunity to fashion my own program, a combined honors degree in forestry and biology. This allowed me to study a broad range of life-science subjects: genetics, biochemistry, soil science, plant physiology, and forest science. Then I discovered ecology, the study of how all living things are interrelated, and how we are related to them. Having grown up in an agnostic household I had always viewed science as a purely technical subject, the objective of which was to dispel mystery rather than to foster it. Now I saw that through the science of ecology one could come to appreciate the infinitely complex nature of the universe and gain an insight into the mystery of life. I realized the feeling of tranquility and wonder I had experienced as a child in the rain forest was a kind of prayer or meditation. Ecology gave me a sort of religion, and with it the passion to take on the world. I became a born-again ecologist.

Upon graduating with honors I was awarded a Ford Foundation Fellowship to enroll in a PhD program at the university of my choice. I picked Washington University in St. Louis, where Dr. David Gates, a leader in research on photosynthesis and food chain energetics, agreed to head my thesis committee. In June of 1969 I drove from Vancouver to St. Louis in my Volkswagen camper microbus, sporting a pretty big Afro, to discover America for the first time. The campus was beautiful but the city center had been burned to the ground the previous summer during the riots following the assassination of Dr. Martin Luther King. A nearby river was so polluted it would regularly catch on fire. It was the height of the Vietnam War and even grad students were being drafted. Fear and loathing darkened the beauty of the campus... I felt like Bilbo the Hobbit witnessing Mordor for the first time. It was certainly no place for a country kid from Canada to study ecology.

So I traveled on through the South and east to Key West, Florida, and back across Texas to California, where I visited the University of California at Davis, known for excellence in agriculture and ecology. There was no burned-out city there, but the dread of being drafted into an unpopular war was the same as in St Louis. I couldn't fathom the idea of being among fellow students who lived in fear every day. I turned tail and headed back to my peaceful home in Western Canada, where I convinced my professors to let me do my PhD at the University of British Columbia.

I didn't realize it at the time, but I was part of what became known as the "reverse brain drain." The brain drain referred to the fact that many young Canadians, after benefiting from publicly funded educations, chose to move to the United States where salaries were higher and taxes lower. For a period of a few years during the Vietnam War this trend reversed as Canadians chose to stay home and many of the brightest Americans came to Canada to avoid the war.

One of my mentors was C.S. (Buzz) Holling, a pioneer in computer modeling of insect population dynamics. He agreed to let me do an interdisciplinary PhD in ecology and environmental science, which allowed me to take courses in any faculty. I studied environmental law, environmental economics, forest ecology, oceanography, marine biology, mineral engineering, and soil science, among other subjects.

Shortly after I began my studies an announcement was made that would help shape the future of environmental policy and law in my home province. Utah Mining and Smelting of San Francisco was developing a large open pit copper mine near the sea on northern Vancouver Island, not far from my home at Winter Harbour. The company had applied for a permit to dispose of 40,000 tons of mine tailings per day into Rupert Inlet, a deep fjord in Quatsino Sound. Over the next 25 years it would produce $3 billion worth of copper and become the world's deepest open pit at 1,200 feet below sea level. A number of the fledgling environmental groups, a few university professors, and 150 or so individuals filed objections with British Columbia's Pollution Control Branch to stop the mine from dumping its waste into the sea. The battle was joined.

I realized this was a perfect subject for my interdisciplinary PhD thesis as it involved the environment, industry, government regulation, communities, pollution, marine science, and economics. The company, backed by consultants, claimed the mine waste would immediately settle to the bottom of the inlet and stay there. My preliminary research contradicted this, predicting the tailings would be stirred into the surface waters due to the tidal circulation pattern in the inlet. With the support of my professors I filed an objection with the Pollution Control Branch, explaining that I had evidence the mining company and its consultants were wrong. The director of Pollution Control denied my objection, along with most of the others. Only one organization, The Pacific Salmon Society, and three lay individuals were chosen to appear at a public hearing. It's hard to imagine today but in 1969 the director had the authority to deny any objector; in fact this was to be the very first public hearing in B.C. on the subject of industrial pollution.

I didn't give up so easily. I contacted the Pacific Salmon Society, found out its members knew relatively little about the specifics of the issue, and invited myself to their next board meeting. After explaining my hypothesis to them they made me vice-president and appointed me as their representative to the public hearings. I then had the opportunity to present my evidence in public, completely disagreeing with the company and its experts. The media, always eager for a good controversy, duly reported this. It was noticed in high places that a certain graduate student was meddling in B.C.'s affairs of state.

It was not long before the head of my thesis committee, forest ecologist Hamish Kimmins, called me into his office. He advised me that the dean had been approached by a high authority who recommended that if I was interested in getting a job with industry or government after graduating perhaps I should "change the nature of my inquiry." I balked at this threat, really got my back up, and with a young man's air of invincibility decided to continue my investigation. I was not just a born-again ecologist now, I was a radical environmental activist and it all happened because I cared more about science than politics.

I fashioned a research agenda that included measuring the turbidity (lack of clarity) and temperature of the water in Rupert Inlet. I did this for a year before the mine began to dump its tailings into the inlet and for a year afterwards. I proved beyond a doubt that the powerful tides mixed the tailings throughout the water column and regularly brought them to the surface. By the time I was supposed to graduate, the mining company had hired two of the five professors on my thesis committee as consultants, and the head of the geology department had forced his way onto my committee. At my oral defense it was obvious I was in trouble, three against three. My defense dragged on for a year with the opposing professors making pathetic claims that there was something wrong with my science. Eventually, the dean of Graduate Studies had to bring in an independent adjudicator, who thankfully sided with me. I got my PhD in ecology.

CHAPTER FOUR

No Nukes Now!

My PhD struggles gave me an introduction to the world of environmental politics and I wanted to make a change. The Don't Make a Wave Committee's plan to oppose U.S. hydrogen bomb tests seemed like a perfect opportunity. About 20 of us gathered regularly in the basement of the Unitarian church to plan this crazy voyage across the North Pacific. Jim and Marie Bohlen were Quakers from Pennsylvania who had immigrated to Canada so that their sons would not be drafted into the Vietnam War. An MIT engineering graduate, Jim had become a pacifist during the Cuban Missile Crisis. He had been designing heat-resistant nose-cones for nuclear missiles when he realized he was part of the problem. Irving and Dorothy Stowe, from Rhode Island, were also expatriate Americans with a similar story. Only Irving was a lawyer and a fierce anti-American orator. The complement was rounded out by a dozen or so Canadians, mostly young like myself and mostly newly arrived to the protest scene.

We had all grown up under the daily threat of an all-out nuclear war between the United States and the former Soviet Union. Everyone knew it would be the end of civilization as we knew it and the environment would take a heavy toll. The prospect of a nuclear winter following a nuclear exchange galvanized us into joining the fight to save the earth from such a fate.

A benefit concert was organized in Vancouver featuring Joni Mitchell, James Taylor, the late Phil Oakes, and a local band called Chilliwack after a local town in British Columbia. This raised $20,000 for the cause, pretty good money at the time, allowing us to charter an 85-foot halibut fishing boat named the *Phyllis Cormack*. The skipper, John Cormack (the boat was named after his wife), was a veteran of the Bering Sea halibut fishery, so he knew the waters at the H-bomb test site and how to get there.

A bit of history. The first successful atomic bomb was tested by the United States in the desert outside Alamogordo, New Mexico, in July of 1945. This was followed less than a month later by the bombings of the Japanese cities of Hiroshima on August 6 and Nagasaki three days later, bringing an end to World War II. The world had suddenly and horrifically entered the nuclear age, with all its threats and promises. The Soviet Union followed the U.S. with a successful atomic bomb test in August of 1949. Then came Britain in 1952, France in 1960, and China in 1964. By 1971, nearly 500 atomic bombs had been detonated in the atmosphere around the world, with the U.S. and Soviet Union each responsible for more than 200 atmospheric tests and dozens of underground tests.

Most people think of the Cold War as an ideological war. But the Cold War was as hot as they come in terms of radioactive fallout. Hundreds of different radioactive elements are created during an atomic blast, including biologically dangerous isotopes such as cesium-137, strontium-90, and iodine-131. In the days, weeks, and even years following a blast these radioactive particles rain down on the land and sea.

Many of the elements in nuclear fallout decay very rapidly and pose little threat. But a few longer-lived isotopes are particularly nasty because they are selectively absorbed and concentrated by plants and animals. Our body can't tell the difference between normal iodine, which is not radioactive, and radioactive iodine-131. Iodine is an essential nutrient, so our digestive system absorbs it from our food, sending most of it to the thyroid gland in our neck. This is why people exposed to nuclear fallout are at high risk of contracting thyroid cancer; their body sends the radioactive iodine to the gland and concentrates it there.

Strontium-90 is even more insidious; it is not an essential nutrient, but it mimics calcium, which is the main element in our bones. We can't distinguish between calcium and strontium, so our blood carries the radioactive strontium-90 right to our bone marrow, where red blood cells are produced. This is why people exposed to fallout are at higher risk of developing leukemia or bone cancer.

Cesium-137 mimics potassium, an essential nutrient that is distributed throughout the body. Our system thinks cesium-137 is potassium and sends it all around, increasing the risk for many types of cancer.

Up until 1951, nuclear bombs were relatively small. The two bombs dropped on Japan, for example, were 15,000 and 25,000 tons of TNT equivalent, or 15 and 25 kilotons. But the development of the hydrogen bomb in 1952 marked the beginning of the thermonuclear age, when the bombs became a thousand times more powerful. The hydrogen bomb depends on nuclear fusion (combining hydrogen atoms) in addition to nuclear fission (splitting uranium or plutonium atoms). Nuclear fusion is the same process that powers our sun.

Scientists soon realized atmospheric fallout from these new, more powerful weapons posed a serious health risk. In addition to the direct threat that humans and other animals would breathe in the radioactive dust, radioactive particles fell on crops and pastures, contaminating food, dairy products in particular. As a result of this knowledge the U.S., U.S.S.R., and Britain signed the Limited Test Ban Treaty in 1963, which banned atmospheric weapons tests. France did not sign this treaty and continued testing weapons above ground until 1974.

After signing the treaty, the U.S. focused on underground testing of atomic bombs in the Nevada desert, where there was a long-established test range. Even these relatively small tests shook the buildings in Las Vegas. It was simply not possible to test hydrogen bombs there; they would break windows in the casinos. Prior to the treaty the U.S. had tested its hydrogen bombs on Bikini atoll in the South Pacific, exposing islanders to large doses of radioactivity. If the American government wanted to continue testing thermonuclear weapons, it had to find somewhere outside the lower 48 states to do so.

It didn't take long for the Atomic Energy Agency to identify Amchitka Island, halfway out the far-flung Aleutians, as the perfect place to play with the ultimate weapon. It was well removed from New York, Los Angeles, Chicago, or any other likely source of complaint. In the era of superpower dominance, it didn't seem to matter that Amchitka was closer to Japan, Russia, Korea, China, and Canada than it was to the U.S., with the exception of sparsely populated Alaska. This turned out to be a bit of an oversight on America's part.

Project Cannikin would be the largest underground nuclear test the U.S. had carried out. Scheduled for October 6, 1971, the five-megaton device was designed to proof-test a warhead for the Spartan antiballistic missile program.

On September 15, 1971, we set off from Vancouver to confront the H-bomb: 11 activists plus Captain J.C. Cormack. It was an epic voyage with terrible storms and serious mechanical breakdowns. But we made headway, taking a straight course from the north shore of the Queen Charlotte Islands across the North Pacific to the first islands in the Aleutian chain. About three days after leaving sight of land a U.S. reconnaissance aircraft buzzed us. Clearly we had the attention of the authorities; no doubt the CIA, the Coast Guard, the Atomic Energy Commission, and even the White House were tracking our progress. Then we received troubling news. The Atomic Energy Commission had decided to delay the test one month; the new date was November 6. October 6 was late enough in the

CONFESSIONS OF A GREENPEACE DROPOUT

This photo was taken in Klemtu on the Central Coast of British Columbia in September 1971, on the way to Alaska to protest the U.S. hydrogen bomb tests. I had become a radical environmental activist and would never look back. Ben Metcalfe is on the left and Bill Darnell, who coined the name Greenpeace, is on the right. Photo: Robert Keziere

season, but the new schedule would push us well into severe winter weather. Suddenly nature became a serious factor in our ability to reach the test site. At the time we believed the delay was an effort to make our mission impossible. We later learned that technical problems in the underground cavity where the bomb would be placed caused the delay.

After a week of being tossed around in the open sea we arrived at the tiny Aleut village of Akutan on the island of the same name. The residents had known John Cormack for many years and we were welcomed as friends. Whiskey costs an arm and a leg in these far-flung places, so they make raisin wine; it's a little rough but it does the trick.

On our second day in Akutan, at anchor in the calm bay, the watchman saw a ship approaching. It turned out to be the U.S. Coast Guard cutter *Confidence* and it was coming right for us. John Cormack's sense of humor mixed with drama as he ordered the anchor weighed, fired up the engine, and motored full ahead up the inlet. It was a dead end, of course, and with the cutter in hot pursuit we eventually had to stop and lower the anchor again. But at least we got a boat chase.

The cutter came to a stop about 200 yards off our stern and we watched as a launch was lowered, boarded by four people, and then motored toward us. It arrived alongside carrying three seamen and the captain. The captain boarded our boat without asking permission, heading to the wheelhouse, where John Cormack was waiting for him.

We found out later we had been interdicted for failing to clear Customs and Immigration before landing in Akutan. It was true we had overlooked

At the height of our campaign against U.S. H-bomb testing, we posed aboard the *Phyllis Cormack* in Akutan Harbor. From the top left: Bob Hunter, myself, Bob Cummings, Ben Metcalfe, Dave Birmingham. From the bottom left: Dick Fineberg, Lyle Thurston, Jim Bohlen, Terry Simmons, Bill Darnell, and Captain John Cormack. Photographer Bob Keziere, who took the photo, and crewmember Rod Marining, who joined later, are not shown. Photo: Robert Keziere

this minor technicality, knowing full well we would have been refused entry if we had checked in with the authorities at nearby Dutch Harbor.

While the skipper of the *Confidence* was reading the riot act to Captain Cormack, one of the Coast Guard crew passed us a hastily typed and crumpled note that read, "If it were not for these military bonds, we would be with you." The entire 16-member crew had signed it (except the captain, of course). The Coast Guard is part of the armed forces, so we were amazed that regular enlisted men would dare to make such a bold statement. We heard later that the Coast Guard crew were subsequently confined to quarters and docked pay. Our media reps immediately relayed the Coast Guard crew's note to the wire services over our temperamental shortwave radio. That night, we made it onto "CBS Evening News with Walter Cronkite," then the number one television news program in the U.S.

Bingo. Greenpeace was on the map and we never looked back. A few people had proven they could reach millions and create a new awareness just by getting up and doing something creative.

Under orders, we retreated to the small fishing village of Sand Point in the Shumagin Islands, a couple of hundred miles back from where we had been apprehended. There played out one of the most intense personal encounters I have ever been party to. The debate that ensued forged lasting bonds and prejudices in all of us. The basic question was, Should we retreat with our tails between our legs or should we defy the Coast Guard and carry on to the test site via international waters? Well, that was the way

CONFESSIONS OF A GREENPEACE DROPOUT

Some of the crew of the Phyllis Cormack around the galley table. From the left, Terry Simmons, Jim Bohlen, Lyle Thurston, Dave Birmingham, Dick Fineburg, Bill Darnell, Bob Hunter, me, and Captain John Cormack. Photo: Robert Keziere

the kamikazes put it. Some of us asked, Should we sail to certain death in winter storms or should we go home knowing we have succeeded in raising the issue? Bob Hunter led the death wish contingent, he really didn't mind dying for the cause. Jim Bohlen, as the senior Don't Make a Wave Committee member on board, who didn't want to die just yet, preached caution. Captain Cormack somewhat sadistically let this argument play out for a few days before he made it clear no bunch of city boys was going to tell him where to take his boat. We headed home.

Even though we were blocked from sailing to the nuclear test site, and even though that 5-megaton explosion did take place on November 6, 1971, we were the ultimate victors. Fueled by our action and the resulting publicity, tens of thousands of protesters blocked border crossings between the U.S. and Canada the day the bomb was detonated. The public opposition to the tests forced President Nixon to cancel the remaining H-bomb tests in the planned series in February 1972. This was at the height of the Cold War and the height of the Vietnam War.

In retrospect this proved a major turning point in the global arms race. Our September 15 departure from Vancouver on our first mission was the birth of Greenpeace. This mission put us squarely on the front lines of the battle to end the threat of nuclear Armageddon. The first major agreement between the United States and the Soviet Union under the Strategic Arms Limitation Talks, the Anti-Ballistic Missile Treaty, was signed on May 28, 1972.

We were made honorary brothers of the Kwakiutl First Nations at Alert Bay on our return from Alaska. This began a long association with aboriginal people around the world. I am in the center with cap in hand. Photo: Robert Keziere

Even though we had been on opposite sides of the debate about whether to go home or go on, Bob Hunter was to become the kind of lifelong friend that rarely comes along. He was a prominent editorial columnist with the *Vancouver Sun*, our city's main newspaper, and he had established himself as an exciting commentator on the emerging environmental movement.

As we made our way back down the coast from Alaska, Bob and I had time for sustained reflection. But there was one conversation that still seems as if it happened yesterday. "Pat, this is the beginning of something really important and very powerful," he predicted. "But there is a very good chance it will become a kind of ecofascism. Not everyone can get a PhD in ecology. So the only way to change the behavior of the masses is to create a popular mythology, a religion of the environment where people simply have faith in the gurus." Today I shudder at the accuracy of his foresight.

On our way home from Alaska we were welcomed into the big house of the Namgis (Nimkish) First Nations, part of the Kwakiutl First Nations, at Alert Bay near my northern Vancouver Island home. They danced for us and initiated us into their tribe as brothers, sprinkling holy water and eagle feathers on our heads. We were given the right to display the Sisiutl crest, a double-headed sea serpent representative of the orca whale.

For Greenpeace, this began a long relationship with aboriginal and indigenous people around the world. Bob Hunter came across a small book titled *Warriors of the Rainbow*. It contained an American Indian prophecy predicting that someday when the sky was black and the birds fell dead

CONFESSIONS OF A GREENPEACE DROPOUT

A depiction of the Warriors of the Rainbow from the book of the same name. Aboriginal people are following the dove of peace to save the environment.

and the waters were poisoned that people from all races would join togeth-er to save the earth from destruction.[15] We soon fashioned ourselves as the "Rainbow Warriors."

After the voyage to Alaska many of the campaigners who put Greenpeace on the map against U.S. nuclear testing moved back to their former lives or moved on to new ones. But a few of us—Ben and Dorothy Metcalfe, Jim and Marie Bohlen, Bob Hunter, Rod Marining, and myself—had be-come addicted to making waves and taking on the nuclear establishment. It wasn't long before we turned our sights on French atmospheric nuclear testing at Mururoa Atoll in the South Pacific.

France had refused to sign the Partial Nuclear Test Ban Treaty of 1963 banning nuclear tests in the atmosphere. Both France and China con-tinued to detonate nuclear weapons in the air, sending radioactive fallout around the world. New Zealand, in particular, had become a hotbed of op-position against the French nuclear tests.

Before sailing on the first Greenpeace voyage, Ben Metcalfe, a for-mer CBC radio news correspondent, had made a reputation as a creative booster for the emerging environmental movement in Vancouver. Ahead of his time, in 1969 Ben paid for 12 billboards at major Vancouver inter-sections so commuters could read in simple bold print, "Ecology? Look it Up! You're Involved." It is hard to imagine today that the word *ecology* was

---

15. William Willoya and Vinson Brown, *Warriors of the Rainbow* (Happy Camp, California: Naturegraph Publishers , 1962).

One of the 12 billboards Ben Metcalfe paid for in 1969, long before the word ecology came into popular usage.

not yet mentioned in the popular press, but at the time one only found it in obscure academic journals.

During the winter of 1971-72 Ben and the rest of us met around kitchen tables to plan our next campaign. We knew that French atmospheric nuclear testing, conducted at Mururoa Atoll in French Polynesia, was the logical target. Soviet and Chinese testing would have been great targets too, if they didn't involve the practical reality of wanting to avoid the prospect of life in the gulag or death in a far-off prison cell. And certainly within the peace movement at the time the West was considered the aggressor. The Vietnam War put an exclamation mark on that perception.

But French Polynesia lay way out in the remote South Pacific. It had been one thing to sail a boat up the coast from my hometown near Vancouver a thousand miles to Alaska; it was quite another to sail from New Zealand, the closest "friendly" country to Mururoa, 2500 miles across the open waters of the South Pacific. There was also the inconvenient fact that our bank account contained only $9000 and we had no boat, no captain, and no crew. But we were not about to let pesky details get in our way.

We decided to issue a press release announcing that Greenpeace's next campaign would be to sail a boat from New Zealand to Mururoa in order to challenge the French nuclear tests. As France was illegally cordoning off thousands of square miles of international waters during the tests (the 200-mile limit was not in force at the time), we planned to position a boat near the atoll in international waters, then only three miles offshore. Any nuclear test would fry the boat and its occupants, something France might want to avoid. It turned out we were a bit overconfident on this point.

Our press release received little notice anywhere but New Zealand, where the major newspapers put it on the front page. Suddenly there was a buzz that this bunch of crazy Canadians were coming down under to raise Cain as they had up north in Alaska. The headlines brought a few phone calls from skippers in the South Pacific but only one call made sense. A certain David McTaggart, an expatriate Canadian from Vancouver, who had been sailing the southern ocean for seven years, telephoned us to volunteer his 36-foot ketch *Vega* for the mission. David had been a Canadian badminton champion and a successful entrepreneur until he fled for bluer waters. Now he wanted to challenge the right of France to take over international waters for its nuclear tests. Suddenly, we had our skipper, we had our boat, and the publicity surrounding the adventure brought financial support from around the world.

Dorothy Metcalfe coined the slogan *Mururoa mon amour* ("Mururoa My Love") after the acclaimed 1959 film *Hiroshima mon Amour*. This became our campaign slogan and we also used it on lapel buttons that we ordered. Ben Metcalfe took the $6000 or so left in our account to New Zealand and joined McTaggart to outfit the *Vega* for the voyage. In the spring of 1972 I traveled to New York with Jim and Marie Bohlen, who came from that part of the world, and we spent a week visiting the UN embassies of the Pacific Rim countries to inform them about the French nuclear tests. The first UN Conference on the Environment was about to take place in Stockholm, Sweden, and there was an opportunity to make the tests an issue from an environmental perspective. It is hard to believe today, but the Western superpowers (the United States, Great Britain, and France) took the position that nuclear weapons and nuclear testing were not environmental issues and should therefore not be raised at the UN conference. We took exception to this. If nuclear fallout spreading around the earth wasn't an environmental issue, what was? And come to think of it, what about the environmental impact of all-out nuclear war?

Yes, that was the "thinkable" reality that gave my generation nightmares for years. I half-jokingly said, "It might rain today, and by the way, total nuclear annihilation is possible on Wednesday." It is hard to express the singular resolve that emerged to fight this possibility. It expressed itself in many countries, in many publics, in many political debates. But I don't think it expressed itself anywhere more fully than in our fledgling troupe of Greenpeace button-wearing ecologists, pacifists, anarchists, and revolutionaries.

The spring of 1972 saw Greenpeace coming into its own with a coordinated effort straddling the globe. While David McTaggart and Ben Metcalfe set sail from New Zealand for Mururoa, a small group of us set off to Europe, where we hoped to "send a flaming arrow into the heart of Western civilization, " to use the hyperbole of that time. Our first stop was Rome, where we had requested an audience with Pope Paul VI in the Vatican. As a man of peace he welcomed us, blessing our flag and sending a message against nuclear testing around the world.

We then proceeded to Notre Dame Cathedral in Paris, where we spent the afternoon leafleting visitors with antinuclear pamphlets and telling them, in broken French, about *le petit bâteau* that was sailing into the test zone as we spoke. As the cathedral closed, we sat in the pews and told the custodians that we were taking refuge in the church and wouldn't leave until nuclear testing stopped. They politely informed us that Notre Dame was not a church but a national monument and we'd better get out or we would be arrested by the *sûreté* (the national police).

We left, but not until we were interviewed by *Le Monde*, France's main national newspaper. The next day's story marked the first time the French public had been informed about opposition to their nuclear testing program in French Polynesia.

Our next stop was Stockholm, where in June the sun barely sets. This was the first United Nations Conference on the Environment and budding environmentalists from around the world came to join the legions of national government and UN representatives. Most of the nongovernment folks attended a "counter-conference," where they had their own agenda composed of spirited rallies complete with full-size whale balloons and a celebration of life.

The big debate at the counter-conference was between Paul Ehrlich, best-selling author of *The Population Bomb*,[16] and Barry Commoner, author of *The Closing Circle*.[17] Ehrlich contended that the biggest environmental problem was overpopulation, especially in the developing countries. Commoner disagreed, stating that the worst problem was chemicals and toxins in our food chain, caused primarily by the industrialized countries.

The people attending from developing countries and their supporters claimed Ehrlich's view was racist and genocidal as it targeted people of color in developing countries and let the superpowers off the hook. In contrast, nearly everyone was happy to blame industrialized countries for toxic pollution, so Commoner won the debate hands down. The repercussions of this quarrel have affected environmental policy ever since.

Greenpeace, for example, has never addressed population growth or poverty as key environmental issues while it has focused heavily on toxic chemicals through the years. There can be no doubt human population is an important environmental issue, because humans inevitably alter their surroundings and impact ecosystems. The human population rose at an exponential rate through the 20th century, increasing from about 1.6

---

16. Paul R. Ehrlich, *The Population Bomb* (Cuthogue, N.Y.: Buccaneer, 1971).
17. Barry Commoner, *The Closing Circle* (London: Jonathan Cape, 1972).

CONFESSIONS OF A GREENPEACE DROPOUT

billion people at the start of the 20th century to more than six billion at the end. But it may well turn out that Ehrlich, and Malthus before him, were wrong in believing that population growth in itself would be the unraveling of civilization or the death knell for a healthy environment.

In *The Population Bomb* Ehrlich predicted that hundreds of millions of people would starve to death in the 1970s as a result of massive food shortages, mainly in Asia and Africa. As he pontificated about apocalypse from his ivory tower at Stanford University an unknown agronomist from the U.S. Midwest was doing something to prevent this disaster from occurring. The late Dr. Norman Borlaug would eventually win the Nobel Peace Prize in 1970 for leading the international research effort to create high-yielding varieties of wheat and rice for the developing countries. This ushered in what became known as the Green Revolution. In a matter of years, countries like India and Pakistan that had depended on grain imports to feed their populations became self-sufficient in grain production and even became net food exporters. Needless to say, Ehrlich's predicted mass starvation never happened.

Ironically Dr. Borlaug, who died in 2009, is relatively unknown in his home country to this day while Paul Ehrlich, who continues to predict doom and gloom, is still held up by activists and the media as a guru.

We three Greenpeacers in Stockholm spent most of our time at the official conference, where we continued to lobby the Pacific Rim countries. We were elated when New Zealand, in defiance of the superpowers, put a resolution against French nuclear testing on the floor. To our delight, the resolution passed by a wide margin, bolstering our cause and putting some wind in the *Vega*'s sails as David McTaggart approached ground zero at Mururoa.

When we returned to Vancouver, we learned the French had sent a frigate to meet the Greenpeace boat in international waters, rammed and disabled the 36-foot ketch, and forced McTaggart to come ashore on Mururoa. David made the mistake of having lunch on the island with the French general in charge of the nuclear testing program. Photos of McTaggart breaking bread with the enemy were broadcast around the world. It appeared to Greenpeace supporters that David was supping with the devil. In retrospect this was a minor setback.

In 1973 the *Vega* returned to Mururoa, this time attracting even more public attention. Upping the ante, French commandos boarded the ketch and beat McTaggart with truncheons, damaging his eye, and then claimed he had fallen on the deck. The French liars didn't know crew member Anne-Marie Horne had photographed the beating, hidden the film canister in her vagina, and sent the film to Vancouver, where we released it to the media. The photos of McTaggart's beating were published around the world, embarrassing France in the international community. The French showed no remorse and censored the photos in France for "national security" reasons. They continued the series of atmospheric tests. Then suddenly, France announced it would end atmospheric testing after 1974, conducting further tests underground. With a few dedicated people and a couple of small boats, Greenpeace had now chalked up two major victories against nuclear superpowers.

In the aftermath of his voyages, McTaggart moved to Paris, where he began a personal campaign through the French courts, challenging France's right to cordon off international waters and seeking damages for the loss of his sight and the damage to his boat. It took three years of hard work, but in 1976 David won a partial victory when the judges ruled he had been deliberately rammed and was owed compensation, which he received.

CHAPTER 5

Saving the Whales

Ideas travel at the speed of thought.
—Paul Spong, founder of the
Greenpeace Save the Whales Campaign

In early 1973 I met Eileen and we fell in love that same day. We had found ourselves, recently separated from our partners of five years each, in a 13-room hippy boarding house, which was named Fowler's Rest Home after the owner, my old school chum Ron Fowler. I had arrived a couple of months earlier, a refugee from a relationship that had begun when I was too young and had never really worked. I was busy writing my PhD thesis in a basement room at Fowler's when Eileen moved in. Vancouver born, Eileen and her first husband, Jim, a jazz drummer, had moved back to Toronto in the hope of finding more work there. That plan fizzled and their marriage didn't make it either, so Eileen came home to Vancouver and found a bed at the home of her old friend Karen's. She got a job serving cocktails at a local nightclub, The Garage, and Karen soon found her a room at Fowler's place. Other notables who called the Rest Home their home were Frankie Allison, the lead guitarist of Wildroot, and Ian Berry, who played sax and keyboards. The band had a steady gig at the Garage. The party at Fowler's began when the band arrived home at two in the morning and we assembled for a communal dinner, loud music, and various intoxicants. We were one big happy hippy family.

It was at one of these gatherings that Eileen appeared, newly arrived, and we struck up a conversation that quickly excluded all others. We both loved plants, trees, and the country. She had followed the story of the

Greenpeace voyage to Amchitka because she knew two of the other crew members, Dr. Lyle Thurston, who had become my good friend, and Bob Keziere, the photographer and PhD chemistry student. Eileen looked nice in a tight red sweater with no bra. It was her night off. How about heading down to the Garage to hear the band? I suggested. After all the Rest Home crowd always got in free. So off we went with half the house in my Volkswagen microbus camper. Eileen and I danced, held hands, embraced, and then went home to my room at Fowler's Rest Home. And we have never left each other since.

In May, with McTaggart's second voyage to protest the French nuclear tests at Mururoa under way and my PhD thesis handed in, Eileen and I set off for Mexico in the microbus. After 20 years of schooling it was the first time I had really "escaped." By this time I wasn't really interested in getting a job with industry or government after I graduated. On our return from eight weeks of exploring pre-Columbian ruins, snorkeling, and generally discovering Mexico from Mazatlan to Puerto Escondido, Eileen and I went to my childhood home in the rain forest at Winter Harbor; we wanted to get back to the land. I went to work in my dad's logging camp as a "bullbucker." A bullbucker looks after a half-dozen tree-fallers, helps them pack their gear into the woods, and fixes their chainsaws. The pay was good and we soon saved enough to start building a house.

By now you can see that I had a very different, and more up close, experience with logging and forestry than the average environmentalist. I understood from the beginning that trees are renewable and what really mattered was that the land was reforested after the trees were cut to make our homes, furniture, and paper products. I knew wood was the most abundant renewable material on the planet. I had no idea at this time that the movement I was helping to build would eventually adopt an anti-forestry campaign.

Dad had a small sawmill with a 54-inch circular blade that could cut timber from a log up to 28 inches in diameter. Eileen and I collected cedar logs from here and there on the weekends and cut all the lumber for a 750-square-foot cabin, and then we built it ourselves over the winter of 1973 and into the summer of 1974. I cut shake blocks from a huge red cedar tree, and Eileen split all the shakes for the roof while I was at work. We had the place roofed and closed in by the fall. It is amazing how much two people can accomplish during evenings and weekends when they set their minds to it. We moved into something of a shell in early 1975, and ever since we have been finishing our beautiful cedar cabin by the sea.

Our idyllic country life was not to last. During our infrequent visits to Vancouver, which lay 12 hours away by road and ferry from Winter Harbour, we maintained contact with Bob Hunter and the others who kept Greenpeace alive through the lull in campaign activity. In the fall of 1974 Bob invited me over to his place to meet a whale scientist who had a new idea for Greenpeace. Paul Spong told us his fascinating story and I was

CONFESSIONS OF A GREENPEACE DROPOUT

Albert Lee, long-time employee at the logging camp, sharpening the 54-inch circular saw in the sawmill where Eileen and I cut all the cedar and spruce lumber for our cabin in Winter Harbour. Photo: Bill Moore

instantly in on the program. Bob and Paul and I, with our partners Bobby, Linda, and Eileen, would spend the next five years together living out a dream—to save the great whales from extinction at the hands of factory whaling ships.

Paul was a native of New Zealand with a PhD in developmental psychology. His arrival in Canada coincided with the first live capture of an orca whale in 1967. At the time orcas were commonly called killer whales because of their predatory nature. The 15-foot orca had been caught in a fisherman's net and had then been transferred to a large pool at the Vancouver Public Aquarium. The whale was named Skana, meaning "supernatural one." Dr. Murray Newman, the aquarium's curator, was interested in studying the whale to determine its intelligence and behavior. Paul Spong was hired for the job.

Paul began to conduct routine psychological tests. For example, one test was designed to determine if the whale could learn to select a single line on one card from a double line on another card to get the reward of a herring snack. He was soon amazed to see Skana learned which card to select a lot faster than the average chicken did. Just as the whale was getting 90 percent on the test it suddenly reversed its behavior, pushing the wrong button nearly 100 percent of the time. Paul was shocked into the realization that the whale was toying with him, turning the tables completely and playing with his mind. Time to rethink the "experiment."

Over the next weeks Paul and Skana's relationship deepened. Skana cultivated Paul's trust so that Paul could eventually put his head in Skana's mouth, surrounded by rows of six-inch sharp predatory teeth, with no fear.

Paul began to invite friends to the aquarium to participate in this evolving relationship. On a moonlit night, flautist Paul Horn played to Skana from the side of the pool. Many of those present—some of them in an LSD-induced trance—felt certain they were witnessing a breakthrough in interspecies communication. Word of the late night séance got out. The aquarium staff claimed that they had found broken glass in the pool. Paul was fired. The management wanted a circus animal for paying customers, not a love-fest between man and whale.

During his time at the aquarium, Paul had gained an abiding interest in whales of all species and began to study their evolution and natural history. He soon learned that one species after another had been driven to the brink of extinction by commercial whaling.

Whales are ancient creatures that first appeared in the fossil record over 60 million years ago. They evolved after the great dinosaur extinction, caused by a large meteor that crashed near the Yucatan Peninsula, ending the Jurassic Age. Among the dinosaurs exterminated were the large marine plesiosaurs and ichthyosaurs. Their disappearance left a big hole in the marine food chain, one that was, in evolutionary terms, filled quickly by whales and dolphins. They evolved from a species similar to the present-day hippopotamus. These creatures swam down a river to the sea and evolved into the largest animals ever to exist on Earth. They lived peacefully for over 60 million years, with no natural enemy except one of their own kind, killer whales, who rarely attacked them. Then we came along, learned to build boats, and in a few centuries nearly wiped them off the face of the earth.

While some cultures, such as the Inuit (Eskimos), Native Americans of the Pacific Northwest, and the Norwegians had been whaling for a thousand years or more, the Dutch, British, and Americans didn't start until the 16th century. Early whaling was conducted close to shore in small, rowed boats with hand-thrown harpoons. In both Western Europe and North America, early whalers often targeted right whales, so named because they were the "right" whale to hunt: They swim slowly and float after they are killed.

By the 17th century the purpose for whaling had become purely commercial, as demand for lamp oil and lubricants increased with industrialization. Whale oil was the first commercially important oil, (it was used mostly to fuel lamps) and was obtained by slow cooking (rendering) the whale blubber. After coastal right whale populations had been significantly reduced, whalers turned to increasingly larger whales in deeper and more remote waters. In addition to whale oil, whalers sought baleen, sperm oil, spermaceti (wax), and ambergris for perfume.

Baleen, or whalebone, are the large, hairy plates that hang down from the roof of a baleen whale's mouth. Baleen whales include the blue, fin, sei, minke, Bryde's, humpback, right, and bowhead whales. They gulp mouthfuls of plankton and fish-rich seawater and then close their mouths, forcing the water, but not the food, back out through the baleen plates that act as a filter. By this method, baleen whales consume tons of shrimp, small fish, and plankton each day. Baleen is flexible and is made of the same material from which fingernails, hair, and claws are made. Baleen was the plastic of its day and was used to make skirt hoops, corset stays, buggy whips, umbrella spokes, and many other products.

Sperm oil and spermaceti came from the spermaceti organ of the sperm whale, a large oil-filled sac that comprises most of the whale's huge head. Biologists believe the spermaceti is an acoustical lens for amplifying sperm whale sounds, the loudest of any animal. The powerful sound may be used to hunt and stun giant squid, cuttlefish, and other prey. One spermaceti organ can contain as much as 1890 liters (500 gallons) of sperm oil, which, even today, is considered one of the finest lubricants. Spermaceti, a waxy substance obtained from the oil, was used until the end of the 19th century in fine candles and for waterproofing clothing.

Sperm whales also provided ambergris, a wax-like substance obtained from their intestines—often encasing the indigestible beaks of the giant squid that are a key part of their diet. Ambergris was used in the finest perfumes to enhance the fragrance's longevity. Due to its rarity, ambergris was, and still is, an extremely valuable substance.

In 1625, a Dutch businessman met with a Basque whaling captain and then built Smeerenburg, or Blubber Town, on the arctic island of Spitzbergen, north of Norway. The whaling facility included a dock where whales could be hauled out whole and dropped into a massive cooker for rendering the blubber into valuable oil. Between 1675 and 1720, whaling records show Smeerenburg whalers killed more than 30,000 bowhead whales.

By the 1840s, more than 700 whaling ships with nearly 25,000 crewmen were plying the world's oceans in search of ever more elusive whales—cramming their hulls full of oil, ambergris, and baleen to feed the ever increasing demand for these substances.

Whaling became even more lethally efficient when fast steamships were combined with the harpoon gun and exploding harpoon tip in 1868. These inventions not only allowed the whalers to keep up with faster whale species, but also allowed them to kill the animals from a safe distance and ensured a quicker kill. No more dangerous "Nantucket sleigh rides" in small, rowed whaleboats towed at frightening speeds by harpooned, wounded whales.

By the late 1800s, whalers had severely depleted the world's oceans of many species of whales. Several, including the California gray whale, had been hunted to the brink of extinction.

Fortunately for the whales, Thomas Edison's lightbulb and petroleum oils were developed around this time. This dramatically cut the price for whale oil and sent many whalers in search of more lucrative professions. These inventions deserve some credit for saving whales from certain extinction at the turn of the century.

Early in the 20th century when the whaling industry seemed to be on its last legs, explorers in the Southern Ocean discovered new and vast whale herds off the coast of Antarctica. It was the answer to the whaling industry's woes. These were mostly baleen whales—blues and their smaller cousins the fin, sei, and minke. Baleen whales sink when killed, so techniques were developed to pump their bellies full of air after they were harpooned so that they would stay afloat. Large factory ships were built to process the whales at sea. Not only were the whalers after oil and baleen, they now sought the meat as well, which for the first time could be preserved in refrigerated storage compartments. Another technology that helped create the Southern whaling explosion was the ability to chemically hydrogenate whale oil to make margarine and soaps.

The magnificent blue whales were the first to be wiped out by the new whaling fleets. Blue whales can grow to more than 30 meters (100 feet) in length and 136 tonnes (150 tons) in weight. Blue whales are the largest animals in the history of life on earth. They comprised about 90 percent of the whale industry's catch in the first few decades of the Southern whaling industry. By the 1930s, some 30,000 blues had been killed in the Southern Ocean and the largest animal that has ever existed was on the brink of extinction.

Next the whalers went after the fin whales. Fin whales can reach up to 27 meters (85 feet) in length and weigh 45 to 64 tonnes (50 to 70 tons) and are sometimes called the "greyhound of the sea" because they swim so fast. After depleting fin whale numbers, the whalers then pursued smaller species, the sei, Bryde's, and eventually the minke. At 7.5 to 9 meters (25 to 30 feet) in length, the latter is the smallest of the baleen whales.

By the 1940s, all of these whale populations had been drastically reduced, just as their northern cousins had. Fortunately, no whale species was hunted to extinction. But many species were on the brink by then, some with only a few hundred individuals remaining.

In 1946 the International Whaling Commission was formed to create a mechanism for the whaling nations to divide up what was left of the dwindling populations. Its members agreed to stop hunting some species and set quotas for the others. But the quotas were always higher than the populations could withstand. By the 1960s, the right, blue, humpback, fin, sei, minke, and sperm whale populations had all been slashed to a tiny fraction of their former size. Some regional populations had been completely wiped out.

Somebody needed to put an end to this senseless slaughter. The world community had to be jolted into action before a whale species actually did go extinct. We arrived a bit late on the scene, but we knew it was better late than never. Paul Spong had come to us because we were the only environmental group that had launched a marine expedition and he saw the possibility of going deep-sea against the whalers. Most environmental groups were good at marching in the city with placards and standing in the mall with a petition. Greenpeace could go where the action was and bring the same attention to the whale slaughter as we had to nuclear testing.

A Save the Whales campaign seemed like a brilliant idea, especially since whales were such huge symbolic creatures in their own right. Through magazines, movies, and television, the public was gaining an appreciation for the complexity of whale behavior, social life, and intelligence. Whales were cool. The television show *Flipper* aired on Sunday nights during primetime from 1964 to 1968 and was incredibly popular. The "songs" of the humpback whale were identified in the 1960s and recordings were sold to the public in 1970.[18]

The hard-core antinuke peaceniks in our group were aghast at the idea of a Save the Whales campaign. What kind of hippy-dippy sentimentalists put whales—big lumps of floating blubber—ahead of the threat of nuclear holocaust? They thought we had gone completely soft, not realizing the whales would become a symbol for the salvation of life itself. Many of us thought if we couldn't save the whales, the largest creatures ever to live on our planet, then what could we save? In the process we lost a few of the antinuke campaigners but we gained an army of supporters for the cause of the whales.

I thought it was a great way to diversify and get beyond a one-issue organization and it added a positive note. There is limited appeal to a campaign focused on mass nuclear death and destruction. The whales were a symbol of life, and the promise of saving them offered a message of hope. I felt inspired by this positive energy and signed on with enthusiasm.

Paul Spong was the inspiration, but Bob Hunter became the leader and driving force that pushed the Greenpeace whale campaign into reality. It is very likely Greenpeace would have come to an end as an organization if Bob hadn't taken up this cause. He quit his job at the *Vancouver Sun*, found office space in the counterculture district of the city, and began to organize. It is not possible in a short account to explain the magic and power Bob brought to this exercise. In all the history of the environmental movement, the Greenpeace voyages to Save the Whales were undoubtedly among the most significant in terms of changing global thinking about the natural world and our relationship with it. Bob's ability with words and his sheer energy and determination helped to launch a new world order of mass consciousness, using what we came to describe as "media mind bombs."

In fact it was Bob who invented the term *mind bomb*, then used rou-

---

18. Paul Winter, *Songs of the Humpback Whale*, http://www.amazon.com/Songs-Humpback-Whale-Paul-Winter/dp/B00000AFPR

Left: The *Phyllis Cormack* and the Vega in Winter Harbour, May 1975, ready for action against the Russian and Japanese whaling fleets. One month later our voyage would be broadcast around the world. Photo: Patrick Moore

Below: The *Phyllis Cormack* in full battle colors, on maneuvers in preparation for the first encounter with the Russian factory whaling fleet. Photo: Patrick Moore

CONFESSIONS OF A GREENPEACE DROPOUT

tinely in the press and eventually reduced to the single word mindbomb. It refers to a video, a photo or a word picture, combined with interesting information, automatically spreading through the electronic media like wildfire. Today this phenomenon is called "going viral." It occurs regularly as a major breaking news story, but it isn't easy to manufacture a mind bomb to make a point about ecology. Bob was a genius at it; he knew how to craft his words to fit the image so that the media found it irresistible. Bob thought of the media as a giant machine screaming repeatedly, "Feed me, feed me." His own mantra in response was, "Eat me, eat me," and he provided fodder.

The first local environmental group in Vancouver was SPEC (Society Promoting Environmental Conservation). Founded by nature lovers Gwen and Derrick Mallard, it gained public support and soon was able to hire a full-time executive director. Gary Gallon was pretty much a thinking person's hippy like Bob and Paul and I, so we got along famously. Gary offered us office space in his building to organize our voyage to save the whales. He taught us a lot about being organized in a business sense. Gary was the first environmentalist I knew who took off his tie-dyed shirt, put on a jacket and tie, and went downtown to knock on CEOs doors to preach ecology. For this I dubbed him the first "ecocrat."

While Bob was putting the campaign together, hiring captain John Cormack again and raising funds, Paul Spong traveled to Oslo, Norway, the headquarters for the International Whaling Commission. Posing as a whale scientist (not a bad disguise as that's what he was), he gained access to the records of the Soviet and Japanese whaling fleet's movements over the years. At this time, in the mid-1970s, they were the only two countries operating deep-sea factory whaling fleets. It turned out that the Japanese fleet spent nearly all its time in the Western Pacific, west of Hawaii, but the Soviet fleet regularly operated off the coast of California in June. Amazingly the American public remained completely unaware that Russian harpoon boats were killing endangered whales just over the horizon off the California coast. This was before the 200-mile limit was established under the UN Law of the Sea treaty, so it was technically legal for other countries to fish and hunt whales up to 12 miles off the coast. There was no way the *Phyllis Cormack*, an 85-foot halibut boat, could really go deep-sea; but there was a chance we could intercept the Soviet fleet 30 to 100 miles off the coast of California. Talk about tilting at windmills—a tiny fishing boat up against the might of the Soviet empire in the biggest ocean on Earth. How were we going to do it? We were going to place ourselves in front of the harpoon boats to protect the fleeing whales as they were chased at 15 knots in rough seas.

Eileen and I were still living and working in Winter Harbour when the campaign was first being organized, and I suggested to Bob Hunter that

Our first encounter with the Soviet factory whaling fleet on June 27, 1975, off the California coast. I am driving the inflatable boat with film cameraman Fred Easton in the bow. The harpoon boats are about to transfer dead whales to the factory ship. Photo: Rex Weyler

our coastal village would make a good base to train the crew in preparation for the confrontation with the whalers. He agreed.

On April 27, 1975, the *Phyllis Cormack*, with the Kwakiutl Sisiutl symbol painted brightly on its single sail, departed Vancouver amid much fanfare with the promise to save the whales. The expedition arrived in Winter Harbour on April 29 and over the next six weeks we hosted the crew. We were joined by the 26-foot sloop *Vega*, formerly owned by David McTaggart and recently acquired by Greenpeace supporter Jacques Longini. I was assigned the task of training the mostly inexperienced crew members in seamanship and small craft operation.

Paul Spong was correct in observing that we were the only environmental group that knew how to put together an ocean expedition. But on the first voyages to Alaska and Mururoa we had remained on the "mother ship" as our main boat came to be called. This time we intended to put people into small rubber inflatable boats, known as Zodiacs after the popular French brand. This would require launching three Zodiacs from the deck of the *Phyllis Cormack* in rough seas and then maneuvering them in front of a harpoon boat while it was pursuing whales. One Zodiac would carry the cannon fodder, an operator and passenger, who would try to get in between the harpooner and the whales to shield them. The passengers in the other two Zodiacs would be a still photographer and a movie cameraman. The logistics of doing this would be difficult enough on a millpond; trying it in typical ocean conditions off Cape Mendocino could be suicidal.

CONFESSIONS OF A GREENPEACE DROPOUT

By getting in front of the harpoon, we created images that were broadcast around the world. Photo: Rex Weyler

It turned out that Bob Hunter got the idea of using Zodiacs from the photos Anne-Marie Horne shot while the *Vega* was being boarded at Mururoa atoll during the anti-French nuclear testing campaign. It was the French commandos who knew how to run Zodiacs, not us, but we could learn.

Bob asked me to join the crew as first mate, so in April I left my job in my dad's logging camp and after six weeks of training we headed for our rendez-vous with the whalers. It is not easy to find a whaling fleet in the Pacific Ocean. We knew where the whalers had been in early June for the past 10 years, but even that was an area of about 250,000 square miles.

Our best bet was to listen for Russian voices on our marine short-wave radio and then use a direction finder to determine their position. After a couple of false alarms, we picked up the crackle of Russian voices and sailed toward the signal. Early on June 27, I was the first one to spot a Russian harpoon ship on the horizon. Then the huge factory ship and seven more harpoon boats came into view. As we steamed toward them, the first thing we came across was a dead sperm whale that had been harpooned and marked with a flag, a radar reflector, and a beacon so that it could be rounded up later. We had come across the Soviet fleet during the thick of a hunt.

The dead whale was small, a baby well under the size limit set by the International Whaling Commission. We launched a Zodiac and Paul Watson got on the back of the whale so we could document its size in comparison to his. We then began to move closer to the whaling fleet.

After three months at sea, we arrive back in Vancouver from the first Greenpeace voyage to save the whales. I am driving the inflatable in the center with Rex Weyler in the bow and Bob Hunter on the right. Paul Watson is driving the second inflatable with Ron Precious on camera and Fred Easton on sound.

The eight harpoon boats were operating like a wolf pack, using their sonar to track the whales underwater after they sounded. When the whales surfaced, the boats were right on top of them. At first the whales just sounded again quickly before the gunners could take aim. But they couldn't catch their breath, so after a few dives they had to stay on the surface to breathe. Then they would end up fleeing as fast as they could on the surface, eventually tiring and being gunned down one at a time. A favorite trick of the whalers was first to kill the dominant male, causing the females in the harem to come to his rescue as he thrashed about bleeding to death. Then the whalers would circle around and systematically kill the entire pod.

There is no way to kill a whale in a humane manner. The tip of the harpoon is a grenade that explodes, preferably in the spine, severing it and rendering the whale immobile. Among the tens of whales we witnessed being harpooned over the years, most died slowly, spouting blood and gasping desperately.

The whalers had no idea who we were. Being off the coast of California with cameras, they may have assumed we were filmmakers from Hollywood. We approached slowly, as we wanted to make sure they realized that we were peaceful, even if we didn't agree with what they were doing. They called off the hunt and waved to us from the decks of the factory ship and the harpoon boats. We launched our three Zodiacs and went alongside one of the harpoon boats. At the advice of people who had been to Russia we had taken along ballpoint pens, some blue jeans, and a copy of *Playboy* magazine. We came alongside one of the harpoon boats

CONFESSIONS OF A GREENPEACE DROPOUT

Eileen and me in San Francisco on July 2, 1975, the day after we arrived with the film footage of the harpoon sailing over Bob and George into a sperm whale. This is a lapel button that we had made by a street photographer as we walked up Market Street, on a high after scoring a victory with the media. Greenpeace was launched as a global movement.

and held out our peace offering. The first English words that were spoken to us by a Russian whaler were, "Hey, you guys got'it any acid?" We hadn't thought of that.

But things quickly turned sour as we made our intentions clear. Our Russian-speaking crew member hollered across to them that we were here to save the whales and we intended to directly interfere with the hunt. The harpoon boats coolly turned to go about their deadly business.

Thankfully there was only a two-foot chop, so we could move along at a reasonable speed. Miraculously we quickly managed to get in front of a harpoon boat as it was chasing a pod of sperm whales. Even more miraculously, Fred Easton had his camera pointed at the harpoon when it was fired, following it and the attached cable as it flew over the heads of Bob Hunter and George Korotva and plunged into the back of a female sperm whale. All this was captured on about three seconds of footage. We didn't save that whale, but eight whales in the pod escaped as the whalers retreated to the factory ship with only two whales. Maybe they realized that in their zeal they had nearly killed two people.

"We have saved eight whales today" stated the media release we broadcast over short-wave radio to our shore station in Vancouver. The story of the encounter was quickly broadcast around the world. The International Whaling Commission was meeting in England and news of our success buoyed the anti-whaling protestors who had gathered there.

When we arrived in San Francisco the next day we were swarmed by the media. We handed our film footage to an independent studio so it could be "pooled," that is, made available to all the networks. That evening we watched from a nearby tavern as our story ran near the top of all three networks' national news programs. Our film footage of the harpoon shot was carried on television stations around the world, including in our home country, Canada. This was before the advent of cable networks like CNN and Fox, when only CBS, NBC, and ABC ruled the tube. As counterculture personality Hank Harrison (father of actress/musician Courtney Love) wrote later, it was the "Greenpeacing of America." We were welcomed into the city of San Francisco as conquering heroes. There was an explosion of support from around the world. Greenpeace would never look back.

CHAPTER SIX

Baby Seals and Movie Stars

While on the whale voyage we read the cover story in a recent edition of *National Geographic* about the annual slaughter of hundreds of thousands of harp seal pups in their breeding grounds off the east coast of Canada. Letter writing campaigns and petitions had failed to stop the killing. It looked like a job for Greenpeace. Plans began for an expedition to the ice floes to save the seals.

Our little committee in a church basement had turned into a full-time job for an office full of people with rent and salaries to pay. To be fair, the salary was between $200 and $300 a month, but in the 1970s it was a subsistence living.

In the fall of 1975 we set about organizing our U.S. branch office, based in San Francisco. While on a talk show with Dr. Bill Wattenburg on KGO in San Francisco, Bob Hunter and I appealed for a volunteer lawyer to help us set up operations in the United States. We knew the key to raising the amount of money we needed to stop the factory whaling fleets was a fund-raising arm in the U.S. We joked among ourselves that with American money and Canadian know-how we would save the earth.

A young lawyer named David Tussman came forward. He seemed sharp, his dad was a famous philosophy professor at Berkeley, and he was plugged into the San Francisco scene. David incorporated Greenpeace USA, got us our tax-deductible status, and helped build a board of directors. He would later betray us.

Nineteen seventy-six saw Greenpeace flower with other branch offices springing up in Portland, Seattle, Los Angeles, Boston, and Toronto. Most of these were spontaneous gatherings of people who identified with what we had done and what we stood for. It was impossible for us to keep up with the growth in support. Some of these new groups were incorporating their own legal entities, thinking they could just take our Greenpeace name and raise funds with it. It proved a somewhat futile effort to keep all this growth coordinated and controlled. It didn't help that our otherwise brilliant leader, Bob Hunter, didn't care much for legal technicalities.

During the winter the story of our plans to stop the seal hunt made headlines across Canada. The annual slaughter of seal pups had been a tradition in Canada for more than 200 years. For the first time Greenpeace was portrayed as the Goliath against poor Newfoundland sealers who needed to put bread on the table. The intelligentsia and media of central Canada tended to side with people over seals. We were no longer white knights in shining armor to everyone.

On March 2, 1976, Eileen and I joined a small group of Greenpeacers who boarded the trans-Canada train in Vancouver for the five-day journey to Newfoundland, where we had announced our intention to stop the baby seal slaughter. We took the ferry from Sydney, Nova Scotia, to Port aux Basques in Newfoundland and rented a van to drive up to St. Anthony at the northern tip of the island. Halfway up the road we encountered a blizzard of arctic proportions. Snow built up on the van's fan belt and threw it off, stranding us in hostile territory in the dark. We knocked on a nearby inn and were welcomed in for the night. The owners had seen us on TV earlier and were happy to have us staying with them. It was our first taste of Newfoundland hospitality.

The situation seemed a little different as we approached St. Anthony, a regional center of 5,000 people, many of whom had a history in the seal hunt and whose families were still employed to harvest the seal pups. What appeared to be a lynch mob had assembled on the outskirts of town. There were a lot of pickup trucks and the boys were drinking mickeys of whiskey and rum. One guy was displaying an actual noose and shook it at us as we approached. But they didn't block our passage; they acted as a kind of escort as we made our way to Decker's Boarding House.

The proprietors, Emily and Nate Decker, were there to greet us, despite the fact that the mob surrounded us when we got out of our van. They jeered and demanded we leave. We tried to make peace with them by explaining that our main target was the big factory sealing ships, not the little guys like them. Eventually the crowd dispersed and we settled into what would be our headquarters for the next two weeks.

The plan was to set up a base camp in tents on Belle Isle, a windswept frozen rock in the strait between Newfoundland and Labrador. We had rented two Bell Jet Ranger helicopters for the expedition. They fer-

The crew and pilots of the first campaign to Save the Seals pose on the ice floes off Newfoundland in March 1976. In back from the left, Bernd Firnung (pilot), Doug Pilgrim (Newfoundland guide), Michael Chechick (film producer), Ron Precious, (cameraman). In front from the left, Paul Watson, Bob Hunter, Jack Wallace (pilot), Eileen Moore, and me.

ried a group of us out to Belle Isle, where we were in range of the sealing grounds, which lay 50 miles off the coast among the ice floes. We put up our tents and bedded in for the night.

Morning ushered in a cold clear day, perfect conditions for flying to the ice. The helicopters arrived early and we set out to find the sealing ships. Within an hour we had spotted them. The potential for confrontation was made difficult by the Seal Protection Regulations, a law that made it illegal to fly lower than 2000 feet above any seal on the ice or to approach within one-half nautical mile of any seal without a permit. Of course we Greenpeacers had no permits. We had, in fact, been refused them. Only the seal hunters had permits.

The ostensible purpose of this law was to protect the seals from the noise of aircraft and to avoid disturbing them in their breeding grounds. Its real purpose, however, was to prevent photos of the hunt being taken, and, in our case, to prevent interference with the hunt. The law should have been titled the Seal Hunt Protection Regulations.

We would have defied the regulations in a second, but our pilots were responsible for half a million dollars worth of helicopters that belonged to the helicopter company. We had no choice but to comply. This meant a long hike across treacherous broken ice fields. About an hour after landing we finally arrived at the scene of the slaughter. There was blood everywhere. The sounds of fear from mother seals and the whack of the hakapik on baby seals' skulls filled the otherwise still air.

Eileen was likely the first woman ever to witness this carnage in its 200-year history. She was certainly the first woman to try to protect a baby seal from a hunter's club as she waded into the fray, throwing herself in

Paul Watson and Bob Hunter pose with a baby harp seal after they stopped the ice-breaking sealing ship in its tracks—probably a Guinness Book of Records first. Photo: Patrick Moore

front of a sealer as he approached his next victim. He pushed her aside, clubbed the pup, and skinned it in 30 seconds. The photographer from Agent-France Presse captured Eileen as she tried over and over to save a seal.

As crew photographer, I was busy with another confrontation. Bob Hunter and Paul Watson had positioned themselves in front of a 150-foot sealing vessel that was pushing its way through the ice. "We're not moving," yelled Bob to a man leaning over the bow. The ship lurched forward, splitting the foot-thick ice floe into shiny chunks. "They're not movin', Capt'n," hollered the watchman. The cameras were whirring and clicking as the big bow bore down on the two tiny men. This was without doubt the first time people had stood in front of a ship at sea to try to stop it.

No more than ten feet from their backs the ship stopped, the captain cursing a blue streak as he backed off. We had stopped the progress of a sealing vessel and slowed the slaughter just a little bit. It was a symbolic victory but that's what we really needed, something to turn the tone in the media. A headline such as "Greenpeace Stymies Seal Hunters" was a perfect tool to get people's attention and to indicate progress in the campaign.

When we got back to the helicopters we discovered that Federal Fisheries officers were charging our pilots with landing too close to a seal. After we had landed a seal had hauled itself onto the ice through its hole and was less than half a mile from the machines. Our pilots were forcibly grounded, so this was to be our last trip to the ice that year. But we didn't give up immediately. We returned to our base camp on Belle Isle, hoping our lawyers could figure out how to get the choppers flying again.

As we settled into our pup tents for the night we felt the wind coming up. In the morning we were greeted by a blizzard with 60 mile per hour winds, which confined us to our three-person pup tents that you couldn't stand up in. The helicopters were grounded back in St. Anthony and we had no radio contact. It was three long days in subzero weather; the only time we left the tents was to do our business, and this was a most unpleasant experience as there was no shelter from the storm. To make matters worse, we ran out of fuel for our small camp stoves and had to resort to burning helicopter fuel. It produced more soot than heat, causing us to dub our shelters "black-lung tents." I had never been in such abysmal conditions in my life. At times we feared we would freeze to death, but we had survival suits and warm sleeping bags and the food rations were sufficient. As far as I could tell we were the only living things in the vicinity with the exception of a big black raven that braved the driving snow. I couldn't imagine what it was finding to eat in this desolate place.

Finally the blizzard ended and we heard the *whup-whup* of a helicopter approaching. We were tired and cold and dying for a hot meal. When the first chopper landed, I was shocked to see Paul Watson, who was the leader of the expedition, get on board, leaving a group of us behind to wait for the second machine to arrive. I'd had a couple of run-ins with Paul before, but this really bothered me. No leader takes off in a risky situation, leaving half his crew, including a woman crew member, behind. We did all get off Belle Isle safely in the end and decided to call it a day. We had made a big splash in the international media with our film and photos of the confrontation and we vowed to return the following year.

Save the Whales 1976

Bob Hunter and Paul Spong were now spending a lot of time in San Francisco working with David Tussman to establish a strong base for fundraising there. We were determined to get a larger boat for the whale campaign in 1976, one that could really go deep-sea and chase the Russians across the Pacific. We found the *James Bay*, an ex-Canadian minesweeper, whose twin 1200 horsepower diesels could make 18 knots, more than enough speed to outrun the factory whaling ships. It took over a month to prepare the *James Bay* for the expedition as the engines needed work, and the interior of the ship had been more or less gutted. I found myself

Working seven days a week, we built bunks and galleys for 32 crew members in what had been an empty shell of a ship. By the time we set sail the M.V. *James Bay* was nicely equipped. Photo: Rex Weyler

cutting plywood for three weeks, building bunks and galleys for the crew. On June 13, 1976, we set out from Vancouver with a complement of 32 volunteers from seven countries.

We made our way down the west coast in favorable weather, then sailed up the Columbia River to pay a visit to our supporters in Portland and to raise awareness of the campaign. While in Portland we received word that a Soviet whaling fleet was approaching the California coast, so we cast off for San Francisco, where we would take on final fuel and provisions for a deep-sea voyage. Our San Francisco office was fully up and running now and had been very successful in raising funds for our mission. We made a quick turn-around from San Francisco and headed out to sea.

As we passed under the Golden Gate Bridge, the wind picked up. By early evening we were bucking into a full gale and had to change course to the north. One by one many of the 32 crew members succumbed to sea-sickness and collapsed in their bunks. The storm raged through the night and by morning only a few of us were left standing. Unlike your typical maritime crew, about half of the *James Bay* crew were vegetarians. This resulted in an interesting revelation. At the height of the storm, I was able to truthfully write on the wall of the ship's head that every single vegetarian was sick in his or her bunk and that the only people capable of operating the ship were the meat-eating, whiskey-drinking, chain-smoking members of the crew. While vegetarians generally cite health or spiritual reasons for their avoidance of meat, this real-life situation suggests what is commonly referred to as a "weak constitution" might play an important role in one's choice of things to ingest. I'm sure there are many people with strong constitutions who choose to be vegetarians, but we didn't

The pride of the Greenpeace Pacific fleet, the *James Bay*, on its first voyage to save the whales, joined by the *Phyllis Cormack* for its second whale campaign against Russian and Japanese whalers. This photo was taken in June 1976 in Sydney, B.C., at the outset of the voyage. photo: Matt Heron

seem to have any on board the *James Bay*. Thankfully, I did quit smoking some years later, after a difficult struggle with the addiction. Meat and alcohol still remain essential parts of my diet, however.

By this time, we had become the fortunate beneficiaries of some inside information. After our first whale voyage, we had befriended Robert O. Taunt III—Bob to us —who joined the San Francisco Greenpeace office as a director. Bob was well connected in Californian political circles. In particular he knew Congressman Leo Ryan, who would later be tragically murdered during the Jonestown massacre in Guyana in November 1978.

It was arranged through Leo's office in Washington that the intelligence services would provide him, on a daily basis, the previous day's position of the Soviet whaling fleets. This information was relayed to our shore-based radio station and from there to the ship via shortwave.

In order to keep the position confidential, we devised a code that could not be cracked unless one had inside information. We took a page at random from the San Francisco telephone directory and made three copies, one for Leo's office, one for our shore radio station, and one for the *James Bay*. The position in north latitude and west longitude was coded by sequentially going down the address column in the directory and then across to the correct letter or number. So the sequence 36-5 meant go down 36 and across 5 in the directory. This system worked for us for three years, even after Leo was murdered, and it was the real reason that it was possible for us to find the whaling fleet in the middle of the Pacific. The funny thing was, no reporter ever asked us why we were so good at finding the whalers.

We kept it a secret, partly because we didn't want to let on that the

U.S. was giving us the Soviet coordinates, but was not willing to give the Japanese whalers' positions. We didn't want to be seen as favoring the American ally and picking on the Cold War opponent because we wanted to be neutral in the political sense. This was not easy because interests in the U.S. administration wanted to use us to promote anti-Soviet agendas. Other interests, also mainly in the U.S., sought to portray the Japanese whalers in a racist light, harkening back to Pearl Harbor. It wasn't easy to avoid political and nationalistic elements in the whale wars.

In early July we confronted the whaling fleet 1400 miles southwest of San Francisco, off Baja California. With our new ship we could stay with the whalers and we were able to successfully interfere with their hunting, reducing the number of whales they killed. The film footage we obtained was broadcast around the world again. We were definitely gaining momentum.

We were no ordinary cruise ship or freighter, so we could do things our own way. When we weren't in the thick of battle, one of those things included going for a daily swim in the deep blue waters of the warm Pacific. It was about 6,000 feet deep and populated by flying fish, blue sharks, and sunfish. We would stop the ship at around noon and up to a dozen of us who were not afraid of 6,000 feet of water would leap off the deck while Captain Korotva stood on the flying bridge with a rifle in case he needed to shoot sharks. We were more concerned that he would hit us and wished he would put the gun away.

One day, as we came to a stop for our daily dip, there happened to be a very large sunfish alongside the *James Bay*. It was about six feet long and deep. If you haven't seen a sunfish before, it is a wondrous thing to behold. They are as deep as they are long and quite thin through the middle; in other words they are shaped like a discus, hence the reference to the sun. They have a mouth with no teeth that opens about two inches wide. Their main food is plankton and jellyfish, which they ingest as they move along. The sunfish has a couple of tiny fins and a small tail and a top speed of about two knots, so it could not outswim a human, never mind a shark or other predator. That is why they are composed of not much more than thick skin and bone, so no predator would ever consider trying to eat them. Because they swim slowly, they become a host to various barnacles and algae that attach themselves to the rear and bottom of the fish. In addition they are accompanied by gleaner fish, which wait for bits of food that get past the sunfish's mouth. They are very much like a floating reef, supporting many other species in a commensural relationship as they ply the surface waters.[19] It was an entire marine ecosystem around a single fish.

There were only six of us on this swim, one of whom was the lovely Caroline Keddy, who had joined us in San Francisco. In snorkel gear, most

---

19. Commensural-a relationship between two species where one species benefits and the other species suffers no harm. Compare to parasitical where one species benefits and the other species is harmed or to *symbiotic* where both species benefit.

CONFESSIONS OF A GREENPEACE DROPOUT

of us approached the sunfish with some trepidation, as it was much larger than we were. Caroline was not even slightly afraid and moved right in alongside the giant fish. Perhaps it was because she was a hippy from the Bay and had never encountered a wild animal before. Soon she was touching the sunfish on the face and rubbing its back. The sunfish was obviously pleased with her attentions as it sidled up to her, making no effort to escape. Seeing this the rest of us joined in the love fest, taking turns petting the fish and observing the many species attached to it or following along. But it was clear the sunfish favored Caroline, perhaps because she was the first to make contact, or because the rest of us were not so attractive.

We lost track of time but eventually George blew the ship's whistle for us to come back aboard. By now we had drifted about 300 feet away from the ship, so it was a bit of a swim back home. Caroline held back a minute to say goodbye to her sunfish and then joined us as we headed to the *James Bay*. No sooner had we begun our return than the sunfish turned and with all its two knots of top speed started to follow us. But the fish wasn't just following us; it was following Caroline. As she emerged from the ocean to climb the rope ladder hanging down the side of the ship, the sunfish looked up at her with its big eyes as if to say "Farewell, I love you." I am not a sappy romantic by any stretch of the imagination, but this was a very moving event. We marked the chart with the location where a sunfish fell in love with a human being in 6,000 feet of water in the middle of the Pacific Ocean, on July 12, 1977.

Back on task, we followed the Soviet fleet across the Pacific to Hawaii, dogging them all the way. We decided to pull in to Lahaina on Maui, where there was a good group of whale-saving supporters, as Lahaina is a major center for viewing humpback whales in the winter months. We were determined to try to find the Japanese whaling fleet so that we could provide a balance to our focus on the Russians. Reports indicated it was operating just west of the Hawaiian Islands. The U.S. Coast Guard offered to take us up in one of their surveillance planes on a routine mission to see if we could find the fleet. We decided we would move the *James Bay* to Nawiliwili Harbor on Kauai as we would be closer to the fleet if they found it.

By this time the strain of the voyage was coming to the surface. On our previous expeditions aboard the *Phyllis Cormack* there were only 12 crew members; the *James Bay*'s crew numbered 32. We were living in cramped quarters and we were a pretty headstrong bunch. The fact that two of the couples on board had broken up coincidentally and that they were now involved in new relationships, which left jealous exes with shattered hearts and nerves, was complicating personal relations. This is bad enough on land where people can get away from one another. On a ship it is positively suicidal. This behavior was, of course, entirely contrary to standing orders. As a member of the crew selection committee, I had made it clear that if

Bob Hunter, myself, and Matt Heron strategize on the movements of the Soviet whaling fleet. Twelve hundred miles north of Hawaii the weather was foggy and foul. Photo: Rex Weyler

you came on board as a single person you went off single and that if you came on with a partner you left with the same one. But it is not always possible to control affairs of the heart, even on a voyage to save the whales.

The morning of July 30 began well with reports of a school of dolphins in the outer harbor. We launched our three Zodiacs and sped out to see them. We found at least 50 Pacific white-sided dolphins in the pod and they came leaping toward us and then followed us along for miles. You could literally reach out and touch them as they surfaced right next to the Zodiacs, making rainbows in the spray. It was a magical experience.

I guess some of the guys needed to let off steam as George, Bob, and Mel had begun to drink straight vodka from the bottle at ten in the morning. They were hooting and hollering among the dolphins when Bob decided to go for a swim off the Zodiac. He picked a bad spot, as he dived into the ocean amid a large coral head. By the time George pulled him into the boat, he was badly lacerated from been dragged back and forth over the coral by the surf. It appeared he had lost a considerable amount of skin.

This put a damper on the morning's fun as we rushed Bob back to the boat for medical treatment. Paul Watson's partner, Marilyn Kaga, was the ship's nurse, so Bob was delivered into her hands, by this time in considerable pain. Mistaking a bottle of rubbing alcohol for hydrogen peroxide, nurse Marilyn poured it all over Bob's wounds causing him to go into a catatonic fit of pain. Captain George and Paul got into a shouting match, which ended with George punching Paul in the head: so much for the peace in Greenpeace. As Bob's eyes rolled back into his sockets, we carried

CONFESSIONS OF A GREENPEACE DROPOUT

him to his bunk, where he screamed for a very long time and refused to be treated for some hours. Eventually we got some antiseptic cream on his cuts and scrapes and settled him down.

With our illustrious leader Bob down for the count, Paul Watson decided to lead a mutiny of the crew. Marilyn's mistake and his beating from the captain embarrassed him. As the rebellion unfolded in the crew's quarters, George and Mel went back out in a Zodiac with their bottle(s) of vodka. By nightfall, they were raging drunk and decided to go to the little discotheque at the end of the pier. Realizing they would never get past the bouncers, they decided to scale the pier up the pilings from the water. We watched as various patrons repelled them with chairs until they retreated to their boat. Later in the evening they managed to ram and hole a small dinghy tied behind a nice sailboat that was at anchor in the harbor. As the dinghy was sinking, Mel leaped into it with a bailing can only to go down with the ship.

Things settled down by midnight, but we knew we had to get out of town before daybreak. We cast off at four in the morning and headed back to Lahaina, where our reputation was not so sullied and waited for word of the Japanese fleet. We made a sincere effort, but after two weeks we gave up on the Japanese, and after reprovisioning in Kahalui we headed back for the Soviet fleet, reported by our shore station in San Francisco to be 1200 miles north of Hawaii. This location is about as far as you can get from land anywhere in the Northern Hemisphere. The weather changed from tropical to temperamental as we entered the Pacific Gyre, where currents circle, keeping flotsam in their grip for hundreds of years. The Russian whaling fleet appeared before us in a misty-grey sea.

As we had done a few dozen times before, we launched two Zodiacs, this time into unusually rough seas. Paul Spong and I were the operators, with Fred Easton on film and Rex Weyler on stills. We no sooner got alongside a harpoon boat than the fog set in, obscuring our mother ship that was now about three miles distant. We decided to stay with the whaler and this was our mistake. Within 15 minutes we had completely lost our bearings, the fog had become thicker, and we were realizing we only had an hour of daylight to get back to the *James Bay*. In addition we had left our ship in the sunshine with light clothing, no survival suits, no radar reflectors, and no food. Some eco-navy.

As panic set in, Paul Spong tried to use his portable radio as a radio direction finder but this didn't help. Among us we reconstructed our route away from the *James Bay* and determined in which direction we should travel. It took nearly that whole hour, but as dusk was falling we first heard the foghorn and then saw our ship coming through the mist. That was the closest I had come to being lost and dead 1200 miles from the beach. Eileen and Bob and the others raised up a considerable whoop as we came into view. The Rainbow Warriors had karma working for them that day.

Seal Campaign 1977

Our second seal campaign, in early March, 1977, was by far the most bizarre scene I have been in, and I have been in some pretty bizarre scenes. First, Paul Watson (again the somewhat self-appointed leader of the campaign) decided to base the expedition out of the north shore of Quebec in the village of Blanc Sablon. Apparently this was to avoid hostilities in St. Anthony, but that's where all the North American media were based. Paul had managed to convince the Swiss animal-rights activist Franz Weber to bring about 80 European journalists, many of them top-flight, to join us in Blanc Sablon. The only public lodging in the village was a motel with beds for 30 in 10 small rooms. I was glad I'd packed my sleeping bag as we managed to cram more than 100 bodies into the place, including Weber and his journalists, 15 Greenpeacers, our helicopter pilots, and a few others I can't recall. Weber had failed to find a helicopter company that would rent machines to him, so he had no way of getting the journalists out to the ice. As in the previous year, the Greenpeace crew established a base camp on Belle Isle, but this time it was bigger and better equipped. Paul, who seemed to think his actions were the most important part of the campaign, initiated things by nearly getting killed and putting the other crew members at risk of injury or death.

Paul had led a small group to the ice in two helicopters, where they encountered very difficult conditions. There were 12-foot swells under the ice floes, so the entire seascape was in motion. Landing more than a mile from the sealing ships, Paul raced ahead of the crew. Our physically fit lawyer, Peter Ballem, was the only one able to keep up to him. Paul approached a sealer who was skinning a seal pup, grabbed his hakapik and threw it into the water in a gap between the floes. Then Paul threw the sealskin into the water. Peter warned him this activity was unlawful. The sealer had the sense to ignore Watson instead of skinning him. These kind of extreme tactics had not been discussed with the crew, never mind our board of directors. Then Paul really went over the top. He pulled out a pair of handcuffs and attached himself to a cable that was about to haul a bunch of sealskins on board a sealing ship. The sealers saw they had a live one and began to winch the skins in, dragging Paul along the ice. About 20 feet from the sealing ship, the solid ice ended and Paul was dragged into frozen slush. The sealers were jeering like fans watching gladiators eaten by lions. The winch operator purposely lifted Paul 10 feet above the water and then dropped him back in. Then the handcuffs broke loose and Paul was floundering in the frozen sea; he would only last five minutes. Peter had dragged a small inflatable skiff across the ice in case they encountered a wide lead between the floes as they approached the sealers. He got in it and pushed himself across the open water toward Paul, which meant getting soaked to the waist himself. A big man, Peter managed to

CONFESSIONS OF A GREENPEACE DROPOUT

drag Paul, a big man too, into the inflatable and got him back to solid ice, where he laid, screaming obscenities at the sealers. Peter pleaded with the sealing crew to take Paul aboard or he would surely die of exposure as the helicopters were more than a mile away and Watson was already turning blue. The sealers eventually realized that it would not look good if they killed someone, so they winched Paul aboard in a stretcher, landing him face down in a pile of bloody sealskins. Peter also boarded the ship, where he and Paul would remain overnight.

Because he raced ahead and acted unilaterally, Paul had failed to have his actions documented on film, a key purpose of the expedition. Rumors about his fate flew around overnight. Some journalists reported that Paul's arm was broken or that he was possibly dead. When he appeared the next day after having been flown to the hospital in Blanc Sablon and released, he looked perfectly fine. This resulted in a credibility gap with the media, we had no film to show what really happened and the whole episode became an embarrassment. Meanwhile the 80 European journalists were getting antsy, as not one of them had made it out to the ice. Paul, who had signed the charter contract on behalf of Greenpeace, had control of the only two helicopters and had now holed himself up in his motel room, obviously traumatized by the recent events. With our erstwhile leader incommunicado, I had to play my hand as representative of the Greenpeace board, as I was vice-president and organizationally senior to Paul. Bob Hunter, who stayed behind during this campaign, had insisted I go along to keep an eye on Paul and to take control if necessary. It had become very necessary. The media were so desperate for a story that one German film crew hired a local man to pose with a stuffed seal pup as if he were about to club it to death. This made the wire service as if it were the real thing.

In the middle of all this, we learned that the French actress Brigitte Bardot had arrived in Blanc Sablon with a six-person film crew and her Polish sculptor boyfriend, Mirko Brozek. They had flown in unannounced and had rented a vacant house in the town. The European media went into a complete frenzy as the world-famous beauty arrived for a media conference at our motel, denouncing the Canadian government and vowing to campaign until the slaughter ended.

The Bardot party had also been unable to find helicopters for rent, so now there were 15 Greenpeacers, Franz Weber, and his 80 European journalists, and Brigitte Bardot, with a top French TV producer and full film crew, all vying for eight seats in our two small helicopters. The media were calling for Watson's and Weber's heads. Then our helicopter pilots informed us that Bardot's producer, Henri, was negotiating directly with them to fly Brigitte and the film crew out to the ice. "He says Brigitte will sit beside us in the helicopter," one of our pilots swooned. Brigitte had been uncharitably described as an "aging sex kitten" in one Canadian paper's headline, but believe me she looked stunning for a woman in her early 40s, or indeed of any age. Our pilots were leaning toward breaching our contract, leaving us with no helicopters to get our expedition out to the ice. Peter Ballem and I decided to take matters into our own hands. We borrowed a snowmobile and made our way to the house that the Bardot party had rented.

Henri eventually greeted Peter and me through a small crack in the doorway. We explained that the helicopters were ours but that we were willing to try to work out an accommodation. At first Henri responded negatively, but we insisted so he went to speak to Brigitte and she gave the nod. There we were sitting around the kitchen table with Brigitte Bardot in an isolated community on the North Shore of Quebec. It was a bit disarming, but we had business to do. It turned out that Brigitte didn't want to see the seal hunt; she just wanted to be photographed with a baby seal. I proposed that we share the helicopters the next morning, taking Brigitte and a bare-bones film crew along with some of the Greenpeace team. We decided we would make a stop at the Greenpeace camp on Belle Isle to introduce Brigitte to the expedition members. Then one helicopter would find a baby seal on the ice for the photo-op while the other would look for the sealing ships. It was a good compromise even though it did nothing to help Franz Weber and his 80 journalists, who were now in full mutiny.

That evening we had a large party. By then Brigitte had realized that Peter and I were cool, and as the beer and wine flowed we engaged in an animated discussion of everything from the seal hunt to the latest movies. Paul Watson finally emerged from his lair and joined the festivities. He agreed to come with us to Belle Isle in the morning.

The weather forecast was not particularly encouraging as we lifted off at 6 a.m. Halfway to the base camp we found out why. It was blowing snow and the wind was picking up fast, so we stayed low to the water over the Straits of Belle Isle. When we came up against the 800-foot cliffs of Belle Isle, we went into a steep ascent into the clouds; but there was still some visibility. We came up over the top of the island, now trying to get our bearings on this huge rock in order to locate the base camp. Within minutes we found ourselves in the midst of a squall with blinding snow, a "whiteout" as they call it in helicopter school. In this situation there is only one option: land the helicopter now. Whiteouts have the effect of completely disorienting the pilot so that he doesn't know up from down. Our pilots were probably being heroic because they had a beautiful VIP on board, but they did get us safely on the ground in challenging conditions.

It was not good that we were stranded, with no radio contact, in an intensifying blizzard. Moreover our helicopters were flimsy with limited fuel for flying and an insufficient amount to keep us warm in the subzero Newfoundland winter. But then again, I was stranded with Brigitte Bardot, the most beautiful French actress, an intellectual, whom the philosopher Sartre had used as a model for a character in one of his novels. Another consolation was the large provision of food we had on board to resupply the camp. And if things got really desperate we had a good stock of rum and whiskey meant for the camp as well. I mean, if we couldn't find the camp in a whiteout it was okay for us to survive on their rations, right? I'm forever thankful that after about an hour the storm lifted long enough for us to get the choppers in the air and find the camp.

The mood at the camp was mainly jubilant, at least on the surface. Most crew members seemed pleased to meet a superstar and there were lots of photos taken and some group discussion about the environment and animal welfare and the seals. However, beneath the veneer of smiles this encounter brought out a deep division in the personal philosophies of the Greenpeace crew. Some of our number thought it belittled the high cause of Greenpeace to associate with an actress who was primarily known for her love of cats, dogs, and horses. Other members, myself included, realized that we could benefit by linking with Brigitte, thus making a more powerful statement for the seals than either one of us could alone. There was no doubting her sincerity, and it didn't matter that we Greenpeacers didn't belong to the upper-class European elite as Brigitte did.

We soon realized that we weren't going any farther out to the sealing grounds on this day. There were blizzard conditions all around and it was another miracle that we were able to return to Blanc Sablon and the relative comfort of our motel rooms, where most of us were sleeping on the floor. But sleep could come later, we had another big dinner planned and the prospect of succeeding tomorrow. Just before dinner I was informed that Paul Watson had declared his legal right to control the helicopters, as he had signed the rental contract. Some members of the expedition had impressed on him their disapproval of Brigitte, as she was not "serious" like we were. I asked Paul to reconsider, but he was determined to assert his authority. I joined the Greenpeace/Bardot dinner with bad news. When I told Henri I could not provide any helicopters, the next day he retorted, "You will never see Brigitte again." I felt crushed, of course, and very disappointed that we couldn't work together any longer.

The next morning a privately owned Bell Jet Ranger helicopter took off at dawn from Blanc Sablon with Brigitte and her crew on board. Henri had worked late into the night to find an alternative now that we had cancelled. They reached the ice, where the seal pups lay about like big white Easter eggs and Brigitte held a baby seal in her arms. The photo appeared on the front cover of *Paris Match* and the accompanying article mentioned her visit to the Greenpeace camp on Belle Isle. I felt vindicated but still wished we had delivered her to the seals ourselves.

The expedition now wound to an end with some bitterness on my part. Paul Watson had behaved like a spoiled child and really undermined our effectiveness. I documented every detail about Paul's misbehavior and wrote to Bob Hunter about my concerns. I was actually a bit surprised on my return to Vancouver that most of the board members agreed with me. They could see Watson was too much of a rogue elephant for a group that prided itself on being a democratic collective.

Immediately after the seal campaign I set out for Europe with two reels of 16-millimeter film footage of the seal hunt. In those days the best way to get footage aired on TV was to deliver it to the studio, where they made a duplicate of it for their archives. They didn't have live satellite feeds in the old days! I traveled to Rome, where Eileen was staying with her sister. Upon landing in Rome about 20 of us were missing our luggage. We insisted that the airline's baggage handlers go back to the plane again and look for it. They claimed they had done so. Unfortunately all our luggage went on to Bangkok and I had to wear my brother-in-law's clothes for the next five days until my bags miraculously returned. They also contained the two reels of film without which my trip to Europe would have been a disaster.

Once my suitcase and film had been returned, Eileen and I set off to deliver the footage to TV stations in Italy, Switzerland, Germany, and France. When we arrived in Paris we were nearly broke, so we were thankful when Brice LaLonde, the founder and head of Les Amis de la Terre (Friends of the Earth), put us up in his large apartment in Montparnasse. I had made friends with the young photographer who was with Brigitte Bardot's group in Blanc Sablon, so we looked him up and met for lunch. He offered to give our regards to Brigitte, who issued an invitation to Eileen and me to have dinner at her Paris apartment that same day. Brigitte's sister and brother-in-law joined us for a delicious vegetarian meal. That evening we discussed all manner of environmental and political subjects. Henri had been wrong: I did see Brigitte again!

CHAPTER SEVEN

Taking the Reins

By April of 1977, it had become clear that Bob Hunter needed a break from leading our fast-growing organization. He was tired and cranky and just plain worn out. Bob asked me if I would take over. As he wrote in his book, *Warriors of the Rainbow,* "There was no doubt who should succeed me: it was obviously Patrick Moore's turn. He had been my own ecological guru for so long, it seemed inevitable to me that sooner or later he would run the organization anyway. Everybody else seemed to have a special focus, whether whales or seals or bombs or nuclear reactors. He was the lone interdisciplinarian. Whether he would be able to lead people or not would depend on himself and the flow of events hurtling about him."[20] This last observation would prove prophetic.

As the new president of the Greenpeace Foundation, I had inherited a fractious organization. Greenpeace had now grown into a full-fledged movement with offices springing up like weeds all over North America and in Europe, and we had not really taken care of the legalities. Bob and most of the rest of us had been focused on campaigning and raising enough money to keep the bank off our back. Meanwhile little Greenpeace fiefdoms were being established in San Francisco, Los Angeles, Portland, Seattle, Boston, Montreal, and Toronto. Not all these new Greenpeacers

---

20. Robert Hunter, *Warriors of the Rainbow* (New York: Holt Rinehart and Winston, 1975), 387.

felt an allegiance to the Vancouver organization, even though they were operating with our name and using our deeds to raise money for their little bureaucracies. The Vancouver organization was deeply in debt, in excess of $100,000, while the new offices were all debt-free and didn't seem compelled to send us any of their money.

I had realized for some time that this was an untenable situation; we couldn't have eight Greenpeace organizations that weren't connected to one another legally. I would spend the next two years, in between campaigns, trying to address this issue and bring the factions together. But as they say, the horses were well out of the barn.

Of more immediate concern was the fact that Paul Watson was now in full rebellion against the "Vancouver office" as the dissidents liked to call it. As if it was just another office and not the founding center of the Greenpeace empire. Paul was going around to the other offices and openly fomenting opposition against Vancouver. This played into the hands of the new people, many of whom hardly knew us and who saw an opportunity to have their very own Greenpeace group. Even worse, Paul made regular announcements about what Greenpeace was going to do next without consulting the committee first. One morning we awoke to read in the daily press that Greenpeace would next head to Africa to save the elephants. This was news to us and we didn't think it was funny. After all Paul was a member of board of directors. It was a clear case of insubordination.

By a vote of 11 to 1 (Paul being the 1), Paul Watson was voted off the board of the Greenpeace Foundation in May 1977. To this day, he tells people he quit, but believe me, Paul is not a quitter: we had to fire him. Paul soon started his own group, the Sea Shepherd Conservation Society, and earned a reputation for ramming and scuttling whaling ships. He fashions himself as a larger-than-life action figure who will defeat the evil overlords of industry. I admire the bravado he demonstrates in his ongoing campaign against Japanese whalers in Antarctica. He has landed a TV series called *Whale Wars* on *Animal Planet*, which highlights his high-seas confrontations with these whalers. The very successful TV series *South Park* based one of their most hilarious episodes, "Whale Whores," on Paul's adventures in Antarctica. Even though it was mercilessly critical, it must have given him a good laugh and put some wind in his sails. I say more power to him on that front.

Now there was an even bigger rebellion under way. Paul Spong and George Korotva had relocated to Hawaii, from where they announced that they would launch the 1977 whale campaign with a new ship. Because Vancouver's Greenpeace Foundation was so deep in debt, they believed it couldn't possibly finance a whale voyage. So they formed Greenpeace Hawaii, as if they owned the brand, and started raising money there. The San Francisco office, and other U.S. offices, pledged to support the campaign. Back at headquarters, we were becoming pretty isolated.

Jerry Garcia playing a benefit for the 1976 Greenpeace Voyage to Save the Whales at Pier 33 in San Francisco harbor. Our ship, the *James Bay*, was the backdrop and the backstage for the event. The *James Bay*'s funnel is behind Jerry.

Spong's and Korotva's defections were not treasonous. The two men were just fanatical about the campaign and didn't have time for legal niceties or bureaucracy. In those days everyone was wearing "Question Authority" buttons, and there were lots of anarchists in our midst. It was hard to question the religious fervor of the whale savers, unless you were responsible for the debt. I suppose I could have moved to another city and started a Greenpeace office myself, but that was not in my nature. I wanted to pull this bunch of renegades together into a stronger, global organization rather then allowing it to degenerate into fractious chaos.

The Hawaiian group found an ex-navy sub chaser that had operated at a speed of 26 knots when it was built 25 years earlier. It was a bucket of bolts when George found it, but it was all they could afford at $70,000, so they bought it and set about a refit. An air of machismo pervaded the whole Hawaiian effort: They would put a boat to sea that would go faster, farther and really stop the whalers in their tracks. They would show that bunch of hippies back in Vancouver how you really put an eco-navy together. There were times when they forgot this war was all about communicating ideas and images to the masses; it was not about defeating an enemy fleet in battle.

In the meantime Bob Hunter and I and the gang back in Vancouver managed to pull off a couple of successful campaigns in our own back yard. In early 1977 there was a proposal to build a supertanker terminal at Kitimat on the northern British Columbian coast to receive the oil from the Alaskan North Slope. Then the oil would travel by pipeline from Kitimat to the lower 48 states. We didn't believe that British Columbia, with its rugged rocky coastline known as the "Graveyard of the Pacific," should bear the risk of a massive oil spill, especially since the coastal waters are rich in sea life, including sea otters, orcas, and salmon.

The pipeline proponents had hired a cruise ship, the *Princess Patricia*, to carry a group of municipal politicians and media to view "the route of the supertankers" as a promotional exercise. We cobbled together a coalition of First Nations, United Church members, union leaders, and other environmentalists and planned to blockade the junket as the 300-foot cruise ship came past Hartley Bay, a First Nations village at the mouth of the inlet leading to Kitimat. We chartered the beautiful 80-foot wooden ship *Meander* for the voyage up the coast, where we were joined by a flotilla of smaller boats. The First Nations and church representatives had radioed to the *Princess Pat*, requesting that they be allowed to come aboard and read a statement that opposed the supertanker port proposal. We all expected that this fairly civilized request would be granted, but the captain didn't answer our hails, even though he knew our radio frequency.

As the cruise ship rounded the point, we could see that it had no intention of stopping, in fact it seemed to be accelerating. The captain had decided that the best plan was to try to run the blockade. He picked a spot where there were fewer of our boats and gunned it. Suddenly all the little boats were converging on the path of the cruise ship. The faster ones managed to get in front and alongside. Horns were tooted and the protesters on board yelled anti-supertanker slogans. As news helicopters swirled around the scene, politicians stood on the cruise ship's deck sipping cocktails. The media were frantically recording this amazing uprising around them. We succeeded in completely upstaging the pipeline promoters, and our protest ran on the local news for two days.

On board the *Meander* we were jubilant until we learned that the *Princess Patricia* had run over two Greenpeace members who were dogging the ship in a Zodiac. The Zodiacs floorboards had buckled in the cruise ship's bow wave, and Rod Marining and Mel Gregory had been thrown out and sucked under the hull. This incident had been captured on video. We had visions of minced Greenpeacers coming out behind the propellers of the ship. But within 10 minutes, one of the Hartley Bay boats arrived with two shivering cold, slightly injured crewmen. They had been spit back out from beneath the hull before they hit the props. This was as close as we had come to losing anyone in six years of hard campaigning.

The media made the captain's decision to run the blockade look callous and public opinion ran hard on our side. Public hearings were called and a year later it was announced that the Kitimat supertanker port was dead. We may have prevented our own version of the *Exxon Valdez* oil spill from happening on the B.C. coast.

Following on the heels of our supertanker campaign, the B.C. government announced that it was going to spray a 50,000-square-mile area of forest with insecticides to control an infestation of spruce budworm. I had studied forestry and pesticides and did not believe that the aerial spraying would solve the problem. I also believed it would do considerable damage to other species. We announced our intention to occupy the forest with dozens of volunteers so the government would have to risk spraying people if it went ahead. There were actually only about six of us, with a few allies among the First Nations communities in the area, but we made it seem like we had a volunteer army. Long before email was common, we made sure that we had lots of coins so that we could place calls to the media from a pay phone by the highway. We made the front page of the *Vancouver Sun* and the *Province* newspapers as a result of our plan to act as human shields to stop the spraying. Twelve hours before the spraying was to begin the premier called a special cabinet meeting and emerged to announce that the decision to spray had been rescinded. We had "saved" billions of budworms. Our opponents couldn't accuse us of only caring about cute and cuddly animals that day! Meanwhile, our thoughts turned back to the plight of the whales.

The gang in Hawaii was taking ages to get its ship, now renamed the *Ohana Kai* (meaning "family of the sea" in Hawaiian), ready for its voyage. It was early June and the whaling season was beginning. Bob and I were concerned that if the *Ohana Kai* didn't get off the dock there would be no campaign and we would lose the two years of momentum we had built up. We decided we had better start organizing Plan B. The *James Bay* was available and was already operational , except for the fact that it needed a minor refit. The owner gave us generous terms and we somehow found enough money to outfit the ship. Affording diesel fuel would be another matter. We stocked cases of Greenpeace T-shirts and whale buttons to sell at stops along the way. I assembled an excellent crew that included Captain John Cormack, who had skippered us on our first voyage to Amchitka and our first whale voyage. I was now the leader of the expedition and could choose a crew I thought would be capable and compatible, and get beyond Bob's frantic style of running things. Bob and I were the best of friends, but we had very different ways of going about our business. Bob generated the chaos from which Nietzsche said dancing stars are born; I was much more methodical and calculating in my approach (or so I like to think).

Within three weeks the *James Bay* was ready to sail. It was a good thing because the *Ohana Kai* was still tied to the dock when we set sail on July 17, heading straight south down the coast off California. Thirteen days later, thanks to the CIA and our friend Leo Ryan, we were in the midst of the Soviet fleet in gale force winds off Baja California. It was too rough to launch the Zodiacs and the whalers didn't seem to be doing much, so we just shadowed them for a couple of days. There was a plan for the *Ohana Kai* to rendezvous with us, but even then they were still in the harbor. Thank goodness we had a Plan B!

After two days the sea calmed a bit, but it was still running a six-foot swell when we saw the harpoon boats go into action. Conditions were marginal for the Zodiacs, especially for the people standing tethered in the bow trying to capture the events on film. Eight sperm whales surfaced in front of three harpoon boats, so we launched two Zodiacs and sped toward them. Rex Weyler and Michael Bailey succeeded in blocking the first harpoon shot, which missed the intended whale. Now we saw another seven harpoon boats bearing down on the fleeing pod. With two Zodiacs and a rough sea we tried desperately to shield the whales during the next two hours as they were gunned down one after the other. The crew watched from the deck of the *James Bay* as blood filled the sea around us, whales screaming and writhing in agony until all was quiet. It was a tough day.

Whereas previously the whalers had adopted a policy of calling off the hunt when we interfered, now they were using the brute force of all 10 killer-boats to overpower us. It was a gruesome scene and ironically it worked very much in our favor. When we docked in San Francisco to refuel, we released the footage of the slaughter to ABC news. It aired nationally, and among the many viewers was President Jimmy Carter. He phoned us after the airing and spoke with Bob Taunt, the most politically connected member of our group. In the news clip I was interviewed about our encounter with the whalers, and I mentioned they were killing whales that were clearly under the size limit set by the International Whaling Commission. President Carter asked Bob if we could supply evidence of this to him so that he could instruct the U.S. delegation to the International Whaling Commission to bring it before the international body. We fulfilled his request, but the IWC never brought formal charges against Russia, even though our evidence was irrefutable.

We had come into San Francisco to refuel, but by this point we had no money. The San Francisco office had committed all its funds to the *Ohana Kai* expedition and the Vancouver office was so far in debt the bank had closed its doors to us. We were desperate to get back on the whaling grounds. Rex Weyler, Mel Gregory, and Caroline Keddy were out when they saw a marquee advertising a Jerry Garcia (of the Grateful Dead) performance at a small club. They entered the club and announced to a biker bouncer that they were from Greenpeace and would like to speak to Jerry Garcia. The biker had heard of us and thought we were cool, so he escorted the boys backstage, where they explained our predicament. "We need about $10,000 for fuel and food," explained Mel. "Will you do a benefit concert for us?" Jerry said, "Sure, as long as Tom Campbell produces it." Rex had never heard of Tom Campbell, but he soon found out Tom was the impresario among benefit concert producers. He was a hippy like most of us and had worked with everyone from Jackson Browne to Bonnie Raitt. "When would you like to do this gig?" Tom Campbell asked Rex. "Friday," said Rex. "Which Friday?" Tom inquired. "This Friday" (it was Monday), Rex replied. "Yah, right," kidded Tom.

It took a while, but eventually a plan was devised. The benefit would be held at Pier 33, where the *James Bay* would be the backstage. This way there was no need to book a venue in advance; all we needed was fair weather. Word would go out on the underground telegraph, radio stations, and street flyers. Tom phoned Maria Muldaur and she agreed to warm up the crowd.

On the day of the concert, the sky was brilliantly blue and a brisk breeze starched the flags and banners flying from the *James Bay*'s rigging. A faithful crowd of Dead Heads and San Francisco hipsters magically appeared and Maria Muldaur opened with her signature number, "Midnight at the Oasis." While pot smoke wafted among the assembled thousand or so the Jerry Garcia Band played for the whales while we counted the money on board our floating backstage home. Eureka! It was exactly enough to fill the fuel tanks and larder and get us back on the high seas.

Or so we thought until certain members of the San Francisco office demanded they get half the loot because we were in their town and the *Ohana Kai* needed money too. For me this marked a turning point. It felt like a stickup by your own side and became the official beginning of a conflict that would last two years. Up until now I had been willing to chalk the rivalry up to instinctual competitive urges. Now I saw it as a dangerous sign of division and betrayal. We put the money in our on-board safe and told the San Francisco office to take a hike. Our lines were cast by nightfall and we slid back into the open sea with full tanks and fresh coordinates for the Russian whaling fleet.

Unfortunately for the *Ohana Kai* expedition, which did eventually leave the dock in Honolulu, our footage of the whale slaughter overshadowed their two encounters with the other Soviet factory whaling fleet north of Hawaii. At the time I could only think it was just deserts for having deserted the home team in the first place. It was all coming into focus, there was mutiny in the ranks. But we had so much campaigning to do that the problem kept slipping through the cracks. As it turned out, our initial campaign encounter on the *James Bay* and the buzz it created would be the highlight of the 1977 whale voyage.

I was arrested for sitting on a seal pup and hauled off to jail. The seal pup was subsequently clubbed and skinned, but this picture appeared in more than 3000 newspapers around the world the next morning. Photo: Rex Weyler

While the two whale-saving voyages were under way in the North Pacific, Bob and Bobbi Hunter set out for new frontiers—the last whaling station in Australia at Albany in Western Australia. By this time, Australia was a somewhat reluctant whale killer, but economics and inertia had kept the practice going. Bob and Bobbi landed in Sydney, where they were met by a typically idealistic yet technologically inept band of volunteer whale-worshipers. They had been promised everything for the expedition would be organized but nothing had been. In an epic journey, they crossed the 2000-mile expanse of the Nulabar Desert in completely worn-out vehicles that broke down at least once a day. Upon their arrival in Albany, the group expected Bob to know how to assemble a Zodiac from scratch; after all he was a leader of the greatest whale-savers on Earth. Actually Bob was about the most technically incompetent member of our eco-navy; instead words were his bag. But as was usual, perseverance furthered the cause, and the Zodiacs were eventually launched from the beach into the Southern Ocean. Unfortunately, the Southern Ocean is the roughest body of water in the world, with normal seas running 20 feet or more—not the place for a 14-foot Zodiac.

The whaling operation was from a shore station, so the harpoon boats operated individually, not in a pack like the factory fleets. In order to confront the killer boats without a mother ship of their own, Bob and his crew had to follow them up to 40 miles from shore and then try to interfere with them. While tactical success was limited by weather and logistics, the campaign made big news across the country and support poured in. The following year, after a Royal Commission was struck, Australia decided to

CONFESSIONS OF A GREENPEACE DROPOUT

get out of whaling for good and took its vote against killing whales to the International Whaling Commission.

With all of us home from the wars we spent the fall preparing for the seal campaign, scheduled for early 1978. I hoped we could bring the various offices together by including everyone in the expedition. By this time Bob Taunt had become my strongest ally in the U.S. Greenpeace universe. He did not share the insurgent mentality of many of his colleagues, due in large measure to his good breeding and allegiance to moral principles. Finally having wrested control of the seal campaign from Paul Watson, Bob and I worked tirelessly to put on the best expedition to date. It would be a multipronged effort.

The head of our Los Angeles office, Phil Caston, was acquainted with animal rights activist Tippi Hedren, who was famous for her starring role in Alfred Hitchcock's 1963 thriller *The Birds* and who is nowadays known as the mother of Melanie Griffith. Tippi asked her friend Pamela Sue Martin to join our expedition, which she agreed to do. (Pamela Sue was acclaimed for her role in the TV series *Nancy Drew*.) In addition, Monique van der Ven, an up-and-coming Dutch actress, agreed to join to provide popular appeal in Europe.

Meanwhile Bob Taunt worked with Leo Ryan to put a motion before the House of Representatives to condemn the Canadian seal hunt. It passed by a wide margin, embarrassing the Canadian government into officially "regretting" that the U.S. was meddling in its sovereign affairs. Congressman Leo Ryan, a Democrat, and Congressman Jim Jeffords, a Republican, agreed to accompany us to Newfoundland to make a bipartisan statement condemning the hunt on behalf of the American people.

In addition we assembled a Greenpeace crew representing all the offices in North America and once again vowed to interfere with the slaughter. This year we would return to St. Anthony and again use Decker's boarding house as our base. Helicopters were hired and the expedition to save the seals was under way for the third consecutive year.

The actresses and politicians piqued the media's interest as they flooded into St. Anthony for the Greenpeace extravaganza. By this time the Canadian government had made it impossible for anyone to go near the seal hunt without a permit. Peter Ballem led the negotiations for the permits, promising we would not interfere with the seal hunt while we were on the ice with our dignitaries. Peter, Bob Taunt, and I, with camera and film crews, accompanied Pamela Sue, Monique, Leo, and Jim to the ice floes, where they were able to witness the scenes of carnage with their own eyes.

During our tour of the hunt, a series of events occurred that could make a grown man cry. We came across a seal hunter who had clubbed a seal pup that was with its mother. The mother seal lunged to attack him, so he beat her over the head with his hakapik and then drove the sharp end of the hakapik into the pup's head and proceeded to drag it away from the mother. The mother seal recovered from the blow and began a desperate full-speed seal waddle across the ice after her pup. The hunter, who could easily outrun the mother seal, stopped and with an experienced hand tore the skin off the pup in 30 seconds and threw it in a growing pile of furs. When the mother seal caught up, she approached her skinned baby and sniffed it before snuggling up to the carcass as if to protect it. I swear that she had tears in her eyes as she mourned the loss of her child. As we left the scene, the mother was still huddled over the remains. The film footage we shot of this event was so powerful that forces in favor of the seal hunt made a concerted effort to claim that it was staged. Years later, Greenpeace took one propagandist, Icelander Magnus Gudmundsson, to court to obtain an injunction against his continued claim that the footage was staged. This was long after I had left Greenpeace, but I was pleased to testify before a judge in Oslo, Norway, that I had witnessed the slaughter myself and that there was nothing staged about it.

Returning to a packed media conference at Decker's, Leo Ryan summed up the feelings of the group when he said, "Just stop this." It was an emotional day and an even more emotional media conference. The footage obtained that day, including that of the mother and her skinned pup, was carried on news broadcasts around the world. The Canadian authorities were reduced to a damage control operation that didn't work very well. We had taken the campaign global and the world was on our side.

With this phase of the campaign over, our four guests departed, leaving us with the job of trying to engineer a confrontation with the sealers on the ice floes. The Canadian government seemed determined to keep us away from the hunt, having had enough bad press for one year. The federal Fisheries and Oceans department had set up a temporary office in a nearby motel room to "manage" the seal hunt, so Peter Ballem and I, accompanied by our photographer Rex Weyler, went there for a visit. We simply intended to inquire about the procedure for obtaining another permit to visit the seal hunt.

As we walked in the door of the "office,", the small staff immediately left the room. We decided to wait for them to return. A few minutes later a Fisheries officer came back with a member of the Royal Canadian Mounted Police in tow, who promptly arrested us for loitering. This scenario was like something straight out of Arlo Guthrie's "Alice's Restaurant." We had difficulty keeping a straight face as we were hauled in for questioning. By the time we were released, the media had thronged the police station and we made the international news once again. It's amazing how the authorities often play right into your hands. These guys could use a course in issues management!

Now the authorities really didn't know what to do with us. Peter Ballem

CONFESSIONS OF A GREENPEACE DROPOUT

pulled out all the stops, contacting the Prime Minister's Office in Ottawa, stating that we had a constitutional right to go out to the ice and that the permits should be issued. We were shocked when we learned that the PMO had issued instructions to the Fisheries officers give us the permits. We had to make a verbal statement that we wouldn't interfere with the seal hunt, but we crossed our fingers behind our backs. Why did they think we wanted to go out there?

Eileen kissed me goodbye for the cameras as we boarded the helicopters and made our way to Cartwright, Labrador, on March 17. The ice and the seals had drifted northward, so we could not reach the seal hunt in a single flight. Fortunately our pilots had access to a fuel cache up the coast of Labrador (Newfoundlanders call it "down the Labrador" even though it is north). The weather forecast called for blizzard conditions the next morning as the crew settled in for the evening in Cartwright. A small miracle brought a bright blue sky the next morning and we took off in the subzero cold of a north Canadian winter. The seal herd was about 50 miles offshore and we landed before noon on the ice floes in the midst of the hunt. We had not told our lawyer, Peter Ballem, what we intended to do, but our mission that day had a single purpose: I had decided to make a statement by sitting on a baby seal and demanding this one seal be spared the hunter's club.

When we landed, we spent some time getting footage and photos of the seal killing and the environment in which this was taking place. Then I spotted a baby seal that lay off to the side of the action and went over to it, sat on its back, and grabbed hold of its flippers in order to prevent it from escaping. I had no idea how strong these little creatures were, and this one wasn't so little either. It was all I could do to hang on to this "tough little bugger, " as I later described the pup. It wasn't long before the Fisheries officers and their RCMP buddies noticed I was astride the pup. They made their way over and gathered around me, along with our film and photo crew, Peter Ballem, Bob Taunt, and a couple of sealers, who were leaning on their hakapiks.

I clung to the seal pup for dear life and announced to the assembled group that I wanted the sealers to spare this one pup, just this one. The sealers could go and find any number of other seals to club, but I was protecting this pup. Surely it was reasonable to spare one pup's life. Of course, the authorities didn't see things that way and, in fact, realized their jobs would be on the line if they allowed me to save even one seal's life, so they told me I must get off the seal or be arrested. The Fisheries officer asked the sealers if they wanted to kill this seal. "Aye bye," one replied. We went back and forth a few times with the camera rolling and Rex snapping shots until the ultimatum was given. Now I am not one to go limp and be forcibly dragged away upon being arrested for civil disobedience. I believe the moment the long arm of the law tells you that you are under arrest you should go peaceably and not resist. That's what the *civil* in civil disobedience means.

So I was arrested and taken off the seal and had to watch while the two sealers who had been pressed into service by the authorities bashed its head in and skinned it. It's not as if I hadn't witnessed this procedure before. When I arrived in the Cartwright jail, they took my belt and shoelaces so I couldn't hang myself in the prison cell. I guess this was standard procedure, but it did seem a bit funny at the time. Thankfully Peter was able to get me out of there before nightfall, and we were all back together in St. Anthony that evening. We had succeeded in getting our confrontation and it was once again broadcast around the world.

In some ways this "seal-sitting" episode was both the most disappointing and the most rewarding campaign action I was ever involved in. It was disappointing because the color film footage, with sound, shot by Steve Bowerman while I was arrested on the seal while pleading for its life, never saw the light of day. We will never know if Steve made a technical error or if sabotage was involved. All we know is that when the film footage arrived at the CBC's Montreal studio for processing it was exposed and useless. Steve had either exposed it by mistake (perhaps he had not closed the camera magazine properly) or someone had purposely exposed the film so that it would never be seen. To this day I suspect the latter, as we all did at the time.

The best news was that Rex's black and white still photos had survived. When he sent them over the wire service, the photo of me sitting on the seal was published the next morning in more than 3000 newspapers around the world. This was the widest distribution of any Greenpeace still image in the history of the organization until then. So the seal-sit was a great success, even though we didn't get the ultimate media hit on TV. You win some, you lose some.

In an extraordinarily petty move the Canadian attorney general filed a charge against our lawyer, Peter Ballem, for "aiding and abetting" my seal-sitting crime. This was probably because Peter had managed to get us our permit and here we had embarrassed the government once more. This meant that Peter could not defend me in court, so we needed yet another lawyer to defend both of us. Longtime Greenpeace supporter David Gibbons, who was one of the most prominent criminal lawyers in Canada, stepped up to the plate. (Gibbons died in 2004.)

As if we hadn't garnered enough attention from the media during the seal hunt itself, we were now faced with a trial in Newfoundland for loitering in a temporary Fisheries office and for sitting on a baby seal without permission from the minister of Fisheries and Oceans. We arrived in Corner Brook, Newfoundland, in early June 1978 to face the charges. Anyone could see this was a trumped-up situation, but the government was serious, so we had to respond in a similar fashion even if it was laughable. With lay Judge Gordon Seabright presiding the proceedings began with the charges against Rex and me for loitering in the temporary Fisheries office. The highlight of the trial came during David Gibbons's closing remarks, when he opined in high court fashion, "Your Honor, Judge Seabright, I must inform you that if my clients are convicted in this matter, it will no doubt go down in the annals of jurisprudence as the shortest loiter in history." We calculated that the loiter had lasted for about seven minutes. "Not guilty," came the verdict. Now we were to move on to the more serious charge: sitting on a baby seal without permission from the minister of Fisheries and Oceans. Oh yes, and the charge that my lawyer had aided and abetted me in this heinous crime, all under the so-called Seal Protection Regulations.

But before we could move on the lawyer acting for the Crown interjected with a complaint. Apparently David Gibbons was not called before the bar in Newfoundland. Without an invitation from the provincial law society, Gibbons could not defend me in a Newfoundland court and we would have to retain another lawyer who was called to the bar. Now my first lawyer had been charged with helping me commit my crime, my second lawyer was disallowed from representing me, so to appear before the judge on our behalf we hired a third lawyer who new nothing of the case.

In the end Peter Ballem was acquitted and I was found guilty of contravening the Seal Protection Regulations and fined $200. It was clear that lay Judge Seabright saw the irony in the case, but there was no doubt that I had broken the law, so he had no choice but to find me guilty. News of the trial and the conviction was widely broadcast, once again bringing attention to the fact that Canada continued a practice that should have been abolished long ago.

CHAPTER EIGHT
Growing Pains

The trial in Corner Brook had been a brief interlude in our preparations for the 1978 voyage to save the whales. We were all disappointed that the *James Bay* was not available, as she had been sold to a group of treasure hunters for service in the Caribbean. We subsequently learned that they had been successful and that the investors in the venture had made a fortune. For a brief moment this made me wonder about the choices one makes in life, but we had our own mission to complete. It might not be a financially rewarding one, but the prospect of saving the whales was such a powerful motivator that I didn't dwell on it.

After a long search, we found the M.V. *Peacock*, another converted minesweeper, in Los Angeles, where she was berthed in San Pedro Harbor. The *Peacock* was not as fast as the *James Bay*, but she could do the job after a major refit and a paint job. Eileen and I moved in with Phil Caston in Sherman Oaks and spent a month commuting to the docks to make the *Peacock* seaworthy. We both felt exhausted from the effort so Eileen and I decided that we would stay ashore for the first leg of the voyage, as there were plenty of seasoned crew on board. Bob Taunt was chosen as the leader of the expedition as he had been on the two previous missions and was a director of the San Francisco organization. It did not bode well for the mission when Bob broke his foot kicking an oil drum on deck in a fit of rage just before the ship was to cast off. We got him bandaged up, and in early July the *Peacock* set sail. The media provided extensive coverage of the launch of our fourth voyage into the Pacific to confront the Soviet factory fleet. ABC's *Good Morning America* featured helicopter footage of the Peacock with flags flying and an enthusiastic crew ready for action on the high seas.

Eileen and I were in Winter Harbour when our old friend, Jim Taylor, who had joined the expedition, phoned to tell us that the *Peacock* had arrived in Honolulu without having met either of the two Soviet whaling fleets. It seemed for the first time that the Soviets were avoiding the whaling grounds off California and were staying west of Hawaii. Perhaps they had received enough bad press already. But that didn't mean they weren't killing whales out there. Unfortunately the mood aboard the *Peacock* had turned sour. Bob Taunt had left the boat and was holed up in the Royal Hawaiian Hotel due to the mutinous nature of the crew. I never really determined whose fault this was, but they obviously needed help. I left Winter Harbour and flew to Honolulu to replace Bob as leader of the expedition. We got the mutiny sorted out and with fresh coordinates for the whaling fleet we headed back out into the north Pacific.

The Soviet whaling fleet was operating about 500 miles north of Hawaii, so we steamed for two days. On the morning of the third day, we arrived among the whalers in rough weather. They found a pod of sperm whales, took up the chase, and we lowered our Zodiacs for the standard confrontation. It was a bit like sleepwalking as we had done this so many times before. Once again we put ourselves in front of the harpoons, filmed and photographed the action, and stymied the odd shot. At the end of the day, though, we really could not prevent them from killing the whales. But we were getting the footage and making the news. We knew what we really needed was a vote against whaling from the International Whaling Commission. To date our efforts had failed there, despite support from many countries, because the majority still sided with the whalers. It was becoming just a little disheartening.

Meanwhile on the other side of the world a new Greenpeace universe was unfolding. Having won a partial victory against the French government for beating him and ramming his boat at Mururoa, David McTaggart had turned his mind to building his own campaign to save the whales in Europe. He had noticed the great success we had in our Pacific campaign and invited Bob Hunter to come to Europe to help raise funds in order to launch a similar effort there. Iceland, Norway, and Spain were all still operating shore-based whaling stations in 1978. Iceland, in particular, was killing the large fin whales in the North Atlantic. Bob appeared with representatives of the World Wildlife Fund on Dutch television, showing footage from our confrontations with the Soviet whaling fleet in the Pacific, and the donations came pouring in.

With the funds raised from Bob's TV appearance, the fledgling European group bought a mothballed British research ship designed for service in the North Atlantic. The 150-foot *Sir William Hardy* was renamed the *Rainbow Warrior*, the brainwave of Susi Newborn, a Londoner who had joined McTaggart's growing band of ecofreaks. Volunteers descended on the new ship. It was soon fit for a voyage against Icelandic whalers, complete with the Kwakiutl Sisiutl crest painted on the funnel.

During the summer of 1978, the *Rainbow Warrior* established herself as the new flagship for Greenpeace, confronting the Icelandic whalers in terribly rough seas. The British media and public were particularly attracted to the campaign as it reminded them of the Cod Wars between British and Icelandic fishing fleets that had taken place a few years earlier. Naval ships from Iceland had systematically cut the lines behind British trawlers to protest the fact that they were fishing within 200 miles of their island. The Brits cheered Greenpeace on as they got in a little payback for the home team.

On the *Rainbow Warrior's* way back from Iceland, the U.K. Mariners Union informed our crew that nuclear waste was being dumped into the Atlantic 200 miles off the coast of Spain. For some years the European countries with nuclear power plants had been pooling their low- and medium-level nuclear wastes, putting them in oil drums and dumping them into the Atlantic. There was some evidence that the U.K. was slipping spent nuclear fuel from naval submarines into the drums. British ships were carrying this out under the auspices of the London Dumping Convention, an international body set up to regulate marine disposal of waste. It caused one to wonder, If it was acceptable to dump nuclear waste in the sea, then what couldn't be dumped? This was clearly a job for Greenpeace.

In the most dramatic confrontation since the first encounter with the Soviet whalers, the crew of the *Rainbow Warrior* piloted their Zodiacs into position beneath the platform where the barrels of nuclear waste were rolled off into the sea. Time after time, the Greenpeacers attempted to block the barrels, only to be repelled by high-pressure water cannons wielded by the dumping ship's crew. Finally a Zodiac positioned itself squarely under the platform as the barrel was jettisoned. The heavily laden barrel fell and crushed the bow of the Zodiac, dramatically flipping the driver into the sea, from where he had to be rescued by his fellow campaigners. All this was filmed and broadcast around the world to an unbelieving audience as no one had ever exposed nuclear dumping before. Greenpeace Europe was now on the map in a big way.

Meanwhile, the *Peacock* arrived back in Los Angeles from the annual whaling campaign to considerable fanfare and the media paid the usual great attention. However, I felt as if we had put on the same show once too often. It was difficult to break through to the top spot in the news and there just wasn't the zing we had had in previous years. Sure there was the big party the night we arrived, which more than a few Hollywood

Representatives gathered for Greenpeace's first meeting to attempt to settle the dispute between the Greenpeace Foundation and the Greenpeace branches in North America, Europe, and New Zealand. David McTaggart, who soon garnered the support of all the branch groups, is in the second row at the far left. I am in the back row at the far right. This photo always brings back a flood of memories. photo: Rex Weyler

celebrities attended. I wandered around the room wondering what more we could possibly do to bring attention to the plight of the whales. We had gone to sea for four years in a row, sailed thousands of miles, confronted the whalers on many occasions and captured it all on film; and yet whaling continued unabated. We had sent representatives to the International Whaling Commission year after year to lobby for the whales and had even recruited small island-nations, such as the Seychelles, to join the IWC to vote against the whalers. Now it seemed all for naught. As the celebration raged into the night, I fell into a state of despair.

There were plenty of reasons for despair in the fall of 1978. Shortly after we returned to Vancouver we heard the grisly news that Congressman Leo Ryan had been gunned down while investigating the People's Temple cult in Jonestown, Guyana. The mass suicide that followed caused revulsion around the world. Greenpeace had lost a great ally.

It had now become clear that our San Francisco office was determined to break away from the Greenpeace Foundation, taking with it our history, our money, and our name. They were simply willing to take advantage of the fact that we had not done our legal homework and that we were weakened by our debt while they had money rolling in. Their attitude emboldened all the other branch offices in the U.S. and Canada to break away too, leaving the founding organization in a very difficult position.

Determined to resolve the situation, we called a meeting in the fall of 1978 that was attended by representatives of all the Greenpeace offices, including the European groups represented by David McTaggart. Dubbed an international meeting, it was the first time all the leaders of the various new groups had come together. It was exhilarating for all of us to meet around the same table at the Vancouver home of our accountant Bill

Gannon. However, the exhilaration did not last as the meeting degenerated into factional disputes over who owned what rights to the Greenpeace name in what country. We adjourned agreeing to think about these issues over Christmas.

In the spring of 1979, we called a second international meeting and chose a neutral ground at the University of British Columbia. The Greenpeace Foundation proposed we form an international board of directors that would see the founding organization in Vancouver in control but that would include a number of key leaders from the other offices. The other offices, San Francisco in particular, asserted that nothing short of autonomy for their organizations was acceptable. After two days the meeting ended with the other offices staging a walkout. The negotiations were over.

Most galling was the fact that David Tussman, the lawyer who had volunteered to help us establish our U.S. group, now led the San Francisco office, and by example the other offices, into open rebellion against the organization that he owed his living to. This was clearly a breach of his fiduciary duty and contrary to everything he had sworn to uphold as a member of the legal profession in California. To this day I believe we should have sued to have his license to practice law revoked for betraying his client. But our backs were to the wall, and we didn't really believe in attacking our own people.

Realizing there was no possibility of resolving the issue through negotiations, in June 1979 the Greenpeace Foundation filed a lawsuit against Greenpeace America in San Francisco for breach of trademark and copyright. The lawsuit focused on the right to use the name Greenpeace for fund-raising and publicity. From a legal perspective the case was cut-and-dried. Peter Ballem, who took on our case without charge, advised us that we were certainly the legitimate owners of the word *Greenpeace*, and because there was no question that we had created the San Francisco organization we would win in court. The political reality was not so cut-and-dried, however.

The political reality hit me squarely in the face in the form of a cream pie when I was ambushed by members of the Seattle group while leaving my office late one afternoon. This surprised and humiliated me, but we had no choice but to stay the course if we wanted to keep Greenpeace whole. In their zeal to become "independent," San Francisco and the other offices seemed oblivious to the fact that if they got their way, then anyone could call themselves Greenpeace and start raising money using the images from our campaigns. The thought of Greenpeace degenerating in this way was my worst nightmare. I wanted desperately to keep the organization together as I realized how powerful it could be if it didn't disintegrate.

Early in the legal battle I made a tactical error that I still regret. It was the campaigner in me that caused me to travel with Eileen to San Francisco to hold a media conference to explain why we were suing our office there. First, the San Francisco media instinctively sided with their locals, so the coverage was not at all good from our perspective. Worse, this gave the San Francisco office the opportunity to use our public utterances as the basis of a counter-lawsuit. They filed a nasty legal action, not against the Greenpeace Foundation but against myself and Eileen personally, for libel and defamation. We had simply explained the nature of the lawsuit to the media, and that we believed that the San Francisco office's effort to secede was illegal. I was served at my home in Vancouver with a writ claiming $1 million in damages. It was clearly an act of intimidation and to some extent it worked, especially as it devastated Eileen.

Having set a lawsuit in motion, I traveled to England in July to attend the International Whaling Commission meeting with the purpose of talking to David McTaggart about the implications of the lawsuit. In what I later found to be typical fashion he refused to meet with me, sending Greenpeace France representative Rémi Parmentier in his stead. I told Rémi that the Greenpeace groups in Europe should be concerned about the legal action because they would also be affected by the outcome. I later found out Remi's report had been interpreted by McTaggart as a threat when in fact it had clearly been meant as a diplomatic communication. I was probably a slow learner, but I was gradually finding out how Machiavellian the politics of environmentalism were, especially when David McTaggart was involved.

Thankfully we received some very good news during that summer of our discontent. The IWC voted 12 to 2 to end the sperm whale hunt in the North Pacific, effectively banning factory whaling in the world's largest ocean. For a few days we all set our differences aside to celebrate a victory that had taken five years of hard campaigning to achieve. It was only the first of many anti-whaling decisions that would see factory whaling banned altogether by 1981.

When I returned home, I realized we were fast becoming surrounded by our own creation. Every Greenpeace office from Seattle to Boston to Toronto to Paris was aligning itself against the people and the organization that had made them successful and famous in their countries, their cities, and their communities. At least the lawsuit gave all these previously disjointed organizations a common cause—opposition to us!

During the summer I made several trips to San Francisco to try to resolve the impasse. At one point David Tussman and a majority of his board agreed to sign a contract whereby funds would be shared among the offices, but at the last minute they refused to do so. We heard that David McTaggart had come over from Europe to visit the Boston and San Francisco offices in an effort to get their support for his proposal. David's idea for Greenpeace was that we should organize on national lines with each country getting one vote. This served his purpose perfectly as he had three countries—England, Holland, and France—squarely in his camp. Canada and the U.S. were the only other countries with substantial organizations, so David's formula would automatically give him control. I had to admit his proposal was at least practical, and I also had to admit he was way ahead of the rest of us as a politician.

Bob Hunter, who was still on our board but had no executive position, staunchly opposed the lawsuit against San Francisco. He preferred the idea that some kind of cosmic intervention would take place and felt that the lawsuit was somehow beneath us. Of course his passive attitude was precisely why we had ended up in such disarray in the first place, but there was no telling him so. He had often said, "May a thousand Greenpeace offices bloom," but he had no regard for the legal mess this approach invited. Bob openly sided with McTaggart, and he managed to convince our lawyer, Peter Ballem, that the case should be settled along McTaggart's lines. Now not only had our San Francisco lawyer betrayed us, but our own lawyer had decided not to take instructions from his client but to "give us advice" that the majority of our board didn't agree with. It was enough to make one wonder about lawyers who offer to work for a charitable cause for free.

All this bickering didn't keep us from starting new campaigns here and there. Earlier in the year we had been approached by Jim Wright, an accomplished landscape photographer and naturalist from Smithers in northern British Columbia. He told us big-game trophy hunters from the U.S. and Europe were coming to Spatsizi Provincial Park and were permitted to kill grizzly bears, mountain sheep, mountain goats, wolves, and just about anything else that moved. "It's one thing to allow such a practice outside the parks," Jim appealed, "but why should we permit trophy hunting for our finest wildlife specimens in a Class A Wilderness Park, where it is theoretically illegal to so much as pick a flower?" After researching the subject, we agreed with his point of view. Trophy hunting, where the main objective is to obtain souvenir parts of the animal for display, certainly can't be compared to subsistence hunting for food. We decided to send an expedition to Spatsizi to confront the hunters and their guides.

British Columbia is divided into Guide Outfitting areas and foreign nationals must employ a guide to hunt wildlife. The guiding license for the Spatsizi Park was owned by the Collingwood brothers, a couple of delightful hayseeds who were well established in the area. They set up tent camps and laid in supplies before the hunting season began. Once it started, they took their clients into the wilderness on horseback for days at a time. They packed a lot of rifles.

We set out from Vancouver in early October, driving 24 hours over two days and then chartering Beaver floatplanes into a public camp at Coldfish Lake. It is a beautiful spot with log cabins and a backdrop across the lake of

The meeting in David Gibbons's office, where the structure of Greenpeace International was determined. From the back left are Michael M'Gonigle, David Garrick, and Bob Hunter. From the front left are Rex Weyler, David McTaggart, lawyers Peter Ballem and David Gibbons, myself, and Rod Marining.

snow-capped mountains that extend well above the tree line. We had our own film crew as well as a reporter from the CBC national radio network.

It wasn't long before we were able to disrupt a hunt by spooking the intended target, while blocking the trail with our bodies. The guides and their clients were not amused. Thus began a three-year campaign that saw us return each hunting season to dog the trophy hunters. It turned out to be a difficult fight.

On the eve of our date in a San Francisco courtroom, David McTaggart arrived in Vancouver, met with his allies, and asked for a meeting with the Vancouver board. It was agreed we would meet in David Gibbons's office: he had been our senior legal counsel for many years and was trusted by all sides. On Sunday morning, October 14, a group of people who had invested a good part of their lives in this thing called Greenpeace sat down to see if we could reach a settlement. By this time I was resigned to the fact that the Greenpeace Foundation would lose control.

We had prided ourselves from the beginning on being transnational in our philosophy because ecology doesn't recognize political borders. So it was difficult to accept an organizational structure that was based on national lines of "one-country, one-vote." But in the final analysis, no one, including myself, could come up with a better idea for the basis of an international constitution. It was agreed that the Greenpeace Foundation did have the legal right to the word Greenpeace. In turn, the Greenpeace Foundation agreed to hand those rights over to a new organization, Greenpeace International, which would be based in Amsterdam. The Greenpeace Foundation would become Greenpeace Canada and would, along with all other national

Greenpeace organizations, sign the Greenpeace International Accord, recognizing the supreme authority of Greenpeace International. Each of the five main national organizations would have one vote on the Greenpeace International Council. The lesser national groups such as New Zealand, Australia, and Denmark would be members of Greenpeace International but would not have a vote until the voting members agreed. Finally, the Vancouver office's debt would be paid off with some of the cash that had piled up in the U.S. and European branches.

In retrospect it was something of a shame McTaggart gained control. He may have been a brilliant political strategist and a Machiavellian thinker, but he had no education in the sciences. Over the years he would allow our organization to drift away from science and logic, eventually adopting policies that were based more on fear and sensation than on facts and reason. But he did help to hold the group together for many years and for that I respect him.

Thus was created the first truly internationally constituted environmental activist organization. Unlike groups such as the World Wildlife Fund and Friends of the Earth, which are loose federations of national groups with a common name, Greenpeace International is a single entity. When the International Council meets, all the money and all the policy are on the same table. This has proved to be a very powerful political formula, allowing for coordinated action around the globe.

I was now the head of Greenpeace Canada and one of five international directors on the International Council. It was good to have the politics behind us, even though control shifted to McTaggart's European base. The important thing was that we had managed to prevent disintegration and we were one organization again. And even more important, we could get back to the reason for our involvement in the first place, campaigning for the environment.

Before returning to the campaign trail, I witnessed the birth of our first child. Jonathan was born to Eileen early on October 20, 1979. I quit smoking for good that very day. Maybe I wasn't smart enough to quit for my own sake, but I wasn't going to blow smoke in a baby's face. Thanks for that, Jon.

CHAPTER NINE

Greenpeace Goes Global

On November 9, 1979, Bob Hunter and I boarded a 747 for London, where we had arranged to join the *Rainbow Warrior* for the passage across the North Sea to Amsterdam. We would be attending the first meeting of Greenpeace International with representatives from all the offices that had sprung up in the wake of our adventures. We both felt quite excited that we had created a truly international organization and could see the power it might wield.

During the overnight flight, Bob and I talked incessantly while he chain-smoked (I had quit two weeks before), and we both enjoyed more than a few drinks. After all, the *Rainbow Warrior* would not sail until eight the next evening, so we could get a good nap before leaving the dock. Not having slept a wink, we arrived in London three sheets to the wind and phoned our London contact to find out the best way to get to the *Warrior*. Whoops, the ship was scheduled to leave the East London Docks at 8 a.m., not p.m., and it was already nearly 7 a.m. "Get on the Underground for Aldgate Station, go up and take a cab to the docks," we were told. We set off at a quick jog. It was easy enough to find the Underground and we were beginning to think we might actually make it when the train stopped one station short of our destination. "This train is reversing, all passengers please get off and wait for the next eastbound train," the speaker droned. So we stepped out and waited on the platform for the next train as time ticked away.

Just as the next train was approaching, I looked down and realized that I had left my leather briefcase on the reversing train. In it were both our return air tickets and our passports. I panicked as I realized we could not get on board the *Warrior* without our passports and that our return tickets would also be useful for a successful journey (This was long before the advent of electronic tickets). Bob was so wasted that he slumped over his baggage in defeat while I raced up the escalator to see if I could find help. Halfway to the surface, I came to a small platform where there was a narrow door on the wall. I knocked and was amazed to hear a loud "come in" from the other side. Entering, I found a small man sitting in a chair in a room about six feet square with a tiny table in the middle on which sat a single black telephone. I rattled off my story. He said it might be four or five days before my briefcase ended up in the Lost and Found if it was ever turned in. I said, "Please, we are on our way to an important meeting," and he offered me a cigarette. I took it. As it turned out, that was to be the last cigarette that ever touched my lips.

The small man picked up the telephone and dialed a number. He asked a few questions and hung up. We waited in deathly silence, puffing on our "fags," for what seemed an eternity and were startled when the phone came to life with a loud ring. "Get down to the platform and wait for the next train," my nicotine-enabling new friend advised. Careening down the escalator, I found Bob in such a deep sleep he was hard to wake. As the train approached, I saw a man leaning out an open window with my briefcase in his hand. Of course Bob was now overbearingly certain of miracles, even though he had been unconscious during my mission-saving effort. We thanked the man profusely and jumped on the next train. Racing off the platform to the surface at the next stop, we were confronted with London morning rush hour. It took a few long minutes to hail a cab. As we approached the East London Docks, we watched for the *Rainbow Warrior*, but she wasn't at the berth we'd been directed to. The cab driver told us a ship leaving from there would have to go through two locks before entering the main stream of the Thames. Our only hope was to intercept the *Warrior* before she left the locks.

As we approached the last lock, we could see the *Warrior* was there. The cab driver pulled up as close as he could, this sort of delivery not being a normal stop on his route. We paid hurriedly and had to leap over various obstacles and train tracks. As we clambered over the gunnels of the *Warrior*, the lock doors opened and within minutes the ship was out into the Thames. Bob and I cheered as we passed by the cranes and derricks along the river. We were on board the flagship of the eco-navy that we had helped to create; we had realized a dream, or was it a miracle?

The voyage across the channel gave Bob and me a chance to meet some of the key campaigners from the European Greenpeace organizations. In some ways they seemed more hard-core than us hippies from Vancouver and San Francisco. They didn't sing about whales and they were very serious about environmental issues. Maybe the movement needed to get past the "revolution is a celebration" stage and get down to real political business. I wasn't particularly convinced of this, but that didn't seem to matter any more.

In Amsterdam the meetings went well: we adopted all the motions that had been agreed to in Vancouver. Some of David McTaggart's loyalists tried to drive a stake through my heart by arguing that Greenpeace Canada should move its headquarters to Toronto. This could have eliminated me from the International Council. Somehow the Vancouver contingent managed to beat this idea back and I would spend the next six years as a director of Greenpeace International.

The creation of Greenpeace International marked the point at which no one person could be directly involved in everything going on in the Greenpeace world. With so many countries and offices, there were now often three or four campaigns occurring simultaneously. From hereon in, I will focus on my own role in the campaigns I was directly involved in.

The Greenpeace Council now met at least twice a year, sometimes three times. For me this was a very enjoyable and productive experience; there were so many issues, and new countries continued to become involved. The structure really worked and even though there were often differences of opinion we tended to sort them out and compromise on funding. The Marine Division was created as a separate budget and management group to operate the *Rainbow Warrior* and a growing fleet of other campaign ships.

Other than returning to Spatsizi to oppose the trophy hunters in the fall, I spent all of 1980 getting with the new international program. We voted via Telex, often after long and convoluted debates, but at least we were making decisions. There was an explosion of new proposals for campaigns in new areas. Acid rain, nuclear energy, uranium mining, whales in captivity, supertanker traffic, driftnet fishing, toxic dumping into rivers and the sea, and kangaroo killing all became targets in the Greenpeace crosshairs. We had not experienced such a burst of energy and growth since we confronted the Soviet whalers in 1975.

Once I had settled into my new role as one of the directors of Greenpeace International, I could turn my attention back to campaigning. Nineteen eighty-one was a very busy year. It began with Greenpeace's first campaign against fossil fuels, a subject that would become increasingly important when concern over climate change emerged later in the decade. In 1981, though, our primary concern was the possibility of a catastrophic oil spill along the coasts of Alaska and British Columbia.

Because we had helped derail the plan to put an oil port in Kitimat to receive tankers from Prudhoe Bay at the end of the Alaskan oil pipeline, oil tankers were now plying the west coast from Alaska to Long Beach,

California, and points in between. (It did cross my mind that perhaps a pipeline from Kitimat to points south would have been safer than tankers.) One of those in between points was the Strait of Juan de Fuca, the international waterway between Canada and the United States that separates southern Vancouver Island from the Olympic Peninsula. Tankers delivered crude oil to two refineries on the U.S. side and navigated the notoriously treacherous waters that lead from the open Pacific to these inland ports. By mutual consent, it had been agreed that tankers on this route would be limited to 125,000 tons of oil. These tankers were about half the size of the really big ones.

The oil interests were not happy with this restriction as it meant two tankers were required to deliver the same amount of crude as one big one could carry. The U.S. Coast Guard, our old friend from the Amchitka days, was somehow pressed into service by the oil companies to rectify the situation. They would oversee a "test," whereby a 189,000-ton supertanker, the B.T. (Big Tanker) *San Diego*, would sail into the Strait with a hold full of water to see if it was "safe" to bring larger tankers into Puget Sound. This was like a red flag to a bull for us. We issued a press release stating that we would send a flotilla to stop the supertanker test. It was one thing to do a controlled experiment in broad daylight, but what about 100 m.p.h. winds at night in the fog? The Coast Guard replied in short order, declaring a 2000-yard "safety zone" around the supertanker to protect us from ourselves. Double red flag. We vowed to defy the so-called safety zone and once again the battle was joined.

We chartered the beautiful 120-foot wooden yacht, *Norsal*, and assembled a veteran crew to challenge the behemoth in the straits. With the motto "Save the Seas" we set sail from Vancouver on January 23 and made for the test area. By this time, we had attracted the main media outlets on both sides of the border, a classic international campaign in a microcosm. The morning was clear and calm as we positioned ourselves in the path of the B.T. *San Diego*. We launched three Zodiacs and proceeded toward the big ship. My God what an enormous ship it was. I was the lead boat with Rex Weyler in the bow doing still photography. A local British Columbia TV camera crew was right behind us and Mike Bailey followed in a back-up confrontation boat. It was a perfect setup for a confrontation. Earlier in the day, I had coined the term "giggle room" for the fictitious place we go to avoid appearing smug in front of the media representatives when the authorities play so perfectly into our hands. We had plenty of opportunities to visit the giggle room on this day.

I piloted our Zodiac right in front of the slow-moving supertanker, edging in close so that we were riding the bow wave about 20 feet in front of the massive ship. News helicopters appeared and the TV crew in our other Zodiac came in close to shoot the action. The B.T. *San Diego* gradually came to a stop. We had halted a 189,000-ton ship with a 14-foot

Rex Weyler and I ride the bow wave of the supertanker B.T. *San Diego* in the Straits of Juan de Fuca (bottom center). Moments later we brought the behemoth to a halt. The authorities were not amused.

Zodiac and a lot of nerve. The Coast Guard reacted by sending four very fast 24-foot cutters into the fray to intercept us. A chase worthy of any Hollywood movie ensued during which we eluded the Coast Guard until they nearly killed us and we finally said uncle. We were taken aboard the Coast Guard cutter and I was handcuffed, but not in the usual manner. As Rex photographed my arrest, he was yelling, "I've been in Vietnam and that is against the Geneva Convention." Then the Coast Guard guys arrested Rex.

Instead of using the normal handcuffing procedure, the Coast Guardsmen, who obviously resented the fact that I had outrun them for nearly an hour, cinched plastic handcuffs around the top of my wrist, where it is excruciatingly painful. This method is used as a form of torture and is forbidden by international law. After cuffing me in this deliberately painful way, they threw me facedown on the metal hatch and held me there with a boot in my back for what seemed a very long time. I asked them several times to please loosen the handcuffs. Once the boat chase had ended, I had not resisted arrest or used abusive language, yet they were behaving like thugs. It was quite a contrast to the first voyage we had

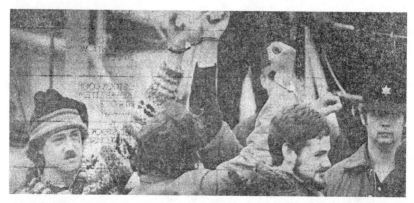

The six of us who were arrested for protesting against the supertanker were handcuffed together in pairs. I am on the left, chained to photographer Rex Weyler. Cameraman Robert McLachlan, second from the right, is attached to one of the other six people who were arrested by the U.S. Coast Guard.

made to Alaska in order to protest U.S. hydrogen bomb testing, when the Coast Guard commander and crew had treated us with respect. It was a reminder that the Coast Guard is a branch of the U.S. Armed Forces, and sometimes its guardsmen get rough.

They finally let me get up and replaced the plastic cuffs with regular metal ones, attaching Rex and me together like convicts on a chain gang. It was then that we found out four others, including two members of the TV camera crew that were in one of our Zodiacs, had also been arrested. Thankfully the Coast Guard had left the *Norsal* alone, presumably because it had not violated the 2000-yard "safety zone."

All six of us were ferried into the dock at Port Angeles, where we were escorted to a police van, taken to jail, fingerprinted, and thrown in a cell. David Gibbons had been on standby and he had us out on our own recognizance about three hours later. It's always good to have a lawyer standing by who can get you out of jail before nightfall!

We were greeted by the rest of our crew who reported that the media coverage of our protest had been awesome. The film and photos taken from news crews in helicopters showed our tiny Zodiac in front of the massive supertanker in classic David and Goliath style. Combined with the boat chase and arrests, it made a great TV and newspaper story. And public opinion in both Canada and the U.S. was clearly on our side.

The Coast Guard announced it would proceed with criminal charges against us because we had entered the safety zone. If convicted, the Canadians among us might be barred from entering the U.S. for life. This would not be a good thing. So we were greatly relieved when we were informed in the end that they would not go the criminal route. Instead they issued each of us with a letter stating that we had been fined US$10,000 apiece for our transgressions. The letter went on to say that if we didn't pay the fine we would be "tried in an appropriate jurisdiction." After pondering what that meant, we realized they didn't have any jurisdiction. So I framed my $10,000 fine and hung it on my office wall, where it remains today. Yet another visit to the giggle room was in order. Then we got the news that the U.S. government had decided not to remove the size restriction on tankers in Juan de Fuca Strait. We had prevailed and our victory had only taken a few weeks to achieve.

In the spring of 1981, the United States was beginning to flex its nuclear muscles under President Reagan. It sent large warships into foreign ports to pay a friendly "visit." New Zealand had banned ships carrying nuclear weapons from entering its territorial waters. The U.S. Navy would "neither confirm nor deny" the presence of nuclear weapons, so the New Zealand edict essentially barred all U.S. warships from entering its waters. Many of us in the Greenpeace Canada group admired New Zealand's courage and thought our country should follow their lead.

It was announced that the USS *Ranger*, a nuclear-powered aircraft carrier, would visit Vancouver to give the crew some shore leave. It was all in the serious tone of cold war rhetoric, staunch allies prepared to confront the Soviet threat. Canadians were being called on to pay fealty to their protectors to the south, a demand many Canadians have always resented. We like to think we are independent while at the same time neglecting to invest in effective defense forces. This means that we ultimately depend on the U.S. for protection. This "have your cake and eat it" attitude is compounded by a smug assertion of superiority: we don't pack concealed weapons, hang criminals, invade other countries, or engage in bullying trade practices. Like most European countries, Canadians enjoy universal health care while the U.S., the richest country on earth, is still deeply divided on the subject. Thankfully some progress has been made under President Barack Obama, but there are strong political forces opposed to universal health care.

I believe this resentment of U.S. dominance, both militarily and culturally, stems partially from the "meat in the sandwich" position Canada was in throughout the cold war. The long-range strategic nuclear warheads were aimed in their thousands from both the Soviet Union and the United States across Canadian soil and airspace. Out of a feeling of helplessness springs resentment against one's closest friend and ally.

Leading up to the USS *Ranger's* visit we noticed that local newspapers were carrying many ads from escort agencies and individual young women offering their services to the servicemen who were about to arrive. I was said to have implied that the visit had less to do with national defense and more to do with randy young sailors looking for women and pot in our liberal social environment. Did I ever hit a hot button! The wrath of God descended on me in editorials and letters to the editor about insulting our allies and impugning the motives of the navy's finest. At least the Canadians who appreciated America's role in defending our freedom came out of the closet. It gave me pause, pondering the great questions of war and peace, hawks and doves, randy young sailors and loose women.

But philosophical musings would not deter us from demonstrating against the awful might of the nuclear superpowers. To give us credit, we always made it clear that we would be equally opposed to a Soviet warship carrying nuclear weapons coming to Vancouver. Any nuclear weapons-carrying ship made our otherwise peaceful shire a first-order target in the event nuclear hostilities broke out.

The *Ranger* was too tall to fit under the Lions Gate Bridge at the harbor entrance, so she would have to anchor in the outer harbor. It was Fred Easton who came up with the idea that we would send in Zodiacs to get under the anchor of the carrier so that the crew couldn't drop the anchor without sinking or perhaps injuring us. We hired the *Meander*, the 85-foot wooden yacht we had used in the campaign against the Kitimat pipeline, and called for a flotilla of fishing boats and pleasure craft to join us.

The harbor was thick with boats of all description as the big carrier entered the bay. More of a picket line than a blockade, we flew banners and carried signs of an unwelcoming nature. I made the best protest picket sign of my activist career. It read simply, "Go Home Death Machine." The lead Zodiac placed itself under the anchor as hundreds of sailors hung over the gunnels to get a look at the spectacle below. The standoff lasted for about 10 minutes until the harbor police approached in a small cutter and ordered the Greenpeacers to get out from under the huge anchor. The Zodiac held firm as the police got out their pike poles and proceeded to poke holes in the Zodiac. No one had thought of that before! The inflatable boat was deflating fast as another Zodiac came in to rescue the crew, taking the crippled craft in tow. Amid the confusion the *Ranger* crew saw an opening and quickly dropped their anchor. The demo was over, but the media coverage played all day and evening. I wondered briefly if maybe with this fight we were in a little over our heads.

It all comes back to whether one believes nuclear weapons are responsible for world peace or whether they should be abolished. Many people firmly believe that dropping atomic bombs on Hiroshima and Nagasaki— an act that ended the Second World War— resulted in more lives being saved from continued combat than the number that were lost in the blasts. And many believe that the deterrence resulting from "mutually assured destruction" can be credited with preventing another all-out World War. Pacifists and antiwar activists take the opposite view, of course, that nuclear weapons are evil and should be abolished as soon as possible.

Is it possible there is some truth in both positions: that we should strive to minimize nuclear weapons and prevent further proliferation, while maintaining enough of them to deter anyone from striking first? As globalization rapidly turns civilization into a single intertwined system, it is hard to predict in which direction this debate will take us. It is especially difficult, however, to imagine that all the countries in possession of nuclear weapons will ever give them up voluntarily. Hopefully, the institutions that are in place to prevent further nuclear proliferation will eventually succeed. And one hopes it will not require another hostile use of nuclear weapons such as Hiroshima and Nagasaki to place this issue at the very top of the global agenda. Recent agreements between the U.S. and Russia on nuclear weapons reduction and the disposal of nuclear materials indicate we are on the right path.

In the summer of 1981, we established Greenpeace Germany in Hamburg. This was a calculated move as David McTaggart realized the future of the green movement lay in the German-speaking countries: Germany, Austria, and Switzerland. For whatever reason they were more swayed than other cultures toward a romantic view of nature and the radical approach to campaigning. It wasn't long before Greenpeace Germany became the most powerful influence in the organization, largely due to its ability to raise funds from a wealthy and sympathetic public.

August 1981 saw our expedition against trophy hunting back in Spatsizi Park for the third year. This time I stayed behind to do the media coordination while a crew of eight experienced Greenpeacers made another attempt to foil the hunters. They followed a hunting party deep into the mountains for three days: the hunters on horseback and the Greenpeace party on foot. On the fourth day, as the hunters were stalking a trophy mountain goat, a helicopter swooped down and landed by the Greenpeace camp. The head of the guide-outfitting company, Reg Collingwood, and three of his employees emerged from the machine. As we had remained on polite, though cool, terms throughout the three years of the campaign, a couple of our crew approached to welcome them. They were met with fists and flying belt buckles as the four men began to ransack the camp, beating anyone who got in their way, including Judy Drake. The little vigilante goon squad proceeded to pile the Greenpeacers' tents, cameras, and camping equipment into a heap and then lit them on fire, all the while breaking noses and bruising the peaceful protesters who did not fight back.

Satisfied that they had put a big crimp in our plans, the attackers took off in their chopper, leaving the Greenpeacers 30 miles from the nearest shelter in the high mountains. They walked out in a forced march and made it to the cabins at Cold Fish Lake before dark. Some months later a sympathetic northern judge gave the guide-outfitters a suspended sentence after which the Collingwoods filed a lawsuit against Greenpeace for interfering with their hunting business. Our lawyers advised us that we would probably lose. We offered the Collingwoods $20,000 and they accepted. Case closed. Campaign lost—for now anyway.

In the mid-1990s, the B.C. government finally put an end to trophy hunting in Spatsizi. So it only took fifteen years to make our point. Today the issue of trophy hunting, especially for grizzly bears and polar bears, remains very controversial. I hope someday trophy hunting in the wild will end, but it is not easy to devise a solution for problem bears. When they start breaking into homes and killing pets, people take the law into their own hands. It's fine to say from a distance that the bears have rights, too, but when you live among them it's not that simple. The issue of managing wildlife and human/wildlife interaction is a philosophical minefield in which mutually agreeable positions are very hard to find.

February of 1982 saw Eileen and me travel with three-year old Jonathan to Australia to make a film about uranium mining and to generate public awareness of both uranium mining and nuclear energy. We were opening up a new front: Greenpeace had been publicly opposed to nuclear energy for many years, but we had never taken on uranium mining, the primary ingredient in nuclear fuel.

Australia has about one-third of the world's known uranium deposits and because it has chosen not to build any nuclear power plants domestically, Australia provides the uranium for a considerable proportion of the world's 436 nuclear power plants. In addition, one of the largest uranium mines, the Ranger Mine, is situated in the middle of the Kakadu National Park in sacred aboriginal territory in Northern Australia near Darwin. These facts created a story we wanted to capture on film, so I planned a journey through the uranium mining regions with director Michael Chechik and cameraman Ron Precious, both of whom had worked on a number of Greenpeace campaigns.

When we arrived in Darwin, we learned that the Ranger Mine was securely fenced off and the owners weren't fond of strangers. Trudging through crocodile-infested swamps in the heat, we circled around to the back of the mine and managed to get through the fence, where we could film the big mine-trucks hauling ore and waste rock. Later we interviewed aboriginal leaders, who showed us where mine tailings had been simply dumped onto the land, leaving it a lifeless wasteland. Then we flew over the vast expanse of the Kakadu wilderness and filmed the contrast between the natural beauty of the park and the scar created by the mine. The footage we shot in Kakadu and other sites in Australia was later combined with footage from Saskatchewan in Canada, another major uranium supplier, to create a film titled *Keep It in the Ground*. Little did I know that years later I would regret this one campaign and that I would openly support nuclear energy as part of the solution to environmental damage and sustainable energy.

CHAPTER TEN

Consensus and Sustainable Development Discovered

Taking a rare opportunity for some down time, Eileen and I stopped over in Fiji on the way back from Australia to Vancouver. We were captivated by the gentle and caring nature of the Fijians, who fawned over our blond-haired three-year-old Jonathan like he was their own. After a few days snorkeling on the Coral Coast, a fairly touristy area, we made our way to the capital, Suva. Here we arranged to travel by boat to the island of Ovalau, where we had booked accommodation in a remote camp. Arriving by bus at a tiny port, we were crowded onto an ancient wooden craft, which was about 50 feet long. People were hanging off the rigging as if this was a normal thing to do. Children were running loose among the various species of livestock and great bundles of food and clothing. "See any life jackets?" Eileen asked a little nervously. "Nope, but the tickets were cheap," I half-joked to lighten things up a little. After all we were well away from the dock and Ovalau already loomed in the distance.

Thankfully the sea was reasonably calm and we arrived off the coast of the island without incident. "Where's the dock?" I asked the nearest crewman. "No dock here," he replied just as the boat's whistle sounded. We came to a stop and could see people scurrying into a small outboard-powered skiff on the shore. The beach was lined with palms, but there didn't appear to be any sand. We were greeted by a skinny young Fijian boy and offloaded into the tiny skiff with all our gear—still no life jackets—and ferried to shore.

It wasn't exactly a vacation resort. We appeared to be the only paying customers in what we soon found out was a kava plantation with a couple of shacks they rented out to unsuspecting tourists. It was nearly dusk as we settled into a one-room flophouse, bare lightbulb and all. Then the mosquitoes arrived, by the hundreds, overwhelming the one mosquito coil we had been issued. During an almost sleepless night, we plotted our escape from this hellhole, having no clue how to get out.

In the morning we learned a truck was leaving for Levuka, the only town on the island. Levuka was the original capital of Fiji under British rule during the days of sailing ships. We rode in the back of a pickup loaded with kava roots while our expatriate Kiwi host navigated the ruts and turns of an impossible road. Breaking over a rise, we saw the idyllic green face of the mountain slope rising from the sea above one of the sleepiest little villages on Earth. There were only two places to stay in town, so we chose the nicest one, the Mavinda Guest House. It was right on the rocky beach, where plumaria trees in bloom filled the air with perfume. Our big mama of a Fijian hostess told us the rent was five dollars a day; she realized that was a lot, but it included a full breakfast and a mosquito net over the bed. The most delicious papaya, known as pawpaw in Fiji, accompanied the full breakfast of bacon and eggs. We would have paid five dollars a day for the breakfast alone.

During my daily walk to the old Ovalau Club—the only place where you could buy a few beers, and at the time still off-limits to the fairer sex—I noticed an oval-shaped thatch hut in the center of the village. Every afternoon at around three, about 15 elderly gentlemen would shuffle into the hut and sit in a circle on the dirt floor. The walls were somewhat transparent, so you could see the men talking in turn as they discussed village affairs. They were the Council of Elders and their job was to try to reach consensus, through dialogue, on the pressing issues of the day. I was struck by the softly spoken, polite manner of their dialogue; no one spoke over top of someone else. In fact each speaker always paused in respect to the previous speaker. Aside from the anachronistic fact that they were all old men (at least they weren't all old white men!) their round-table, consensus-based approach impressed me. Little did I know at the time that in a few short years I would help bring this approach to modern-day environmental issues.

While the elders were meeting the *thunk-thunk* sound of a young man beating kava roots filled the air. The root of the kava plant is difficult to chew, so it is chopped into pieces and placed into a length of steel pipe capped with a heavy screen on the bottom. A steel rod is then used to pound the kava. This process releases the juice of the roots into a bowl below the pipe. When the elders emerge from their deliberations, the kava is ready for them, and they switch to cocktail hour with the other villagers, all still sitting in a circle. Kava contains kavalactones that have a narcotic effect, giving the body a warm feeling and stimulating thought. Judging by the effect the kava had on me, I wouldn't be surprised if the elders reached more agreements after their private huddle than during it.

Our time in Fiji gave us a chance to get our heads above water, and under it as well. We had been going full-on for the six years since the whale campaign began and really hadn't stopped to think about our future. Eileen and I had enjoyed snorkeling in Mexico soon after we first met. Now we were in a snorkeling paradise, and we took to it like ducks.

I don't think there is a better remedy for stress than a coral garden teeming with fish of implausibly bright and diverse colors. Sharks, barracuda, giant clams, and moray eels swam around us. Both of us realized we were completely at home in this otherworldly environment, not fearful at all. Ever since, we have been seeking the perfect snorkel. We've taken up scuba diving as well.

A few weeks later, I made my way to Halifax to join the *Rainbow Warrior* crew for the 1982 seal campaign. I had agreed to lead the campaign after being out of the main action for a couple of years while we sorted out the internal struggles that had given birth to Greenpeace International. We felt we might be on the verge of a breakthrough as the European Parliament was considering banning seal pup skins from entering the European market. Now was the time to put the pressure on, so we drew up a blockbuster plan to get the media attention we needed.

There was always a hare-brained idea or two that would emerge in Greenpeace. This year Mike Bailey and his action team had come up with hovercrafts. Apparently we were going to fly over the ice floes in these machines and interrupt the slaughter more effectively. I remained skeptical, knowing the conditions out there: ice pans piled eight feet high and huge waves rolling beneath them. But it would make a good impression on the media, so I went along with the plan.

We decided to show off our hovercraft fleet to the media in Halifax Harbour. We had rented one big one, the kind the Coast Guard might use for rescue missions, and two tiny ones about 12 feet long for close combat. We called a media conference at the Halifax docks, where we would unveil our, until now, secret armada. The idea was to have the media assembled and then to have the hovercrafts arrive in a cloud of spray from farther down the harbor.

As the spokesperson, I was with the media waiting for our secret weapons to arrive. It began to snow as we waited. And waited. Soon it was approaching blizzard conditions and the snow began to stick to us and build up on the windward side of our heads. Thirty minutes later there were still no hovercraft. Finally, the two small hovercraft arrived, a rather pitiful sight, but at least there was some action and noise. As they circled around, we learned the big hovercraft was not going to show up, ever. We were quietly informed that as it was warming up, a big piece of metal cowling had been sucked through the wooden propeller, reducing it to a nub. There was no spare prop.

Despite this significant setback, we got a lot of media coverage for the launch of our expedition aboard the *Rainbow Warrior* the next day. Pulling out of Halifax into a wintry sea, we headed for the Gulf of St. Lawrence, where the first phase of the seal hunt traditionally takes place. As we rounded Cape Breton Island, we could see the ice pans ahead. None of us could imagine what came next. We spent eight days and nights pushing our way through the ice, traveling dead slow, as the *Warrior* was no icebreaker. It was amazing to hear the groans and growls of the ice as we threaded our way among the leads in the ice fields, often stopping and reversing to try another lead. On the evening of the eighth day of the voyage, we broke into open water at sunset. Hundreds of seals swam and leaped out of the water all around us as the colors of the late sun reflected from a glassy sea. We knew the hunters were just ahead and anticipated a chance to confront them in the morning.

While I surveyed one of the most beautiful natural scenes I had ever witnessed, I was summoned to the radio room for a media call from Brussels. "The European Commission has voted to recommend a ban on seal skin imports. What do you think of this?" Tears welled in my eyes as I composed myself to tell the reporter about the scene we had just come upon, seals leaping in a glorious sunset as if they had already heard the news. We had put our hearts and souls into this effort for seven years and now all but the final nail was in the coffin of this unfortunate ritual. I provided the reporter with the mandatory victory statement and we all sank into our bunks with a grateful feeling.

The seal hunt was never a simple issue, and it isn't to this day, as Greenpeace was never able to obtain a complete ban on killing baby seals for fur or meat. Many people equated Greenpeace's baby harp seal campaign to the whale campaign, wrongly assuming that the harp seal was an endangered species. Others felt it was immoral for anyone to kill a seal, even the Inuit of the Canadian north and the Eskimos of Alaska. I have always believed that the reason for the seal campaign was very different from the whale campaign, even though they both involved marine mammals.

The campaign to save the whales was truly about endangered species. They are the largest animals that have ever lived and have brains larger than our own. I would argue that whales, dolphins, and porpoises should be given a special status; sacred cows if you wish, and we should respect them as symbols of living creation. The campaign to stop the baby seal slaughter was about the unethical practice of wading into the breeding colony of a wild animal and bludgeoning the nursing young to death by the hundreds of thousands. In other words, it is more an issue of animal welfare than it is of conservation. The seals are not an endangered species and they are in a different evolutionary class from whales. But no one would support the mass slaughter of the nursing young of other wild mammals—baby deer, for example—just to get their spotted hides for wallets and purses. So I can't see why it is an acceptable practice with seals. I do, however, think it is acceptable for people to hunt adult seals for subsistence, in the same way that it is acceptable to hunt deer for food.

In 1984, after a Royal Commission, Canada announced an end to the annual slaughter of harp seal pups. Great rejoicing ensued, but it was unfortunately premature. After some years passed, the seal hunt was reinvented and during the past three years more than 250,000 seal pups have been taken annually in the slaughter. The difference? Now they wait a week or so longer until most of the pups are weaned, but they are still babies. I don't use the word *babies* lightly because it is so emotional, but that's how I feel about this outdated practice. Surely it will end some day.

Upon my return to Vancouver after the victory, I opened an envelope containing an invitation that would change my thinking forever. After the Conference on the Environment in Stockholm in 1972, the UN had established the United Nations Environment Program (UNEP) in Nairobi, Kenya, in 1974. It was the first UN agency to be established in a developing country and its role was to build an international program of research and education in environmental issues. In order to provide a focus for nongovernment environmental organizations to interact with UNEP, the Environment Liaison Center was established and my old friend Gary Gallon, the ecocrat from Vancouver, was hired as the first executive director.

Gary had sent the invitation and it was an opportunity to join in a meeting with 85 other environmental leaders from around the world to celebrate the 10th anniversary of the Stockholm Conference. In 1972 the environmental movement was just getting its wings. By 1982 we were a force for governments and corporations around the world to contend with. We 85 environmentalists attending the meeting in Nairobi represented the global influence that had been achieved in those 10 short years.

The central purpose of our three-day meeting was to fashion a statement representing our demands for improvements in environmental laws and regulations around the world. The first day was pretty rough as environmental leaders from developing countries, such as Brazil and India, tried to make sense of the antidevelopment thinking of environmentalists from North America and Europe. Environmentalists from the industrialized countries were largely against "megaprojects" like large hydro dams, water diversion projects, and massive nuclear plants. The environmentalists from developing countries explained that being against development would get you laughed out of the room where they came from. We soon realized that we had to be in favor of some kind of development, the kind that would not destroy the environment. The concept of sustainable development was born there in Nairobi.

It was Tom Burke, leader of Friends of the Earth UK, whom I first heard use the term *sustainable development*. It must have been very recently coined if I hadn't heard it already as I was right in the thick of the movement. Tom seemed to naturally fill the position of chairman of our newly acquainted band of activists. Much of the discussion over the next few days revolved around this new idea, what it meant and how it could be put into practice.

Many people imagine the term sustainable development was a compromise between environmentalists and developers or industrialists. This is not so. It was a compromise between environmentalists from developed countries and environmentalists from developing countries. Development was all right as long as it was sustainable, whatever that meant, and a debate about the meaning of the term continues to this day.

The second I heard the words I was catapulted into a sudden realization of what this meant for the future of environmental thinking. It meant a great synthesis was about to occur in the collective conscience of people looking for a solution to the deep conflicts between the environmental movement and industrial civilization. This would require balancing environmental, social, and economic values rather than stressing one at the expense of the others. And it would necessitate cooperation and compromise among competing values rather than perpetual confrontation.

So long as Greenpeace had addressed issues such as nuclear testing and whaling it was not really necessary to consider the social or economic ramifications. Not many people at the time would argue nukes were good for society and it wasn't as if whale meat or oil were central to the world economy. The whaling industry, and the sealing industry, did make the argument that local people would be thrown out of work, and in Canada this had backfired on Greenpeace. But on a global level the benefits of ending nuclear testing, whaling, and baby seal bashing clearly overwhelmed any small benefits.

As Greenpeace and the rest of the environmental movement broadened their campaigns, they began to take on issues that impacted far more directly on the economic and social aspects of civilization as a whole. Subjects like agriculture, forestry, mining, fisheries, energy, and manufacturing have an impact on every individual on Earth and they are essential for the survival of our whole civilization. It is simply not possible to address these issues with environmental values alone. The social and economic values must be considered equally unless one is willing to ignore the existence of nearly seven billion people and their daily needs.

Another way of looking at it is while there are some specific practices that should be banned (e.g., dumping toxic waste in rivers and seas, driftnet fishing, nuclear testing), most large issues are best dealt with by campaigns for reform rather than outright banning. We can't ban farming, forestry, or mining. Activist groups are much better at dealing with issues that can be portrayed as black and white and good versus evil. That is partly why they have now arrived at positions such as "ban clear-cutting worldwide," "ban nuclear energy," "ban genetically modified food crops," "ban chlorine and PVC (vinyl)," and "ban submarine mine tailings disposal." This zero-tolerance approach is useless when it comes to providing our civilization with the materials and energy it needs to survive.

On the other hand it had become abundantly clear, and this was one of the main messages of the environmental movement, that industry and government must take environmental values into greater account in all their decisions. In other words the new environmental values we had helped forge had to be integrated into the traditional economic and social values governing public policy and our individual daily behavior. This process of incorporating environmental values into our decision making lies at the heart of sustainable development theory (nowadays simply called sustainability). It's not about pitting the environment against the economy and society, as if we could have one without the others, it's about finding an appropriate balance among them.

When the human population was low and technologically unadvanced, people did not need to consider the environment. We needed the environment 500 years ago as much as we need it now, but we weren't causing much of a negative impact on it back then. Therefore we really didn't need to be "aware" of it or to make laws to protect it. As the population and technology grew, they began to impact the environment severely enough that they began to undermine the very resources we depend on for survival in the first place.

An important exception to this relatively low impact before industrialization was the early extinction of many species of large mammals and birds as humans migrated to new lands. When people arrived in Australia about 60,000 years ago, they hunted many species of slow-moving large animals to extinction. These species had survived for many millions of years without any humans to bother them. They could get away with being slow because they were bigger than any native predator. But they weren't ready for spears and clubs. The same pattern developed in the New World when humans arrived by land bridge and raft about 15,000 years ago. The mammoths, mastodons, sabre-toothed tigers, and many other large mammals were exterminated for food. Interestingly, many other large mammals that had evolved with humans in the Old World: wolves, caribou, grizzly bears, and moose migrated to the New World with the humans and are here to this day.

The transformational power of sustainability theory is that it turns a foot soldier fighting environmental wars into a diplomat looking for peaceful solutions. It steers one from a stance of confrontation, telling people what they should stop doing, to trying to find consensus about what we should do instead. There is simply no escaping the fact that more than seven billion people wake up every morning on this planet with real needs for food, energy, and materials. Sustainability is partly about continuing to provide for those needs, maybe even providing more food and energy for people in developing countries, while at the same time reducing our negative environmental impact. Not all my colleagues at the meeting in Nairobi agreed with this approach. Many, especially those from the developed countries, rejected the idea of sustainable development because it seemed too much of a compromise. It meant they would have to abandon the "good guy– bad guy" approach to environmentalism and recognize we were all in the same boat. It meant they might become "assimilated" by the established order.

I came away from Nairobi a changed person. I now realized that as an environmentalist I could either act as if the more than seven billion people didn't matter (or pretend they didn't even exist) or I could expand my thinking to include them as part of the challenge. The latter approach seemed both more honest and more intellectually stimulating. It got me outside the box of purely environmental thinking and into the real world of recognizing the entire system. Early in the evolution of the environmental movement, Barbara Ward had written a book titled *Spaceship Earth*.[21] I thought, "Why not One Human Family on Spaceship Earth" as a way of describing this vision for sustainability.

I would stay with Greenpeace as an international director for another three years, but these new thoughts of sustainable development were never far from my mind. We'll return to this theme in greater detail later in the book. However, for now let's get back to some good old Greenpeace campaigns.

---

21. Barbara Ward, *Spaceship Earth* (New York: Columbia University Press, 1966).

CHAPTER ELEVEN

Jailed Whales, Curtains of Death, Raising Fish, and Sinking Rainbows

Many of us had felt for a long time if there was one thing that should be banned it was the live capture of orca whales for display in aquariums. Ever since Paul Spong had studied Skana, the first captive orca in Canada, we had followed the subject closely. But because we viewed the factory whaling issue as so much more important, we had put all our energy into that campaign. When the International Whaling Commission voted to ban factory whaling altogether in June 1981, the job was done, so we could turn our attention to ending the practice of capturing orcas from the wild.

By the time we geared up in earnest, 56 orcas had been taken from their pods since 1967 along the west coast of Canada and the United States. They were transported to aquariums all across North America, including the Vancouver Aquarium and the four large Sea World facilities in California, Florida, Ohio, and Texas. It was eventually determined by the identification of individual orcas that there were only about 300 whales in the wild from Alaska to California. In other words, nearly one-sixth of the population had already been taken. The United States ended live whale capture in 1973, putting more pressure on Canada and causing the collectors to go farther afield to Iceland and Japan to satisfy the demand. Many of the whales died shortly after being taken into captivity, usually from bacterial infections, so there was a constant demand for replacements. In the early years there was virtually no success at captive breeding. We felt these two facts alone indicated inhumane conditions. Orcas were simply too large for a small pool and should be left in the wild, where they usually live for more than 30 years. Some have lived into their 70s.

Today it seems like motherhood to be against capturing whales and putting them in zoos, but at the time we managed to bring upon us the wrath of a significant portion of Canadian society. None other than Pierre Trudeau, the prime minister of Canada, was on the board of the Vancouver Aquarium Society, and the other members weren't exactly working-class either. The local newspapers had openly sided with the aquarium, arguing that captive whales were good for education and acted as ambassadors for their wild counterparts. Greenpeace was publicly ostracized while the papers ran exciting photos of whales leaping in front of appreciative crowds. We felt the whales had been violently stolen from their close-knit family pods and placed in prison, where they were forced to do tricks for food. The practice was unacceptable.

In September 1982 the Canadian Department of Fisheries and Oceans issued a permit to Sealand of the Pacific, based in Victoria, to capture up to four orcas at Pedder Bay on southern Vancouver Island. We announced that Greenpeace would attempt to foil the capture.

We set up a tent base camp near Race Rocks, complete with shore-based marine radios. Fred Easton's dad loaned us his cabin cruiser, the *Cat's Meow*. For some reason the base camp's radio handle became "Crispy Critter," so it wasn't long before the boat became know as the "Kitty Litter." Mel Gregory got a hoot out of hailing us from shore, "Kitty Litter, Kitty Litter, Crispy Critter here. Come in, Kitty Litter." As usual we found lots to laugh and sing about as we prepared for a showdown with the whale-nappers.

Sealand had perfected a capture method that took advantage of the fact that pods of orcas would chase a school of herring around Race Rocks and then corral them in Pedder Bay, where they would take turns feasting on them. A seine-fishing boat lay in wait on one side of the bay with a huge drum of fishnet on the stern, one end of which was tied to the beach. As soon as the whales entered the bay, the seine boat was to steam across the bay laying out the net to prevent the whales' escape. As intelligent as they are, orcas will not leap over a net even though they can easily do so. Our job was to make sure the whales didn't enter the bay in the first place.

We were getting a reasonable amount of coverage in the media, but it wasn't until one of our crew lost power in his Zodiac that we really hit the press. Mel Gregory was rounding Race Rocks late in the day when his outboard motor failed. The strong currents swept him out into Juan de Fuca

Strait and into the shipping lanes. As fate would have it, he was rescued by one of the cruise ships known as the Love Boats and became an instant celebrity on board. The media loved this angle and suddenly our little band of whale-savers was front-page news. We had been at our station for more than a week when this incident occurred, and it was only two days later that we spotted a pod of orcas coming around Race Rocks heading for the bay. By this time a flotilla of smaller volunteer boats had joined the *Cat's Meow*. We converged on the path of the whales while the seine boat fired up its engines and prepared to pull its net across the bay.

As the whales approached, we came to a stop and began banging oars, bailing cans, and whatever else we could find against the sides of our boats. Whether it was a miracle or predictable, the whales immediately changed course and went back out to sea while the would-be captors watched us foil their efforts. This would be the last time anyone tried to capture an orca in Canadian waters. Sealand of the Pacific voluntarily gave up due to the overwhelming public opposition we had generated.

The statistics for captive orcas are not encouraging. Their life expectancy in captivity is six years, which is about one-fifth what it is in the wild. Of 110 orcas taken from the ocean from 1967 to 2007 only 13 are still alive. The good news is that after years of failure, the aquariums have now learned to successfully breed orcas in captivity, and they now live longer than they did in previous years. Of the 42 whales currently in captivity 29 of them were born in captivity. Unfortunately, a total of 152 captive whales have died, 97 of which were born in the wild and 55 of which were born in captivity. At last it appears live captures in the wild have come to an end—a short but brutish period in our relationship with a magnificent species of marine mammal.

Curtains of Death and the Gulag

In 1983 the *Rainbow Warrior* sailed through the Panama Canal into the Pacific for the first time. We had been campaigning against the use of deep-sea driftnets in the north Pacific by the Japanese for a few years but had never actually confronted them at sea. Greenpeace Hawaii did the research and knew where to find the driftnet fleet—large ships that strung nets 30 miles long and 100 feet deep. This "curtain of death," as we called it, caught thousands of dolphins, diving seabirds, turtles, and nontarget fish as well as the intended catch. This activity occurred far from land and out of sight of the public and the media. We aimed to change this practice, just as we had with whaling and sealing. It worked. Our underwater footage of dolphins and birds trapped in the nets went around the world on television. This made the public aware of this cruel practice and brought about worldwide support to end the driftnet fishery. David McTaggart briefed Ted Turner on the issue and he gave us funding to produce a documentary on the subject. We took the issue directly to the UN, where a resolution banning the practice was eventually passed in 1989. Once again Greenpeace demonstrated that direct nonviolent action, going to the scene and documenting the subject for all to see, was capable of creating real change.

In what became the common practice of "serial campaigning" the *Rainbow Warrior* proceeded from the driftnet fishery directly to the northern Kamchatka Peninsula, where a Russian whaling station was still operating. The Russians were killing the gray whales that migrate annually from Baja California up the coast of North America and into the Bering Sea. Long since protected in Mexico, the U.S., and Canada, the grays were still being ground up for fertilizer and pet food in Russia.

Bob Cummings joined the crew in Alaska as media coordinator, and I camped out in my living room in Vancouver for the marathon media-relations exercise that ensued. In a bold move, a group of eight Greenpeacers landed Zodiacs on the shore of the Kamchatka whaling station and began to document the operation. They were soon apprehended by Soviet authorities and taken to prison while the *Rainbow Warrior* made for U.S. waters with a huge Soviet warship in hot pursuit.

One of the Zodiacs involved in the landing had managed to escape capture, and the driver had the film footage of the whaling operation and the Soviet soldiers taking the eight Greenpeacers away. He headed for the *Rainbow Warrior* but was knocked out of his boat by a large Soviet helicopter using its prop wash to try to stop him. The Soviets picked him out of the water, but the zodiac was left doing circles without a driver until the *Rainbow Warrior* returned to it. Miraculously, the film canister had remained in the Zodiac and was retrieved.

Just as the warship was gaining, the spunky Greenpeace ship crossed the U.S. territorial border in the Bering Sea and the Soviet ship quit the chase and turned back. As soon as the *Warrior* landed in Alaska, Bob Cummings got on a plane with the footage. I met him in Seattle, where the raw film was fed to all the news networks' satellites while I narrated it, explaining who was who and what had happened. It hit the global airwaves in true mindbomb fashion and the heat was on the Russians to set our people free. The drama lasted for days as Soviet authorities dithered and only made their dilemma worse. A week later the eight Greenpeacers were released to fanfare and fame. One more victory for the whales.

In 1983 I met Russ George, a free-thinking biologist who turned me on to a book that has influenced me ever since. *Seafarm: The Story of Aquaculture* was written by Elizabeth Mann Borgese, from the Mediterranean island of Malta. She had been a central figure in the negotiations leading to the Law of the Sea Treaty at the United Nations in the 1970s. As she traveled around the world to fishing nations, Elizabeth became impressed by the growing practice of aquaculture, farming lakes, rivers, and the sea for fish and shellfish. She realized this was the future of seafood, that the wild fisheries could provide only so much until they became unsustainable. I agreed with her thesis and realized that just as people had turned to farming the land 10,000 years ago we must learn to tend the seas; to make the transition from hunting and gathering to farming. After a year of mulling over the concept of sustainable development I had found a way to make my transition from problems to solutions. I would start a salmon farm at my childhood home in Winter Harbour.

The farming of fish goes back at least 3,000 years in China, where carp and other freshwater fish are still the main contributor to worldwide aquaculture production. Trout have been farmed for more than a hundred years around the world and catfish have been successfully domesticated in the U.S. South. Marine shellfish such as oysters and mussels, have also been farmed for centuries. But it wasn't until 35 years ago that scientists and fish farmers cracked the life cycle of marine finfish.

It was the coastal people of Norway who pioneered the art and science of salmon farming in the 1970s in the sheltered fjords along their rugged coast. Decades of overfishing had reduced the Atlantic salmon runs there to mere remnants as fleets from two-dozen European countries ravaged the northern seas. Fishermen had discovered that salmon congregated beneath icebergs near Greenland, so they pulled huge nets beneath the bergs, decimating both European and North American populations. The demand for wild salmon could no longer be satisfied, so necessity became the mother of invention.

Salmon became the first marine fish species to be successfully farmed for a simple reason. Unlike most ocean fish, salmon breed in freshwater, returning to their natal streams to spawn, where the young fry hatch and rear before returning to the sea again. It had been relatively easy to figure out how to build hatcheries beside the streams and rivers, take eggs and sperm from the returning adults, hatch the eggs in incubators and grow the fry in ponds or tanks. This greatly increased the survival rate over the wild and thus returned more fry to the sea. Salmon enhancement of the wild populations became common practice in the Atlantic and the Pacific. But it would ultimately fail in the Atlantic partly because there were just too many fishing boats and not enough fish. By contrast, in the north Pacific there were only four countries—Canada, the U.S., Russia, and Japan—competing for wild salmon. The Pacific Salmon Commission was formed in 1989 to control the catch.

The Norwegians figured out how to take the fry from freshwater salmon hatcheries and transfer them to "netpens" in the sea, where they were given a formulated feed and were grown out to market size. The entire life cycle was now brought into domestication and a new revolution in seafood production began. I am convinced that aquaculture is the future of healthy protein and oils to feed a growing world population.

My mom's dad, Art North, was a grizzled west coast salmon fisherman, who, with his three brothers, pioneered the salmon trolling fleet out of my home village of Winter Harbour in the 1930s. When I stayed with him and Granny Mary, he would take me out to sea at four in the morning, where among the rolling swells he pulled the silver salmon into his hold. I was always seasick and vowed never to become a fisherman. But I learned a lot from Granddad Art, as he taught me how to carve a toy boat and to gut fish. Later in life I questioned him about the practice of killing sea lions as a way of increasing the amount of fish available to fishermen. In the 1950s the Canadian fisheries authorities mounted machine guns on the bows of their patrol boats. They would visit sea lion colonies on islands and rocks off the coast and "thin" their populations. I asked,

"Granddad, did you catch more salmon after they killed the sea lions?" He scratched his head and replied, "I guess they didn't kill enough of the bastards." He was the gentlest, kindest man you could ever meet. How attitudes toward marine mammals have changed with the times!

I told my brother-in-law, Peter Taylor, about the idea of salmon farming. Winter Harbour would be a good location to build a hatchery and netpen operation. A few pioneers had already established small salmon farms farther down the coast. We met them and learned the basics of what we needed to get started. Quatsino Seafarms was born, named after the inlet of which Winter Harbour is a part, and the First Nations people who first settled there. I was involved in a positive effort to farm the sea for the first time in my part of the world. It was as exhilarating as the first voyage to stop the H-bomb tests; maybe a bit more down to earth, but easily as meaningful. It was part of a bold new movement for the sustainable use of the sea. It would prove to be a challenge as great as any campaign to save the planet.

Excited by the fact that I was participating in a sustainable new industry and producing good food, I approached my fellow Greenpeacers for support. "You know, we are against whaling, sealing, drift-net fishing, bottom dragging, and just about every way people are getting food from the ocean," I said, then added, "How about if we come out in favor of sustainable aquaculture as a solution to the depletion of wild sea life?" I was surprised with the sharp rebuke. "No way; aquaculture is causing the destruction of coastal mangrove forests in the tropics," one of my fellow Greenpeacers shot back "Okay," I replied, "Let's not endorse that kind of aquaculture. In fact, why don't we define the meaning of sustainable aquaculture for the world so that we become leaders in providing the solution to getting food from the sea?" My entreaties fell on deaf ears. The only other scientist in the organization, Sidney Holt, was a staunch anti-aquaculture advocate who had the ear of Greenpeace chairman, David McTaggart. I thought, If

Greenpeace is against farming fish, what on earth are we in favor of? It was my first brush with disillusion over a question of environmental policy. I let it slide and got on with the business of building our salmon farm.

My younger brother, Michael, agreed to live in Winter Harbour and manage the operation. He had just returned from Europe, where he had married Sophie, who was from southern France. Eileen and I, Peter and Marilyn, Mike and Sophie and our families spent the summer of 1984 building a small salmon hatchery on the shore near the mouth of the Galato River. It rained every day of August as we laid out nearly a mile of 6-inch PVC waterline up the river to supply the hatchery. We purchased 100,000 Chinook salmon eggs and placed them in incubators. (The eggs were surplus to the government's wild salmon enhancement program.) The farming had begun. We started to build the net pens and floating walkways we would need when the young salmon were ready to go in the sea.

A wonderful biological transformation occurs in the lifecycle of salmon when they prepare for the transition from freshwater to saltwater. This is one of the more fascinating metamorphoses in nature, changing from the need to keep water out of the body in fresh water to the challenge of keeping water in the body in seawater. Chinook salmon are about four inches long when they suddenly turn from dark gray to shiny silver. This transformation is called *smolting*, derived from the same origin as *smelting*, as in smelting metals like iron and silver. The smolts, as the newly transformed salmon are called, are as silvery as a newly minted ingot and the sight of thousands of them circling in a big pond in the hatchery is mesmerizing.

Under the Rainbow

We had already put our first batch of smolts in the net pens when I traveled to Auckland, New Zealand, on July 10, 1985, with a small group of international directors to greet the arrival of the *Rainbow Warrior* and her crew. The *Warrior*, affectionately known as the R-Dub by insiders, was about to embark on another campaign against French nuclear testing at Mururoa, now conducted underground in the fragile coral atoll. The *Warrior* had recently been refit with two tall masts and auxiliary sails, giving her a beautiful profile at sea.

We arrived on board the ship in time for lunch and spent the afternoon sitting in the galley shooting the breeze with the crew and exchanging the latest Greenpeace gossip. Everyone felt upbeat about the campaign, as there was some hope France's new socialist president, Francois Mitterrand, might be more sympathetic to the antinuclear movement than his right-wing predecessors. As it turned out, that was a very bad call.

After sharing dinner with the crew, the rest of us were driven to a rowing club graciously loaned to us for our stay. By midnight we were mostly settled into our bunks in the dormitory. At 10 past midnight the phone rang and Steve Sawyer answered it. Hardly able to speak, he reported to us that the *Rainbow Warrior* had been sunk at the dock 10 minutes earlier by two violent explosions. Our photographer, Fernando Periera, was missing. While Steve arranged for a taxi, I put in a call to David McTaggart, who was attending the International Whaling Commission meetings in Brighton, England, where it was midday. David immediately knew the French had sabotaged our ship and I concurred. Who else would do such a thing? We got in the taxis and made for the harbor, where we found a distraught and demoralized crew.

The beautiful *Rainbow Warrior* was sunk in 20 feet of water with her bow and wheelhouse protruding at an unnatural angle. Media people were beginning to congregate, police were everywhere, and the crew found refuge in a harbor building at the top of the dock. We began the process of piecing events together.

The first explosion had jolted the ship just before midnight, while a few crew members were still enjoying a nightcap around the galley table. Most were still out at the pub. Captain Jon Castle immediately went below to assess the situation and saw water gushing in through a gaping hole in the hull in the engine room. She would sink quickly, so he ordered everyone to get off. It was an easy step onto the dock. But Fernando had $10,000 worth of camera gear in his bunkroom in the stern compartment, so he rushed aft and down the hatch to retrieve it. The second explosion rocked the ship a minute or two after the first one, and it came from the stern, where Fernando was packing up his gear. He never emerged.

The saboteurs had been methodical. They placed the first bomb next to the engine room, a large compartment below decks, to sink the *Warrior* quickly; they put the second one at the propeller/rudder assembly to disable the boat for good. At this they proved successful. The *Rainbow Warrior* would never sail again.

It fell to me, as someone who remains calm in times of trauma, to take on the task of liaison with the authorities and to act as spokesperson with the media. The media wanted to know who had done the deed, and I had to be very careful at first to insist we didn't know. We quickly determined it was almost certainly an act of sabotage, but you don't accuse a country of terrorism unless you have some proof. The proof wasn't long in coming. The police found a small Zodiac inflatable boat abandoned on the other side of the harbor. It had a label that said, "Made in France." This was a clue of Inspector Clouseau proportions. Later it would be revealed that the French government, right up to President Mitterrand, had authorized the operation.

Of course the French denied any involvement, and even when it became clear the French military was involved, the politicians proclaimed their innocence. It was soon learned that French operatives had illegally entered New Zealand waters in a sailboat two months before the bombing,

CONFESSIONS OF A GREENPEACE DROPOUT

smuggling the Zodiac, explosives, and dive gear into the country. They infiltrated the Greenpeace New Zealand offices, found out when the *Warrior* would arrive, and laid their evil plan. It was determined that two frogmen, trained as the French equivalent of the U.S. Navy Seals, had placed plastic explosives on the *Rainbow Warrior's* hull. At the time I believed they were meant to explode simultaneously. I still can't think of a reason to have them go off a minute or two minutes apart. I suppose the timers were not synchronized perfectly. This tiny technical imperfection caused the death of a fellow campaigner, the first and only death a Greenpeace member has suffered in action.

Two of the French operatives, Sophie and Alain Turenge, later identified as Commander Alain Mafart and Captain Dominique Prieur of the French secret service, were apprehended at the airport before they could get out of the country. Charged with murder, they plea-bargained and were tried and convicted of manslaughter and sentenced to 10 years in a New Zealand jail. A few months later, under increasingly brutal trade sanctions imposed by France, New Zealand allowed them to be transferred to Hao Atoll in French Polynesia, where France promised they would serve out the remainder of their sentence. Within two years they were both repatriated to France to a hero's welcome. So much for justice in the Republic of France.

But there was some justice. United Nations Secretary-General Mr. Xavier Perez de Cuellar stepped in as mediator and awarded Greenpeace an $8 million settlement for the loss of the *Rainbow Warrior*. Not bad when you consider it had been purchased for about $47,000 in 1978. Fernando Periera's estranged wife was also awarded an undisclosed settlement, rumored to be of a similar magnitude. All parties except Fernando and his young son received adequate compensation.

One of the best slogans in Greenpeace's history found itself on a button commemorating the first anniversary of the bombing: "You Can't Sink a Rainbow." If it hadn't been for the loss of life, it would have been the biggest giggle room affair in our history. France overreacted to such an extreme that it deserved the ridicule heaped on it. No other story in Greenpeace's history has received as much media coverage as the bombing of the *Rainbow Warrior*. France handed Greenpeace its biggest mindbomb on a platter. I still won't order French wine in restaurants; it's overpriced and it reminds me of France's dastardly deeds in the South Pacific. And what makes France think it has a right to continue to subjugate the people of Polynesia under colonial rule in today's world?

I departed from New Zealand with a renewed determination to chart a different course. I could understand how the bombing might cause some in Greenpeace to harden their resolve to fight French nuclear testing, and I supported that view. But it wasn't for me. I was simply exhausted from carrying the flag for 15 years and I needed a fresh start. I wanted to move from constant confrontation, always telling people what they should stop doing, to trying to find consensus about what we should do instead. I had been against three or four things every day of my life for the past 15 years. I now decided to figure out what I was in favor of for a change. I wanted to find solutions rather than problems and to seek win-win resolutions rather than unending confrontations. The salmon farm was starting to look like a pretty good exit strategy from my 15-year Greenpeace apprenticeship.

I had personal reasons to move on as well as professional ones. My two boys, Jon and Nick, who was born in October, 1984, were growing up with a mostly absentee father. I had been living out of a suitcase for far too long. There was also the fact that I had gone into my Greenpeace career straight out of university. It was the only job I had known other than my stint in the logging camp. I wanted to go back and take care of the home fires for a change. I wanted to make a contribution to sustainable development in my home province of British Columbia.

CHAPTER TWELVE

Greenpeace Sails Off the Deep End

A quaculture wasn't the only issue that gave me reason to question my continued involvement in Greenpeace. Beginning in 1982 a campaigner from Greenpeace Germany, Renate Kroesa, had led the effort to end the production of the herbicide 2,4,5-T, otherwise know as Agent Orange. It had gained notoriety during the Vietnam War when it was used to defoliate vast areas of forest to expose Viet Cong troops. The only factory still manufacturing this chemical was in New Zealand, so Renate traveled there and eventually succeeded in closing it down. This was the first Greenpeace toxics campaign involving dioxin and other chlorine-containing chemicals.

Soon after, scientists discovered that the effluent from pulp and paper mills contained small amounts of dioxin. The detection of dioxin was due to the radically improved diagnostic tools for measuring minute quantities of substances, down to parts per billion and parts per trillion. The dioxins were being formed by a reaction between the chlorine gas used for bleaching the paper and organic matter in the pulp. Dioxins are known carcinogens, so it wasn't long before Greenpeace launched a campaign for "chlorine-free" paper mills. This became a worldwide campaign but was particularly targeted at the Canadian pulp and paper industry.

As soon as the industry became aware of this problem, it began working to solve it. At first it seemed likely pulp mills would need to eliminate chlorine altogether and switch to much more costly ozone and oxygen bleaching processes. As it turned out a combination of secondary treatment, similar to advanced sewage treatment, and switching from chlorine gas to chlorine dioxide, did the job of reducing dioxin to below detectable levels. (Chemists never assume that any substance is at zero; we can only be certain down to the level at which we are technically able to measure a substance.) Then there was the communications challenge of explaining that using something called chlorine dioxide eliminated dioxins! From the time of detection, it took one of the world's largest industries only five years to research, develop, and implement the solution. But Greenpeace has never accepted this approach, sticking to its "chlorine-free" position to this day.[22]

In fact it wasn't long until the paper campaign morphed into a much broader one—a campaign for a global ban on chlorine in all industrial processes, including polyvinyl chloride (PVC), often simply referred to as vinyl. This is when Greenpeace really lost me. As a student of advanced biochemistry, I realized chlorine was one of the 98 natural elements in the periodic table and that it is essential for life. You don't just go around banning entire elements, especially when life without them would be impossible! This was the first time I really noticed that none of my fellow directors, including Chairman David McTaggart, had any formal science education. They could variously be described as political and social activists, or as environmental entrepreneurs, looking for a career in the now highly popular environmental movement. These were perfectly acceptable orientations, but we were now dealing with very complex issues of chemistry and biology. The great divide between the physical sciences and the social sciences was making things extremely difficult.

I reminded my fellow directors that chlorine was one of the building blocks of the universe and questioned "whether banning an element was within our jurisdiction." I reminded them that adding chlorine to drinking water represented the biggest advance in the history of public health and saved hundreds of millions from death due to cholera, typhoid, and other water-borne communicable diseases. I explained that more than 75 percent of our pharmaceuticals, including antibiotics, were based on chlorine chemistry. And if that wasn't enough I said, "The best way to deliver the slightly chlorinated drinking water to the public is in a PVC pipe." The other Greenpeace directors behaved as though these were minor exceptions to the general rule that chlorine should be banned worldwide, so I had to leave. Simple science made me a Greenpeace dropout.

---

22. Paper Buying for Individuals: Go Ancient Forest Friendly, Greenpeace International, December 3, 2008, http://www.greenpeace.org/international/campaigns/forests/solutions/paper-buying-for-individuals

To this day I am proud of most of the things we accomplished during my 15 years with Greenpeace. We got many things right in the early years of the movement: We stopped the bomb, saved the whales, and ended toxic discharge into the water and air. In retrospect the only issue I feel we got wrong was nuclear energy, and that was a big mistake with significant consequences. But with the decision to ban chlorine for all human uses, Greenpeace began to adopt a number of campaigns that were wrongheaded and in no way based on science or logic.

For me, this was when what had been science-based policy turned into a kind of religion based on belief rather than facts or evidence, as Bob Hunter had predicted years before. Greenpeace now calls chlorine the "devil's element" and refers to PVC as "the poison plastic," even though there is no evidence to show that it is toxic. And there are the following points to consider:

- Table salt is sodium chloride (NaCl), about two-thirds chlorine by weight. It is an essential nutrient for plants and animals, including humans. This is why farmers put salt licks out for their livestock. The acid in our stomach that digests our food is hydrochloric acid. It is doubtful any form of life would be possible without chlorine.
- There is more chlorine in the earth's crust than there is carbon, which is the most essential element for life. Chlorine is the 11th most abundant element in the earth's crust.
- PVC is the most important plastic used in the construction of buildings. It is found in water and sewer pipes, electrical conduits, wiring insulation, siding, roofing, decks, flooring, and wall coverings. It is particular important in health care facilities, where it is used for blood bags, intravenous tubing, gloves, caps, flooring, and wall covering. Because it is smooth and impervious, it can easily be disinfected, making it easier to control the spread of staph infections and super-bugs.

There was some irony in the fact that at the same time Greenpeace was adopting a zero-tolerance policy on chlorine and PVC, I was busy building a fish hatchery in which all the plumbing was made from PVC pipe. I glued together thousands of feet and hundreds of fittings and marveled at what an efficient material PVC was to work with. The idea that it could be labeled "poison plastic" seemed way over the top to me. I had become intellectually alienated from my own organization.

No one can deny that many of the substances used in daily life are toxic when ingested in large doses. Try chasing a cup of table salt with a cup of gasoline, to name two such substances. As every toxicologist knows, "the poison is in the dose," not in the substance itself. Many chemicals that are essential nutrients at low doses, such as table salt, are fatal at high doses.

Anyone who has siphoned gasoline knows it is not an essential nutrient, and yet it is unlikely to cause any harm at low doses.

None of this matters to the "chemophobes," those who generally fear chemicals. They tend to want to ban anything that has the potential to be toxic. If they had their way, today many elements in the periodic table would be eliminated, thus severely damaging the fabric of the universe, or at least the fabric of civilization. There are campaigns against lead, mercury, cadmium, chlorine, fluorine, bromine, tin, arsenic, and, of course, uranium. These elements all have important uses in health, technology, energy production, and lighting. We have been bombarded into thinking lead is deadly, yet many of us drive around with about 30 pounds of it in the battery of our cars.

It is natural, I suppose, to think that it would be good to get rid of everything "toxic." But then how would we disinfect our water and how would we kill the bacteria that are trying to kill us? The reason chlorine is the most important element for public health is precisely because it is toxic. The fact is we need toxic substances to survive. Even herbal medicine is partly based on using plants that contain chemicals that are toxic to infectious agents that would otherwise overwhelm our own defenses.

Here I was one of five international directors of Greenpeace and there was nothing I could say or do to reverse this slide into voodoo science. Not one of my fellow directors had any education in science and yet they were making judgments about complex issues that involved chemistry and biology: Chlorine must be banned for the good of the environment and human health—*human health* for Pete's sake. I guess junk science started before Greenpeace adopted the anti-chlorine campaign, but this was my first direct encounter with it and I was flabbergasted. Renate Kroesa was supposed to be a chemist, but she was the most fanatical of all in promoting this crazy idea. Most Greenpeace folk had no chemistry and simply bought into the rhetoric about the devil and the poison and then, of course, there were the evil chlorine-producing multinational corporations bent on subjugating humankind.

Somewhere in the middle of all this, Greenpeace, and most of the environmental movement, lost its way. Whereas early campaigns were based on an honest concern for human survival, whale extinction, and really toxic waste, they gradually drifted into sensationalism, fabrication, and downright lies in order to gain public support. I watched, helpless but for the pleas for common sense, as the organization I had helped found and build became my adversary in relation to a growing number of issues. This was not in my plans, for a time I tried to convince my fellow directors that they should stick to the facts. But the combination of David McTaggart's political instincts and the growing power of the movement corrupted the organization. It was way past the time for me to move on.

On January 31, 1986, I drew my last Greenpeace paycheck and joined

Quatsino Seafarms full-time to help take the salmon-farming venture from start-up to production. Our first year-class of salmon was already in the sea pens, and the second year-class was hatching in the incubators. Brother Mike had his hands full running the operation and it was time for me to start looking for markets and planning for future expansion. I took the job on with enthusiasm, adding more capacity to our hatchery, as there was now a growing demand for salmon smolts from farms that didn't have a hatchery. In our third year we produced 300,000 smolts, selling 200,000 of them to other farmers and making the hatchery a profitable operation in its own right.

In the early summer of 1986, I attended the first formal meeting of the fledgling B.C. Salmon Farmers Association. Brad and June Hope and Tom and Linda May were joined by a dozen or so folks who had either started farms or wanted to find out more about how to get into the business. Brad said we needed a spokesperson to deal with the media and the concerns about our industry among the public. They elected me president because I had a lot of experience with the media and could hold my own in a discussion or debate. Within a month I found myself publicly defending salmon farming against charges from the environmental movement, including Greenpeace. It was easy to see how I could be portrayed as a turncoat.

The activist campaign against salmon farming has grown steadily, keeping pace with the growth of the industry worldwide. Since its beginnings in Norway in the 1970s, salmon farming has become established in Scotland, Ireland, Chile, Canada, Australia, New Zealand, and the United States. Salmon are a cold water species, so they do best in the abundant sheltered waters found in northern and southern coastlines, where glaciers once carved deep fjords and inlets. Salmon farming has proved controversial everywhere it operates, partly just because it is new and partly because it competes with existing wild fisheries. But the opposition has been most virulent in British Columbia. Today the province houses a small industry of full-time activists who are bent on damaging the salmon farming industry and its markets.

It's clear to me that aquaculture, including salmon aquaculture, constitutes the future of healthy protein and oil, nutrients that we need to feed a growing population. Worldwide, aquaculture is now the fastest-growing food-producing sector, and there are good reasons for this.

First, the wild fisheries have been largely tapped out; there has been no increase in the global catch for about 15 years. Some wild fisheries are severely overfished and must be allowed to rebuild, a process that may take decades or longer. The Atlantic cod fishery is a classic example. Cod are large predatory fish, which are caught above the continental shelves in the North Atlantic. In the 1850s, 43 sail-powered schooners from the port of Beverly, Massachusetts, hauled in nearly 8,000 tons of cod from a portion of the Scotian Shelf each year. Mind you, back then the men fished using single-hooked hand-jigged lines dropped from small, two-man dories. Compare that to 1999, when 90 modern ships equipped with the latest fish-spotting sonar and massive nets hauled in only 7,200 tons from the entire Scotian Shelf. Scientists used the old ships logs to calculate that the current tonnage of adult cod in the North Atlantic is just 4 percent of what it was in 1852. This means the stocks have been depleted by 96 percent. The only practical way to increase seafood production and reduce the pressures on the wild fish stocks is aquaculture, which now provides nearly half of the world's seafood and will soon produce more than half of it.[23] [24]

Second, fish are two to three times more efficient at converting feed into food for people than are land animals like cows, pigs, and chickens. There are two reasons for this: Fish are cold-blooded, so they don't have to expend energy keeping their insides warm as mammals and birds must do. And fish live in a neutrally buoyant environment, so they don't use energy to remain upright fighting gravity as we and other land animals do.

Third, the protein and oils from seafood are healthier than those from land animals. The omega-3 oils in seafood, especially in oily fish like salmon and tuna, cut the incidence of fatal heart attacks by up to 50 percent.[25] And it has been shown in a number of studies that these oils can also reduce the risk of Alzheimer's disease by more than 50 percent.[26] [27] A number of studies have shown omega-3 oils reduce stress, something many of us would benefit from.

The anti-aquaculture activists who belong to Greenpeace, the David Suzuki Foundation, the Coastal Alliance for Aquaculture Reform, and many other pressure groups do not share my views. These organizations claim to support the salmon farming industry, but only if it adopts "closed containment" technology. There is only one small catch: there is no such thing as "closed containment." It would be like telling chicken farmers they can't take the chicken manure out of the chicken coops and spread it on their fields. All agricultural systems have inputs and outputs – farming can't be done in a vacuum. But the idea of a salmon farm that has no outputs seems to appeal to some people, so much so that the opposition political party in British Columbia has adopted "closed containment" as a condition for its support of salmon farming. Watch it wriggle out of that one if it wins an election someday.

Initially the activists demanded salmon farms be placed on the land where they couldn't "pollute" the ocean. My initial response was to sug-

23. Steven Hedlund, "FAO: Aquaculture Nearly Half of Global Seafood Production," *SeafoodSource*, March 2, 2009, http://www.seafoodsource.com/newsarticledetail.aspx?id=2678
24. UN Food and Agriculture Organization, "World Review of Fisheries and Aquaculture," ftp://ftp.fao.org/docrep/fao/011/i0250e/i0250e01.pdf
25. Optimal Heart Health, "Heart Attack and the Benefit of Fish Oil," http://www.optimal-heart-health.com/benefitoffishoil.html
26. Laterlife, "Oily Fish Reduces the Risk of Dementia and Alzheimer's," May 2004 http://www.laterlife.com/laterlife-oily-fish.htm
27. Martha Clare Morris et al., "Consumption of Fish and n-3 Fatty Acids and Risk of Incident Alzheimer Disease," *Archives of Neurology* 60, no. 7 (July 2003).

gest that maybe we should put the dairy cows and chickens in the sea in order to avoid polluting the land. Seriously though, salmon need seawater to grow and placing farms on land would mean pumping huge volumes of ocean water uphill into shore-based tanks. This would require a tremendous amount of energy, likely from diesel-electric generators in remote, off grid locations, which would spew out air pollution and greenhouse gases. This would hardly constitute an environmental improvement. Faced with this fact the activists changed their demand to "closed containment" in the sea. They provided no suggestion of what to do with the waste from the fish or how to get new water in and let old water out. Basically, their "solution" would mean an end to the practice of salmon farming.

Let's look at the laundry list of complaints activists make on a daily basis about what I maintain is one of the cleanest industries on the planet and one that produces the healthiest food in the world.

Salmon farms are polluting the ocean with fish waste.

Activists compare salmon farms to "cities of 500,000 people, dumping their raw sewage" into the environment.[28] The primary reason for concern about untreated human waste is disease transfer, not the waste itself. For centuries before sewage was treated, diseases such as cholera and typhoid were transmitted by water contaminated with human waste. Once human waste is treated and sterilized, it is a perfectly good fertilizer, and fish waste is no different except that there are no diseases that can be transmitted from fish to people. Fish waste consists of carbon, oxygen, hydrogen, potassium, nitrogen, phosphorous, calcium, iron, zinc, and the other nutrients essential for life.

It is possible to have too much of a good thing. If a fish farm is situated in shallow water where there is no tidal flushing and the farm is heavily stocked, it can cause the form of pollution known as eutrophication, or simply too many nutrients. Excess nutrients cause excess plankton (algae) growth, depleting the water of oxygen when the plankton die. The lack of oxygen kills fish and reduces a farm's productivity. One of the best features of fish farms is that they are self-regulating in this regard. If a salmon farmer pollutes the water at the farm site, it is the fish in the pens that will suffer the most harm. Fish that live outside the pens can swim away, but the farmed fish must live or die in an enclosed area. They are like the proverbial canary in a coal mine in that they suffer first, the farmer either adjusts or goes broke, and the pollution ends.

If a farm is properly located where there are strong tidal currents, the nutrients are dispersed widely and actually increase the the area's produc-

28. Salmon Farming Backgrounder, Wilderness Committee,
http://wildernesscommittee.org/what_we_do/salmon_farming_backgrounder

tivity. It is no secret that prawn and crab fishermen often set their traps close to fish farms due to the abundance of marine life in their vicinity. What would I do with a wheelbarrow full of fish waste? I'd spread it on my vegetable and flower gardens, knowing it would make them grow faster and produce more food and blooms.

In this case the activists are employing the propagandist tool of using words like sewage and waste that conjure up foul smells and negative impressions, as if fish waste were some kind of toxic chemical when it is actually beneficial where farms are properly sited. In the great food chains of life, one species' waste is another species' food. Three cheers for fish poop.

Farmed salmon may escape and breed with wild salmon and even displace the wild fish.

To cut to the chase I sum this one up as follows, "Some people are more worried about which fish are mating up a river than where their own kids are at night." The concern is that if a farmed fish escapes and mates with a wild fish the offspring will be inferior and unable to compete in the wild. Then there is another concern that if a farmed fish escapes it will overpower the wild fish and displace it, which will result in an inferior stock of fish. Activists can't have it both ways. Either the farmed salmon are inferior and won't be able to compete, or they're superior and will outcompete. Or they could just blend in. In fact the critics are wrong on both counts because in the wild the rule is the fittest will survive. If the escaped farm fish really were more fit, then they would deserve to survive. Transplanted chinook and coho salmon from the North Pacific have adjusted to the Great Lakes and they thrive there. Rainbow trout from the Pacific Northwest—from British Columbia in particular—are now well established in lakes and rivers around the world. People generally feel happy about this because they like to catch and eat the salmon and trout.

Most of the farmed salmon raised in British Columbia and Washington State are Atlantic salmon. It isn't possible for them to breed with Pacific salmon, so there is no genetic concern as is the case in Norway and Scotland, where farmed Atlantic escapees could breed with their wild cousins. But activists fear Atlantic salmon might become established in the Pacific and displace the native species. After 15 years, during which time thousands of Atlantic salmon have escaped, there is no evidence that the Atlantics have become permanently established. This is likely to remain the case as there have been many attempts around the world to establish Atlantic salmon outside their natural range and all have failed. It would appear that, unlike Pacific salmon, Atlantic salmon are difficult, if not impossible, to transplant.

Even if Atlantic salmon were to become established, would it be such a bad thing? There are already eight species of salmonids in Pacific Northwest rivers and they don't "displace" one another. Perhaps a ninth species would simply add to biodiversity. The oyster farming industry in the Pacific Northwest is based upon the cultivation of Japanese oysters in the ocean. In some warmer inlets they have become established as self-perpetuating populations. In other words they have become naturalized and it seems to me this is a pretty natural state of affairs. There is no evidence that the Japanese oysters are displacing native species of shellfish.

In Norway and Scotland activists charge that escaped Atlantic salmon will wipe out the wild stocks. They neglect to mention the reason salmon farming was invented in Norway was because the wild salmon had been so badly overfished that there weren't enough to satisfy the demand. If anything, the salmon farms allow some of the fishing pressure to be taken off the wild stocks so they might rebuild. In a recent agreement Greenland has stopped commercial fishing for Atlantic salmon with financial support from Denmark and the US.[29] One can only hope this will increase ocean survival so that more fish will return to spawn in their native rivers in Europe and on the Atlantic Coast of North America. In the absence of the salmon farming industry, this agreement would have been more difficult to achieve.

Salmon are fed large amounts of antibiotics that spread into the sea.

During salmon farming's early years, it was common to medicate fish fairly regularly to control a number of diseases to which they were susceptible. Today, antibiotics are used very seldom because vaccines have been developed for most diseases. Whereas pigs and chickens are on antibiotics for over 50 percent of their lives, salmon are on medicated feed for only 3 percent of their lives. Many salmon farms are now completely antibiotic-free and some even qualify for organic status.

It amazes me that activists are so negative about the use of modern medicine in animal husbandry. It is perfectly reasonable for veterinarians to prescribe medication for diseased livestock, and reasonable to use low-dose antibiotic feed to promote rapid and healthy animal growth. These practices partly account for why our agriculture flourishes today. It would be nice if there were no diseases in this world; but such a world is a fantasy that could never be real.

Salmon farms spread disease to wild fish.

The anti-fish farm set give people the impression that salmon farms somehow manufacture diseases and then spread them to wild fish. In fact the reverse is true. All the diseases that farm fish contract come from the wild.

---

29. West Greenland Commission, "West Greenland Fishery Sampling Agreement," 2008,
http://www.nasco.int/sas/pdf/wgc(08)06.pdf

Farm fish go into the ocean disease-free from hatcheries and sometimes contract the natural diseases from the waters around them. If the disease outbreak is severe, they can be treated and cured, unlike wild fish, which get diseases and transfer them to both other wild fish and to farm fish.

Salmon farms are spreading sea lice to wild fish, causing their populations to plummet.

This is the claim anti-salmon activists are pursuing most aggressively today. It is a completely trumped-up fabrication, repeated so often that the media, and thence the public, tend to believe it.

The story goes like this: sea lice, which are a mildly parasitic relative of shrimp and crabs, attach themselves to farmed salmon and breed on them so prolifically that the pens become a reservoir for infecting wild fish swimming by. Lice from salmon farms attack and kill juvenile pink salmon when they come out of the rivers and go to sea. In 2002 a large run of pink salmon returning to spawn in rivers near the Broughton Archipelago, on British Columbia's central coast, crashed to less than 10 percent of its previous size. This is blamed on sea lice.

It is a great story for the activists, as it argues that the fish farming industry is a direct threat to the wild salmon populations. Whereas the aquaculture industry argues, correctly in my view, that farming helps take the pressure off wild stocks by providing a farmed product, the activists now have an argument that suggests the opposite is the case. Let's examine the facts.

There is no direct evidence that lice from salmon farms harm wild salmon stocks. The crash of 2002 was clearly a natural phenomenon caused by overpopulation in the 2000 year-class of salmon. The salmon simply ate themselves out of house and home and collapsed. This pattern occurs in most populations of wild species; it is a typical boom and bust cycle. The activists never mention that the 2000 and 2001 pink salmon populations were the highest recorded since records have been kept. They don't mention that salmon farms were established for 15 years before the crash occurred. And they certainly don't talk about the fact that in a number of years before salmon farms existed on the coast the populations were even lower than in the crash year of 2002. You can be doubly sure they will never volunteer the fact that in 2003, 2004, 2009, and 2010 the population rebounded, quickly coming back to a level higher than the 50-year average for the region. Meanwhile the activists continue to claim sea lice from salmon farms are "threatening wild pink salmon with extinction."[30]

---

30. Stephen Leahy, "Fish Farms Pushing Wild Salmon to Extinction," December 14, 2007, http://ipsnorthamerica.net/print.php?idnews=1218

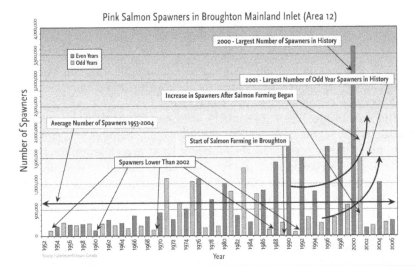

Pink Salmon Spawners in Broughton Mainland Inlet (Area 12)

This graph shows that there have actually been more salmon spawning in the Broughton Archipelago since salmon farming began than there were before. In 2009 nearly one million fish returned to the spawning beds, despite predictions by activists that they faced extinction.

This debate has raged in British Columbia for more than 10 years, culminating in the publication of an article by the anti-salmon farm activists in the influential magazine *Science* in 2007.[31] It reads in part:

Rather than benefiting wild fish, industrial aquaculture may contribute to declines in ocean fisheries and ecosystems. Farm salmon are commonly infected with salmon lice (*Lepeophtheirus salmonis*), which are native ectoparasitic copepods. We show that recurrent louse infestations of wild juvenile pink salmon (*Oncorhynchus gorbuscha*), all associated with salmon farms, have depressed wild pink salmon populations and placed them on a trajectory toward rapid local extinction. The louse-induced mortality of pink salmon is commonly over 80% and exceeds previous fishing mortality. *If outbreaks continue, then local extinction is certain* [my emphasis], and a 99% collapse in pink salmon population abundance is expected in four salmon generations.

One year later, fisheries scientists from the Pacific Biological Station of the Canadian Department of Fisheries and Oceans replied:

Krkosek et al. (*Reports*, 14 December 2007, p. 1772) claimed that sea lice spread from salmon farms 'placed wild pink salmon populations on a trajectory toward rapid local extinction.' Their prediction is inconsistent

31. Martin Krkosek, Jennifer S. Ford, Alexandra Morton, Subhash Lele, Ransom A. Myers, Mark A. Lewis: "Declining Wild Salmon Populations in Relation to Parasites from Farm Salmon," *Science* 318, no. 5857 (December 14, 2007): 1772–1775.

with observed pink salmon returns and overstates the risks from sea lice and salmon farming. [32]

In other words, in typically understated language, the fisheries experts did not agree that the evidence supported the conclusion that pink salmon would become extinct because of salmon farms.

The media have been particularly irresponsible in their reports on this subject. It seems quite obvious that they enjoy helping to create the myth, rarely if ever presenting the facts listed above. As a group the news media have given the anti-salmon farm activists nearly all the airtime and ignored scientists with real credentials and long experience in the field. They have given credence to the illogical musings of Alexandra Morton, an expatriate American who claims to be a biologist, though her credentials in marine biology have been disputed, and deservedly so in my estimation. She has been fashioned as a kind of earth mother, who cares so deeply for the salmon while resorting to ridiculous fabrications, which are dutifully reported by an uncritical provincial and national media. I have dealt with controversial environmental issues for a long time, so I know you can't always simply blame the media. In this case, however, I believe it is justified. Only a couple of small, local newspapers in the salmon-farming region have attempted to provide some balance to the one-sided reporting.

There is no doubt that salmon farms, sea lice, and wild salmon exist in the ocean. Sea lice do attach themselves to farmed salmon, and a percentage of wild pink salmon fry do have sea lice on them as they pass by salmon farms. So where are the sea lice coming from? It turns out that wild salmon were infested with sea lice long before salmon farms existed. Government-funded research has shown that sea lice are present in the billions on many other species of wild fish besides salmon. Sticklebacks, which abound near the outlets of the streams the pink salmon come down, are loaded with lice. They and other wild species are the most likely source of sea lice that attach to the wild salmon. This same research has found no evidence that the lice on the wild salmon cause any damage to the population. Yet hysteria seems to rule the day.

Researchers have developed a treatment for sea lice on farmed salmon called SLICE. It is a medication that is put in the salmon feed and it kills the lice. Activists are now campaigning against the use of this medicine, even though it has been approved by health and environmental authorities in many countries. This is typical: they are against the lice, claiming the lice will exterminate wild salmon, and then they are against the cure, even though there is no evidence of harmful side effects.

Amid the claims of wild-eyed activists that the pink salmon were

---

32. Brian E. Riddell, Richard J. Beamish, Laura J. Richards, John R. Candy: "Comment on 'Declining Wild Salmon Populations in Relation to Parasites from Farm Salmon'," *Science* 322, no. 5909: 1790 (December 19, 2008). DOI: 10.1126/science.1156341

CONFESSIONS OF A GREENPEACE DROPOUT

going extinct, 2009 saw a bountiful run. This extended from Alaska to Washington State, including the Broughton Archipelago and the Campbell River, where there is the greatest concentration of salmon farms.[33] There were so many fish that the Department of Fisheries and Oceans opened the pink salmon fishery for commercial boats in order to prevent an over-abundance of salmon in the spawning streams. In 2009 nearly one mil-lion pink salmon reached the spawning grounds. This is pretty much as much proof as you can get in the real world that they are not going extinct and that the salmon farms are not damaging wild salmon stocks. Yet these zealots don't give up easily.

The runs of coho, chinook, and chum salmon were also plentiful in 2009. The only salmon run that was really depressed that year was the Fraser River sockeye. Over 10 million were expected and only 1.7 million showed up. Alexandra Morton immediately blamed the shortage of sock-eye on lice from salmon farms in the Broughton, far from the Fraser River, something she had never mentioned before. She and her partners in dis-tortion completely ignored the huge pink salmon returns. And a willing media complied in one of the most blatant examples of bias and fabrica-tion I have seen. Not one major Canadian newspaper reported that the pink salmon run had returned in abundance, completely disproving the trumped-up charge that they were nearly extinct.

If the bountiful pink salmon runs of 2009 were not sufficient to con-vince the media and the public that sea lice are not a problem, then 2010 leaves no doubt. Not only did the pink salmon once again return in near-record numbers, the Fraser River sockeye run was estimated at 34 million fish, the largest run in nearly a century.[34] Yet the willing accomplices in the media (such as Mark Hume of the Toronto *Globe and Mail*) have remained silent and the activists warn that one good run doesn't mean much. Their credibility has been shattered beyond repair with both the public and fish-eries scientists. Carl Walters, arguably the most knowledgeable salmon population biologist in Canada, put it this way, "My personal opinion is that the claims about fish-farming effects on either of those species [pink and sockeye] are bogus. It is certainly not a matter of fact that fish farming has affected those populations. It is quite unlikely that fish farming has anything to do with the changes in sockeye-salmon numbers that we've seen, the downs or ups." [35]

Wild salmon populations are subject to a wide range of environmental factors that influence their survival. Perhaps the most important of these

---

33. Fisheries and Oceans Canada, "Facts About Sea Lice," November 3, 2009,
http://www.dfo-mpo.gc.ca/aquaculture/lice-pou/lice-pou04-eng.htm
34. "Sockeye Run Estimates Upped to 34 Million," Michael Loubet, *FIS Canada*, September 1, 2010,
http://fis.com/fis/worldnews/worldnews.asp?l=e&country=O&special=&monthyear=&day=&id=37982&ndb=1&df=0
35. "Critics Claim Wild Fish Still At Risk From Farm Stock," Carlito Pablo, Straight.com, September 2, 2010,
http://www.straight.com/article-341759/vancouver/critics-claim-wild-fish-risk-farm-stock

is what researchers call "ocean conditions". During their years at sea, salmon are subjected to predators, disease, fluctuating abundance of feed, varying temperatures, and competition from other species. All these factors combine to determine their success at returning to their natal streams to spawn. The past ten years have demonstrated that it is difficult to predict with accuracy how many salmon will return in a given year because there are many variables and the fish are far at sea where direct observation is impossible. But we can conclude that the evidence is overwhelming that sea lice are not a significant factor in salmon survival.

The feed for farmed salmon contains fishmeal and oil from wild fish. This results in a net loss of protein for a hungry world because it takes two to three pounds of wild fish to make one pound of farmed salmon.

It is true that a portion of the feed for farmed salmon is fishmeal and oil from wild fish. The omega-3 fats in fish oil are essential for good health in salmon and other farmed fish. But it is not true that the use of these products results in a net loss of protein for consumers. When you think about it, why would fish farmers be so stupid as to employ a system that made less food for people? The fact is they don't; aquaculture produces more food for people or it would not make any sense. An independent study done for the European Union Research Director concluded, "Globally the efficiency of consuming fish directly and eating animals fed on fishmeal and fish oil is about equal. Feed conversion figures for salmon suggest that it is more efficient to consume salmon derived from aquaculture than wild caught fish."[36]

Fishmeal and fish oil are derived from three main sources: the scraps from processing wild and farmed seafood, undesirable fish caught incidentally while fishing for other species, and from fisheries that target fish such as menhaden and anchovies caught specifically for fish meal. The anti-salmon farm brigade focuses most of its attention on the anchovy fishery, a well-managed and sustainable harvest that lands five million tons per year, or about 5 percent of the global wild seafood catch. The gist of the its criticism is that salmon farmers are taking food from the mouths of poor Peruvians and producing food for affluent consumers in rich countries. And by feeding the fishmeal and oil made from anchovies to salmon there is a net loss of protein as it takes two to three pounds of anchovies to make one pound of salmon. It's a great story about corporate greed and abuse of poor people, but there isn't a speck of truth to it.

First, not even poor people want to eat a regular diet of anchovies. We do have to take people's tastes into account. It might well increase the

---

36. European Parliament, "The Fish Meal and Fish Oil Industry: Its Role in the Common Fisheries Policy," December 2003, http://www.consult-poseidon.com/reports/EP%20Role%20of%20Fish%20Oil-Meal%20in%20the%20CFP.pdf

food supply if we all ate algae paste three meals a day, but that isn't likely to become a fad anytime soon. Second, anchovies spoil very quickly after they are caught: that is why they are usually canned in oil with a lot of salt. Some people, myself included, enjoy the occasional one on a Caesar salad. But the only other way to keep them for a reasonable time is to freeze them. There simply isn't a market for five million tons of frozen anchovies. That is why they are converted to meal and oil. If people wanted to eat them as anchovies, there would be a market for them and they would not be rendered down. Food fish always command a higher price than fish that go into rendering plants. I suppose one could argue that the government of Peru should buy all the anchovies and give them, and a deep-freeze, and the power to run it, to the poor. The export of anchovy meal and oil is one of Peru's largest income earners. It surely does Peru more good to bring in foreign currency than it would to make the people eat five million tons of anchovies every year. Yet the activists, and even some wooly-headed academics, continue to argue this point.

Whatever your thoughts on developing countries and poor people, it doesn't make sense to blame salmon farmers for keeping Peruvians down on the farm. And only about one-third of the world's fishmeal and oil is consumed by aquaculture, the majority is fed to chickens and pigs. Why? Because it's good for their health just as it's good for our health. As aquaculture grows, it will consume a larger share of these feeds, because fish have better conversion rates, so fish farmers can afford to outbid land-based farmers. Eventually the limited supply of fishmeal and oil will become a constraint to the growth of aquaculture. That's why a tremendous amount of research is now focused on replacing fishmeal and oil with substitutes such as soybeans and other crops grown in abundance on land. Already a genetically enhanced soybean has been engineered to produce omega-3 oils. This and other innovations will eventually revolutionize the human diet and the diets of our domestic animals, with positive results all around for health and nutrition.

Fish farmers feed salmon artificial chemical dyes to make them look pink like wild salmon.

This is one of the most preposterous allegations, but it is repeated in the activist rant against aquaculture. Again it is simply the use of propagandist language—turning a good thing into a toxic threat—that gives consumers the impression farmed salmon is somehow "artificial."

True, naturally occurring chemicals called carotenoids are added to salmon feed and this gives the salmon a distinctive color. These are, in fact, the same carotenoids that make wild salmon pink. They come through the food chain from the plankton that produce them in the first place. These same carotenoids also make shrimp and crabs pink and that is why shrimp farmers add them to their feed as well.

It is also a fact that these carotenoids—namely, astaxanthin and can-thaxanthin—are produced synthetically and used as additives in the feed of fish and of poultry (to give the skin and egg yolks a brighter yellow color) and as colorants in and on a wide variety of foods. These carotenoids benefit human health and are essential nutrients for salmon.[37] They are powerful antioxidants, sold as health food supplements and sunless tan-ning treatments.[38]

Carotenoids make carrots orange (and they *are* good for our eyesight), daffodils yellow, and prepared meats pink rather than gray. Adding them to food for nutritional or aesthetic reasons is perfectly safe and in many cases beneficial. It is no different than adding vitamin C to fruit juice as a dietary supplement—and, yes, vitamin C (ascorbic acid) is also made synthetically and is no different from the "natural" vitamin C produced in citrus fruits. Should products with added vitamin C be labeled "contains the artificial chemical ascorbic acid"?

Farmed salmon contain high levels of cancer-causing PCBs and dioxins.

Enter the classic food scare, complete with images of pregnant women and babies threatened by toxic chemicals in their diet. It is a fundraiser's delight and millions of dollars are spent, and even more millions raised, on orchestrated media campaigns to make sure the scare is spread far and wide. How about some facts?

Yes, farmed salmon contain minute traces, in the parts per billion (equal to one penny out of $10,000,000), of PCBs and dioxins. But so do milk, cheese, butter, beef, chicken, and pork. The levels of these chemicals in all these foods are so far below what is considered a risk to health that it isn't worth talking about; but it is worth fear-mongering in order to fabricate campaigns, make media headlines, and bring in the big grants and donations.

Interestingly, scientists have new evidence that some long-lived chem-icals thought to be entirely human-made pollutants, such as polybromin-ated diphenyl ethers (PBDEs)—the latter are used as flame-retardants in furniture and clothing—actually have significant natural sources. Most of the PBDEs found in the blubber of a stranded True's beaked whale, which was found in Virginia in 2003, were found to have a natural origin.[39] The

37. Mera Pharmaceuticals, "Carotenoids,"
http://www.astaxanthin.org/index.php?option=com_content&view=article&id=3:carotenoids&catid=14:general&Itemid=4#Q2
38. Health Marketplace, "Canthaxanthin," http://www.health-marketplace.com/Canthaxanthin.htm
39. Emma L. Teuten, Li Xu, Christopher M. Reddy, "Two Abundant Bioaccumulated Halogenated Compounds Are Natural Products," *Science* 307, no. 5711 (February 11, 2005),: 917-920.
http://www.sciencemag.org/cgi/content/abstract/307/5711/917?hits=10&RESULTFORMAT=&FIRSTINDEX=0&maxtoshow=&HIT
S=10&fulltext=whale+pcb&searchid=1&resourcetype=HWCIT

natural sources of PBDEs found in the whale are still unknown; scientists only know they aren't from human activity. Even more important from a health perspective is the fact that these natural chemicals likely explain why whales, humans, and other animals have enzymes that can break down PCBs, PBDEs, and other pollutants. That's why, from a health perspective, the parts per billion of these chemicals in our foods is of no health consequence.

This is a story of conspiratorial proportions with politicians, lobbyists, fishermen, charitable foundations, and activist groups all lined up to deliver the knock-out punch to salmon farming. Yet farmed salmon sales continue to rise, and one must admire the intelligence of the consumer who sees through the hype and buys one of the healthiest foods on the market, one that is available year-round at a reasonable price.

In January 2004 the journal *Science* carried a report that concluded that farmed salmon had higher levels of PCBs than did wild salmon.[40] PCBs, now banned, are an oily compound that was used in power line transformers as a coolant. The activist scientists who conducted the research were paid by the Pew Charitable Trust. The latter is an advocacy group based in Philadelphia that has billions of dollars in assets as a result of a legacy from the Sun Oil Corporation. Coincidentally the advisory board to Pew included a former governor of Alaska and a representative of the Alaska seafood industry. It just so happens that the main competition for "wild" Alaskan salmon sales in the U.S. is farmed Chilean and British Columbian salmon (we will get to why I put "wild" in quotations shortly). Other powerful figures to wade into this campaign were Alaskan Frank Murkowski, then governor, and his daughter, U.S. Senator Lisa Murkowski. The *Science* article made headlines around the word while salmon farmers watched and wept. The whole episode was framed as a threat to health posed by farmed salmon. Most media reports did not even mention the fact that wild salmon was also shown to contain PCBs, although supposedly at lower levels. The impression was given that farmed was toxic and wild was safe.

On September 3, 2003, the Netscape News proclaimed that farmed salmon was "contaminated with high levels of cancer-causing chemicals" when PCBs have never been shown to cause cancer in humans, even at thousands of times the levels found in salmon and other foods. The story, which was based on reports from the *New York Times* and Reuters, should have read, "[farmed salmon] contain extremely low levels of substances that have never been shown to cause cancer in humans." But that wouldn't have made a good headline, unlike the loaded word *contaminated*, which has little scientific meaning in this context.

---

40. Ronald Hite et al, "Global Assessment of Organic Contaminants in Farmed Salmon," *Science* 303, no. 5655 (January 9, 2004),: 226-229. http://www.sciencemag.org/cgi/content/short/303/5655/226

The study that the *Science* article was based on contained numerous flaws. The wild salmon that researchers selected included species like pink salmon, which have a much lower fat content than farmed Atlantic salmon. Because PCB and other fat-soluble contaminants concentrate in fat, it is predictable that pink salmon, which are not farmed because they are not as desirable as Atlantic salmon (partly for the very reason they have a lower fat content!), would have a lower PCB content. But pink salmon also have a lower omega-3 fat content and are therefore not as effective in preventing heart attacks as farmed Atlantic or wild king (chinook) salmon, both of which have a similar high (good) fat content.

An even more glaring shortcoming of the *Science* paper was that it failed to reference two previous studies that provided examples of wild salmon containing higher PCB levels than farmed salmon. One of these reports analyzed the famed Copper River sockeye salmon from southeast Alaska. It is usually the first fresh wild salmon on the market. It appears in stores in May, so it commands a high price. The report, done by the environmental organization The Circumpolar Conservation Union, showed Copper River sockeye contained about five times the level of PCBs found in farmed salmon.[41] Another well-known report demonstrated that wild king and silver (coho) salmon in Puget Sound, Washington, contained two to three times the levels of PCBs found in farmed salmon.[42] Both these reports were widely circulated among scientists before the *Science* article was published, yet no mention was made of them. Selective sampling of salmon and selective omission of previous studies makes for a biased report.

Nowhere in the *Science* article or in any of the anti-aquaculture literature is there a mention of the fact that the average North American consumer ingests about eight times as many PCBs from beef and about three times as many from milk as they do from eating farmed salmon. Yet all the warnings are about salmon and the facts are ignored. The famed Canadian activist Dr. David Suzuki said to a *Toronto Star* reporter, "I would never feed farmed salmon to a child. It's poison."[43] He should retract that statement if he wants to leave a credible legacy.

The fact is eating salmon has many benefits and carries so little risk that it makes sense to to eat it regularly. The American Heart Association states categorically that eating oily fish, such as salmon, reduces the risk of a fatal heart attack by 50 percent. According to the association, for every

---

41. Sierra Williams, Jon Buchholz, Krystin Habighorst, and Will Newberr, "Persistent Organic Pollutants in Alaskan Consumers," March 22, 2004,
http://seagrant.uaf.edu/nosb/papers/2004/soldotna-pops.html
42. James West, Sandra O'Neill, Greg Lippert and Stephen Quinnell, "Toxic Contaminants in Marine and Anadromous Fishes From Puget Sound, Washington: Results of the Puget Sound Ambient Monitoring Program Fish Component, 1989-1999," August 2001, http://wdfw.wa.gov/fish/psamp/toxiccontaminants.pdf
43. Susan Sampson, "The Great Salmon Debate," *Toronto Star*, September 15, 2004, http://www.beattystreetpublishing.com/confessions/references/the-great-salmon-debate

100,000 people who eat salmon only 400 will suffer fatal heart attacks. The Environmental Protection Agency, which tends to exaggerate risk by orders of magnitude, estimates that eating farmed salmon more than once a month will result in one additional cancer in 100,000 people in a 70-year life span. I make that a 400 to 1 justification for a regular feed of salmon, pretty good odds in my book. And one might ask how these people lived to be 70 years old in the first place: they probably ate a lot of oily fish like salmon.

And it's not only the American Heart Association that underlines the benefits of eating salmon. The World Health Organization, the U.S. Food and Drug Administration, Health Canada, and the U.S. Council on Science and Nutrition all recommend increasing our intake of seafood, particularly oily fish, as a way of improving our health. The activist campaign against salmon farming alarms people unnecessarily. Rather than heeding it, they would be much better off to ignore these scare tactics and eat more salmon—farmed or wild.

In order to save the wild salmon we should boycott farmed salmon and only eat wild salmon

Whoever thought up this lunatic idea should get the Nobel Prize for anti-logic. How can you save wild salmon by eating more of them? Yet a whole gaggle of goofy groups has succeeded in convincing chefs, restaurant owners, and consumers that a boycott of farmed salmon will somehow be good for wild salmon. Activists are blackmailing chefs and restaurateurs by threatening to picket and harass them if they don't take farmed salmon off their menus. Of course the deadly sea lice fabrication comes in handy here: Get rid of the salmon farms and wild salmon will no longer be decimated by the lice from the farms, activists say. As if the fishermen are not decimating the wild salmon. Oh no, they are just "harvesting" them, a nice term for "killing." *Every time you eat a farmed salmon you are saving a wild salmon.*

Every year tens of millions of wild salmon are killed by commercial, sport, and aboriginal fisheries just as they are about to go up rivers and spawn. This is somehow twisted into being "good" for the wild fish. If you ask me, what's good for the fishery is not necessarily what's good for the fish. I am not opposed to fishing for wild salmon, I do it myself, but fishermen are unquestionably impacting salmon numbers far more than fish farmers. There isn't any conclusive evidence that salmon farms harm the wild fish in the slightest, but there is no doubting the body count in the wild salmon fisheries.

It is interesting that the anti-aquaculture set have allied themselves with commercial wild fishing interests. Obviously the wild fishery opposes aquaculture; it represents a direct competitive threat. It doesn't cost as much to grow a farmed salmon as it does to catch a wild one. Moreover, one has to chase around for wild salmon in big power boats, which burn fuel. Of course this is why people began to farm plants and animals on the land 10,000 years ago; it is more efficient than hunting and gathering.

So why do so-called environmentalists side with the people who are killing the wild salmon? It has to do partly with a romantic notion about going back to a time when brave men went to sea and sometimes died trying to earn a living and bring food to hungry villagers. Partly it is an opportunistic move to play upon the public's notion of this romantic theme. In fact there is nothing romantic about risking your life and possibly capsizing and drowning in an angry sea. Just ask the widows.

But the single biggest driver is the competition for sales in fish stores and restaurants from Los Angeles to New York. This is a very good example of "environmental" campaigns today that are simply piggybacking on trade disputes, competition for market share, and antiglobalization agendas. Salmon farming just happens to be one of the issues in the crosshairs. In the case of salmon farming, it's all about U.S. interests (read the Alaskan salmon fishery) versus the growing imports of less expensive, consistently fresher, higher quality, available year-round, high in omega-3 fat content, farmed salmon from Chile and British Columbia. It really has nothing to do with the environment and everything to do with raw competition, a good thing when the consumer has the right information. Activist groups, who advertise themselves as environmentalists, make sure that the public doesn't have the right information and they raise money on the misinformation they spread.

It is no coincidence that most of the money flowing into British Columbia and Chile to combat salmon farming comes from the U.S.. For example, the David and Lucile Packard Foundation of California funds the anti-salmon farming activities of the David Suzuki Foundation in Vancouver. (Packard made his fortune by founding the Hewlett-Packard computer company.) Thus local Canadian activist groups are taking money from wealthy American foundations and acting as fronts for U.S. commercial interests.[44] It's a winning formula for all concerned, except the salmon farmers and their customers in American stores and restaurants.

Let's look for a moment at the so-called wild Alaska salmon fishery, which is so proud to be wild rather than farmed. The fact is much of the Alaskan salmon fishery is based on what is called "salmon ranching." Every year eggs are stripped from returning adult females, fertilized with milt (sperm) from returning males, and placed in hatcheries just like the ones salmon farmers use. When the eggs hatch they are "ponded" into

44. The Demarketing of Farmed Salmon, Vivian Krause, April 23, 2010,
http://fairquestions.typepad.com/files/demarketingfarmedsalmon30s.pdf

large tanks, where they are fed the same fish feed farmed salmon get, complete with synthetic canthaxanthin as a nutrient/colorant. When the smolts are ready to go to sea, they are transferred to net pens in the ocean, just like farmed salmon, and are fed on a diet that contains the same fish-meal and oil that farmed salmon enjoy. If they get sick, they receive the same antibiotics farmed salmon have the privilege of receiving. Some months later they are released to the open ocean to forage for themselves.

About 1.5 billion salmon are released into the wild each year from these aquaculture facilities in Alaska. After this point, they must compete with the truly wild salmon that have not been artificially spawned, hatched, reared, fed, and medicated. While promoters of Alaskan salmon go on about the amount of wild fish used to feed farmed salmon, their own industry churns out ranch salmon that consume about 20 times more wild feed than the entire Canadian salmon farming industry. The Alaskan ranched salmon are competing directly with the wild salmon for feed in the ocean while the farmed salmon are confined to their pens, where they feed on anchovies, soybeans, and wheat germ.

This is the reason I placed "wild" in quotation marks earlier on. The practice of salmon ranching is about as wild as the practice of cattle ranch-ing. Who would insist that cattle, reared on the farm and then released to the range, be classified as "wild" when they are rounded up for slaughter? I say ranching is a type of farming! Yet the activists who decry the sal-mon farming industry endorse salmon ranching. This is another clue that the anti-salmon farm campaign has little to do with the environment and everything to do with an unholy alliance between commercial fishermen and political activists, who effectively act as their agents.

I wouldn't have used up so much ink on this subject if I didn't think it was vital to our future health and the health of the world's oceans. Allow me to spend a little more time discussing aquaculture in order to present a positive vision, as the negative side of it has already received far too much attention.

First and foremost, aquaculture is the only feasible way to increase seafood production while at the same time managing the wild fisheries on a sustainable basis. More seafood is good for us; the health benefits of the Mediterranean diet and the longevity of Japanese people attest to this. And if it is done in an intelligent manner, aquaculture can even help increase the productivity of many wild fisheries.

The Japanese abalone and scallop fisheries are good examples of combining high-tech aquaculture with traditional fishing methods. All around the coast of Japan are found modern solar-powered hatcheries, where abalone and scallops are bred and reared. The juvenile shellfish are fed on algae and grown until they are the size of a penny. They are then seeded by the millions into the ocean at appropriate spots, where they grow to market size. In the south of Japan, where the sea is warm, they are harvested by women who dive for them in a traditional costume. In the north, where it is too cold for free diving the shellfish, they must be harvested with long poles from small boats, in the same way it has been done for centuries.

Another fine example of sustainable aquaculture is the abalone farming practiced in Monterrey, California. Juvenile abalone are purchased from a commercial hatchery and placed in cages, which are then suspended by ropes beneath the fisherman's pier. The cages are hauled up regularly for cleaning, sorting, and harvesting and then filled with California giant kelp (*Macrocystis*) harvested from nearby reefs. The kelp provides the staple diet for the abalone, along with algae and other marine species that grow inside the cages. California giant kelp grows very quickly, up to three feet a day, so the kelp is easily sustainable in quantities that can feed a lot of abalone.

Over 100 species of finfish and over 50 species of shellfish are now grown in commercial or experimental aquaculture operations around the world. Tilapia, which is now available in Costco and other large chains, makes a firm white fillet. Tilapia production is growing rapidly in tropical and subtropical countries, as is basa, a Vietnamese variety of catfish that is popular in many North American restaurants. Farmed Atlantic cod and sablefish (Alaska black cod) are already on the market and other species, such as sturgeon, halibut, and tuna are not far behind.

While fish farm production can still increase considerably in sheltered inshore waters, with the currently available feed supply there are three ways in which production could become much larger.

First, aquaculture operations can move offshore, where the pens can be anchored below the surface to avoid the destructive power of storms. There are already a number of pilot offshore aquaculture operations in service around the world. A float at the surface is tethered to a submerged feeding tube that can be pulled to the surface by a ship servicing tens of such cages along the continental shelves. The activists are so strongly opposed to fish farming that they have set themselves preemptively against open ocean fish farms, where all of the previously mentioned supposed environmental harms have even less validity. In the U.S., the National Oceanic and Atmospheric Administration has proposed greatly expanding fish farming in the internationally recognized Exclusive Economic Zones that extend 200 miles from each nation's shoreline. The U.S. wants to sell multiyear leases to fish farmers based on a percentage of their sales. In these open waters, wastes from the fish are greatly diluted and washed away with the currents to be absorbed by algae. Experimental offshore fish farms miles from shore have raised halibut, cod, red snapper, and tuna. The response from the environmentalist community has been predictable wailing over the "industrializing" of the seas by greedy big business. Anne Mosness with the anti-biotech, antidevelopment Institute for Agriculture and Trade Policy told the *Seattle Post-Intelligencer* that the U.S.'s open ocean proposal is "the equivalent of having a hog farm in a city park flushing its wastes into the street."[45] Pure nonsense.

Second, if geneticists can enhance land crops like soybeans and corn so that they contain omega-3 oils and other essential nutrients, this will vastly increase the feed supply. It will then make more economic sense to feed these crops to fish rather than to less efficient land animals. Don't worry: there will still be steaks for the barbecue and bacon for breakfast, but it would be very good for all of us who eat meat if fish consumption went up and consumption of red meat went down.

Third, we will learn how to use the waste from fish farms as a way of feeding shellfish grown nearby. The beauty of shellfish, such as oysters, mussels, and clams, is that they obtain their food from plankton growing in the ocean: there is no need to feed them directly. Plankton thrive on the nutrients from fish waste. Designed properly, the combination of finfish and shellfish farming could dramatically increase seafood production while simultaneously removing any excess nutrients from the ocean.

There is every reason to believe that we could increase seafood production by five to ten times over the next century while at the same time improving the environment for wild fisheries. We are quite capable of managing wild fisheries sustainably. The real problem is our inability to manage fish stocks that spend their time in international waters or migrating from one country's territory into another's. The collapse of the Atlantic cod and Atlantic salmon were both the result of 15 or more nations' fishing fleets competing for the same fish with no coordinated management plan. In the North Pacific, where only four countries—Canada, the U.S., Japan, and Russia—had fleets, they were able to create formal agreements that resulted in considerable success in managing halibut and salmon sustainably.

The greatest obstacle to the sustainable management of many fisheries is the classic "tragedy of the commons." It is virtually automatic that a species will be overfished if it is a public resource with no effective management system in place. As each fisherman or fishing fleet tries to maximize its catch, so do all the others. This leads to declining stocks and declining catches, which spiral downward and end in collapse. It is easy to blame this on "corporate greed" and other such scapegoats, but it is really the lack of any institutional framework for effective management that is to blame.

One of the most effective ways to overcome this tragedy is to establish a system of allocations known as individual tradable quotas (ITQs). Each fisherman buys or is granted a quota, allowing him or her to catch a certain

---

45. Bruce McClure, "Bush Seeks Expansion of Offshore Fish Farms," *Seattle Post-Intelligencer*, June 8, 2005, http://www.seattlepi.com/local/227623_fishfarms08.html

amount of a given species with a particular type of gear. The sum of the individual quotas is the allowable catch, which can be raised or lowered, affecting everyone's quota proportionally. The quotas can be bought and sold on the open market, so the healthier the stock the more value the quotas have. Therefore it is in every fisherman's interest to ensure that the stocks are healthy, and so they will support reductions in catch when necessary. Through private interest a self-policing system emerges that results in the opposite of the tragedy of the commons. It is the triumph of self-interest, transforming "greed" into "need."

The only problem with the ITQ system is that many so-called environmental groups, entrenched fishing interests, and leftist activists remain vehemently opposed to it. Even though there are well-established successful examples, such as the Alaskan salmon fishery and the Dungeness crab fishery, they object to the "privatization" of a public resource. They argue that because fish are a public resource all members of the public should have access to them and that ITQs amount to turning public property into a private monopoly. Certainly there are some good examples of socialism, like universal health care, but free-for-all fishing isn't one of them. Under the ITQ system, the public, through government, receives their rent from the fishermen through a royalty, some of which can be used to enhance the fishery. In the end, it is the seafood-consuming public that is the real beneficiary, certainly more so than if the species were wiped out through lack of effective management.

CHAPTER THIRTEEN

Round Tables and Square Pegs

Back to late 1989 at Quatsino Seafarms. I received a call from Lee Doney, then Deputy Minister of the Environment for British Columbia. He wanted to know if I would be interested in joining a new initiative, the B.C. Round Table on the Environment and the Economy. I was thrilled and jumped at the chance.

The United Nations report, *Our Common Future*, which had first publicized the concept of sustainable development five years after I heard it discussed in Nairobi, put forward two other important ideas. It suggested governments, at all levels from local to national, should appoint round tables, with representatives from all walks of life, to provide elected bodies with advice on how to achieve sustainability. The round tables would operate according to the principles of consensus, in other words, not by Robert's Rules, where a majority vote defeats a minority. In addition the report suggested that not enough land was protected from industrial development. The figure then was about 4 percent globally. The report advocated that it be tripled to 12 percent on the basis of representing the many varieties of ecosystems (forests, grasslands, wetlands, alpine regions, etc.).

The call from Lee Doney was like someone had read my mind during the five years I struggled with moving from confrontation to consensus. I felt lucky I was a Canadian because Canada took up the round table movement like no other country. This was due in large part to the fact that two Canadians were instrumental in producing the report. Maurice Strong, who had chaired the 1972 UN Conference on the Environment in Stockholm and would go on to chair the UN Environment Summit in Rio de Janeiro in 1992, was an influential member of the United Nations that produced the report . And Jim McNeil, a former deputy minister in the federal government, had written the report. Needless to say they had strong connections in Ottawa and Canadian society in general and they pressed their colleagues into making their recommendations a reality. By early 1990 the national government, all 10 provincial governments, and both territories had announced the formation of round tables on the environment and the economy. A short-lived revolution in Canadian political life had begun.

Following the publication of the Brundtland Report, as *Our Common Future* was also known, the former president of the University of British Columbia, David Strangway, was asked by the provincial government to write a report on the feasibility of establishing a round table to consider the issues around sustainability for British Columbia. His report formed the basis for our province's entry into the round table movement in Canada. CBC Radio News carried the B.C. government's announcement that a round table would be formed to our short-wave radio in Winter Harbour. They were looking for volunteers. I phoned the toll-free number and put my name in the hat.

By this time, in the summer of 1990, our little family-run salmon farm was foundering. Since we had begun in 1984, much had changed in the industry. Where there once had been a few pioneers with homemade equipment, there were now large corporations investing millions in state-of-the-art facilities. Where there had once been limited supply and high prices, there was now a lot of farmed salmon on the markets and prices fell steadily. And now the new farms were switching from growing Pacific chinook salmon to Atlantic salmon, a costlier investment, but a faster growing fish less susceptible to disease. Our profit margin shrunk until it went below the waterline.

None of us had much money, so we could not operate at a loss for a long period. The consolidation of the industry was just beginning as companies with deep pockets bought up smaller companies even though they were losing money, just to stay in the game. I could see the writing on the wall and realized we probably wouldn't make a go of it in the long run. Salmon farming had clearly become big business and that wasn't us.

The round table provided a perfect opportunity for me to begin the transition from salmon farming back into environmental work, only this time in the context of sustainability. Here was a chance to be around the same table with thinking people from all walks of life to discuss how we could balance the needs of the people with the needs of the environment. Unfortunately the environmental groups weren't quite as thrilled to get an invitation as I was. In all of British Columbia, the birthplace of Greenpeace, only two other people with green credentials agreed to join the process. One was Bob Peart, a member of the Canadian Parks and Wilderness Society, who turned out to be a very thoughtful participant and one who genuinely sought consensus. The other was Vicky Husband of the Sierra Club, a firebrand and no friend of the forest industry, nor any industry for that matter. She had joined reluctantly after much arm-twisting. The government needed to have an environmental activist on board and she had finally consented.

It turned out Vicky was one of the very few environmental activists in the whole of Canada to join the 13 round tables formed in 1990. Her reluctance to join was partly due to pressure from her colleagues to turn down the invitation. Not a single Greenpeace representative ever joined the effort, even though many were asked. For me, this confirmed my conclusion that activists in the environmental movement had become so insular that they chose to boycott the very process that could bring their ideas into the mainstream. But they didn't want to talk about sustainability or consensus, they wanted to continue to fight a war through the media, a war in which they were the good guys and their targets were branded as the enemies of the earth.

I joined in the meetings with enthusiasm. There were 30 of us, chosen from a wide range of professions and regions of the province. There were mayors and ex-mayors, labor leaders and business people, ranchers and foresters, tourist operators and fish farmers. Most of us were chosen because we had multiple perspectives, mine being environmental activism, aquaculture, and forestry. Chuck Connaghan, a seasoned labor/management negotiator, was appointed facilitator and Lee Doney was given the full-time job of heading our secretariat. Our budget exceeded $2 million, so we had the resources to pay for travel, per diems, and consultants. A new kind of think tank was born. We were a true citizens' group with real resources and access to the highest levels of decision making in our government.

There were not many published guides to running a round table with 30 different perspectives on sustainability. One book that helped us get oriented was *Getting to Yes.*"[46] In it Roger Fisher and William Ury present four principles for negotiating agreements:

- Separate the people from the problem.
- Focus on interests rather than positions.
- Generate a variety of options before settling on an agreement; and
- Insist that the agreement be based on objective criteria.

---

46. Roger Fisher and William Ury, *Getting to Yes: Negotiating Agreement Without Giving In* (New York: Penguin Books, 1983).

This approach influenced the entire round table, consensus-based movement in the early 1990s and provided a base from which to move forward.

We soon realized the scope of our task was enormous. We had been charged with developing sustainability policy recommendations for all aspects of society, the economy, and the environment. Needless to say it took us a while to get a sense of direction. Many of the early meetings were simply about discussing the meaning of sustainability and getting to know one another. There was a wide range of opinions and attitudes, which spanned the spectrum from very preservationist to outright capitalistic. The beauty of sustainability is that it allows for this wide range. There is a place for total preservation and a place for relatively unfettered commerce. There is a place for community and there is a place for globalization. There is a place for culture and for science.

But the other beauty of sustainability is that there is no place for misinformation, dishonesty, dogma, or prejudice. One must come to the table with an open mind, an honest demeanor, an interest in facts, and a willingness to try to understand diverse points of view. One-sided attitudes about people and politics don't fit with the effort to balance all points of view. People who come with hidden agendas and insincere motives are soon discovered, as the round table process is rigorous and thorough. This is why "politicos" don't like the process. They have an ideological approach to the world and they already know who is right and who is wrong. They aren't there to learn from other perspectives but only to push their own narrow agendas. In the end they are boring.

The intellectual stimulation of the round table proved infectious. Nearly all of us were excited by the exchanges and the conversations and the debates. Almost miraculously, within six months, members with disparate interests bonded: we came to like people with whom we had intense philosophical and political differences. We realized political differences were partly about social separation and the context of our daily lives. When we were forced to sit opposite one another and experience one another's points of view first hand, we developed an empathy that hadn't existed before. Heaven help us, we "understood" one another better.

It wasn't as if there weren't irreconcilable differences among some of our members. But at least we could separate the person from the problem and begin to focus on interests rather than positions. Just learning to speak to the "other side" in a civil manner made all the difference in the world.

The main result of our deliberations was a series of documents on various aspects of sustainability and the consensus process. We covered sustainable transportation, urban design, energy, education for sustainability, and wrote our own version of how to get to yes. The latter involved a series of case histories of previous successful resolutions to difficult conflicts in B.C. and other regions of Canada.

We published a guide explaining how local round tables could be set up and operated. I chaired this committee. As a result I developed a keen interest in the role of the facilitator in round table procedure. A facilitator takes the place of the traditional chairperson, playing a very different role with a different set of skills.

Here is an excerpt from an essay I wrote some years later titled "From Confrontation to Consensus"

Consensus process is not a rigid, rules-based, system such as Robert's Rules that govern directors meetings and the like. But it is not a free-for-all either. The dialogue must be structured in such a way as to achieve an understanding of each other's points of view among all the participants. This can only be achieved if certain principles and methods are adopted and adhered to.

First and foremost, it is important that a professional facilitator, who understands the nature of consensus and has had experience with it, is retained to help guide the process. The facilitator is not "in charge" like a chairperson but rather provides a service function, helping to steer the group towards mutual understanding.

Second, and just as foremost, *consensus process does not mean unanimous agreement about everything*. While it may be nice to think about an ideal or theoretical definition of consensus meaning perfect harmony, in practical terms this is never possible. The practical definition of consensus must recognize there will always be differences of opinion and therefore differences in the position taken by various participants in the Round Table process. This is where the talent of the professional facilitator is needed.

The job of the facilitator, in the final analysis, is to help the Round Table produce a consensus document, which expresses the areas of unanimous agreement among the participants, and where there is not unanimous agreement, an expression of the disagreement in words unanimously agreed to by all the participants.

The above definition of consensus can usually be achieved, providing the facilitator is capable and the participants are genuine in their desire to reach agreement.

Round Tables are not a substitute for government. They don't make policy like the Fijian elders; they provide policy advice to democratically elected bodies, whether these are national, state/provincial, or local. For this reason it is not usually appropriate for Round Tables to be ad hoc (self-constituted) in nature. It is usually best if Round Tables are appointed by, and answerable to, a democratically elected body that is in a position to make decisions based on the Round Table's advice.

There are many variations on this theme. For example, if a private company wants to foster the creation of a Round Table to consider an industrial proposal, it can do so by working with the appropriate level of government. If an environmental group wants to employ the Round Table process to focus attention on a development it believes is harming the environment, it can also do so by working with the appropriate elected body.

It is nearly always desirable that the appropriate elected body be responsible for determining or approving the terms of reference, appointing the members, and appointing the facilitator for the Round Table. Then the Round Table is consultative to, and answerable to, the democratic system. Private sector proponents can fund local Round Tables, providing they do not control the membership or direction of the process. This creates a situation where the credibility of the process is in the hands of elected government. If the government body loses confidence in the process, it can be disbanded.

The membership of a Round Table has an initial meeting with the appointed facilitator in order to review the terms of reference and to provide any feedback to the conveners of the process, such as the elected government that appointed it. At this stage the members must be satisfied all legitimate interests have been included in the make-up of the Round Table. If they think additional members are required they must indicate this. Also, the members must be satisfied with the terms of reference; that they are not too limited in scope but also not too open-ended. All members must agree at the outset that no interest group is missing and the terms of reference are correct. A good facilitator can usually help the group reach consensus on these two points. If new members need to be appointed it is up to the facilitator to go to the authority and convince them to do so. The principle is that the Round Table must be inclusive, excluding no legitimate or even possibly legitimate interest. Beginning with these basic issues, if all members of the Round Table agree to the membership and terms of reference they have already reached consensus on important points. The process has begun!

Once the Round Table is comfortable with its membership and mandate, it can move on to the next stage, the identification of issues and concerns. Issues are real points of substance that most members agree are important to the dispute or task at hand. Concerns are like worries, not always accepted by a majority of the members, but they must be given consideration even if only one member has the concern.

The process of identifying issues and concerns begins to allow the members to stop stating their positions, and to identify the reasons why they hold those positions. Instead of saying, "I am against the uranium mine", they are asked to say why, such as "uranium mining may cause water pollution". The process of identifying issues and concerns should be an exhaustive one; no stone should be left unturned. Even after all issues and concerns have been identified, this agenda item should be

CONFESSIONS OF A GREENPEACE DROPOUT

left open throughout the process, for additions if necessary. As a general rule in consensus process, the agenda should always be open to make it clear nothing has been cut off from discussion.

The issues and concerns should then be listed in some logical or methodical way. Sometimes a group of issues will come under a single general heading. The identification of issues and concerns will usually require two or three full meetings.

Then begins the process of working through the issues one at a time. For each issue, a process for information gathering is determined. Documents, maps, and experts are identified. All members of the Round Table should be able to put any information before the group and should be able to suggest experts who might shed light on the issue. This often requires a budget for bringing people to the table. In addition, it is often beneficial to go on field trips to see the location(s) involved in the dispute or discussion. For each issue or concern, all members should be satisfied the information-gathering phase has been sufficiently exhaustive and all relevant information is now before them.

The next stage involves the facilitator's attempt to help find common ground on as many issues and concerns as possible. It is quite usual for the Round Table to reach unanimous agreement around many issues. In the case of a uranium mine, for example, it is likely the statement "Occupational exposure to radiation must be strictly monitored and controlled" would be unanimously adopted. But other statements, such as "Uranium mining should be banned in this country", will likely not find unanimous support.

At this point the facilitator's most important task is at hand. The facilitator must draft a document, outlining the nature of agreement or disagreement for each issue and concern, finding wording that is accepted unanimously by the Round Table members. This means producing a document expressing clearly where there is unanimous agreement, and where there is disagreement, a description of the nature of the disagreement(s) in words unanimously accepted by the members.

Thus, a consensus document can be produced even though there is disagreement on some points. The great benefit of this process is it provides the actual policy-makers, government, with a very clear expression of public opinion. Compared to the war of headlines in the media that often characterizes land use and other resource issues, the Round Table approach brings clarity and coherence to the forefront of the debate.

The Consensus Document should then be distributed widely in the community, and formally presented, in person, to the level(s) of government involved in decision-making. Then it is up to the political process to make decisions that bring public policy more in line with the round table's advice. It is a very powerful tool because it is difficult for governments to ignore a clearly stated set of recommendations where everyone has agreed with the language.[47]

We would find out later this is one of the reasons governments don't always like round tables, sometimes they cast too much light on the subject.

Global Warming: The Early Years

In the autumn of 1989, the B.C. government published a paper reporting on the amount of carbon dioxide being emitted from various industries and sectors in the province. This was early on in the province's discussion of climate change and this was an important inventory as it provided a baseline for consideration of policies that might reduce greenhouse gas emissions. The report indicated that the forest industry was the largest emitter of carbon dioxide, followed by the transportation sector, heavy industry, and commercial and residential buildings. I studied the report and soon realized the forest industry was being unfairly used as a whipping boy. It had become a kind of national sport to attack the evil tree killers at every opportunity and here was another example of how they were messing up the environment.

Upon careful reading it became clear that most of the carbon dioxide emitted by the forest industry was from burning waste wood, bark, and biomass in sawmill and pulp mill operations. In other words, the industry was using renewable energy rather than fossil fuel. This prompted me to do two things. First I wrote an essay titled "Are All Carbon Atoms Created Equal?" in which I made the case that carbon dioxide from renewable fuels (biomass) should be treated differently from carbon dioxide from burning fossil fuels, even though they are chemically identical.[48] This is because biomass fuels are part of a cycle of carbon dioxide first absorbed by plants, in this case trees, then released by combustion, and then absorbed again by new growing trees. There is no cycle with fossil fuel combustion. Fossil fuels are a one-way trip taking carbon that was stored in the ground for millions of years and releasing it into the atmosphere as carbon dioxide. This concept of distinguishing between CO_2 from renewable fuels versus nonrenewable fuels has since been accepted by the international community of climate scientists and has been incorporated into the Kyoto Climate Change Treaty and the Intergovernmental Panel on Climate Change policy.

Second, I paid a visit to Ray Smith, a friend of my dad's and the president of MacMillan Bloedel, which was then B.C.'s largest forest company.

47. Patrick Moore, "From Confrontation to Consensus," April 1998, http://www.greenspirit.com/key_issues.cfm?msid=32
48. Patrick Moore, "Are All Carbon Atoms Created Equal?" October 19, 1991,
http://www.beattystreetpublishing.com/confessions/references/are-carbon-atoms-equal

I explained to Ray how the greenhouse gas inventory unfairly targeted the forest sector as the worst culprit. I also explained that the defense coming from spokespeople for the forest industry was just as misleading and off the mark. It had become standard practice among foresters to claim it was good to cut the old forest down and plant new trees because young trees were growing and absorbing more carbon dioxide than old trees that had stopped growing. While this is true, it is only half the story because when you cut trees down much of their stored carbon gets released in the form of carbon dioxide. In balance, forestry is close to neutral, but it can be a net carbon dioxide emitter (source) and it can be a net carbon dioxide absorber (sink). No matter what, forestry is far more in balance than fossil fuel combustion. But the industry wasn't doing itself any favors by painting a rosier picture than it deserved. Ray took all this in and agreed it would be useful to create an initiative aimed at getting a better understanding of the carbon cycle, especially as it applied to the forest industry. He introduced me to his vice-president for research, Dr. Otto Forgacs. We got along famously.

Otto and I developed a plan and applied to the British Columbia Science Council for funding for research and meetings. We succeeded in bringing together, into regular round table meetings, all the significant emitters and regulators of greenhouse gases in the province as well as the hydro-electric utility and a representative from Greenpeace. We called our group the BC Carbon Project. Its aim was to develop a common understanding among all parties of the role each played and could play in greenhouse gas emissions reductions. We commissioned an independent review of the relationship between forest management and greenhouse gas emissions, which was eventually tabled with the provincial government and all other interest groups. We established clearly that biomass energy was in a different category from fossil fuels and that it was transportation, moving people and goods, which accounted for the highest carbon emissions.

War in the Woods

About six months after I was appointed to the B.C. Round Table on the Environment and the Economy, I received another phone call, this time an unsolicited one. It was Jack Munro, president of the forest worker's union, and he had an invitation for me. At the time it seemed harmless enough. He wanted me to join a new citizens' group, the Forest Alliance of B.C., which was being formed by the major forest industry companies in British Columbia to help them with their environmental issues, which included public concerns about clearcutting and old-growth forests. This was an initiative of the CEOs and they had asked Jack, a career labor union leader, to chair the citizens' group. Jack had a reputation for being a tough negotiator, but he was also the kind of union guy who would share a meal with the bosses. Over time he had proven to be pragmatic rather than just "hard left" as were many of his contemporaries and rivals in the union movement.

Jack explained that forest companies were concerned about the negative publicity they were receiving from environmental groups in B.C. Collectively polls showed that only 34 percent of the province's public believed companies were doing a good job of protecting the environment. That was quite a condemnation in a province that was responsible for half of Canada's forestry production, which amounted to about US$12 billion per year. And there was a growing threat from large export markets, Germany and the U.K., in particular, that they would boycott B.C. forest products. North American environmental groups such as Greenpeace, the Sierra Club, and the Rainforest Action Network were fueling this campaign.

Ninety-five percent of the commercial forestland in B.C. is Crown land, meaning land that is publicly owned and therefore controlled by the provincial government. Unlike in the U.S., where most public land is federally owned, in Canada public land is nearly all provincially owned. The forest companies operate under various forms of license, giving them the right to cut timber in approved areas in return for paying a royalty, called "stumpage," to the government. This worked fine until there were accusations of bad forestry practices. The companies quickly pointed out that the government had approved all the forestry plans so that was where responsibility rested. The government became very good at deflecting attention to the companies: after all they were the ones cutting the trees. Government promised to crack down on offenders and the environmental groups were happy to attack the companies in the name of corporate greed and environmental destruction. The War in the Woods was to define environmental politics and, to a large measure, politics in general, during the 1990s in B.C.

The industry initially reacted like a deer caught in the headlights. Its leaders could not understand why none of the existing mechanisms, such as its own communications and public relations departments, the industry associations, or even the government, could get a handle on deteriorating public perception. A group of industry CEOs began to meet informally to discuss their growing dilemma. They hired the Canadian office of one of the world's largest public relations companies, New York–based Burson-Marsteller, to advise them on strategy. Its advice was to create a citizen's advisory board, modeled after the chemical industry's Responsible Care program, which had helped that sector with its environmental issues. So Jack Munro and the CEOs began to draft prominent citizens from all walks of life across the province. The only interests they didn't invite were the activists who were campaigning to boycott the industry. In that sense the Forest Alliance was not a true round table; not all interests were to be included. Yet it was a kind of hybrid in that most of the members were

CONFESSIONS OF A GREENPEACE DROPOUT

non-forestry industry people and the group was to operate independently of the companies and to provide them with recommendations.

Not only was I personally intrigued by the project, my family's 75 years in the forestry business compelled me to lend a hand. Here was an opportunity to apply the knowledge I had gained in the environmental movement in assisting the industry my grandfather and father had been involved in all their lives. My dad had worked very hard to improve the image of the working people who were now being accused of "rape" and "desecration" of nature, the very people who provide us with the wood to build our homes and the paper to make our books. And Jack Munro was a close friend of my father's: they sat on various labor-management boards together and saw eye-to-eye on worker safety and the need for fair wages. I accepted Jack's invitation with enthusiasm. My wife, Eileen, said it would cost us dearly with regard to our environmentally oriented friends. She was right.

During the four years since I had left Greenpeace, there had not been much public notice of my new direction. My role as president of the B.C. Salmon Farmers Association had brought me into some conflict with environmental groups but the anti-salmon farming campaign was still pretty low-key at that time. My membership on the B.C. Round Table was mainstream enough. But I was not prepared for the firestorm of public and private invective that followed my acceptance to be one of 30 directors of the Forest Alliance.

And that wasn't the only problem. Even before we had our first meeting, the newspapers were full of exposé-style articles about the new initiative, especially about the fact that Burson-Marsteller had been hired as the public relations advisor. Much was made of allegations Burson had advised various notorious and nefarious polluters, military dictatorships, and other bad actors in the past. In particular the media alleged that the firm had given counsel to the Argentinean military junta during the time 30,000 people disappeared, many of them having been thrown out of helicopters into the sea. It turned out Burson had been retained by Argentina's Ministry of the Economy to advise them on how to attract more foreign investment. One of the key recommendations Burson offered was that it would be easier to attract investors if the killing stopped. This detail was lost on the left-wing media types who continued with their feeding frenzy despite the facts. Ironically our public relations advisor had become our worst public relations problem before we even sat down.

When we did get together in June of 1991 it was to a pretty rocky start. Jack Munro's style was somewhat heavy-handed for some of the recruits. He was fond of saying that we weren't going to operate by Robert's Rules, we were working under Jack's Rules. He was a fairly benevolent dictator, a bit of a diamond in the rough, something one might expect from a man who had worked his way up from being a blacksmith in a railyard to becoming the leader of one of Canada's biggest workers' unions. It didn't take too many meetings until we got used to Jack's tough-talking yet jovial nature.

Early on some of us felt that the citizen's board needed to be independent and not just window dressing controlled by Burson and the forest companies. In this I found an ally in Dan Johnston, an experienced young lawyer who specialized in mediation and understood how to structure organizations. We agreed that the Forest Alliance should become a formal nonprofit organization, constituted under the BC Society Act, rather than remaining an ad hoc committee. In other words, we took control of our destiny, insisting we direct our own budget and policy. After all we had been assembled to help the forest industry and we wouldn't be much use if it were obvious we had no authority or independence. At first this rankled some of the CEOs and Burson folks, but in the end it proved to be the right model. The companies deposited their financial contributions into our bank account and we decided what to do with them. With an annual operating budget of about $2 million, we managed to accomplish a great deal in the following years.

We were immediately faced with some difficult issues. Partly due to the public's dissatisfaction with the forest industry, the probusiness government was defeated in 1991 elections by the socialist New Democratic Party. The party pledged to crack down on the corporations just as we were getting up and running. In particular the new government planned to enact legislation to control forestry practices. The forest companies opposed a legislated Forest Practices Code, arguing that it should be voluntary. Our first useful piece of advice to the companies was that they should accept the idea of a legislated code and they should become actively involved in providing input as to what it required of them. The public viewed the industry too negatively to accept that the companies would do the right thing voluntarily. The companies took our advice and we began the process of defining sustainable forestry. We had begun to help the industry to get out in front of the environmental agenda.

Many people in the forest industry believed they had a public relations problem; if only they could explain the situation to the uninformed citizens everything would be put right. We told them categorically, "It's not what you're saying that's the problem, it's what you're doing." In other words this isn't a communications problem, it's a performance problem. The public simply didn't like the way the forests were being managed; in particular, it didn't accept vast clearcuts from one mountaintop to another. For me this was an opportunity to help do what I knew was needed, to bring forest practices out of the old ways into a style that recognized sustainability, biodiversity, and environmental values. It was like Greenpeace all over again, only this time my old colleagues were on the other side. That's because Greenpeace and their allies were fundamentally against industrial forestry, believing in some kind of ecoforestry that didn't involve cutting many, or any, trees. Certainly not enough to provide housing, furniture, printing paper, packaging, and sanitation for everyone. I felt I was finally finding the balance.

Another key issue in the early 1990s was the proposal to increase the amount of land, forested land in particular, which was permanently protected as parks and wilderness. A movement had developed, led by the Valhalla Wilderness Society, and supported by the Parks Branch of the government, to double the protected area of the province from the existing 6 percent to the Brundtland Commission's recommended 12 percent, which was triple the 4 percent protected globally at the time. This would result in a considerable loss for the forest industry because much of the area proposed for new parks was commercially valuable forest land. Predictably the companies opposed the proposal. We convinced them otherwise.

Our reasoning was quite clear. The 6 percent of the province originally set aside for parks and wilderness was largely what the environmental community referred to as "rocks and ice." Proportionally little commercially valuable forested land was included and the existing protected area was certainly not representative of the many and varied ecosystems in the province. This was understandable, as the term *ecosystem* didn't exist in the early 1900s when these parks were created, mainly for their scenic splendor rather than anything to do with ecology or biodiversity. Back then it simply didn't make sense to "protect" land that had economic potential. How times change.

We were able to convince the forestry companies that doubling the area of parks and wilderness was a good idea for two reasons. First, even though it would mean a one-time loss for the forest industry it would be a good thing for the province in general to have a world-class protected area system for tourism and future generations. Second, rather than kicking and screaming through what might be an inevitable process it made sense for the industry to agree to the concept of doubling the parks because they might then get some say in which areas would be protected and which would remain available for forestry. They agreed with us and now we were really out in front of the agenda. The next 10 years would see the Forest Alliance effectively help the industry become a more progressive element in British Columbia society.

We had succeeded in helping the forest industry to engage with the government and the public on the two most important issues, forest practices and protected areas. Many of the companies now began to play active roles, assigning their chief foresters to participate in the Forest Alliance and to work with government agencies to define sustainable forestry and to delineate new areas for parks and wilderness. By the mid-1990s the Forest Practices Code was enacted and the process of doubling the parks was well under way. By 2000 British Columbia could boast of having one of the best and most representative system of parks and wilderness areas in the world. This was done with a lot less pain to the forest industry than if it had remained opposed to moving forward. There was certainly a reduction in employment due to the loss of land base but much of this was due to mechanization, a factor that has had an impact in all industries as new technologies make it possible to produce more with less labor. In the balance we helped to cushion the social and economic blows while assisting with some desirable, and inevitable, environmental advances.

None of this came easily. The entire time we were trying to steer the forest industry onto a more sustainable path they were being assailed by local, national, and international environmental groups accusing them of crimes against the planet. Apparently the people who used wood to build their homes, print their books and magazines, and wipe their bottoms were not to blame. It was the loggers and most particularly the multinational forest corporations who employed them who were the real evildoers, according to activist theory. So our job in the Forest Alliance was not just to help bring the industry into the environmental age. We had to explain to members of the public that they were the ones using the forest products, and that trees and the wood they produce are the most abundant renewable materials on this earth. Nothing else even comes close. Ironically, the fact that trees are living organisms leads people to have sympathy for them while they have no such feelings for nonrenewable resources like steel, plastic, and concrete. This emotional aspect of the anti-forestry movement is not easily approached with logical arguments. And one wonders why the general public doesn't have the same emotional reaction to the plants and animals we kill for food every day as it does to trees. Never mind the fact that most of our food is grown where forests have been cleared for farming. If there is an enemy of trees, it is farmers, not foresters. No one promised a logical situation and we certainly weren't faced with one.

While our job description was to help industry improve its environmental performance, this proved relatively easy compared to the challenge of convincing the public that forestry is a worthy occupation in the first place. Greenpeace, the Sierra Club, the Rainforest Action Network, and even the usually more temperate World Wildlife Fund gave the impression that forestry was a morally questionable activity. The same tone continues to this day and has been responsible for environmental groups receiving hundreds of millions of dollars in revenue, donations from individuals and foundations that believe there is something fundamentally wrong with cutting trees while they continue to consume products made from wood every day. Forestry provides one of the most perfect examples of hypocritical political correctness, preaching against using the most abundant renewable resource while at the same time telling people to use more renewable resources. There is no shortage of examples on this point.

Despite the vociferous and sometimes angry campaign against forestry, the Forest Alliance proved to be a very successful model. I believe it succeeded because it promoted a reasonable balance among the competing interests: more protected areas, better forest practices, economic development for families and communities, and the utilization and renewal of an ecosystem with a miraculous range of uses, from wildlife to lumber to paper to fuelwood to carbon fixation to cleansing air and water. In the end the single-use, narrow visions of forests as being either only for industry or only for preservation lost out to an approach that recognized the multifaceted nature of sustainability. When the Forest Alliance was founded only 34 percent of British Columbians agreed that the forests were being properly managed. When we wound down 10 years later that figure was 75 percent, a strong testament to the power of the round table, consensus-based model of working toward win-win solutions. Winston Churchill said, "democracy is the worst form of government except for all the others." For me, the round table, multi-stakeholder, consensus process is not perfect, just better than all the other approaches to resolving environmental and resource-use conflicts.

While I continued with the Forest Alliance until its winding down 2001, the B.C. Round Table on the Environment and the Economy did not fare so well. When the socialist New Democratic Party swept the provincial election in 1991, less than two years after we were commissioned, many of us on the round table assumed the new government would support a citizen's group working on sustainability and the environment. This was not to be the case.

The environmental movement had a strong contingent within the New Democrats. They didn't like the round table because they thought it was a place were the environment was being compromised on the altar of the economy and other unsavory considerations. The socialist politicians had the incorrect impression that the round table was a creature of the previous center-right government when it was in fact part of an international movement. The bureaucrats didn't like the round table because it knew too much and presumed to give policy advice to politicians. Bureaucrats easily forget that their job is to carry out policy, not to make it. The new government slowly killed us, eventually sending two cabinet ministers dressed in oversized suits to announce our demise. It was a classic case of small minds destroying something much larger than themselves. I think they secretly feared us; I know I fear them and the repression of intellect and reason they represent.

With the round table behind me and the BC Carbon Project wrapping up, my time was now largely taken up with work for the Forest Alliance. I was appointed chair of the Sustainable Forestry Committee, which was charged with developing Principles of Sustainable Forestry. I had an excellent group of practicing foresters and academics on my committee, including forest ecologist Hamish Kimmins, who had been the head of my PhD thesis committee over 20 years earlier. Our task was to create a set of principles, covering all aspects of forestry and the environment, which could be signed in public by the CEOs. It would then be our job to receive regular reports on progress toward compliance with the principles. It took six months of intensive meetings to arrive at the following set of principles:

Environment

- Roads should not be built where there is a risk of severe soil erosion. Where roads are built they must be up to standards that will ensure long-term erosion control. Temporary roads should be removed to provide more space for growing trees. Harvesting methods, such as skyline cable systems and helicopter logging, that reduce the area disturbed by roads should be used wherever practical.
- Logging operations must be planned on the basis of watersheds. The clearing of excessive areas within a given watershed can lead to flooding, soil erosion, and damage to fish-bearing streams and rivers.
- Fish habitat must be protected through careful planning along waterways. Buffer strips of forest should be maintained on major streams and rivers to maintain stream bank stability, provide shade, and maintain water quality.
- Wildlife habitat must be protected by ensuring that critical features such as deer winter range, bird nesting trees, and woody debris are provided.
- Biological diversity in its totality must be protected by ensuring that representative areas of all successional stages, including old-growth or original forest, are present in each forest ecosystem.
- The forest industry's contribution to greenhouse gas emissions, and hence to the potential for climate change, should be minimized through energy efficiency, wildfire control, soil conservation, and rapid reforestation of harvested land.

Forestry

- Government and industry must ensure there are up-to-date and accurate inventories of all forest resources on which to base forest management plans and to determine sustainable harvest levels.
- Care must be taken to use harvesting practices and equipment that minimize soil disturbance and damage to the remaining vegetation and wildlife habitat.

- Where some form of clearcutting is determined to be an appropriate harvesting practice it must be done in a manner that satisfies all the other Principles of Sustainable Forestry. Other harvesting systems, such as selection and partial cutting, should be used where they are appropriate from a silvicultural perspective.
- All commercially valuable wood that is cut during logging operations should be utilized to avoid economic waste. This must be balanced with the need to leave sufficient woody debris and organic matter to provide wildlife habitat and nutrients for the next generation of trees.
- All logged areas should be rapidly reforested either by natural regeneration or by planting with appropriate species. Forest practices such as brushing and thinning should be employed to ensure the survival of the new forest and to improve the quality of wood production.
- The use of conventional chemical pesticides must be minimized by employing alternative methods of pest and weed control wherever practical and environmentally sound.
- Burning must be carefully prescribed and used only where it is necessary to ensure reforestation, prevent wildfires, and improve wildlife habitat.

Other Commercial Values

- Other commercial uses of the forest must be protected and taken into account when planning logging operations. These values include tourism, livestock grazing, hunting, fishing, trapping, honey production, and berry, mushroom, and foliage picking.

Public Involvement and Recreation

- Local communities must be directly involved in decisions that affect their stability, employment, economic viability, and quality of life.
- Communities and individuals have a right to access information, to be involved in forest planning, and to monitor industrial performance.
- Forests should be managed with concern for recreational use by the public. This includes the appearance of roadsides and harvested areas and assistance in providing campsites, picnic areas, boat ramps, and trails.
- Visual impact should be taken into consideration when planning logging operations near communities, recreation areas, and along major travel corridors.

- Environmentally appropriate practices, such as recycling, waste oil recovery, solid waste reduction and management, energy efficiency, pollution control, the appearance of industrial sites, and a positive attitude toward environmental programs, must be incorporated in all forest industry operations.

Research and Monitoring

- Research and development programs must be undertaken to increase knowledge of forest management, to generate more value-added products, and to protect the environment.
- There must be an independent forest practices monitoring system that reports its findings to industry and the public.

The Principles of Sustainable Forestry were signed by 13 industry CEOs at a public media conference on February 28, 1992, in Vancouver. This represented well over 90 percent of the forest industry in B.C. Over the next five years a tremendous amount of work was done to bring the companies policies in line with the principles. Today all these points are virtually taken for granted and are considered standard operating procedure. The Forest Alliance taught me real progress could be made, and relatively quickly, when well-meaning people roll up their sleeves and work to get the job done. Just as we did to stop the hydrogen bomb tests in the early years of Greenpeace!

In 1991 I had been recruited into my first environmental consulting job by the architect and planner, Arnie Fullerton, who was working with the chemist Ron Woznow, who had recently been appointed head of the newly established BC Hazardous Waste Commission. Arnie and I were tasked with making recommendations for the collection of toxic wastes and the establishment of treatment facilities. The reaction from environmental groups, including Greenpeace, was that there shouldn't be any toxic waste and therefore that it was not necessary to have treatment facilities and that if we did attempt to build any they would try to stop us. It was clear they weren't seeking solutions and were determined to make it very difficult for anyone who was.

Around this time an old acquaintance of mine, businessman Ross McDonald, got in touch with me to talk about how he could become involved in environmental issues. He encouraged me to join him in forming a new initiative and asked me what an appropriate name for such a venture might be. I came up with Greenspirit in late 1991 and have operated under that banner ever since. The *green* allowed me to keep the green in Greenpeace, where I had campaigned for years, and the *spirit* had a double meaning: it reflects both the spiritual side of ecology—we're all one—and the feeling of team spirit as in a sports contest. Ross and Arnie and I formed an informal partnership, rented office space in downtown Vancouver, and worked to find projects we could all be involved in. It never really gelled but we learned a lot from one another before gradually drifting our separate ways. But Greenspirit was born!

My work with the Forest Alliance was already under way and I was gaining other clients who were eager to join the movement for sustainability and corporate responsibility. I soon became the senior consultant and lead spokesperson for the Forest Alliance, reporting at first to Jack Munro and then to Tom Tevlin, who had been hired from Burson-Marsteller to be the executive director of the group. Tom and I have had a close professional relationship ever since. I reported to him as a consultant, and he reported to the Forest Alliance Board, of which I was the most active member. We developed a strong partnership during the 10 years of Forest Alliance work. Then in 2001, along with our colleague, Trevor Figueiredo, we incorporated Greenspirit Strategies Ltd. to offer advice to government and industry on the wide range of issues encompassed by environment and sustainability. We leased an office in the old warehouse district of Yaletown in downtown Vancouver, and continue working there today.

In the autumn of 1992, the World Wildlife Fund published a thick document titled "Forests in Trouble," which gave its view of the "crisis" facing the world's forests.[49] It contained a section on Canada, which was entirely about British Columbia and which repeated many of the false claims being spread by the anti-forestry campaign. This was at the height of the effort by activists to orchestrate a boycott of B.C. forest products in Europe, a boycott focused largely in Germany and the U.K. It appeared the report's author, Nigel Dudley, had simply interviewed the anti-forestry folks in B.C. and had neglected to check any of his "facts" with the relevant government agencies or with the industry associations. For example, the paper claimed the rate of timber harvesting was increasing when, in fact, it had been falling for the past three years and everyone knew it would continue to fall. The report stated all the old-growth forest would be gone in 15 years. That was nearly 20 years ago and there are nearly 100 million acres of original forest remaining in the province today.

We made a public fuss about the sloppy nature of the report, which was all the more damaging because it had been published by the well-respected WWF. They responded by offering us a meeting with the head of their Canadian organization, Monte Hummel, with whom I had become acquainted during the Greenpeace campaign against trophy hunting. I attended along with Jack Munro and Tom Tevlin for the Forest Alliance; WWF was represented by Monte and his chairman, Adam Zimmerman,

---

49. Nigel Dudley, "Forests in Trouble: A Review of the Status of Temperate Forests Worldwide," WWF International, September 2002, http://www.equilibriumresearch.com/upload/document/forestsintroubleexsum.pdf

then president of Noranda, one of Canada's largest companies and the majority owner of MacMillan Bloedel, B.C.'s largest forest company. The meeting began cordially but soon turned sour as we presented our complaints, about 40 of them, set out clearly in point form. I guess the old Greenpeace campaigner came out in me, as I was more aggressive than diplomacy of this nature called for. Monte became offended and at the end of the meeting, when I offered to buy him a beer, he said that would be a cold day in hell. The meeting broke up and the Forest Alliance contingent invited Adam Zimmerman, a long-time friend of Jack Munro, for a beer and debriefing in the hotel lounge.

Realizing this was a somewhat historic occasion I phoned my old pal Bob Hunter to see if he could join us. Adam Zimmerman, now retired, is one of those rare examples of a senior corporate executive who is also a genuine intellectual. He wrote about sustainable development and how it applied to resource industries like forestry long before it became fashionable for companies to issue annual Sustainability Reports. And Jack Munro, more labor populist than intellectual, is equally comfortable with his Harley Davidson–riding crowd and sipping tea with the Queen of England. Bob Hunter arrived to see his old Greenpeace buddy Pat sitting with the president of the biggest forest company in the country and the former head of the largest forest worker's union in North America. I didn't realize it at the time as the conversation was quite good-humored, but Bob went away from the gathering convinced that I had sold my soul to the devil. He promptly commenced writing a six-part series in the *North Shore News*, a local Vancouver weekly paper in which Bob had maintained a regular column during the years since he left Vancouver for Toronto. It was a scathing personal attack and there was no one in our circles who didn't read every installment.

Bob reflected the mood of the environmental movement and much of the public at the time: the forest industry represented all that was evil in the corporate world. Rape, pillage, plunder, devastation, loss of virginity and innocence—these words were all used to denounce the tree-cutters and the providers of wood and paper. It was in these columns that I was described as an "eco-Judas." In his inimitable talent for coming up with clever phrases Bob accused me of "schlepping for the stumpmakers." In the aftermath about half my friends disowned me, buying into Bob's claim that I was a sellout and a traitor to the cause. It's amazing how fickle some friends are. While I spent 15 years on the frontlines of the movement living on a subsistence income, some of my doctor and lawyer friends were bringing in six figures, cheering me on all the way. They were generous with their time, volunteering on many occasions. But they didn't dedicate the best years of their lives to the movement. Many of them fit the description "millionaire socialists" as they were all for the underdogs in society, even though they were decidedly not among them. Our lawyer friend,

Me posing in front of a 100-year-old second-growth Sitka spruce tree on our land in Winter Harbour. You have to live in the rain forest for half a lifetime to appreciate the cycles of disturbance and growth.

the late David Gibbons, denounced me as a "quisling," not a nice thing to call a guy.

In retrospect I believe they were upset because I was no longer serving *their* ideological ambitions, no longer living out their fantasy of how to save the planet. How dare I decide to carve out a future focused on how I see the world rather than doing their bidding for the rest of my life?

It's funny how a single event can shape the rest of your life. I had thought my discovering the science of ecology and then my conversion to sustainable development had been the major turning points in my personal evolution. But it was the trial-by-fire of public humiliation that really made me take a stand for what I believed in. I didn't care how many insults were hurled my way; I knew sustainable forestry was not only possible but also essential to balancing the needs of civilization with the protection of the environment. I realized it was my old friend Bob and many other good and not-so-good friends who were barking up the wrong tree. But in this case their bark took a real bite out of my reputation. I entered a period of wholesale shunning by the environmental community and its friends in the media.

Shortly before he died, Bob Hunter offered me a prolific apology over a few glasses of wine in my kitchen in Vancouver. This was witnessed by my wife, Eileen, and by my then eco-warrior buddy, Rex Weyler. Bob realized that he had made the mistake of attacking the person rather than debating the issue. *My rule–put family and friends above politics.*

None of this daunted me. I was determined to do what I knew was right. I really had no choice. I either caved in to people who I did not agree with or I followed my conscience. I knew it would be a long struggle because so many environmentalists, and so many people who lived in cities, had already made up their minds on the subject. Indeed nearly 10 years would pass before I could claim to be vindicated in my beliefs. During those 10 years, from the early 1990s to the early 2000s, I endured attack after attack, usually in the form of name-calling. The media made a willing conduit for this style of assault, repeating the "eco-Judas" slur time after time. If I thought I had developed a thick skin during my time with Greenpeace, that was nothing compared to the hide I developed during these years. It culminated in 1996 with the launch of the "Patrick Moore is a Big Fat Liar" website by the Forest Action Network, a band of anti-forestry campaigners who thought nothing of using misinformation and distortion to further their cause. They published what they claimed to be my "Ten Top Lies." Realizing it is possible to get away with saying nearly anything on the Internet, I seriously considered suing for libel but then, instead, published "Patrick Moore is Not a Big Fat Liar" on my own website.[50] Over the years people who read the material on both websites get a pretty good idea of my position. So in a way the name-callers did me a favor. It's always gratifying when you can use your critics words to your own advantage.

In retrospect the anti-forestry campaign was the beginning of a trend in the environmental movement that targets the people who produce the material, food, and energy for all of us. This pits the vast number of people who live in urban environments against the very people who work hard in the country to provide the essentials of civilized life. The irony of this is that the very people who demand the food, energy and materials to support their urban lifestyles are the people who accuse their providers of raping the earth. It is a modern version of Aesop's Fable "The City Mouse and the Country Mouse," only today the city mice are in a huge majority and control the major media outlets. They can usually drown out the protestations of loggers, farmers, miners, energy producers, and fisher folk. They bite the hand that feeds them. It is time to change that pattern and to give the people who do the hard work in the hot sun and driving rain their due.

On a dark and rainy morning in December 1992, Eileen and I were awakened by a crashing sound outside our front door. Upon going downstairs to investigate Eileen hollered up that I had better come down and take a look. Someone had dumped eight giant garbage bags of horse manure on our front porch and steps. A note was left with "Tree Killer" scribbled on it. It wasn't a pretty sight or smell.

Eileen did not want the embarrassment of our neighbors noticing 400 pounds of horse crap on our porch. I quickly dressed and went out into the

---

50. Patrick Moore, "Patrick Moore is Not a Big Fat Liar," 1996, http://www.greenspirit.com/logbook.cfm?msid=44

torrential downpour, grabbed a shovel and the wheelbarrow, and spread all the manure over our front and back flower beds before daylight. The next spring and summer our garden was more beautiful with blooms than it had ever been. Embarrassment was avoided, and talk about making a silk purse out of a sow's ear!

In 1995, nearly 10 years after I left Greenpeace, an event occurred that made it even clearer I had made the right choice in leaving the group. Shell Oil was granted permission by the British environment ministry to dispose of the North Sea oil storage platform, Brent Spar, in deep water in the North Atlantic Ocean. Greenpeace immediately accused Shell of using the sea as a "dustbin." Greenpeace campaigners maintained that there were hundreds of tonnes of petroleum wastes on board the Brent Spar and that some of these were radioactive. They organized a consumer boycott of Shell and the company's service stations were fire-bombed in Germany. The boycott cost the company millions in sales. Then German chancellor Helmut Kohl denounced the British government's decision to allow the dumping. Caught completely off guard, Shell ordered the tug that was already towing the rig to its burial site to turn back. They then announced they had abandoned the plan for deep-sea disposal. This embarrassed Britain's prime minister, John Major.

An independent investigation subsequently revealed that the rig had been properly cleaned and did not contain the toxic or radioactive waste Greenpeace claimed it did. Greenpeace wrote to Shell apologizing for the factual error. But the group did not change its position on deep-sea disposal despite the fact that on-land disposal would cause far greater environmental impact.

During all the public outrage directed against Shell for daring to sink a large piece of steel and concrete, it was never noted that Greenpeace had purposely sunk its own ship off the coast of New Zealand in 1986. When the French government bombed and sank the *Rainbow Warrior* in Auckland Harbour in 1985, the vessel was permanently disabled. It was later refloated, patched up, cleaned, and towed to a marine park, where it was sunk in shallow water as a dive site. Greenpeace said the ship would be an artificial reef and would support increased marine life.

The Brent Spar and the *Rainbow Warrior* are in no way fundamentally different from each other. The sinking of the Brent Spar could also be rationalized as providing habitat for marine creatures. It's just that the public relations people at Shell were not as clever as those at Greenpeace. And in this case Greenpeace got away with using misinformation even though it had to admit its error after the fact. After spending tens of millions of dollars on studies, Shell announced that it had abandoned any plan for deep-sea disposal and supported a proposal to reuse the rig as pylons in a dock extension project in Norway. Tens of millions of dollars and much precious time wasted over an issue that had nothing to do with the environment and everything to do with misinformation, misguided priorities, and fundraising hysteria.

To make matters worse, in 1998 Greenpeace successfully campaigned for a ban on all marine disposal of disused oil installations. This will result in hundreds of millions, even billions of dollars, in unnecessary costs. Many of these rigs and their components cannot be recycled in a cost-effective manner. One obvious solution would be to designate an area in the North Sea, away from shipping lanes, for the creation of a large artificial reef and to sink obsolete oil rigs there after cleaning them. This would provide a breeding area for fish and other marine life, enhancing the biological and economic productivity of the sea. But Greenpeace isn't looking for solutions, only conflicts and bad guys.

CHAPTER FOURTEEN

Trees Are The Answer

You may ask, If trees are the answer, then what is the question? I believe trees are the answer to many questions about the future of human civilization and the preservation of the environment. Questions like, "What is the most environmentally friendly material for home construction?" "How can we pull carbon dioxide out of the atmosphere and how can we offset the greenhouse gas emissions caused by our excessive use of fossil fuels?" "How can we build healthy soils and keep our air and water clean?" "How can we provide more habitat for wildlife and biodiversity?" "How can we increase literacy and provide sanitary tissue products in developing countries?" "How can we make this earth more green and beautiful?" The answer to all these questions and more is "trees." From the most practical question of what to build a house with to the most aesthetic issue of how to make the world prettier, trees provide an obvious solution. In other words I am a tree-hugging, tree-planting, tree-cutting fanatic. Trees show us there can be more than one answer to a question, and sometimes the answers seem to contradict one another. But I hope to demonstrate that just because we love trees and recognize their environmental value doesn't mean we shouldn't use them for our own needs.

Forests, and the trees that define them, are the most complex systems we know of in the universe. To a computer scientist or a molecular biologist, this statement may at first seem exaggerated, but it is a fact. To begin with, we don't know of any other planet that harbors life. On Earth it is undeniable that forested ecosystems are home to the vast majority of living species. Every needle and leaf on every tree is a factory more complex than the most sophisticated chemical plant or nuclear reactor. We may be capable of genetic modification and producing atomic energy but we can't imitate photosynthesis, never mind the infinitely more intricate systems that make up the entirety of a forest. There is every reason, despite our considerable talents, to live in wonder of the natural world and, I would argue, of forests in particular. As far as we are concerned, photosynthesis might just as well be magic.

Our species was born of the forest, descended from primates that came down from trees to the savannah, got this two-legged habit of mobility and made history. The males among us excelled at running across the open plains, spears and clubs in hand, replacing even the lion as "king of the beasts." But in our new posture the forest was no longer our primary home. The forest was more dangerous than the savannah because predators could find cover there and make a surprise attack. We evolved from a forest-dependent species to a species that distrusted and disliked the forest. Then we learned to use fire. The forest provided the firewood and when we used fire to clear the forest we made more productive grazing land for the animals we hunted for food, bone, sinew, and hide. Then we invented the axe.

If you observe the dwellings of people who live in Africa and other tropical regions today, you will see they keep vegetation away from their huts. A couple of million years of experience with snakes, scorpions, and lions has resulted in a scorched earth approach to yard maintenance. As humans spread out across the other continents, they took with them the habit of making large clearings around their homes. In colder climates this has the added benefit of letting the sunshine in. Trees provided the building materials for shelter and the fuel to keep the homes warm. When we began the transformation from hunting and gathering to agriculture, the axes really came in handy. The forest was an obstacle to be overcome. Over the past 10,000 years we have converted nearly one-third of the world's forests into cities, farms, and pastures, the best one-third in terms of fertility and productivity. Thus our species became a dominant force in shaping landscapes to our own design. No wonder we became too sure of our ability to overcome all natural obstacles as we transformed the earth to serve our growing needs for food, energy, and materials.

As long as the human population was reasonably small compared with the vastness of global forests, deforestation remained a very local issue. But as numbers grew and more land was cleared for crops and grazing animals, we began to take our toll on the natural world. It went reasonably well, other than the frequent wars and short lifespan, until the Industrial Revolution and the exponential increase in the use of wood for fuel, fuel

CONFESSIONS OF A GREENPEACE DROPOUT

for heating, fuel for smelting iron and copper, fuel for glassworks, and eventually fuel for steam engines to run the factories, ships, and trains. During the 18th and 19th centuries forests of the industrialized European countries were rapidly decimated and wood soon came into short supply.[51]

We began to learn how to farm trees in the same way we had learned to farm food 10,000 years earlier. The art and science of silviculture, more commonly known as forestry, emerged in central Europe as a way to increase the wood supply to feed the growing demands of industry. Up until about 250 years ago forests had merely been exploited and the land was either converted to farm land or left to grow back on its own, often with trees not as stately or useful as the ones that preceded them. Now people began to replant harvested areas with new trees of desirable species for timber production. Over the past 200 years the forested area of Europe has tripled from about 10 percent to about 30 percent, due almost entirely to the transition from pure exploitation to forest management.

Similar patterns have occurred more recently in China and India, where the demand for wood products from an emerging middle class has resulted in a doubling of forest area in recent decades. During the past 20 years, China has added more new forest than any other country and has adopted an aggressive reforestation program that will continue into the foreseeable future. The forests of Canada, the U.S., Australia, New Zealand, Chile, South Africa, and Japan are all stable or growing in area due to the application of sustainable forestry management. And even though there is a net loss of forests in Brazil and Indonesia due to clearing for farming, there is also a major effort afoot to establish sustainable plantation forestry over large areas.[52] In general it is the industrialized countries that have avoided further deforestation while it is the tropical developing countries that continue to experience loss of forests.

It may seem ironic that with few exceptions the countries that use the most wood have a stable or growing area of forest whereas the countries that use the least wood are losing forest as more land is cleared for agriculture. There are two reasons for this apparent contradiction. First, the adoption of intensive agricultural practices in the industrialized countries makes it possible to grow much more food on the same amount of land. Advances in technology, chemistry, and genetics have brought about a five-fold increase in productivity over the past 100 years. This has resulted in a vast increase in food production without the need to clear any more forested land. Second, it is precisely because we use so much wood that the area of forest is maintained. We may think that when we buy wood from a lumberyard we are causing a bit of forest to be lost somewhere. But what

51. John Perlin, *A Forest Journey: The Story of Wood and Civilization* (Countryman Press, 2005),
http://www.wikio.com/book/a-forest-journey-the-story-of-wood-and-civilization-0881506761-2996385,b.html
52. UN Food and Agricultural Organization, "State of the World's Forests," Rome, 2009,
http://www.fao.org/docrep/011/i0350e/i0350e00.HTM

we are really doing is sending a signal into the marketplace to plant more trees to produce more wood to supply the demand in the lumberyard. It is no different from any other renewable crop, it's just that trees take longer to mature than annual farm crops. Forestry is more comparable to tree-fruits like apples and oranges where it takes some years before there is a harvest. But trees are no different from farm crops; as long as the demand for wood is steady and strong, landowners, both private and public, will plant trees to supply that demand. Take note this is the polar opposite to the contention that the way to save forests is to stop cutting trees.

We learned to farm trees nearly 300 years ago, so you would expect people might be familiar with the concept by now. There is an interesting comparison here with the debate over salmon farming. Activists are clearly against cutting trees that grow in the wilderness, yet they insist it is better to eat wild salmon and to boycott farmed salmon. This kind of logical inconsistency creates confusion and fails to recognize that farming trees and farming salmon both contribute to the sustainability of the resource. That's why we evolved from simply exploiting wild species of plants and animals to farming them.

Imagine a scenario in which our morning newspapers carry headlines warning that new research shows tomatoes cause cancer. Tomatoes would rot on the grocers' shelves and no farmer would be foolish enough to plant them the next season. But imagine if the headlines announced that tomatoes cured cancer. They would all be sold as fast as stores could stock them and farmers would line up to buy seed, purchase more land, and take out bank loans to increase tomato production. Trees and wood are no different. Take North America as a perfect example. There is the same area of forest in both the U.S. and Canada today as there was 100 years ago; in fact the area of forest has been growing in recent years. This is despite a tripling of population and an even larger increase in the consumption of food and wood products. About 85 percent of timber production in the U.S. is from private lands. Those millions of individual landowners could easily remove the forest from the land and grow crops like corn or cotton or raise cows for beef. But they choose to grow trees because they know they will get a good price for them to pay their taxes, send their children to college, and live a good life. Because landowners choose to grow trees the land remains forested, providing habitat for other plants and wildlife, pulling carbon from the air, protecting soil from erosion, and making the landscape beautiful. Rather than illustrating the common belief that forestry destroys the forest it is truly a win-win solution for the environment and the economy, maintaining the land in a forested state while providing an income for the owners.

A great disservice to public understanding of forests is the allegation that the forest industry is the main cause of deforestation. Of course when you think about it, forest companies are in the business of growing trees,

CONFESSIONS OF A GREENPEACE DROPOUT

not removing them permanently. Reforestation, that is, the practice of replanting trees after they are harvested, is the opposite of deforestation. Once we realize deforestation is caused primarily by clearing forests to make way for farms and cities it becomes obvious that deforestation is not an evil plot by multinational forestry corporations. It is something we do on purpose in order to grow our food and house our population. The more intensively we grow our food, the less forest must be cleared. And the more wood we use sustainably, the more incentive there is to keep the land forested to provide that wood. Next time you fly over a country landscape of farms and forests, note the patterns of land use that are caused largely by the relative demands for food and timber products.

Deforestation isn't something that happens and then is done forever. Deforestation is a continuing process of purposeful human activity aimed at preventing the forest from growing back. Farmers plow their fields regularly and encourage the growth of crops, working hard to keep other plants, insects, and animals off their land. Cattle farmers do the same. Roads are continually repaired (so we hope). If roads were left disused for a few years, grasses and other plants would take root and within a few decades those roads would have all but disappeared with a profusion of new growth, including trees, rapidly taking over.

Of course it is important to maintain large areas of land as parks and wilderness, and make them off limits to industrial development for factories, managed forests, or farms. The World Wildlife Fund, one of the largest nature protection groups, states that 10 percent of the world's forests should be protected from development. I would have no problem with 15 percent or even more in some cases. In California about 25 percent of the natural range of the coastal redwood forest is completely protected. The redwood is a unique tree, the tallest in the world, and creates such a beautiful ecosystem, that it is reasonable to protect a significant percentage as natural forest. But some anti-forestry activists are never satisfied. They would fight until every tree was protected as if using trees for wood products was unnecessary. Redwoods produce a unique wood that is both durable for outdoor use as well as beautiful in color and texture. Therefore it is also reasonable that large areas of the redwood forest be sustainably managed for timber. The most important thing is to make sure that as much of the forest as possible is retained either for protection or forest management, and as little as possible is deforested and converted to non-forest uses.

The Aesthetics of Landscapes

We have all been told since childhood that you can't judge a book by its cover. Yet we are easily inclined to think that if we like what we see it is good and if we don't like the looks of what we see it is bad. Beauty is in the eye of the beholder but beauty is often only skin deep. This tendency to judge things by their appearance is one of the greatest obstacles to public understanding of land use in general and forestry in particular.

We like the looks of things that are neat and tidy. We don't like things that look messy or out of place. We prefer order to disorder. Perhaps there are good reasons for this instinct, but it does not serve us well when judging the merits of various landscapes and land uses. Neat and tidy are not virtues in ecology, messy and jumbled often indicate a healthy ecosystem. Let's consider some examples.

No one thinks a wheat field shimmering in the sunlight is ugly. Yet from an environmental point of view, a wheat field represents the total destruction of a diverse native ecosystem, replacing it with a monoculture crop. If the wheat is grown in North America, South America, or Australia it is further an exotic species since wheat is only native to Europe and Asia. But most people think a recently harvested forest, with stumps and jumbled-up limbs and debris, is unsightly, even ugly. Such a scene is often judged as the complete and permanent destruction of the forest ecosystem. Despite the fact that a new forest of native trees will soon be planted on the site we judge it to represent the destruction of the environment. So we think a monoculture of exotic wheat in nice neat rows looks good, but we judge a recent clearcut in the forest to be unacceptable.

All manner of agricultural crops planted in rows look pretty, even though the original ecosystem has been completely destroyed and replaced with species not native to the region. We even think recently plowed fields, with nothing growing on them, look better than the mess of a recently harvested forest. Yet there is more biodiversity in an area of recently harvested forest than there will ever be on an area of farmland. We actually prefer the sight of an asphalt parking lot marked with fresh yellow lines to a recently logged landscape. We like the looks of a fancy new car parked in front of an upscale hotel, but we do not like the clutter that results from harvesting trees. We judge the book by its cover and we reach a fundamentally incorrect verdict on the health of ecosystems as a result.

Imagine you are sitting at a high spot looking down at sheep grazing peacefully in a grassy meadow on a warm summer day. It is a scene of tranquility and peace; all is well with the world. Yet in truth you are looking at the deforestation of a landscape where there were once majestic oaks, beeches, and pines. The sheep are an exotic, domesticated species originating in Mesopotamia. You are looking at the permanent removal of the forest and the destruction of the native ecosystem.

Now imagine you have stopped beside an area of recently harvested native forest. You may be shocked by the fresh carnage of sawed-off stumps and jagged limbs. You may believe that an ecosystem has been destroyed for profit and forever ruined. But in all likelihood it will not be long before tree seedlings, of the same native species that were cut, grow back from native seeds or are planted here. And within a few years a thriving new forest will emerge, complete with native animals, birds, shrubs, and wild-flowers. And don't forget, the farmer grazing his sheep in the meadow is also trying to make a living.

We tend to judge landscapes by how pretty a postcard they would make; that's art, not science. I dwell on this because I believe we need to get a new pair of eyes to view the landscapes around us; to get beyond the immediate impression of ugly versus beauty and to understand a little more about science, ecology, and biodiversity. Otherwise we will never get beyond an emotional rather than a logical approach to understanding the look of the land around us. It is not a difficult concept but unfortunately it is not instinctual, it must be explained with clear examples showing the difference between a parking lot and a recently harvested forest, between deforestation and reforestation. And we must realize that a snapshot in time is not the whole story. A landscape that looks ugly today may be beautiful in a few years as the ecosystem recovers from disturbance.

As if the hurdle of getting over our aesthetic intuition were not a large enough barrier to understanding the ecology of landscapes there is an-other confusing factor. This is the fact that in order to prepare a plot of land for farming it must first be logged. It is likely that any usable timber cleared from the land will be used to make lumber or that it will be burned as firewood. Therefore it is easy to get the impression that the deforesta-tion is caused by loggers rather than farmers even though the reason for clearing the land had nothing to do with forestry. Anti-forestry groups work hard to reinforce this false impression

Disturbance versus Destruction

The anti-forestry folks have become very good at using strong language to reinforce the impression that forestry destroys the environment. Forest companies are accused of "rape," "desecration," "pillage," and "plunder" when they harvest trees for lumber to build our homes, furniture, and other wood products. Propaganda is largely about associating words and ideas with positive or negative descriptors, loading them down with verbal baggage that triggers an emotional reaction. A critical part of critical thinking is the ability to recognize when you are being misled by loaded language.

Take the word *clearcut*, for example. Many people associate this word with forest destruction as for them it implies the forest has been *wiped out*, *eliminated*, and otherwise lost forever. And yet the word *clearing*, as in the phrase *a clearing in the forest*, has no such negative connotation. In fact a clearing is a nice place where the sun can get in and one can build a home and plant a garden. Clearings are pleasant whereas clear-cuts are nasty.

In truth clearcut is a forestry term that means to cut all the trees in a given area, large or small. But the clearcut will be reforested, as that is what forestry requires. A clearing, on the other hand, is usually a permanent feature, making way for a new farm or urban development. Clearcuts are reforested while clearings usually equal deforestation.

The science of ecology is partly about how ecosystems develop and how they recover after disturbances caused by fire, drought, floods, disease, volcanic eruptions, and ice ages. The process of recovery is called *ecological succession*, where landscapes that have been decimated by natural disasters are able to recover and return to their original splendor. Because these processes are natural, ecologists prefer to use the more neutral word *disturbance* as opposed to the negative term *destruction* to describe the impact of natural forces. In this light, forest harvesting is just another form of ecological disturbance. But are the loggers "natural"? And is the disturbance caused by logging comparable to the disturbance caused by fire, flood, volcanoes, and glaciers?

The word *natural* is one of the most misused terms in our language. The opposite, of course, is *unnatural*. How do we decide which situations are natural and which are unnatural? Are all human activities unnatural? If not, which human activities are natural and which are unnatural? And are all nonhuman activities natural? What does this word mean anyway? What has it got to do with *nature*?

Clearly natural is good and unnatural is bad; in other words these are value judgments, not objective descriptions. Activities viewed as natural by one person might be seen as unnatural by another person. These are ethical and moral judgments. Many people think homosexuality is unnatural, and yet many others think it is natural. Most people believe incest is unnatural but in some cultures, the Hawaiian royalty, for example, inbreeding was purposely employed to produce "superior" offspring.[53]

The use of the word natural as a judgmental term is entirely different from our use of the word nature to describe the natural world. Here the issue is not so much about whether or not people and their actions are *natural* but rather about whether or not humans are a part of *nature*. You might say, of course, humans are part of nature, but you would never know it based on the pronouncements of many activists. They tend to think in terms of "humans versus nature" rather than "humans as nature" or "humans in nature."

In the sense that we are part of nature everything we do is natural. So from an environmental and scientific point of view there is no such thing as unnatural. The term unnatural should be reserved for judgments of

---

53. Joanne Carando, "Hawaiian Royal Incest: A Study in the Sacrificial Origin of Monarchy,"
http://www.luckyulivehawaii.com/incest.htm

one's character and behavior at a social level, not as a way of judging our impact on the environment.

Looked at in this light, the disturbance caused by logging falls into the same category as disturbances caused by other natural factors. While there are differences in the impacts of fire, floods, volcanoes, glaciers, and logging they are similar in that the ecosystem is capable of recovering from all of them. In particular, when the fire goes out, the floodwaters recede, the volcano stops erupting, the glaciers retreat, and the loggers finish their work, the forest immediately begins the process of recovery. The time it takes to recover depends, to a large part, on the severity of the disturbance. The impacts of logging are generally less severe than a hot wildfire, a prolonged flood, a volcanic eruption, and certainly less than an advancing glacier.

The truth is, forests and all the species in them are capable of recovering from total destruction without any help from us. They have been doing so for hundreds of millions of years as ice ages come and go and as fires regularly ravage the landscape.

Forests and Climate Change

In recent years anti-forestry activists have claimed forest harvesting and forestry in general has a negative impact on climate change. The group ForestEthics (an offshoot of Greenpeace) claims forestry amounts to a "carbon bomb," referring to the release of CO_2 from decomposing wood immediately after harvesting.

It is true that there is a net release of CO_2 as a result of harvesting, but the activists fail to take into account that new trees are soon established and that they absorb all that CO_2 back over time as they grow into a new forest. And they fail to take into account the reduction in wildfires in managed forests, which reduce the amount of carbon that goes into the atmosphere. A hot wildfire not only burns trees but it also burns soil, causing a far greater release of carbon than just harvesting the trees. And most important, the wood harvested is used to build homes where the carbon in them remains stored for many years. In addition, when we use wood we avoid the use of nonrenewable materials such as steel and concrete, which require large amounts of energy to manufacture, putting more CO_2 into the atmosphere. In the final analysis, the combination of harvesting trees and then reforesting the area, suppressing wildfire, storing carbon and using renewable wood instead of nonrenewable materials has a large net positive impact in terms of greenhouse gas emissions. Yet in order to further their anti-environmental aim of curbing the use of wood, activists distort the truth and mislead the public. They make these claims despite the fact that both the Kyoto Protocol on climate and the Intergovernmental Panel on Climate Change (IPCC) have clearly recognized the benefits forest management bring to reducing greenhouse gas emissions.

Here is the language used by the IPCC to describe the relationship between climate change and forestry:

7.2 Technologies for Reducing Greenhouse Gas Emissions in the Forest Sector

Forest management practices that can restrain the rate of increase in atmospheric CO_2 can be grouped into three categories: (i) Management for carbon conservation; (ii) management for carbon sequestration and storage; and (iii) management for carbon substitution.

Conservation practices include options such as controlling deforestation, protecting forests in reserves, changing harvesting regimes, and controlling other anthropogenic disturbances, such as fire and pest outbreaks.

Sequestration and storage practices include expanding forest ecosystems by increasing the area and/or biomass and soil carbon density of natural and plantation forests, and increasing storage in durable wood products.

Substitution practices aim at increasing the transfer of forest biomass carbon into products rather than using fossil fuel-based energy and products, cement-based products, and other non-wood building materials.[54]

The IPCC could not be clearer about the benefits forest management and wood production have for reducing CO_2 emissions. And yet anti-forestry activists, including Greenpeace and ForestEthics, continue to spread the opposite story. They will twist the truth in any way they can to support their contention that we should cut fewer trees and therefore use less wood. The IPCC knows that a sensible environmentalist would support a policy of growing more trees and using more wood.

The Kyoto Protocol on climate change takes a similar view of the role of forest management, pointing out that when we plant trees we pull carbon out of the atmosphere and that when we use wood we avoid putting it in the atmosphere in the first place.[55]

---

54. UN Intergovernmental Panel on Climate Change, "Forest Sector: Technologies, Policies and Measures for Mitigating Climate Change," November 1996, http://www.gcrio.org/ipcc/techrepl/forest.html
55. D. Schoene and M. Netto, "The Kyoto Protocol: What Does It Mean for Forests and Forestry?" Unasylva 222, 56 (2005), ftp://ftp.fao.org/docrep/fao/009/a0413E/a0413E02.pdf

So the anti-forestry crowd is happy to take the concerns of the IPCC and Kyoto about climate change and exaggerate them into apocalyptic proportions but then fail to listen to the same organizations when they tell us growing more trees and using more wood are solutions to the problem.

Wood Is Good

Wood is the material embodiment of solar energy. The chlorophyll in the leaves of trees catalyzes the combination of carbon dioxide from the air, water from rainfall, and a smattering of minerals from the soil to make the miraculous substance known as wood. When we burn wood to heat our homes, we are simply releasing the energy of the sun the tree captured while growing in the forest. When we use wood to build our homes, we are storing solar energy and the carbon the wood contains.

When it comes right down to it we must recognize that wood is the most abundant and most environmentally friendly renewable source of both materials and energy resources on earth. About 75 percent of all our renewable energy comes from wood, used mainly for cooking and heating but also for making charcoal, drying lumber, and producing pulp and paper. Wood provides more than 90 percent of our renewable materials for buildings, furniture, packaging, and sanitary products. One of the great ironies of the "environmental" movement today is that it claims to support all things renewable on the one hand while at the same time ignoring or rejecting the fact that wood is far and away the most important renewable resource. Environmental activists place huge importance on solar panels made from aluminum, silicon, and gallium arsenide when in fact *the most important solar collectors on earth are the leaves and needles of trees and other plants.* I believe this is one of the most important facts for everyone to recognize.

With our incredible knowledge of science we are able to produce genetically modified plants and split atoms to make nuclear energy. But we haven't come close to developing the ability to replicate photosynthesis, the most important process for life on earth. Without photosynthesis not only would our lives be impossible but so would the lives of nearly every other plant and animal on the planet.

About one-third of the human population, more than two billion people, depend on wood for their primary energy source, mainly in the tropical developing countries, where wood and charcoal are the main fuels for cooking and heating. Unfortunately the practice of sustainable forestry has not been adopted in all of the developing countries. But this is changing quickly as countries like China, India, Indonesia, Brazil, and others begin to understand the benefits of managing forests rather than simply exploiting them. This must be a primary goal of international aid and technology transfer, the conversion from simply harvesting wood for timber and fuelwood to the sustainable management of forests, for forests provide the most abundant renewable resource on earth.

Building Green with Wood

There is probably no better way to make trees the answer than to use more wood for our buildings and other infrastructure. Yet much of the "green building" movement has failed to recognize the importance of wood in contributing to the "greenness" of our built environment. Most buildings that get certified as green under the LEED (Leadership in Energy and Environmental Design) standard of the Green Building Council are built mainly of steel and concrete. This is due to the anti-forestry attitude of many of the environmentalists who influence the LEED standard. This must change if we are to advance the idea of truly green building.

The LEED standard for green building requires that wood be certified as originating from sustainably managed forests. This is as it should be but only the Forest Stewardship Council, another activist-oriented organization, is accepted as a certifier. There are a number of other legitimate certifiers of sustainable forest management, including the Sustainable Forestry Initiative (SFI), [56] the Canadian Standards Association (CSA),[57] the American Tree Farmers,[58] and the Programme for the Endorsement of Forest Certification (PEFC).[59] The U.S. Green Building Council (USGBC) does not recognize these systems. This means most of the wood certified as sustainably produced does not qualify for points under the LEED green building standard. This is clearly discriminatory but the activists within the Green Building Council have so far prevailed against the protestations of the majority of forest owners and managers.

Even more discriminatory is the fact that the LEED standard does not recognize construction lumber as a renewable material. LEED does recognize all kinds of marginal building materials, such as wheatboard, bamboo flooring, and strawboard. But USGBC manages to exclude lumber by naming the category "Rapidly Renewable Materials." This term is then defined as "renewable materials that renew themselves in less than ten years." Because it takes trees anywhere from 25 to 100 years to reach a size where they become suitable for sawmilling they are excluded. These people don't think trees grow fast enough to qualify as "renewable." If you

56. SFI, "Sustainable Forestry Initiative," http://www.sfiprogram.org/
57. CSA SFM, "Canadian Sustainable Forest Management," http://www.csasfmforests.ca/home.htm
58. American Forest Foundation's Center for Family Forests, "American Tree Farm System," http://www.treefarmsystem.org/cms/pages/26_19.html
59. PEFC, "Caring for our Forests Globally," http://www.pefc.org/

needed any evidence that anti-forestry activists have hijacked the USGBC, then this should do the trick.[60]

The "Green" Olympics

The 17th Winter Olympic Games were held in Lillehammer, Norway, in 1994 and were the first Olympic Games to have guidelines for sustainable infrastructure. Norwegian leaders and architects quickly realized this meant maximizing the use of renewable wood for the Olympic venues. They pioneered the use of wood to create large arched beams in the arenas for indoor events, such as hockey and speed skating. This marked the beginning of Greenpeace's campaign against the use of wood in Olympic buildings.

By the year 2000, Greenpeace had quietly succeeded in convincing the government of Australia that native wood and PVC should be banned from the Games of the 27th Olympiad, the Sydney Summer Games. In return, Greenpeace agreed to let Australia call the Games "The Green Olympics." Ironically this meant the Olympic venues for the 2000 Sydney "Green" Olympic Games were built almost entirely with steel and concrete.

The engineers who built the venues could get by without native wood (they imported wood from other countries), but they weren't going to give up using PVC pipes for water and sewers, electrical conduits, wiring insulation, etc. They laid PVC pipes for water and sewers in the foundations. Greenpeace arrived with a backhoe and TV crews and dug up some pipes, declaring through the media that the government had broken its promise to ban "The Poison Plastic." This embarrassed the government and caused concern among suppliers and industry groups. Many letters were written and many meetings were held at the end of which the government pledged to conduct materials specification and procurement policies in a more transparent manner in future.

In 2002 we learned that Greenpeace had gained control of the Sustainability Committee for the Toronto bid for the 2008 Olympics. Working with the wood and vinyl industries we managed to obtain a copy of the recommendations from the Sustainability Committee to the organizing committee in charge of the bid. Building on the Australian campaign the document recommended that most wood products, PVC, tin, and cadmium be banned. We were amazed that Greenpeace seemed to ignore the fact that most cameras, cell phones, and laptop computers use batteries made with cadmium. Did they plan to ban most battery-operated devices from the Games? Even more incredulous was the inclusion of tin

---

60. U.S .Green Building Council, "LEED 2009 for New Construction and Major Renovations Rating System," November 2008, http://www.usgbc.org/ShowFile.aspx?DocumentID=5546

The interior roof of the speed-skating arena for the Vancouver 2010 Winter Olympics was made entirely of engineered wood.

in the committee's list. To this day we don't know why it was included, but apparently Greenpeace and the committee members were not aware that bronze is made of tin and copper. A few days later, just before Bid Committee was to accept the Sustainability Committee's recommendations, we placed an opinion editorial in a major Canadian national newspaper that was headlined, "No Bronze Medal at the Green Olympics." The phones in the Ontario premier's office lit up and we soon learned that the recommendations had been rejected. Beijing eventually won the bid for the 2008 Games.

The experience we gained during the Toronto bid put us in a good position to help Canada with the Vancouver bid for the 2010 Winter Olympics, which Canada did win. Canada also won the most gold medals (14) and the gold medal in hockey, our national sport. This last triumph was the most gratifying. At the Greenspirit head office in downtown Vancouver we witnessed more than 150,000 people celebrate the victory in the streets.

One of the main features of the Vancouver Olympics was the extensive use of native wood in the skating arenas.[61] In addition, the new Convention Center on the waterfront showcased British Columbia wood in a stunning manner. Premier Gordon Campbell, in his third term of office, personally supported the use of as much wood as possible. He linked it to the fact that wood is renewable and beautiful and results in reduced greenhouse gas emissions. Hundreds of thousands of people from around the world

61. CNW, "The Aesthetic Experience at the Richmond Olympic Oval: 'It's the Wood,'" February 26, 2010, http://www.newswire.ca/en/releases/archive/February2010/26/c5439.html

CONFESSIONS OF A GREENPEACE DROPOUT

witnessed this display of wood's warmth and beauty and were no doubt impressed. It was a proud moment for Vancouver and British Columbia.

Wood in Residential and Commercial Buildings

For many years building codes in Europe and North America restricted the height of wood-framed buildings to three, or at most four, stories. Advances in architecture and an increasing awareness of the environmentally beneficial qualities of wood have resulted in many jurisdictions raising the maximum height to six, eight, and even nine stories in the case of the record-holder in the U.K. Built properly, wood frame buildings of this height have better resistance to earthquakes than similar concrete structures.

In the United States and Canada, the Wood Works! organization,[62] [63] a project of the Canadian Wood Council[64] and the Binational Softwood Lumber Council,[65] works with architects and builders to promote the strength, versatility, beauty, and environmental attributes of wood. There is a tremendous potential for wood to replace steel and concrete in low-to-midrise commercial buildings.

All things considered it makes sense both environmentally and economically to use more wood in our buildings, especially where it is not exposed to the elements and kept dry. If wood is protected from water and sunlight, it will last for hundreds of years. The more wood we use, the more trees we must grow and therefore the more land will remain forested. That is the real win-win solution for the environment and the economy.

62. Wood Works!, "Richmond Olympic Oval," http://www.wood-works.org/
63. Ibid.
64. Canadian Wood Council, http://www.cwc.ca/
65. Paul Perkins, "The Binational Softwood Lumber Council," April 13, 2007, http://www.cofi.org/library_and_resources/annual_convention/2007/pdfs/Perkins.pdf

CHAPTER FIFTEEN

Energy to Power Our World

About 10 years ago I had a revelation—it wasn't my first one but it was a beauty. Like almost every other environmentalist I had been a staunch foe of nuclear energy from the beginning. Nuclear war was our worst nightmare and we lumped nuclear power in with nuclear weapons as if all things nuclear were evil. I finally realized that I had been wrong. This chapter explains why I came to the conclusion that nuclear energy is our most important source of clean power and how it fits in with other technologies that will inevitably be part of our energy future.

I had long been aware that James Lovelock, the independent British scientist who developed the Gaia Hypothesis, favored nuclear energy as a way to reduce fossil fuel use and greenhouse gas emissions. My old Greenpeace buddy Rex Weyler had introduced me to Lovelock's first book in 1979. He was perhaps the first prominent environmental thinker to accept nuclear energy as a solution rather than a threat. The antinuclear folks conveniently ignored his consistent support for nuclear energy while at the same time rallying to his increasingly dire warnings about climate change.

In 2002 I decided it would be enlightening to meet Jim Lovelock in person if he would receive me at his West Country home in England. Out of the blue I emailed him, asking to discuss the future of the world and he replied, Come on over. We spent a full day and an evening together. He picked me up at 10 a.m. and the cab came to take me back to my B&B around 10 p.m. In the morning we walked the cliffs above Bristol Channel, deep in discussion about everything under the sun. My main question concerned nuclear energy, but I was also keenly interested in the climate change issue, having formed the Carbon Project years earlier. I did not come away disappointed.

Jim Lovelock is a very compatible soul. He had a lifelong experience with the scientific method as both a PhD chemist and a medical doctor. He knew we needn't be irrationally afraid of chemicals. And he immediately won me over to the idea that nuclear waste was not going to hurt me or my children's children. He said, "Patrick, I would be perfectly willing to take a bundle of used nuclear fuel, properly contained, put it in my swimming pool, and use the heat from nuclear decay to pipe heat into my house." I didn't have to think too long to realize he was right. So long as radioactive materials are properly contained there is no risk of exposure. We are very good at making containers that last a long time. The pyramids at Giza are more than 4000 years old and yet their insides still remain dry and secure. We are also good at repackaging should the original container deteriorate with time. I lost my fear of nuclear energy.

The discussion of climate change took a very different track. Jim had already carved out a pretty radical position, stating that the three Cs, "cars, cattle, and chainsaws" would lead to the demise of our planet if we didn't smarten up. These philosophical musings did interest me, but I was focused on the science: does CO_2 cause global warming? And if so is that a good thing or a bad thing? Coming from northern Vancouver Island I was not so sure a warmer world would be a bad idea.

The discussion went something like this:

P.M. "So Jim, the Gaia Hypothesis states that all life on Earth is acting to control the chemistry of the atmosphere so as to make the environment more suitable for life. Are humans a part of Gaia and if so aren't our emissions part of Gaia's plan?"

J.L. "We are a rogue species and are about to pay the price."

P.M. "But what if Gaia's strategy is to increase CO_2 in the atmosphere, to make the world warmer and jump us out of this Ice Age period we have been in for the past 2.5 million years?

J.L. "If we don't act quickly we will be doomed to global heating."

P.M. "I think it is reasonable to assume we do not know the future of the global climate. How do we know an increase in CO_2 emissions won't be good for life and people? This requires a bit more study."
J.L. "Humans are the biggest threat to civilization, and they must stop CO_2 emissions."

You can't sum up a day of discourse in a few words but the bottom line was that I now believed that nuclear energy was not something to be feared and Jim Lovelock still feared catastrophic climate change. So much for *my* powers of persuasion.

It seems a stretch to conclude that the human species is the only "rogue species" in all creation. It's too much like the idea of original sin in fundamentalist religions. I'm even willing to accept original sin in the context that humans stoop to murder, sexual assault, and theft, but that is not the same as branding us a traitor to Gaia, to Mother Earth. If that were the case, then every farmer, miner, logger, fisher, and industrial worker would be an enemy of the planet. It makes for great media but we should remember the media are mainly about entertaining the masses and securing advertising revenue (or state revenue in the case of state-financed media).

Climate scientists tend to insist that their computer models of the global climate reliably predict what the climate will be like in 50 or 100 years. We do not have a computer program that can look into the future with accuracy. There is actually no proof we are causing the observed changes in weather and climate we are observing. The climate has been changing from the beginning of the earth's creation, billions of years before we were here. How presumptuous is it for us to think we are suddenly the main cause of climate change?

Energy Powers Everything

Energy underlies virtually every aspect of our lives and the lives of every other living thing. Motion requires energy, so without energy, time would stand still.

We get the energy from our food to walk, talk, and type. We are able to turn sugars, starch, fats, oils, and proteins into the energy that makes our bodies alive. All these sources of energy are produced by photosynthesis in plants. The animals we eat, in turn, ate those plants. Of course plants are the original "green."

Energy is a vast and complex subject, partly because there are so many different types of energy and so many ways to harness them. For practical purposes energy can be divided into electrical energy and thermal energy (heat). To confuse matters, most of our electrical energy is produced using heat from burning fossil fuels and uranium. Then we often turn the electrical energy back into thermal energy to toast our bread or heat our homes. There is always a chain of energy events that leads from the original source to the end use.

While most people have access to sufficient thermal energy for cooking and heating (much of it in the form of wood), 1.5 billion people have no access to electricity.[66] There are 580 million people in India and 500 million in sub-Saharan Africa with no electric service. Interestingly, in China, where 56 percent of the population is poor, the vast majority of people have access to electricity. This suggests political will and organization are even more important than income in determining who gets to plug in and who doesn't.

While it is possible to survive without electricity, it is not possible to achieve a high quality of life. Whether it is literacy, education, health care, public transit, industry, or entertainment, electricity forms the foundation of a civilized life. Of the 13 terawatts (one terawatt equals one trillion watts) of commercial energy used each year in the world, 86 percent is currently supplied by oil, coal, and natural gas.[67] Even if we include the noncommercial burning of wood, dung, and crop residues by two-fifths of the world's people without access to commercial energy, fossil fuels supply about 80 percent of the total amount of global energy.[68]

By 2050, many experts believe the world's larger, more affluent population will demand 25 to 35 terawatts of commercial energy. The International Energy Agency predicts a 40 percent increase in demand by 2030. One reason for this is that China and India, with 40 percent of the world's population, are only now entering the automobile and air conditioning era in a significant way, where commercial energy consumption increases rapidly.

Some argue we should simply reduce our energy use across the board, conserving our way to a significant reduction in fossil fuel use. The problem with this approach is so many people on the planet already live in total energy poverty. One-third of the world's population lives without electricity or any other modern energy supplies. Another third has only limited access. Without electrical energy, life is difficult and often miserable. People naturally don't want to remain energy poor. Even the slightest increase in energy use by the poorest two-thirds of humanity will overwhelm any conservation savings we can accomplish in the developed world. This is not to suggest conservation isn't worthwhile. Wherever we can economically increase energy efficiency, in our vehicles, homes, and appliances, we should do so. But at some point you can't diet your way out of starvation. Conservation cannot conserve what is not produced.

66. International Energy Agency, "World Energy Outlook 2009 Fact Sheet: Why Is our Current Energy Pathway Unsustainable?" http://www.worldenergyoutlook.org/docs/weo2009/fact_sheets_WEO_2009.pdf
67. Estimates vary as to the amount of noncommercial energy produced globally. The International Energy Agency estimates that biomass accounts for 11 percent of the world's total energy supply, mostly the burning of wood, crop residues, and other combustible biomass.
68. International Energy Agency, "Share of Total Primary Energy Supply in 2007," 2009, http://www.iea.org/textbase/stats/pdf_graphs/29TPESPI.pdf

Others suggest replacing fossil fuels with renewable energy sources, such as hydroelectric, geothermal, wind, solar, and biomass. These are all viable, and in some cases limited, alternatives that have either been used for decades (such as hydroelectric energy) or are beginning to be adopted on a larger scale (such as geothermal energy and wind power). However, the challenge lies in getting these renewable sources to add up to enough energy to make a dent in global fossil fuel consumption—and doing so even as global energy use increases.

Simple arithmetic tells us that if we want to cut fossil fuel consumption in half we must at least triple the amount of energy derived from all non-fossil sources. If total energy consumption doubles or triples, we need to increase the non-fossil energy by six or eight times by the end of the century. Is this even possible? Yes, but only if we are willing to include every cost-effective non-fossil option available to us, especially nuclear energy.

Nuclear energy currently supplies nearly half of the world's non-fossil commercial energy and, along with hydroelectric energy, represents the most feasible, lowest cost alternative to fossil fuels. Without nuclear energy, cutting our use of fossil fuels by half while doubling total energy consumption would require a 12- to 32-fold increase in energy from the remaining alternatives. Without nuclear energy, the job literally becomes impossible.

A single 1000-megawatt nuclear power plant can provide the equivalent electricity of 500 of the largest wind turbines at a lower cost. Moreover, the nuclear plant produces power continuously and is always able to meet the demand for electricity, unlike wind energy, which depends on weather that is intermittent and often unpredictable.

Yet many environmentalists have rejected nuclear energy entirely, recommending that instead of increasing its use we eliminate it completely. How did we get to the point where environmental groups reject the most cost-effective, feasible, and timely solutions to the very problems they are most concerned about?

Later in the chapter we will explore the arguments for and against nuclear energy in more detail. Suffice it to say for now that there are over 400 commercial reactors operating in 36 countries and of the three serious nuclear accidents that have occurred during the past 60 years, only one, the Chernobyl accident, has caused loss of life due to radiation exposure. Not one person has died from a radiation-related accident in any of the 104 reactors now operating in the U.S., yet nearly 40,000 people are killed in automobile accidents every year and there is no movement to ban cars.

Globally, of the 14 percent of commercial energy that comes from non-fossil sources, 6.7 percent is from hydroelectric, 6.6 percent is from nuclear, and about 0.8 percent is from biomass, geothermal[69], wind, and

---

69. The term *geothermal* is confusing because the same term is used to describe two entirely different energy sources. One type

CONFESSIONS OF A GREENPEACE DROPOUT

solar combined. Unless there is an unforeseen breakthrough in energy technology, these are the choices we have to reduce reliance on fossil fuels. With global energy demand rising rapidly nothing short of an aggressive expansion of renewable and nuclear energy production can accomplish the task of reducing fossil fuel use.

Now let's look at the energy policies of the majority of environmental groups today. While they claim to be in favor of renewable energy, they oppose building more hydroelectric dams and are even campaigning to tear down existing dams. Many environmental groups, Greenpeace included, are entirely opposed to nuclear energy, calling for a phase-out of existing capacity. If you add up the numbers above, you can see that the environmental movement opposes 95 percent of the non-fossil commercial energy currently produced and if it had its way it would reduce this source of commercial energy rather than increase it. They also oppose continued use of fossil fuel. This means they support only 0.8 percent of current global energy production. This is ridiculous in the extreme and yet the movement is very successful in achieving support for its agenda.

So on the one hand the movement demands reductions in fossil fuel consumption while on the other hand it presents the greatest obstacle to achieving that goal. Activists vigorously support the Kyoto Protocol on climate change yet they oppose or ignore the most effective technologies that would result in reduced greenhouse gas emissions. This is an entirely self-defeating approach.

Fortunately there is a sensible and practical pathway to reducing fossil fuel use while continuing to provide the energy that is necessary to support civilization. But there is no single technology that can accomplish this goal; we must be willing to use all the available, affordable, non-fossil energy sources. These include hydroelectric, biomass, both types of geothermal, nuclear and solar hot water heating. Although nuclear energy is nonrenewable, it must be included because the task simply can't be accomplished with renewable energy alone. And while it is not renewable, nuclear energy is sustainable over the long term (thousands of years).

Thankfully I am no longer a lone wolf as an environmentalist who supports a combination of nuclear and renewable energy as the sensible solution to reducing fossil fuel consumption. In recent years a number of prominent environmental leaders have joined in the call to rethink the movement's position on nuclear energy.

James Lovelock, lifelong independent scientist, has made the strongest statement. "Civilization is in imminent danger," he warns, "and has to use

---

of geothermal is based on near-surface volcanic activity, where the high temperatures are used to make steam to drive electrical turbines. This type of geothermal energy is very localized and is used in California, Italy, Iceland, and New Zealand. The other type of geothermal energy, called geothermal heat pumps, uses the stored solar energy in the soil, lakes, or oceans to heat and cool buildings. This type of geothermal, also referred to as geoexchange, or simply geo, is universal and can be tapped under or alongside any building anywhere on Earth.

nuclear—the one safe, available energy source—or suffer the pain soon to be inflicted by our outraged planet."[70]

While I may not be quite so strident as my friend James Lovelock, it is clear that whatever risk there is from increased CO_2 levels in the atmosphere, it can be offset by an emphasis on nuclear energy.

Stewart Brand is the founder of the Whole Earth Catalogue, a mail order cornucopia that back-to-the-landers considered a bible in the 1960s and 70s. In the May 2005 edition of the Massachusetts Institute of Technology's *Technology Review*, Brand wrote that nuclear energy's problems can be overcome and:

> The industry is mature, with a half-century of experience and ever improved engineering behind it. Problematic early reactors like the ones at Three Mile Island and Chernobyl can be supplanted by new, smaller-scale, meltdown-proof reactors like the ones that use the pebble-bed design. Nuclear power plants are very high yield, with low-cost fuel. Finally, they offer the best avenue to a "hydrogen economy," combining high energy and high heat in one place for optimal hydrogen generation.[71]

Hugh Montefiore, a former Anglican bishop, was a founder of Friends of the Earth UK in the 1970s and served as a director for decades. When he stated in 2004, "I have now come to the conclusion that the solution [to global warming] is to make more use of nuclear energy."[72] he was forced to resign his post. Here is hard evidence of the extreme green movement's intolerance of any divergent opinions on key environmental issues. Disagree with the dogma and you're fired. There's not much room for intelligent debate in that kind of atmosphere.

One of the founders of the Italian environmental movement, Chicco Testa, has written a book explaining why he has converted to nuclear power.[73] He now actively supports Italy's decision to build between four and eight nuclear plants, now put on hold in the wake of the incident at Fukushima, Japan. Italy is a classic case of a country that can benefit from nuclear development. They have no coal, oil, or natural gas. They have limited hydroelectric resources, and they have a growing economy that needs new energy supplies.

In 2009 Stephen Tindale, the former executive director of Greenpeace UK, announced that he now supports nuclear energy. He was joined by three other prominent conservationists: Lord Chris Smith of Finsbury, the

---

70. James Lovelock, "Nuclear Power Is the Only Green Solution," the *Independent*, May 24, 2004, https://secure.hosting.vt.edu/www.choicesandchallenges.sts.vt.edu/2007/docs/Lovelock%202004.pdf
71. Stewart Brand, "Environmental Heresies," *Technology Review*, May 2005
72. Amanda Griscom Little, "Green vs. Green," *Wired* Magazine, February 2005, http://www.wired.com/wired/archive/13.02/nuclear.html?pg=5
73. Chicco Testa, *Tornare al nucleare?* (Torino, Italy: Giulio Einaudi editore, 2008)

chairman of the Environment Agency, Mark Lynas, the author of the Royal Society's science book of the year, and Chris Goodall, a Green Party activist and prospective parliamentary candidate.[74]

Among well-known personalities to declare support for nuclear energy are Bob Geldof, the musician and antipoverty activist for Africa, and the late Paul Newman, actor, liberal political activist, and philanthropist.

Although it is not his primary designation, I'm sure U.S. President Barack Obama would call himself an environmentalist. His personal support for new nuclear plants in the United States is perhaps the most effective action to date to help activists and members of the Democratic Party who previously opposed nuclear power to see the wisdom of changing their position on nuclear energy.[75]

Many Choices in the Energy Palette

Some forms of energy are "on demand" while other forms are intermittent. If you have a large enough woodpile, you can make a fire to heat your home whenever you want. If you store water behind a dam, you can make electricity whenever you wish, so long as you do so sustainably. These are examples of energy on demand.

Solar panels are an intermittent form of energy because you can't make them work at night or when it is cloudy. The same is true of wind energy; it is only available when the wind blows. If tidal or wave energy were ever harnessed successfully, they would also be intermittent sources of power. Some proponents of wind and solar energy believe we will eventually develop storage systems that convert these technologies into on-demand energy. This may be so but we are not there yet as there is no proven, cost-effective way to do it.

Before we discuss the strengths and weaknesses of the various energy choices we have for the future, I will give a brief description of each of the energies we can choose from.

Biomass energy refers to all energy derived from plants, wood used for cooking and heating, for example. *Biofuel energy* refers to biomass that has been converted into liquid fuel for vehicles. Plants use about seven times as much energy each year from the sun as is consumed by all human civilization. Trees are by far the largest consumers of solar energy. The majority of biomass energy used by people is derived from trees and other woody plants. *Biomass accounts for about 75 percent of all our renewable energy consumption.* The majority of this is fuelwood for cooking and heating in the tropical developing countries, but large amounts are also used in the pulp

74. Steve Conner, "Nuclear Power? Yes Please....," *Independent*, February 23, 2009,
http://www.independent.co.uk/environment/green-living/nuclear-power-yes-please-1629327.html
75. On the Issues, "Barack Obama on Energy and Oil," http://www.ontheissues.org/Celeb/Barack_Obama_Energy_+_Oil.htm

and paper industry for process heat and drying the pulp. In addition there is a growing biofuels industry that produces transportation fuels.

Hydroelectric energy starts as the sun's heat evaporates water from oceans, lakes, and landscapes, transports it into the atmosphere, where it eventually falls as rain at higher altitudes, flows down rivers into man-made dams, and is directed through turbines to make electricity before returning to the sea. Hydroelectric energy provides about 20 percent of electricity worldwide, so between them wood and hydroelectric energy account for about 95 percent of all renewable energy. One of the greatest ironies and logical disconnects of our time is the fact that many "environmentalists" generally oppose felling trees and strongly oppose large hydro dams.

Fossil fuel energy is by far the largest portion of total energy consumed; about 86 percent of our energy comes from petroleum, coal, and natural gas. These fuels have proven to be the most convenient and versatile for so many applications. Most of the world's electricity is produced by burning coal and natural gas. Nearly all our forms of transportation are fueled by petroleum products. Most buildings are heated with natural gas and other fossil fuels. Fossil fuels are the primary energy source in manufacturing and other industrial production.

Even though the fossil fuels were originally derived from ancient forests and plankton, grown on solar energy, they are classified as nonrenewable because they do not replenish themselves. At the present rate we will end up consuming more than 300 million years of fossil fuel creation in a few centuries. This is hardly a model of conservation.

Nuclear energy is unique in that it is a major energy source that is not based on solar energy. Uranium is a naturally occurring element that is slightly radioactive. Natural uranium is composed of two main isotopes: 99.3 percent is uranium-238, which has a half-life[76] of 4.5 billion years, 0.7 percent is uranium-235, which has a half-life of 704 million years. It is the uranium-235 that produces the nuclear reaction in a conventional nuclear reactor. Uranium is one of the rarest elements in the earth's crust, but because it contains so much energy it has the potential to provide fuel for thousands of years. One kilogram of natural uranium has the same amount of energy as 10,000 kilograms of coal. One kilogram of uranium-235 has the same energy as 1,500,000 kilograms of coal.

I apologize for the many numbers in the last paragraph. But they are nothing compared to the complexity of nuclear physics and nuclear engineering. We will leave it at that for now, but we will encounter a few more

---

76. The half-life of a radioactive element (isotope) is the time it takes for half of the element to decay. Ten half-lives are sufficient to effectively eliminate the element, transforming it into either another radioactive element or a stable element that is not radioactive.

numbers when we discuss nuclear energy in more depth. A nuclear power plant is our most brilliant engineering achievement. Yet a single leaf on a tree is more complex in nature.

Among them, fossil fuels, hydroelectric, nuclear, and biomass energy account for about 98 percent of all our energy use. There are a few other energy technologies that deserve mentioning:

Geothermal energy refers to two different technologies, both based on the heat in the earth (geo means earth, thermal means heat). One form of geothermal energy, often called "hot rocks," relies on local areas where heat from the earth's core comes close to the surface. The Old Faithful geyser in Yellowstone National Park is an example. California, Iceland, Italy, and New Zealand obtain considerable energy from geothermal by using the earth's heat to make steam to run turbines that turn generators to make electricity. Hot rocks geothermal energy is generated by the radioactive decay of uranium and thorium in the earth's interior and is therefore a form of nuclear energy.

The other type of geothermal energy is known as a ground source heat pump or a geothermal heat pump. Nearly half the sun's energy striking the earth is absorbed at the surface by the land, lakes, and sea. The heat pump, which uses the same technology as a refrigerator, is able to tap into this stored solar energy and use it to heat buildings, to make hot water, and, by reversing the heat pump, to provide air conditioning. This form of geothermal energy can be applied to any building in the world, unlike the hot rocks form of geothermal, which is only practically available in a few locations.

Wind energy is based on the movement of air in the atmosphere. There are two factors that cause the wind to blow. When the sun heats the earth's surface this in turn heats the air and causes it to rise. When the air rises, it creates a kind of vacuum that pulls surrounding air in, thus creating wind. The variable heating of the land and sea results in areas of higher and lower pressure in the atmosphere. Air moves from high pressure areas to low pressure areas. The other factor is the earth's rotation. Because the atmosphere is a gas rather than a solid, it doesn't really want to follow the surface of the earth as it rotates. This is why there are "prevailing westerly" winds in both the Northern and Southern Hemispheres. The combination of the earth's rotation and the sun's heat create the wind and weather patterns that change with infinite complexity.

Wind energy has been used for centuries to power ships for exploration, trade, sport, and pleasure. Windmills were invented to use the natural energy in the air to grind grain into flour and to pump water from wells. More recently wind has been harnessed to produce electricity both on and off the electrical grid. When used off the grid, the energy is often stored in batteries, making it possible to have electricity on demand when the wind is not blowing. When wind energy is fed into an electrical grid, it allows the operators to shut down other electric plants while the wind is blowing. The negative aspect of this is that whenever a wind energy facility is established it is necessary to build a suitable backup plant to produce energy for when the wind is not blowing. The best geographical locations for wind energy will produce about 20 to 30 percent of the energy that would be produced if the wind were blowing at an optimum speed all the time. In other words, when a wind company claims it has installed 1000 megawatts of wind energy, it has really installed about 200 to 300 megawatts. The promotional material invariably talks about the *installed capacity* of 1000 megawatts when, to be more honest, it should reveal that the *capacity factor* is 20 to 30 percent thus actually producing 200 to 300 megawatts.

Solar energy is derived directly from the sun. There are a number of ways to convert sunlight directly into energy. The most widely recognized is the solar photovoltaic panel, usually just called a solar panel or PV. It produces electricity by converting the photons in sunlight into a flow of electrons from the panel, either directly into the grid or in off-grid applications to a battery that stores the energy for use when the sun is not shining. Even in the best locations solar panels will produce electricity only 15 to 20 percent of the time. This is the most expensive way to produce electricity and also one of the most unreliable.

Sunlight can also be used to heat water in solar water heaters. This is much more cost-effective than photovoltaic panels. In sunny climates it is a very efficient way to produce hot water for washing. China leads the world in adopting solar hot water heating.

Passive solar energy refers to building designs that absorb, reflect, or store solar heat in a way that reduces the need for heating and cooling with other fuels. Much more use could be made of passive solar energy if our homes and other buildings were better designed with the sun's daily movement in mind.

To Grid or Not to Grid

The distribution of electricity through the electrical grid represents one of the greatest advances in the history of energy technology. When you think about it, it is almost a miracle that huge amounts of energy can be transmitted through relatively tiny wires over great distances with no moving parts. But, in fact, there are moving parts—quadrillions of invisible electrons traveling through the wires to run motors, charge batteries, power computers, TVs and other electronic equipment, heat our homes, and cook our food.

The grid allows everyone on it to be connected to a number of different electrical plants, often ones based on different technologies. All grids must have sufficient capacity to satisfy peak demand plus a surplus to allow for individual plants to be shut down for repairs or refueling. This provides continuous power to all consumers unless there is not sufficient surplus to deal with demand or in the case of an unexpected failure. Ice storms, tornados, and earthquakes can disrupt the grid for days or weeks while repair crews struggle around the clock to restore power. It is during these events that we come to recognize just how important the grid is to our daily lives. Civilization as we have come to know it would be impossible without the grid.

Many people have a romantic notion that it would be desirable to "get off the grid." This is no doubt linked to their wish to be independent and self-sufficient. While this is a noble aim in some circumstances, electricity is not one of them. Winter Harbour, the small community I was born and raised in, was off the grid during my childhood. Photovoltaic panels did not yet exist, and wouldn't have worked very well in a rain forest anyway, so the only choice for electricity was a gasoline or diesel generator. They are noisy, dirty, expensive, and they break down regularly. And the owner of the infernal machine is usually the one who ends up having to fix it.

The hamlet of Winter Harbour is, to this day, divided into two tiny towns, the fishing village and the logging camp. In the fishing village each home and business is separate. The residents, mostly independently minded folks, never did agree on a central "light-plant," so during my childhood it was everyone for themselves. The personal generator ran only in the evening for lights. Many were the nights when the man of the house had to go out and monkey- wrench the generator in the dark. Refrigeration was only possible with kerosene fridges that needed filling every few days. Freezers were nonexistent and we made toast on top of the oil or wood stove.

The logging camp where I grew up was a company town of about 60 people and 20 buildings. Because there was an organization it was possible to install a central generator and to build a small grid to service all the buildings. The camp mechanic was in charge of running and repairing the system, which allowed the rest of us to go about our business. In the early years the generator was used mainly for light to read and work by and to provide power for the machine shop. At 10 to 10 each evening, the lights blinked twice, warning us that the plant would be turned off in 10 minutes. This allowed the nighthawks time to light their gas lanterns. Eventually larger generators were purchased, with a back-up plant in case of breakdown, and then the power was on 24 hours. This allowed the use of electric fridges and freezers, electric light whenever you wanted it, and electric appliances like toasters and washing machines. The good life had arrived, but not for the fishing village, where it was still everyone for themselves.

While those of us in the logging camp enjoyed 24-hour power for 20 years the folks in the fishing village carried on with their independent ways. Then in 1991 I joined a small delegation from Winter Harbour before the British Columbia Utilities Commission. We explained that the hard-working people of our village had provided millions of dollars worth of fish and timber into the economy and had paid their taxes faithfully. For this reason, we argued, Winter Harbour should finally be connected to the provincial electric grid. The Commission found in our favor, so long as we paid a higher rate to cover part of the cost of the transmission line. Not one resident, especially in the fishing village, minded paying the premium for the seven years it took to retire the debt. Even at three times the regular rate it was a lot less expensive than a gasoline or diesel generator. And there was the blessed convenience of power on demand at the flick of a switch. But the really pleasant surprise was the sound of silence now that 20 or more generators no longer howled day and night, drowning out birdsong and frogs croaking in the roadside ditches.

More recently, Eileen and I bought a village lot and built a cottage in the town of Cabo Pulmo on the Baja Peninsula of Mexico. The village of about 100 homes and cottages is off the grid with no electricity or phone lines. Trust Eileen and me to pick a place that reminds us of our Winter Harbour home, complete with a rough gravel road to get there. There are a few native Mexicans in Cabo Pulmo, mostly ranchers and their families, some of whom run restaurants, diving shops, and other businesses that cater to tourists. Most of the homes are owned by Americans and a few Canadians who visit Cabo Pulmo for a few weeks or months each year. Some have retired there.

Very few, if any, of the Mexican homes are equipped with solar panels for electricity. They can't afford the $10,000 cost of a typical system that includes the solar panels, inverters, and storage batteries. They can buy a two-kilowatt gasoline generator for under $500. That's all they need for power tools, lights at night, and a TV set, but it does not allow refrigeration and it makes for a noisy lifestyle. Ice is imported by truck to keep meat and produce fresh in big coolers.

Nearly all the homes owned by visitors and expatriates have solar systems that provide 24-hour power to run lights, highly efficient refrigerators with freezers, satellite Internet, sewage treatment systems, mini-stereos, espresso machines, and blenders. They can afford solar panels because they are relatively wealthy people from very wealthy countries. But it has become clear to me that it is a very romantic notion that solar power is the answer for people in developing countries. It is so much more expensive than every other option that there is no way it can provide widespread electrification. It is so important to remember that sustainability includes economics as well as the environmental and social priorities. A more cost-effective approach than solar panels is required if the 1.5 billion people without electricity are to enjoy a better life.

Strengths and Weaknesses of Electricity-Producing Technologies

The previous section began to bring into focus the fact that every energy technology has strengths and weaknesses. While solar electricity is quiet and clean, it costs 5 to 10 times more than most other electricity-generating technologies. Seeing that energy is required for nearly all our goods and services, it is obvious that if energy costs more, then goods and services will cost more. This does not seem to matter to activists who think solar and other "renewable" technologies are somehow morally superior to other forms of energy, and therefore a bargain at any price. And their attitude indicates they don't really care how much energy costs, even to people who are already struggling.

Biomass Energy and Biofuels

As previously mentioned, the term "biomass energy" generally refers to solid fuels such as wood, sawdust, straw, and dung whereas the term "biofuel" is used for liquid fuels derived from biomass. Both, of course, are derived from plants that are ultimately the product of photosynthesis.

Biomass energy is typically used to produce heat for space heating and water heating or to make steam for electricity production. Biomass energy accounts for over 70 percent of all renewable energy. Biomass is an effective substitute for fossil fuels for many applications. Much of the energy used in sawmilling and in the pulp and paper industry is derived from wastes such as bark, sawdust, and shavings. In the Kraft pulping process nearly 50 percent of the wood, the lignin and hemicellulose, is digested into "black liquor" that is burned to provide most of the energy for pulp-making.

Sweden produces 32 percent of all its energy from biomass, including about 8 percent of its electricity. Biomass, mainly wood-waste from forestry, sawmilling, and pulp and paper industries, has now surpassed oil as the main source of all energy in Sweden.[77] While not every country has the ability to reach such a target, Sweden provides a model for the world in producing realistic, cost-effective renewable energy in an industrialized economy.

---

77. "Biomass generates 32 percent of all energy in Sweden", Renewable Energy World, July 2, 2010, http://www.renewableenergyworld.com/rea/news/article/2010/06/biomass-generates-32-of-all-energy-in-sweden

Unlike inherently intermittent sources of renewable energy such as wind and solar, biomass can be easily stockpiled and therefore provide reliable energy on demand. There is a great potential for increasing biomass energy, especially in countries with large forest cover and major forest industries.

Biofuels are liquid fuels that have been produced from plant sources such as sugar cane, corn, and palm oil. Unlike biomass energy, which requires little processing or manufacturing, biofuels are produced in sophisticated refineries similar to petroleum refineries. Biofuels are used almost exclusively for transportation, as an additive to or substitute for fossil fuels.

Brazil has traditionally been the world leader in biofuels due to its policy of self-sufficiency and the fact that until recently it had no fossil fuels of it own. Vast areas of land were converted to sugar cane plantations in the 1970s to produce ethanol for passenger vehicles. Today the United States produces about twice as much ethanol as Brazil, mainly from corn, and between the two countries they produced 88 percent of the world production of 23 billion gallons (87 billion liters) in 2010.[78] Biofuels now account for about 1.5 percent of global transportation fuel.

The countries of the European Union, where diesel provides over half the transportation fuel, produce about 70 percent of the world's biodiesel, mainly from rapeseed. Palm oil and soybeans are also used to produce biodiesel.[79]

Virtually all of the biofuel produced today is from sugar, starch, and oil, the edible carbohydrates produced by plants. These are the primary energy supply for the human population and therefore there is a real conflict between human food and transportation fuel. On average it takes about 10 people's food to fuel one car. The realization that increased biofuel production will eventually result in an unacceptable level of competition with the food supply has led to a large investment in alternative biofuel research and development. The feedstock for alternative biofuels will consist largely of wood and other woody materials such as corn stover (the stem and husk) and wheat straw. These are commonly referred to as "cellulosic biofuels". The waste from forestry and agricultural, and trees grown specifically for biofuels, could provide much more feedstock than the traditional carbohydrates, and would not compete so directly with the human food supply.

It is technically more difficult to convert woody materials into liquid fuel than to convert sugar, starch and oils. Therefore much of the research on cellulosic biofuels is focused on reducing the cost of production. A number of commercial-scale plants are now operating and more are

78. Wikipedia, "Ethanol fuel", http://en.wikipedia.org/wiki/Ethanol_fuel

79. Masami Kojima, Liquid Biofuels: Background Brief for the World Bank Group Energy Sector Strategy, World Bank, March 2010, http://siteresources.worldbank.org/EXTESC/Resources/Biofuel_brief_Web_version.pdf

under construction. They have all been heavily subsidized in hopes that production costs will eventually come down.

The future of biofuel production very much depends on the price of oil. Whereas it was thought by many that "peak oil" was just around the corner, recent offshore discoveries and unconventional oil sand and shale oil developments have brought this into question. Still, the International Energy Agency predicts a continued increase in global oil consumption of one percent per year from the present 83 million barrels per day to 105 million barrels per day by 2030.[80]

Whatever the timing, it is likely that as demand for liquid fuels rises, and as oil becomes scarcer and more expensive, that biofuels will play an increasingly important role in transportation energy supply.

In the 1970s, anti-nuclear energy campaigners commonly used the homespun slogan, "Split Wood, Not Atoms". Wood was recognized as a renewable energy source for cooking and heating in back-to-the-land communities. Then came the anti-forestry movement in the 1990s and the idea that wood is a "primitive" fuel that should be replaced with modern renewables such as wind and solar energy. It was no longer fashionable to split wood. Thus came about the environmental movement's rejection of wood, the world's most important source of renewable materials and energy.

Today, Greenpeace flatly rejects both biomass energy and biofuels even though they are clearly a form of renewable energy. They contend that because land that might otherwise be left as wilderness must be cleared to grow the crops needed to produce biofuels, that biofuels derived from trees and plants should not be used.[81] [82] They have adopted the terms "land-based biofuels" and "harmful biofuels" to describe biofuels that are produced from plants grown on the land.

In 2011, Greenpeace launched the Rainbow Warrior III, a $32 million custom-built ship designed for campaigning around the world. Equipped with state-of-the-art electronics for satellite transmission of their protests against oil drilling and tuna fishing, it is equipped with sails to assist with propulsion when the winds are favorable. This is a far cry from our first Rainbow Warrior, a surplus British fishing research vessel that was purchased for £40,000 and refit for a few thousand more.

Greenpeace's first campaign on the Rainbow Warrior III was to protest a coal-fired electricity plant in the Netherlands. A photo on their website showed the coal-plant under construction amid a sea of wind turbines

---

80. Alexander Kwiatkowski and Rachel Graham, IEA Cuts 2030 Global Oil Demand Forecast on Economy, Bloomberg, November 10, 2009, http://www.bloomberg.com/apps/news?pid=newsarchive&sid=ab8gxNuuOayl

81. First biofuels, now biomass: is the EU driving another BioMess? Greenpeace EU, 2011, http://www.greenpeace.org/eu-unit/en/Publications/2011/biomess-briefing/

82. Report: Sustainable Alternatives for Land-based Biofuels in the European Union, Greenpeace EU, 2013, http://www.greenpeace.org/eu-unit/en/Publications/2013/CE-Delft-Report/

on the Dutch coast. In a media release a Greenpeace spokesperson proclaimed, "This ship is driven by super-efficient electric motors and sails that set a standard for sustainable shipping. It will be powered by the wind."[83] They do have good writers at Greenpeace.

Nowhere is it explained how the "super-efficient electric motors" are driven. Electric motors, however efficient, require electricity. Indeed, two large diesel-powered engines turning generators provide the electricity to drive the electric motors. But of course Greenpeace is using biodiesel? No, they are using fossil fuel diesel because they are opposed to biodiesel.

Here is a description of the propulsion system from a shipping industry website:

> "Ship propulsion—Rainbow Warrior III is a sailing ship mostly dependent on wind energy. It, however, has a back-up engine - Volvo Penta D65A MT 1850 HP - that runs on diesel-electric propulsion. The back-up engine is used during bad weather conditions and has a speed of up to 11kt.

> The ship, running on the back-up engine, moves at a maximum speed of 11kt. Power from the diesel-electric engine reaches the propellers through an electromotor. The ship's speed can be increased by connecting the main engine, which can elicit a maximum speed of 16kt. The main engine powers the propellers mechanically. However, this increases the emission levels."[84]

It is a bit of a stretch to call an 1850 HP diesel engine a "back-up engine". And then there is the "main engine", the horsepower of which is not disclosed. As a mariner myself, I cannot accept the assertion that the ship is "mostly dependent on wind energy" and that the engines are only used during "bad weather". I suppose "bad weather" includes when there is no wind, or when the wind is blowing in the wrong direction for the ship's movement. In fact, this is a motor-powered vessel with what is commonly know as "sail-assist", and there is nothing wrong with that, if only they would be honest about their dilemma. Greenpeace is sailing on a fancy fossil fuel-powered ship with a bit of wind to help them on their way.

Back to the coal-fired power plant on the Dutch coast that was the target of the Rainbow Warrior III's first campaign. If Greenpeace can have a fossil fuel "back-up" for their wind-powered ship, why can't Holland have a fossil-fuel back-up for their wind turbines, to provide electricity when the wind is not blowing, which is about 75 percent of the time? Such is the

---

83. Clean Energy Now: Rainbow Warrior in action, Brian Fitzgerald, Greenpeace International, October 26, 2011, http://www.greenpeace.org/international/en/news/Blogs/makingwaves/clean-energy-now-rainbow-warrior-in-action/blog/37537/
84. Greenpeace's Rainbow Warrior III Vessel, Netherlands, http://www.ship-technology.com/projects/rainbow-warrior/

hypocrisy of self-appointed activists who demand other's do as they say and not as they do.

Solar Electric Energy

It is easy to find glowing reports from promoters who claim that both solar and wind energy are not prohibitively expensive and prices will come down dramatically in the future. Anton Milner, the spokesperson for the European Photovoltaic Industry Association, claims, "Europe will save 300 billion Euros by switching to 12 percent of solar power by 2020." This is due, he says, "to the fact that solar installations are cheaper than any nuclear or coal facility, and that sunshine is free".[85] Perhaps he means a small solar installation costs less than a nuclear plant that produces more than 100 times as much energy. Regardless, it is a reckless statement and holds no truth.

I don't mean to beat up on Bobby Kennedy Jr. all the time, but at least it's a change from picking on Greenpeace. The blurb announcing his keynote presentation to the 2009 Solar Power International conference in Anaheim, California, states, "Mr. Kennedy argues a sophisticated, well-crafted energy policy will help sharpen American competitiveness while reducing energy costs and our national debt and offers a bold vision to restore U.S. economic might, safeguard our environment, and reestablish America's role as an exemplary nation." He has a lot of nerve implying solar energy will "reduce energy costs" and help "sharpen American competitiveness." It is so preposterous it leaves one short of breath. Does he realize the Chinese are producing most of the world's solar panels but can hardly afford to use them themselves? And that when they do use them they can just tack the price onto the ones they sell to wealthy countries where they are subsidized to the hilt?

In 2008, China exported 98 percent of the solar panels it manufactured. Most of these panels were sent to Germany, Spain, the U.S., and Japan, rich counties that can "afford" to squander taxpayers' money to subsidize ridiculously expensive, politically correct solar technology. This has led to the adoption, in 2009, of a 70 percent subsidy for large solar installations in China in order to get some domestic uptake of the technology.[86] I'm not holding my breath; it might take a 90 percent subsidy to get anything moving.

One of the strengths of solar power is it tends to track the demand for electricity in the summer when the air conditioning load is highest. The

---

85. Henning Wicht, "Europe Could Gain by Switching to Solar Power," *iSuppli*, February 23, 2009, http://www.isuppli.com/Photovoltaics/MarketWatch/Pages/Desire-to-Become-Energy-Independent-and-Lower-Emissions-Has-Translated-into-Global-Leadership.aspx
86. Liu Angi, "China to Pay 70 percent Subsidy for Solar Power," CCTV, July 23, 2009, http://www.cctv.com/program/bizchina/20090723/111018.shtml

longest, sunniest, and therefore hottest days are the best days for solar panels. If they were able to produce electricity at a reasonable cost, they would be a welcome addition to the grid. This is why it makes sense to put research and development funds into solar technology. A breakthrough in price would be an important advance.

In addition to its much higher cost, solar electric power is also intermittent and unreliable. It does not work at night, during cloudy days or cloudy periods, or in the early morning or late afternoon when the sun is low in the sky. In other words, solar panels are automatically powerless for about 16 out of 24 hours on average during the year, or two-thirds of the time, even when there are no clouds. Depending on the cloudiness of the location where the solar panels are installed, they may actually provide useful power for only 15 percent of the time over the year.

The term *capacity factor* is used to describe the amount of electricity actually produced compared to the potential if the generator were operating at 100 percent of its capacity, 24 hours a day, 365 days a year. Large baseload power plants, such as coal, nuclear, and hydroelectric, typically have capacity factors of 90 percent or higher as they run continuously, except for repairs and refueling in the case of nuclear power plants.

An analysis of 12 large solar installations in the United Kingdom concludes they have an average capacity factor of 7 percent. That is the main reason why, at the standard cost of electricity in the U.K., it will take between 45 and 290 years to pay for these systems.[87] Not even solar panels last that long. It doesn't take a genius to realize solar power is a waste of good money on the grid. In the words of a sustainability director in one of the five New York City boroughs, solar panels are a "wealth-destroying technology." If quiet, sustainable, and clean are the main criteria then there are other, more cost-effective technologies that can deliver much more energy at lower cost and with even fewer emissions. Let's look at some real examples of the prices consumers are being charged for solar electricity.

In 2004 the government of Germany passed the *Renewable Energy Sources Act*, requiring electrical utilities to pay a fixed price for solar energy. It did so to encourage individuals and companies to buy solar panels, install them on rooftops, and connect them to the national grid.

The price utilities must pay for solar energy is called a "feed-in-tariff." The average price for rooftop solar is 50 euro cents per kilowatt-hour (kWh), or about 70 US cents per kWh. (A kilowatt-hour is the amount of electricity required to power 10 100-watt lightbulbs, or 40 compact fluorescent bulbs of the same brightness for one hour.) This does not include the delivery cost over transmission lines to the eventual consumer.

---

87. "Rooftop Solar Power in the UK – Real World Data," March 10, 2009,
http://lightbucket.wordpress.com/2009/03/10/rooftop-solar-power-in-the-uk---real-world-data/

Consider that coal and nuclear energy are sold into the grid for less than 5 US cents per kWh on average across the United States; you can calculate that German solar energy costs 14 times as much as U.S. coal and nuclear power. Over the past decade billions of dollars have been invested in solar power and yet today it produces less than 1 percent of Germany's electricity at a cost of over US$3 billion per year. A wise German would hope the percentage of solar stays below 1 percent.

Feed-in-tariff laws have now been enacted in France, Spain, Italy, and Greece as solar hysteria continues to grip the European community. But there is a growing realization that the pace of solar installations can't be sustained at recent levels. In late 2008 Spain reduced the feed-in-tariff to 46 US cents per kWh and placed a cap on the amount of new installations for 2009. This is clearly due to the unsustainable cost increases solar energy imposes on electricity prices.

The only jurisdictions in North America to have introduced feed-in-tariffs are Ontario and California. In Ontario, the *Green Energy Act* of 2009 required initially that the electrical utilities pay 42 cents per kWh, about half the German rate. The average cost of electricity for residences in Ontario is 7 cents per kWh. So at 42 cents solar is six times more expensive than the average cost of electricity.

Predictably, the Ontario Sustainable Energy Association rejected the original 42-cent rate as insufficient. They are correct that it is not possible to pay back the investment in a reasonable time at 42 cents. They lobbied actively for a rate as high as 86 cents per kWh, more than double the legislated price. In their aptly named document, "Renewables Without Limits," they claim it is not possible to make a profit on solar energy unless it is priced 15 times higher than the average cost of power.[88] They succeeded in getting the government to raise the price for solar to up to 80.2 cents, nearly 14 times the cost of conventional power.[89] And they did so in all seriousness as if this was obviously the right thing to do. It was a case of unbridled moral certitude that negated any concern for cost to the economy or human welfare. It was a complete rejection of competition in the market and a blind (or not so blind) adherence to feel-good policies that will surely pave the road to hell with good intentions.

As of early 2013, California was the only state in the U.S. to adopt a feed-in-tariff for solar energy. The renewable energy community has declared it a failure from the start because it offers only up to 31 US cents per kWh.[90] Even in one of the sunniest states in the country, five times

88. Paul Gipe, "Renewables Without Limits," Ontario Sustainable Energy Association, August 29, 2007, http://www.cpfund.ca/pdf/updating-ontarios-standard-offer-program.pdf
89. "Renewable Energy Feed-in Tariff Program," Ontario Power Authority, 2010, http://fit.powerauthority.on.ca/Page.asp?PageID=122&ContentID=10543&SiteNodeID=1103&BL_ExpandID=260
90. David Erlich, "Who's Lining Up for California's Feed-in Tariff?" Cleantech Group, February 20, 2008, http://cleantech.com/news/2483/whos-lining-up-for-californias-feed-in-tariffs

the rate for conventional baseload power won't support intermittent and unreliable solar energy.

Most U.S. states have shied away from feed-in-tariffs, possibly because the obviously inflated cost would result in consumer outrage. Instead, several states have adopted Renewable Portfolio Standards (RPSs), a bureaucratic term that the average person has never heard of, never mind knows what it means. I would love to see Jay Leno out on the sidewalk asking people what they thought of the Renewable Portfolio Standard. The word *energy* is entirely absent, as if there is a standard for renewable portfolios. A more understandable term would be Renewable Energy Mandates, or Renewable Energy Dictates because what it means is that government has forced the utilities to acquire a certain percentage of their electricity from approved renewable technologies, almost regardless of price. But large-scale hydroelectric power, by far the most important renewable electricity source in the U.S., and the world, is not accepted as part of most states' Renewable Portfolio Standards. That's because many activists don't like dams and they have lobbied successfully to exclude the most important renewable electricity technology from the renewable category. This in itself makes a mockery of the policy.

It would be funny if it weren't so serious. To date, 28 states, including the most populous ones, have adopted RPSs and many others are considering doing so. While the objectives vary from state to state, most require between 20 to 30 percent of electricity from approved renewable sources by 2020 or thereabouts. The federal government is considering a national RPS of 20 percent by 2020 as well. This means an 8- to 12-fold increase in renewable energy from the present 2.5 percent of the national electricity supply.[91] Given the existing choices, this will invariably be mainly wind and solar energy. Such a program could conceivably increase the cost of electricity in the U.S. by 50 percent, thus making nearly everything Americans do and every item they purchase considerably more expensive. Politicians will no doubt blame the electrical utilities for the consequences of these energy dictates, despite the fact the utilities are being forced into them against their better judgment in many cases.

In mid-2010 the wheels began to come off the heavily subsidized solar industry in Europe. Spain has reduced the subsidy by 30 percent and may retroactively reduce the tariff it guaranteed for 20 years.[92] Spanish solar companies are being investigated for selling solar energy at night. It is presumed they were running diesel generators and sending the power through the meters that measure solar output. Such incredible distortions

91. "U.S. Electric Industry Net Generation," U.S. Energy Information Administration, January 21, 2010, http://www.eia.doe.gov/cneaf/electricity/epa/figes1.html
92. Lawrence Solomon, "Nightfall on the Solar Industry," *Financial Post*, June 17, 2010, http://opinion.financialpost.com/2010/06/17/lawrence-solomon-nightfall-on-the-solar-industry/

to market prices are bound to lead to this kind of fraudulent activity.[93] Germany and France have begun to cut their subsidies for solar energy. This has resulted in a collapse in new installations. The German government has had to face the fact that after committing over US$100 billion for solar energy it is producing well under 1 percent of the country's electricity.[94] Solar electric energy is clearly a bubble that's beginning to burst. As of early 2013, the value of most publically traded solar stocks had fallen to less than ten percent of their value during the peak years of 2007-2008. The governments of Germany, Spain, and Italy are scaling back their subsidies as the huge government-guaranteed commitments for future payments are beginning to weigh heavily on national budgets.

Wind Energy

Wind energy is more cost-effective than solar panels, but it too is relatively expensive.

Looking again to the German feed-in-tariff that provides real numbers instead of optimistic projections, the price paid for wind energy is between 10 to 15 US cents per kWh. In Ontario, the tariff price is 13.5 Canadian cents, much higher than prices paid for hydroelectric, coal, and nuclear power.

And wind energy also suffers from some inherent weaknesses. Like solar energy, wind is intermittent and unreliable. It has a higher capacity factor than solar, between 15 to 30 percent, depending on the location of the wind farm. But unlike solar, wind does not track the demand for electricity. The peak periods for electricity demand are during the coldest and hottest days of the year. Very often these are calm, clear days in the winter and summer. This means if wind is used for either baseload or peaking power there must be a reliable backup that can be brought online when the wind is not blowing. So when you build a wind farm you must also build a gas plant or another generator of equal capacity to back it up. Then why bother with wind farms?

In some cases there is good reason to build wind farms because when the wind blows we can avoid burning natural gas. This contributes to the conservation of a nonrenewable resource and reduces greenhouse gas emissions. On the other hand, the more wind farms we build, the more gas we must burn to back them up during the periods when the wind is not blowing, or not blowing hard enough to run the windmills at sufficient capacity to meet demand. In the final analysis building wind farms guarantees more and more natural gas will be required. This will likely

93. "Solar Bubble Bursts in Spain Amid Subsidy Cuts, Fraud Allegations," *Climate Wire*, May 6, 2010, http://www.windaction.org/news/27146
94. Jeremy van Loon, "German Clean-Power Boom 'Breaks' System, Ex-Lobbyist Tells Handelsblatt," June 21, 2010, http://www.bloomberg.com/news/2010-06-21/german-clean-power-boom-breaks-system-ex-lobbyist-tells-handelsblatt.html

result in increased CO_2 emissions, the opposite of what one would expect from wind energy.

The only exception to this is where there is abundant hydroelectric energy. When the wind is not blowing the hydro can be turned on. It is capable of "following the load" as it can be turned on and off quickly and can be ramped up and down with ease. This can allow better management of the hydro capacity because when the wind blows the water behind the dam can be conserved to be used another day.

Wind energy and other energy technologies can be converted into baseload, continuous power by using what is called *pumped storage*. When the wind blows and the power is not needed on the grid, the energy generated can be used to pump water up into a reservoir. Then when the energy is needed the water can be passed through turbines, exactly as with hydroelectric power, to a lower reservoir, 450 feet lower, where the water can be stored until it can be pumped up again. Or there must be a sufficiently large river where water is pumped up to the reservoir and released back to the river after flowing through the turbines. The problem with using wind for pumped storage is that it costs too much to begin with and after pumping water back into a reservoir it costs even more

The clever Swiss buy very inexpensive nuclear energy from France late at night, when there is a large surplus on the grid, and they use it to pump water into dams in the Alps. In the morning they run it through hydroelectric turbines and sell it to the Italians at a profit. But the economics work because the nuclear energy costs less than a penny a kilowatt-hour. With wind you are pumping with energy that costs 10 to 15 US cents per kilowatt-hour. And you have to build all the reservoirs and hydroelectric turbines, so the wind energy ends up costing much more than 15 cents. It is unlikely this approach will be used widely with wind energy in the near future.

Intermittent Versus Continuous Energy Sources

There is a popular perception, encouraged by activists and renewable energy advocates, that technologies such as wind and solar could replace conventional sources such as hydroelectric, nuclear, and fossil fuels. These activists fail to recognize the fundamental difference between technologies that are intermittent and those that produce power continuously. Continuous production is referred to as *baseload* as it is able to satisfy the main load all the time. Power plants are also used intermittently to satisfy *peak loads* when demand is especially high, such as in the afternoon on hot days when air conditioning operates at its peak. Natural gas plants are often used for "peaking" because they can be turned on and off quickly, whereas coal plants and nuclear plants can't be turned on quickly and turning them off quickly is not convenient for the operators. Even peaking plants work best if you can rely on them at all times. But intermittent technologies, such as wind and solar energy, are not available whenever we want them.

We have discussed how much more expensive wind and solar energy are to produce than conventional systems. But the *cost* to produce the energy is only one aspect. The *value* of the energy produced, how much it is *worth*, is a different matter. Regardless of the cost of producing the power, reliable continuous power is worth more than unreliable intermittent power. It is not worth much to have a lot of wind and solar energy when there is no demand for it. And technologies like wind and solar energy inevitably produce a percentage of their energy when it is not needed. In a very readable essay on this subject Glen Schleede states, "In fact, few people in the general public, media or government know the facts about the high true cost and low true value of electricity from wind."[95]

One can only conclude that wind energy and particularly solar energy are investment bubbles that will eventually burst. Only very rich countries that think they have money to burn can afford these technologies. To expect that countries in Africa will adopt them without huge subsidies from rich countries is far-fetched. It appears equally far-fetched that rich countries will provide such subsidies. In many ways these very expensive technologies are destroying wealth as they drain public and private investment away from more affordable and reliable energy-generating systems. It seems this lesson will be learned the hard way.

Hydroelectric Energy

Hydroelectric technology was the first large-scale producer of electricity. Thomas Edison did build a steam-powered generator in New York three weeks before he launched the first hydroelectric system in Appleton, Wisconsin, in September 1882. But for years after hydroelectric energy became the primary source of electricity. Eventually the hydroelectric system around Niagara Falls became the powerhouse that spurred industrial growth in New York and Ontario. The Tennessee Valley Authority's 30 hydro dams and the Bonneville Power Authority's 31 hydro dams contribute to a system of hydroelectric facilities that provide 7 percent of U.S. electricity, nearly three times as much as all other renewable electricity technologies put together.

Hydroelectric energy is, in many ways, the best source of electricity. It is renewable, clean, relatively emissions-free, available on demand for baseload power, and in suitable sites is the least expensive of all the major electricity technologies. That is why energy-intensive industries, such as

---

95. Glenn Schleede, "The True Cost of Electricity from Wind Is Always Underestimated and Its Value Is Always Overestimated," February 4, 2010, http://www.scribd.com/doc/26394311/Glenn-Schleede-1-High-Cost-Low-Value-of-Electricity-From-Wind

aluminum smelting, tend to locate their factories where large hydro projects can supply the power even when this means shipping the bauxite ore thousands of miles. The airplane manufacturers—Boeing in the U.S., Bombardier in Canada, and Embraer in Brazil—have in common the fact that they are located where there is abundant, inexpensive hydroelectric power to manufacture aluminum. Boeing benefits from the Bonneville Power dams on the Columbia River. Bombardier is in Quebec, where more than 90 percent of the electricity comes from the huge James Bay hydro project. Embraer takes advantage of the fact that Brazil produces 85 percent of its electricity from hydro power. The main weakness of hydropower is that it is limited by geography and rainfall. Some regions have abundant hydro potential while others regions have little or none.

Most environmental groups oppose large hydro dams because they flood valleys. It is true that a hydro dam completely alters the ecosystem, transforming a valley into an artificial lake. But a lake is not an undesirable environment. It's not as if the valley is being turned into a toxic waste dump. Fish can thrive in hydro reservoirs, boaters and cottage owners can enjoy holidays there and in many cases the dams provide flood control and improved irrigation. It's not as if there are too many lakes or too few valleys in this world. While a hydro dam means the end of a valley, it also means the birth of a new lake environment.

It is therefore highly irrational for environmental activists to have a zero-tolerance policy toward all large hydroelectric developments. Hydroelectric energy is the most important renewable source of electricity and will probably remain so into the distant future. Yet many Renewable Portfolio Standards in the U.S. do not classify large hydro as renewable energy. Environmentalism is supposed to be about all things renewable. Are solar panels made from aluminum that is produced with hydroelectricity somehow morally superior to the hydro dam that produced the aluminum? Are wind turbines that require backup with large fossil-fuel plants better than renewable hydro plants that provide power around the clock? And perhaps most important, would anti-dam activists rather see countries build more coal-fired plants instead of hydro?

Based on their opposition to hydropower, Greenpeace and other activist groups managed to force the World Bank to withdraw financial support for the Three Gorges Dam in China, the largest hydro project in the world at 22,500 megawatts. Thankfully China had enough economic muscle to go ahead on its own. New cities were built to relocate over one million people who lived near the flood zone. The Three Gorges Dam is equivalent to 40 large coal-fired plants.

In recent years China has become the world's largest producer of hydroelectric power, surpassing Canada, Brazil, and the U.S. I think this is a good thing as otherwise it would surely have built even more coal-fired plants, of which there are more than enough already. China gets more than

15 percent of its energy from hydro dams and is building more. But over 80 percent of China's electricity comes from coal, only 2.5 percent is nuclear.[96] Clearly hydropower is the most important renewable energy technology in China, without which there would be considerable more use of coal.

Some countries produce a large percentage of their electricity with hydropower. As mentioned, Brazil gets 85 percent of its power from hydro, one of the main reasons it accounts for about 50 percent of industrial production in Latin America. The Itaipu dam on the Parana River, on the border between Brazil and Paraguay, is the world's second largest dam at 14,000 megawatts. This one dam provides 26 percent of all Brazil's electricity and 78 percent of Paraguay's.

Canada produces more than 60 percent of its electricity from hydropower, mainly in Quebec, British Columbia, Manitoba, Newfoundland, and Ontario. When you add the 15 percent coming from nuclear generation, Canada can boast that 75 percent of its electricity is non-fossil fuel, among the highest such percentage in the world. Sweden produces 45 percent of its electricity from hydropower, 48 percent from nuclear energy, and 6 percent from biomass (wood). Therefore it has one of the least fossil-fuel dependent electrical systems in the world. Switzerland is also nearly fossil fuel free with 54 percent of its electricity coming from hydropower and 41 percent from nuclear energy. And France is also almost fossil fuel free, with 79 percent nuclear, 11 percent hydroelectric, and 10 percent from other renewables and natural gas.[97] That is the main reason why Switzerland, Sweden, and France have the lowest CO_2 emissions per capita in Western Europe—approximately 6 tonnes (6.6 tons) per person per year. This is less than one-third of U.S. emissions of about 19 tonnes (21 tons) on a per person basis.

In Eastern Europe it is interesting to compare Latvia with Poland, countries with similar per capita incomes but widely different electric energy profiles. Latvia produces 60 percent of its electricity with hydropower, while Poland depends on fossil fuels, mainly coal, for 98 percent of its electricity. As a result, Poland emits about 4.5 tonnes (5.0 tons) of CO_2 per person per year, more than double Latvia's per capita CO_2 emissions of 2.2 tonnes (2.4 tons) per year.

The above examples that show lower per capita CO_2 emissions from countries that produce more of their electricity from hydro and nuclear power, and therefore less from fossil fuels, may seem obvious, but this is seldom reported in the media. This is due to the fact that there is often a built-in bias against both nuclear and hydro in the activist community and among journalists who specialize in environmental reporting.

Consider the major energy sectors: electricity, transportation, build-

---

96. "China: Electricity," U.S. Energy Information Administration, July 2009, http://www.eia.doe.gov/emeu/cabs/China/Electricity.html
97. "Hydroelectricity," Wikipedia, http://en.wikipedia.org/wiki/Hydroelectricity#Countries_with_the_most_hydro-electric_capacity

ings, and industrial production. Only electricity production has such a varied mix of technologies among different countries. Transportation is nearly all driven by fossil fuel, with minor exceptions such as electric trains powered by nuclear and hydroelectric energy, and ships using nuclear propulsion. Most buildings are heated with fossil fuels, and industry is largely fueled by coal and natural gas. Therefore it is primarily the mix of electricity-producing technologies—fossil fuels versus renewables and nuclear energy—that differentiates per capita CO_2 emissions in countries with comparable economies.

Of course there is an even stronger determining factor; the relative wealth of countries as commonly measured in gross domestic product (GDP) per capita. China uses fossil fuels to produce most of its electricity, but because it has a relatively low GDP per capita of US$6000 per year, China's per capita CO_2 emissions are also relatively low at about four tonnes (4.4 tons) per year. Sweden, with a very high GDP of US$37,300 per year, has per capita CO_2 emissions of about six tones (6.6 tons), a low figure for a highly industrialized country but one that is 50 percent higher than China's. Yet Sweden's CO_2 emissions are only one-third of Australia's, even though Sweden has a per capita GDP about equal to Australia (World Bank figures).[98] Australia produces about 80 percent of its electricity from coal.

These two variables, relative wealth and differing mixes of electricity-generating technology, are at the bottom of much of the inequality in CO_2 emissions among countries. This leads to great difficulty in reaching a binding international agreement on greenhouse gas emissions. Two questions make this clear. Why should Sweden be required to reduce its emissions when they are only one-third of Australia's emissions, largely because Sweden does not use fossil fuels for electricity production? And why should China, even though it uses a lot of fossil fuel to produce electricity, be required to reduce its emissions when they are only one-fifth that of the U.S.? In the chapter on the science and politics of climate change, we will explore this and other aspects of the global debate on climate in greater detail.

Geothermal (Ground Source) Heat Pumps

Ground source heat pumps—also known as geothermal heat pumps, or simply geo—are one of the most important renewable energy technologies for the future. They are probably the third most important renewable resource after biomass and hydroelectric energy. *They are more important for the future than wind and solar energy combined.* Yet they are not

---

98. "List of Countries by GDP (PPP) per Capita," Wikipedia,
http://en.wikipedia.org/wiki/List_of_countries_by_GDP_(PPP)_per_capita

well known and most people who have heard about them do not know how they work. Part of the reason for this is that they are not visible: the heat pump is in a dark room in the basement and the pipes bringing the earth's heat to it are buried in the ground or submerged in a water body. But the technology itself is also difficult to comprehend. The earth beneath your house is not hot, not even room temperature unless you are in the tropics. How can a heat pump turn "cool into warm"? Thankfully one does not need to discuss the physics in detail to explain how this works. If you would like to read an explanation of the physics, see the reference below.[99]

Most people are also mystified by how their refrigerator, freezer, and air conditioner work. That's because they are also "heat pumps," using the same technology as a geothermal heat pump. The concept is relatively simple: a heat pump pumps heat from one place to another. In the case of your refrigerator, the heat is being pumped from inside the fridge into your kitchen. Note that when the fridge is running heat comes out the back. I used to assume the heat came from the motor or the compressor, but, no, it is the heat from inside the fridge. That's why it's cold in there! A freezer is exactly the same; only more heat is pumped out to make it even colder. An air conditioner treats your whole house as if it is a fridge, pumping the heat out of your house into the outdoors.

Geothermal heat pumps are made possible because the earth, including lakes and oceans, absorbs nearly 50 percent of the sun's energy in the form of heat. That heat can be tapped by putting pipes in the ground or a body of water and circulating water through them where the water picks up some of the stored solar energy in the earth or water. The slightly heated water then goes to a heat pump, where the heat is extracted and concentrated and put into your home. Even though the earth beneath your home may be at 10 degrees Celsius (50 degrees Fahrenheit), the heat pump makes it possible to concentrate that heat to 55 degrees Celsius (130 degrees Fahrenheit), which is hot enough to make your domestic hot water and more than hot enough to heat your home to a comfortable 22 degrees Celsius (72 degrees Fahrenheit).[100]

In summer the heat pump can be reversed and operated as an air conditioner, pumping heat out of your house into the ground. In this mode, it is more efficient than a conventional air conditioner. It is an amazing device, which can replace the gas, oil, or propane furnace, the gas, propane, or electric hot water tank and the conventional air conditioner with a single unit that is about the size of a gas furnace.

Geothermal heat pumps can be used in any building, anywhere on earth. It is possible to extract heat from permafrost in the High Arctic, and

99. "Heat Pump," Wikipedia, http://en.wikipedia.org/wiki/Heat_pump
100. "What Is a Ground Source Heat Pump?" International Ground Source Heat Pump Association, http://www.igshpa.okstate.edu/geothermal/geothermal.htm

it is possible to cool a building with heat pumps in the tropics more efficiently than with a conventional air conditioner. The most cost-effective applications are where there are both a high heating requirement and a high cooling requirement, such as in the cases of the continental climates of middle and eastern North America and central and northern Europe and Asia. Geothermal heat pumps are also the most effective way to reduce fossil fuel consumption in buildings.

The most advanced applications of geothermal heat pumps use tanks of hot or cold water to store energy. In this way the heat pump can operate at night when there is surplus power on the grid, producing and storing hot or cold water to be used for heating and cooling the following day. An in-home computer can tie into the weather forecast and determine whether to store hot water or cold water and what the expected demand for heating or cooling will be over the next few days. This fits in nicely with smart meters that charge for electricity according to the time of day it is being used.

The geothermal heat pump is as close to a perfect technology as one can imagine. It is based on stored solar energy, so it is renewable. There is enough stored solar heat under every city lot to supply more than 10 houses, so it is virtually inexhaustible. Heat pumps are a distributed rather than a centralized energy generator, a quality often cited as superior by environmentalists. Geothermal energy is a baseload, or on-demand technology because the energy is available 100 percent of the time. It has virtually no environmental footprint because the heat pump is in the building and the piping, or "loop," is in the ground. Unlike electricity, it is easy to store large amounts of energy by simply using water tanks. So geothermal is not only on-demand; it can also be stored at times of low electricity demand and then used during times of high electricity demand. And it is cost effective and pays for itself over a relatively short time.

A geothermal heat pump system installed in a new home will cost nearly twice as much as a conventional gas furnace, gas hot water heater, and air conditioner. But the increase in the monthly mortgage due to the increase in capital cost for the home will be less than the monthly saving on the energy bill. In other words, a geothermal heat pump installed in a new home pays for itself from day one. A geothermal system retrofit into an existing home can't usually be included in the mortgage, so it will result in a higher cost until the unit is paid for, after which there will be a net saving. This is all without any subsidy or government incentive.

But there are a number of barriers to the rapid adoption of geothermal heat pumps:

- Geothermal systems cost more to install than conventional furnaces, water heaters, and air conditioners. This increased capital cost is a barrier even though geothermal heat pumps typically result in a 50 percent reduction in operating costs for these services. Builders tend to be more concerned with competing for lower construction cost, as they will generally not be paying for the operating costs over the 50-year life of a building. Home buyers are often more interested in features like granite counters and a three-car garage than they are in adding to the cost of heating and cooling equipment that is concealed in the basement. Most people tend to avoid higher initial cost even when there is a reasonable payback due to lower ongoing costs. For example, many people avoid paying four dollars for a compact fluorescent lightbulb when they can buy an incandescent bulb for one dollar. The four-dollar bulb, which uses one-quarter of the energy and lasts two to four times as long as the one-dollar bulb, is clearly the best choice. Yet for some reason it seems we have to rely on environmental conscience rather than economic logic to rationalize paying more up front.

- Most homebuilders and homeowners do not realize that geothermal is the superior technology from an environmental and economic perspective. This is beginning to change in some countries, but it is difficult to break old habits as everyone knows what a gas furnace is, but very few people really understand what a geothermal heat pump is.

- There are not enough trained professionals to install or service geothermal equipment. Geothermal heat pumps are quite different from conventional technology. They are not more difficult to install or service, but they require specialized training. A number of organizations and associations now provide training for geothermal technicians, including the Canadian GeoExchange Coalition[101] and the International Ground Source Heat Pump Association in the U.S.[102]

Many countries, including the U.S. and Canada, have adopted incentives in the form of grants, rebates, and tax exemptions for the installation of heat pumps in new and existing residential and commercial buildings. This can cover as much as 30 percent of the total cost, making geothermal competitive with all other technologies.

A number of European countries have succeeded in overcoming the barriers to geothermal installation in new buildings. As a result of public awareness campaigns and a common sense approach to energy, geothermal now has a 90 percent penetration into new residential construction in Sweden. Switzerland can boast nearly 75 percent geothermal in new hous-

101. "CGC Quality Training Commitment," Canadian GeoExchange Coalition,
http://www.geo-exchange.ca/en/cgc_quality_training_commitment_p35.php
102. "Certified GeoExchange Designer Course," International Ground Source Heat Pump Association,
http://www.igshpa.okstate.edu/training/cgd.htm

ing units. Norway, Finland, and Austria are all close to 25 percent followed by France and Germany at around 5 percent. In the U.S. and Canada only about 2.5 percent of new homes are equipped with these heat pumps. Clearly North America, and some European countries, have a long way to go to catch up with Sweden and the other leading European countries.

It is not as if your home uses less energy when you install a geothermal heat pump, even though your utility bill will be reduced by at least one-third. It still takes the same amount of energy to heat and cool the home, but now about 50 percent of the energy for heating and cooling is coming from the earth, free except for the cost of pumping it in and out of the ground. Now if you improve the home's insulation and install better windows, you can really save money in the long run.

When you install a geothermal heat pump, you virtually eliminate the use of fossil fuel for heating and cooling in your home. If the source of electricity that runs the heat pump, other appliances, and lights is either renewable or nuclear, your entire home is now nearly fossil-fuel free. This makes a very big difference to your overall emissions of pollutants and CO_2.

When it comes right down to it, our houses and cars are the greatest consumers of energy and materials we own. Here is a formula for drastically reducing your material and energy consumption as well as your overall footprint on the planet:

The next time you buy a car, buy a modest one with really good fuel economy. Don't worry about the image your car gives you, just focus on practicality and common sense. Guys usually want a big fancy car with 350 horsepower just to get to work and back. Sure, you can have a stereo with seven speakers and heated seats, but buy a small hybrid or conventional car that gets good mileage. This will give you big savings; a luxury car with a big motor won't offer such savings. And a small car will use fewer resources and create much less air pollution. Then take the money you save on your car and put a heat pump in your house. The heat pump will probably be in a dark little room in your basement. Lighten up that basement room, paint your heat pump a bright color, put racing stripes on it, and take your friends and family down there and brag about what you have done for the environment. Forget the gas-guzzler as your pride and joy. Celebrate the 50 percent reduction in your personal use of fossil fuels!

Hot Geothermal Energy

As mentioned in the introduction, there are two distinct technologies that use the term *geothermal*. One of these is based on the fact that the earth's inner heat comes close to the surface in certain locations where the earth's crust is thin. In some locations it is possible to tap into steam generated from these hot spots and to generate electricity with turbines on the surface. Today 24 countries generate about 0.3 percent of the world's electricity by this method and scientists believe this could be increased substantially. Five countries—El Salvador, Kenya, the Philippines, Iceland, and Costa Rica—generate more than 15 percent of their electricity from geothermal sources.

Deep geothermal energy may have great potential and is definitely worth investing in as a renewable and sustainable energy resource. Difficulties include the high cost of drilling deep boreholes, uncertainty about the sustainability of the resource, the fact that every site has unique geology and therefore unpredictable circumstances, and the geographically limited nature of locations where it is hot enough to produce steam close to the surface.

In areas where it is not hot enough to produce steam, it is often possible to tap geothermal heat directly for district heating in towns and cities. In 1892 Boise, Idaho, became the first city in the U.S. to develop a district heating system with direct geothermal heating.

Nuclear Energy

Nuclear energy supplies about 16 percent of the world's electricity, a percentage similar to hydroelectric power. Among the 30 countries with nuclear power plants, 21 countries obtain 15 percent or more of their electricity from nuclear energy, ranging from Canada at 15 percent to France at nearly 80 percent. In the U.S. about 20 percent of electricity is produced by 104 nuclear plants, nearly one-quarter of all the world's nuclear power. The more than 400 nuclear plants that operate in 30 countries today are producing clean, reliable, reasonably priced electricity for hundreds of million of people.[103] And yet nuclear energy remains the most controversial form of power, so much so that some countries and regions have passed laws against it, either pledging to phase it out altogether or placing bans on further development.

However, there is a powerful sea change under way, which is bringing nuclear energy back into favor and targeting coal as the villain in the piece. This evolution in public opinion and government policy has come about very rapidly. It is due to the convergence of a number of factors, primarily the concerns over global climate change, energy security, and air pollution from fossil fuels.

Nuclear energy came by its controversial reputation honestly. Two atomic bombs killed nearly a quarter of a million people on August 6 and August 9, 1945, in Hiroshima and Nagasaki. This was our first experience with nuclear technology on a grand scale. A deep fear was indelibly impressed into the human consciousness. Now we could annihilate whole

---

103. "Nuclear Power by Country," Wikipedia, http://en.wikipedia.org/wiki/Nuclear_power_by_country

civilizations in seconds. Now genocide had become suicide. The course of evolution had been altered and the nature of culture and politics were changed forever.

We will never answer the question, "Was it worth it to avoid prolonging the war?" Many historians believe there would have been far more casualties on both sides if the U.S. had invaded Japan. But we cannot know the outcome of refraining from using the atom bomb. Some say the only reason it has not been used since is because it was used then. Others contend that the existence of nuclear weapons provides a deterrent to mutually assured destruction. Still others believe nuclear weapons are evil, an atrocity waiting to happen, and the sooner we can rid the world of these weapons of mass destruction, the better. This debate will likely outlive us all. But that should not stop us from working to reduce the number and the threat of nuclear weapons.

I visited Hiroshima recently as part of a public speaking tour on nuclear energy. The head of the Hiroshima Memorial Peace Museum gave me a tour of the exhibits, including models of the city and photographs showing the scale of devastation caused by the bomb. One could not avoid being deeply moved by the personal accounts and images that showed the horrible effects of the bomb on what appeared to be living corpses of men, women, and children. We must never forget.

I was guided to the courtyard where a gas flame burns as a memorial to the victims. Our tour leader explained the flame would burn until the last nuclear weapon was eliminated from the face of the earth. "Do you call it the eternal flame?" came to my lips. My host had to admit that was a good question.

In the wake of World War II, the arms race began with the U.S., Russia, and then Britain and France engaging in atmospheric nuclear testing and a buildup of nuclear weapons to be delivered by bombers and missiles. Throughout the 1960s and 1970s the world lived in constant fear that there would be an all-out nuclear war. My generation was born into that world and by the time I came of age, the Beat Generation had had its heyday and the hippy years of the late 1960s had just begun. We celebrated life in the face of the death machine that had been assembled to annihilate us all. Through altered consciousness we escaped into a world best captured by the Beatles film *Yellow Submarine*. Many of us became radicalized and turned against the establishment that was preparing for what seemed like our inevitable annihilation.

In 1953, U.S. President Dwight D. Eisenhower and Secretary of State John Foster Dulles had announced the Atoms for Peace program to use nuclear fission to produce energy rather than bombs.[104] Many of us believed this had been a cover for the continued buildup of nuclear

---

104. President Dwight D. Eisenhower, "Atoms for Peace," December 8, 1953, http://www.iaea.org/About/history_speech.html

weapons. Cold War rhetoric made us cynical as did the eventual advent of the Vietnam War. We concluded that everything nuclear was evil and the waste from weapons manufacturing and nuclear power generation was a toxic legacy that would poison our children for generations. We lost trust in the established order, and for good reason. We focused our attention on turning the tide of ever-increasing arms production—more missiles, multiple warheads, and submarines that were so deadly that one alone could wipe out an entire nation (they are still cruising around out there).

Meanwhile the U.S. and many other countries embarked on programs to build nuclear reactors in order to produce electricity. Most of the nuclear reactors that operate around the world today were built during the 1960s, 1970s, and into the 1980s. During those early years of the nuclear energy industry, there was an optimistic outlook and it seemed nuclear power would sweep the nations of the world. That all changed at 4.00 a.m. on March 28, 1979, when Reactor 2 on Three Mile Island in Harrisburg, Pennsylvania, had an accident involving loss of coolant water, which caused a meltdown in the core of the reactor. A wave of fear spread across the country in the aftermath of the accident. I was nearly 2500 miles away in Vancouver when I woke up to the news and I felt afraid. There was no way a nuclear reactor accident in Pennsylvania could possibly harm far-away Vancouver, but I got swept up in the mood of the time.

It didn't help that the hit movie *The China Syndrome*, starring Jane Fonda and Jack Lemmon, had been released only two months before the accident. In the movie, a nuclear plant accident, which results from a meltdown of the reactor core, threatens the world with destruction. The Three Mile Island accident seemed eerily similar; it was as if fiction had suddenly become reality. For days the news was dominated by the unfolding events in Harrisburg. Pregnant women and young children were evacuated, President Carter tried in vain to calm the populace, and then it was over. The containment structure around the reactor, five feet of steel and heavily reinforced concrete, did its job and prevented the radioactive material in the core from escaping into the environment.

In the aftermath of the accident, many follow-up health studies focused on the people who lived near the reactor. In the end there was no negative impact on the public or the workers in the plant.[105] In many ways the accident at Three Mile Island turned out to be a success story. It was a major mechanical failure, but no one was injured, never mind killed. Three Mile Island was a huge wake-up call for the nuclear industry, not only in the U.S., but in all Western countries that had reactors. All the safety systems and operating procedures were gone over and strengthened to make sure

105. "Backgrounder on the Three Mile Island Accident," U.S. Nuclear Regulatory Commission, April 7, 2009, http://www.nrc.gov/reading-rm/doc-collections/fact-sheets/3mile-isle.html

such an accident would not be repeated. Since then there has not been a meltdown accident in any reactor in the West.

Unfortunately the Soviet Union still lay behind the Iron Curtain in 1979 and the Three Mile Island accident had no effect on its nuclear program. Years earlier the Soviets had begun to build reactors around the country for power production. They took a short cut and simply copied the design of their nuclear weapons production reactors, failing to include a containment structure and adequate safety systems. It was like putting a nuclear reactor in a warehouse. The RBMK class of Soviet reactors was an accident waiting to happen. And it did.

There were four identical reactors at the Chernobyl nuclear complex in the Ukraine. In 1986 a group of engineers was assigned to do a test on Unit 4, which had the best operating record in the group. Ironically, the test was designed to improve the safety of the reactors. When the operators contravened basic safety procedures, the test went horribly wrong and the reactor blew up, breaking through the roof and spewing the radioactive contents of the core downwind over the Ukraine, Belarus, and on to Sweden.[106] There, at a Swedish nuclear reactor, alarms went off indicating elevated radiation levels. At first the Swedish operators thought there was a radiation leak at their own reactor. Two days later the Soviets finally admitted there had been an accident at Chernobyl.[107]

In many ways, Chernobyl was symptomatic of everything that is wrong with the Communist system: secrecy, central control, shoddy engineering, and lack of concern for human life.

It took a week to put out the fire because of the huge graphite moderator in the reactor core. Graphite is pure carbon and when it catches fire it is extremely difficult to extinguish. Thirty-four people died, either during the explosion or from radiation and burns they suffered while trying to put out the fire that continued to spread radiation into the atmosphere for a week after the explosion. When the fire was finally extinguished, a large area downwind had been contaminated with strontium-90, cesium-137, iodine-131, and other fission products.

After the accident the Iron Curtain was opened briefly as the Soviets sought help from nuclear scientists in the West. They helped to modify the other RBMK reactor's safety systems and operating procedures so such a situation could not be repeated. No other serious accident has occurred, even though the other three reactors at the Chernobyl site continued to operate for 13 years after the accident. Even today there are 10 RBMK class reactors operating in Russia. Thankfully they will eventually be shut

106. Wm. Robert Johnson, "Chernobyl Reactor Accident, 1986," June 11, 2006,
http://www.johnstonsarchive.net/nuclear/radevents/1986USSR1.html
107. "Chernobyl Nuclear Power Plant Accident, Detection and Monitoring," Answers.com,
http://www.answers.com/topic/chernobyl-nuclear-power-plant-accident-detection-and-monitoring

down and replaced with reactors with containment structures and better safety systems.

The antinuclear movement in the West used Chernobyl as proof that nuclear energy should be rejected and all existing reactors should be closed. Just as the Cold War was coming to an end, there was a new cause to replace the campaign against the buildup of nuclear weapons. In a way, nuclear energy simply replaced nuclear weapons as the cause of the day. The Greens in Europe made ridiculous claims that 300,000 people had died in the aftermath of Chernobyl. To this day Greenpeace claims that there were more than 90,000 deaths.[108]

A Chernobyl-like accident could not possibly occur in the reactors operating outside the former Soviet Union. Whereas the Three Mile Island accident involved a loss of cooling water from the reactor that, in turn, caused a meltdown of the core due to the heat of radioactive decay in the fission products, the Chernobyl accident was a runaway nuclear reaction. One of the most serious flaws of the RBMK reactor design is that it has a "positive void coefficient," which makes it possible for the reactor to experience a rapid, uncontrollable power increase.[109] This could not happen in the reactors in the West, most of which are designed to have a negative void coefficient. The Candu reactor design has a small positive void coefficient that is easily managed in the case of a power surge.

In 2003 the United Nations established the Chernobyl Forum, an investigative body composed of seven UN agencies, including the World Health Organization, the UN Environment Program, and the International Atomic Energy Agency as well as Russia, Ukraine, and Belarus.[110] In 2006, 20 years after the explosion, the forum published its findings on the impact of the accident. Two facts stand out. First, it concluded that only 56 deaths, including the 34 people who died in the explosion or fighting the fire, could be directly attributed to the accident. Second, they acknowledged the worst effect of the accident was the forced evacuation of 350,000 people from the contaminated zone into tenement blocks on the outskirts of Kiev. The incidence of suicide, drug and alcohol addiction, marriage breakdown, and mental illness and trauma that resulted from living in these crowded urban quarters far outweighed the possible effects of the slightly increased radiation exposure they would have experienced if they had been left in their country homes. The evacuation was ordered with the best of intentions, but it would have been better had most of the people been allowed to stay in their own communities.[111]

108. "Chernobyl Death Toll Grossly Underestimated," Greenpeace International, April 18, 2006,
http://www.greenpeace.org/international/news/chernobyl-deaths-180406
109. "Chernobyl - Appendices: Positive Void Coefficient," World Nuclear Association, March 2001,
http://www.world-nuclear.org/info/chernobyl/voidcoef.htm
110. "Chernobyl Forum," International Atomic Energy Agency, February 3, 2003,
http://www-ns.iaea.org/meetings/rw-summaries/chernobyl_forum.htm
111. "Health Effects of the Chernobyl Accident," World Heath Organization, 2006, www.who.int/ionizing_radiation/chernobyl/en/

Despite the unfortunate fact that injury and death were caused at Chernobyl, nuclear energy is still one of the safest technologies we have invented. Every industry, whether it be construction, farming, mining, steel production, forestry, financial services, transportation, or energy production, has risks associated with it. For the amount of power it produces and the number of people involved in its operations, the nuclear industry is a very safe place to work.

In 2008, workers in the U.S. nuclear industry experienced an accident rate of 0.13 accidents per 200,000 worker-hours. The accident rate for all manufacturing industries combined in the U.S. was 3.5 per 200,000 worker-hours, 27 times higher than for the nuclear industry.[112]

U.S. Bureau of Labor statistics confirm that it is safer to work in a nuclear plant than it is to work in either real estate or financial services.[113] A study of 54,000 nuclear workers conducted by Columbia University and published in 2004 found these workers had significantly fewer cancers, less disease, and lived longer than their counterparts in the general population.[114] If it is that safe to work inside nuclear plants, surely we can feel confident that it is safe to live near them. When asked by a reporter for MSNBC if I would be willing to live near a nuclear plant, I replied, perhaps a bit flippantly, "I'd be happy to live in a nuclear plant." When you think about it, there are not many safer or more secure places to be.[115]

Compare the record of the nuclear industry to other major energy technologies. An accident in the turbine room of Russia's largest hydroelectric dam caused 69 deaths in July 2009.[116] In February 2010 the Connecticut Kleen Energy natural gas plant exploded, killing five plant workers.[117] In April 2010 an explosion in a coal mine in West Virginia resulted in 29 deaths (about 5000 workers die in coal mines every year, mostly in China).[118] Later that same month, 11 workers were killed when a British Petroleum oil rig blew up and sank in the Gulf of Mexico.[119] By contrast, no nuclear worker has ever been killed in a nuclear plant accident in the

112. "Nuclear Power in the United States," Wikipedia, http://en.wikipedia.org/wiki/Nuclear_power_in_the_United_States#Worker_safety
113. "Safety Indicators Show U.S. Nuclear Industry Sustained Near-Record Levels of Excellence in '07," Nuclear Energy Institute, April 14, 2008, http://www.nei.org/newsandevents/newsreleases/safetyindicators/
114. Geoffrey R. Howe, Lydia B. Zablotska, Jack J. Fix, John Egel, and Jeff Buchana, "Analysis of the Mortality Experience Amongst U.S. Nuclear Power Industry Workers After Chronic Low-Dose Exposure to Ionizing Radiation," Radiation Research 162 (November 2004): 517-526.
115. Zbigniew Jaworowski, M.D., Ph.D., D.Sc., "The Truth About Chernobyl Is Told," 21st Century Science and Technology Magazine, Winter 2000-2001, http://www.21stcenturysciencetech.com/articles/chernobyl.html
116. "Confirmed Death Toll in Dam Disaster Rises to 69," AFP, July 23, 2009, http://www.france24.com/en/20090823-sayano-shushenskaya-russia-siberia-hydroelectric-plant-accident-death-toll-69
117. Edmund H. Mahony and Eric Gershon, "Five Killed in Connecticut Power Plant Blast," Los Angeles Times, February 8, 2010, http://articles.latimes.com/2010/feb/08/nation/la-na-conn-blast8-2010feb08
118. Howard Berkes, "Massey, Federal Officials Investigated In Mine Blast," National Public Radio, April 30, 2010, http://www.npr.org/templates/story/story.php?storyId=126422117
119. Patrick Jonsson, "C'mon, How Big Is the Gulf of Mexico Oil Spill, Really?" Christian Science Monitor, May 1, 2010, http://www.csmonitor.com/USA/2010/0501/C-mon-how-big-is-the-Gulf-of-Mexico-oil-spill-really

West and only one accident has caused fatalities. The Chernobyl accident was the exception that proves the rule that nuclear energy is one of the safest industries we have.

Fukushima

At 2.46 pm, March 11, 2011 Tokyo Time a massive 9.0 magnitude earthquake struck 24 kilometers (15 miles) below the surface off the coast of Honshu. At the nearby Fukushima Daiichi nuclear plant, a six-reactor complex situated right by the sea, reactor units 1, 2, and 3 shut down automatically as programmed. Units 4, 5, and 6 were already shut down for routine inspections. The earthquake cut the plant off from electrical power on the grid, causing the emergency diesel generators to come on automatically to supply cooling water to the reactors.[120]

When a reactor is shut down the heat of decay from the fission products would melt the fuel unless cooling water is kept circulating. For the first hour after the earthquake it seemed that all was going well.

At 3.27 pm a massive 15-meter (49-foot) tsunami struck the nuclear plant, drowning the emergency diesel generators and washing away their fuel tanks. This resulted in one of the worst nightmares for nuclear operators, "station blackout", or complete loss of electrical power. Emergency power was provided for a short time by backup batteries but when they were discharged the cooling systems quit and a state of emergency was declared. Everyone except emergency workers was evacuated within a three-mile radius of the plant. Over the next few days things went from bad to worse as fuel meltdowns occurred in all three reactors, followed by hydrogen explosions that blew the roofs off all three reactor buildings. Radiation leaked into the air and into the sea and by April 16 evacuation of everyone except emergency workers was completed within a 20-mile radius from the plant. Iodine tablets were distributed to everyone who was evacuated and people were advised not to drink milk or leafy vegetables from the region.

During the following weeks the situation was gradually brought under control as off-site power was brought back online, cooling systems were provided, and decontamination of water containing radioactive elements began. There is every reason to believe that the situation will continue to improve, although it will take ten years or more for the cleanup and decommissioning of the plants to be completed. In the wake of the accident it is reported that two engineers died when the tsunami struck, 26 workers were injured by the hydrogen explosions, and a number of workers required decontamination of radioactive materials on the skin and clothing.

---

120. "Timeline for the Fukushima Daiichi Nuclear Plant Accident", Nuclear Energy Agency – OECD, August 24, 2011, http://www.oecd-nea.org/press/2011/NEWS-04.html

There is no indication that anyone, including workers in the plant, have suffered injury or death from radiation.

On March 23rd an editorial was published on the New Scientist website calling for the immediate establishment of a long-term study on the health effects of radiation released from the plant.[121] It was suggested that the Hiroshima-based Radiation Effects Research Foundation would be the ideal organization to carry out such a study. They have followed the health histories of more than 100,000 people who survived the atomic bombings of Hiroshima and Nagasaki.[122] On March 24th Evan Douple, Associate Chief of Research with the foundation, was interviewed by National Public Radio on the issue of a long-term study of Fukushima residents and workers. When asked, "What do you think about the idea of studying health effects from the Fukushima Dai-ichi accident?" he replied, "I think it would be very unwise. There just isn't any evidence that there are enough exposed people at high-enough doses to expect to see any health effects that are measurable." and concluded, "On the basis of our current estimates, there shouldn't be measurable numbers of cancers. So you won't be able to count them, ever."

Six months after the incident, an article in the Journal of American Physicians and Surgeons reported that "From personal dosimetry and a standard hazard-function model, risk of deterministic effects of ionizing radiation on exposed recovery workers can be calculated. Barring an exceptional event that caused the 250 mSv/y limit to be greatly exceeded, such effects in Fukushima workers are unlikely."[123]

There are a number of factors contributing to the fact that people working and living in and near the Fukushima plant will not suffer the casualties experienced at Chernobyl.

- At Chernobyl the bulk of the radiation release occurred instantly when the reactor blew up, spreading its contents downwind in a short period of time. At Fukushima there was no radiation release until the hydrogen explosions began the day after the tsunami.
- Soviet authorities did not acknowledge the Chernobyl accident until two days after the release of radiation. At Fukushima citizens were evacuated before significant release of radiation occurred.
- The people exposed around Chernobyl were not given iodine tablets, thus resulting in about 5000 cases of thyroid cancer, mainly in children, all but a few of which were cured. No such result can

---

121. Debora MacKenzie, "Act Now to Track Health Effects of Nuclear Crisis", New Scientist, March 23, 2011, http://www.newscientist.com/article/dn20275-act-now-to-track-health-effects-of-nuclear-crisis.html
122. Radiation Effects Research Foundation, http://www.rerf.or.jp/index_ea.html
123. Bobby R. Scott, "A Guide to Radiation Hazard Evaluation Applied to Fukushima Recovery Workers", Journal of American Physicians and Surgeons, Volume 16, Number 3, Fall 2011, http://www.jpands.org/vol16no3/scott.pdf . See also: http://www.marketwatch.com/story/fukushima-recovery-workers-probably-safe-scientist-explains-2011-09-06

be expected at Fukushima where all evacuees were given iodine tablets.

- Due to the secrecy of the Soviet authorities there was no warning issued to avoid drinking milk or eating dairy products. This resulted in the uptake of iodine-131 around Chernobyl and the resulting thyroid cancers. At Fukushima a ban was placed on milk consumption immediately, as well as on leafy vegetables that may have been contaminated.
- The Fukushima incident resulted in about ten percent of the radiation release compared to Chernobyl. But whereas nearly all the release from Chernobyl went into the atmosphere, and then into populated areas, most of the radiation released at Fukushima went into the sea where it will eventually be buried in marine sediment. It is likely that the exposure to radiation among people living around the Fukushima plant was less than one-thousandth of that received at Chernobyl.

The International Atomic Energy Agency has categorized the Fukushima incident as 7 on a scale of 1-7, the same rating given to Chernobyl (Three Mile Island was rated as 5). This has resulted in widespread belief that the Fukushima indent was equally damaging compared to Chernobyl. Unfortunately the IAEA scale does not distinguish sufficiently between the technical scale of the event, the degree of mechanical failure etc., versus the extent of damage to people in terms of health, injury and death. On that level Fukushima is clearly far less damaging than Chernobyl. Whereas Chernobyl did directly cause 56 deaths and thousands of injuries from radiation, Fukushima has resulted in no injuries and no deaths from radiation and is not expected to in the future.

While the health effects from Fukushima are too small to measure, the political fallout has been harmful to the support for nuclear energy in a number of countries, including Japan. Much of this was due to the incredible hyperbole of major media outlets, which often gave the impression that the nuclear incident was the cause of the death and destruction. In a classic case of misplaced cause and effect the Reuters news agency reported that, "The month-long nuclear crisis that has gripped Japan following an earthquake and tsunami has claimed up to 28,000 lives and the estimated cost stands at $300 billion, making it the world's most expensive disaster."[124] Of course it was the tsunami that caused nearly all the deaths (now estimated at 18,000) while the Fukushima nuclear plant had 2 deaths, both also caused by the tsunami.

---

124. Shinichi Saoshiro and Mayumi Negishi, "Japan Raises Nuclear Crisis to Same Level as Chernobyl", Mail and Guardian Online, April 12, 2011, http://mg.co.za/article/2011-04-12-japan-raises-nuclear-crisis-to-same-level-as-chernobyl

While most countries, including the U.S., France, China, South Korea, Britain, Vietnam, Canada, and Finland have reaffirmed their commitment to nuclear energy in the aftermath of Fukushima, Germany and Italy have rejected nuclear energy. While Italy has no operating nuclear plants, Germany has relied on nuclear energy for about 25 percent of its electricity. The German Green Party and Greenpeace Germany have long campaigned to reject nuclear energy and Fukushima gave then the ammunition they needed in the form of scary headlines and sensationalist rhetoric. They have succeeded over the years in convincing a majority of Germans that nuclear energy should be banned. No one has ever died from radiation from a nuclear plant in Germany, yet in June 2011 an outbreak of E. coli from organically grown bean sprouts killed 53 people and caused life-long injury to over 800. One wonders about the collective wisdom of what is otherwise a very successful nation.

Even before the decision to shut eight nuclear plants immediately and to phase out the remaining nine plants by 2022, Germany was importing nuclear energy from France. Chancellor Merkel has indicated that the lost nuclear power will be replaced with wind and solar energy, but in fact Germany is embarked on building a large new fleet of coal- and gas-fired power plants to replace the nuclear energy.[125] There are 13 Gigawatts of coal- and gas-fired power plants under construction in Germany as of late 2011, the equivalent of 13 nuclear reactors. Another 10 Gigawatts of coal- and gas-fired plants will be required to replace the nuclear reactor fleet when it is shut down in 2022. This flies directly in the face of Germany's, and the European Union's policy of reducing fossil fuel consumption and greenhouse gas emissions, hence the political strategy of using renewables as a cover for a major addition of fossil fuel plants.

The Fukushima incident has also resulted in the derailing of Italy's plans to build between four and eight nuclear plants in the near future. This has now been postponed indefinitely even though Italy has no domestic fossil fuel resources and limited hydroelectric potential. This decision has placed Italy in a precarious energy security position and it is not clear how this will be resolved.

Six months after the incident it was reported that the three reactors that experienced melting of their cores will be brought to a stable condition by the end of 2011. This has been confirmed by the International Atomic Energy Agency.[126] I predict that the Fukushima incident will have a minor impact at the global level as most countries with nuclear energy or aspiring to nuclear energy realize that it is safe, clean and reliable when compared

125. Henry Edwardes-Evans, "Germany 'Needs 10 GW of New Plant' Following Nuclear Phase-Out", Platts, May 31, 2011, http://www.platts.com/RSSFeedDetailedNews/RSSFeed/Coal/8936549
126. Alex Devine, and Tony Barrett, "Japan's Fukushima Cool-Down Forecast Supported by UN Agency", Bloomberg Businessweek, Sept 29, 2011.
http://news.businessweek.com/article.asp?documentKey=1376-LRRQQ91A74E901-7CDQNQHQ2STAI4D9OETFSSUU3K

with other energy technologies. One can only hope that Germany, Italy, and Japan realize this as the future of nuclear energy unfolds.

One of the more interesting results of the Fukushima incident was the conversion of George Monbiot into a nuclear energy advocate. A prominent environmental writer with the left-leaning British newspaper, the Guardian, Monbiot shares many of the views of the extreme environmental wing, including those of Greenpeace. He has now forcefully joined the debate, all the while enduring sharp and personally abusive attacks from his erstwhile environmental allies.

While many commentators lamented the "catastrophic" accident, Monbiot realized the obvious. If Fukushima was the worst-case scenario, and caused zero deaths from radiation, then it is clearly one of the safest technologies we have.

Perhaps his most incisive point was made in a column following the failed Kyoto Protocol meeting in Durban, South Africa in December 2011:

"This year, the environmental movement to which I belong has done more harm to the planet's living systems than climate change deniers have ever achieved.

As a result of shutting down its nuclear programme in response to green demands, Germany will produce an extra 300 million tonnes of carbon dioxide between now and 2020. That's almost as much as all the European savings resulting from the energy efficiency directive. Other countries are now heading the same way. These decisions are the result of an almost medieval misrepresentation of science and technology."

If only the mainstream environmental groups could see the same logical conclusion and embrace nuclear energy as the best technology to reduce fossil fuel consumption.

A report on nuclear safety that had been in the works since 2007 was released by the US Nuclear Regulatory Commission in February 2012, nearly one year after the Fukushima incident. The study, titled "State-of-the-Art Reactor Consequence Analyses (SOARCA)" concluded that "the calculated risks of public health consequences from severe accidents (modeled in the severe accident study) are very small" and that there was "essentially zero risk" of early fatalities due to radiation after a severe accident.[127] It also concluded that the risk of eventually contracting cancer as a result of radiation exposure was "less than one in a billion". Those are pretty good odds and I'll take them over driving a car down the highway or walking across a busy intersection.

---

127. Scott DeSavino, "Nuclear Accidents Pose Little Risk to Health, Say Regulators", Insurance Journal, February 2, 2012, http://www.insurancejournal.com/news/national/2012/02/02/233853.htm

Fear of Radiation

The fear of radiation fuels much of the opposition to nuclear energy. I attended a public hearing in Vermont, conducted by the US Nuclear Regulatory Commission to receive comments on whether or not the Vermont Yankee reactor should be granted a 20-year license extension. A young woman came to the microphone with a small child in her arms and proclaimed that she had moved to a house near the reactor and she knew her child was going to get cancer from the radiation being released into the environment. My immediate thought was, If you really believe your child will get cancer from living near this plant, surely you should move somewhere else. Apparently this is not a politically correct thought, as my colleagues advised me later. Why would someone stay where they think their child will inevitably get cancer? Was she just grandstanding for the crowd? Or did she genuinely feel concerned? It is not for me to judge.

One of the most helpful and annoying aspects of radiation is it is so easy to detect at minuscule levels. You can buy a radon test kit for $25 and determine if you have unusually high radon levels in your basement. The natural geology of many regions contains higher than average levels of uranium, which decays into the radioactive gas, radon. The radon can seep up through cracks in the foundation of your house and concentrate in the basement. This can result in exposure to radiation that is considered unsafe, especially if the basement is occupied. Your 25-dollar test kit can easily detect very low levels of radon, and you can easily rectify the problem by improving the ventilation in your basement.

Not all environmental hazards are so easy to detect. Detection of toxic chemicals requires highly trained technicians to collect samples, analyze them with expensive equipment, and interpret the results, all of which takes considerable time. Radiation can be measured instantly from levels that pose no harm to levels that should be avoided. This makes it very easy to monitor radiation levels in and around nuclear facilities. The second radiation is present it can be detected and then its source can be discovered. There is no radiation-related health hazard around any of the nuclear power plants operating in the world today.

But it is annoying because antinuclear activists are fond of detecting minute amounts of radiation near nuclear plants and then claiming the radiation came from the nuclear plant and that it will cause widespread cancer. The "Tooth-Fairy Project", conducted by the stridently antinuclear group Radiation and Public Health Project, collects baby teeth and analyzes them for strontium-90, one of the fission products from nuclear explosions and nuclear reactors.[128] They claim the levels of strontium-90

---

128. "Tooth Fairy Project," Radiation and Public Health Project, http://www.radiation.org/projects/tooth_fairy.html

in the teeth "may" cause an increase in cancer among people who live near nuclear plants.

A quick search finds that 99 percent of the strontium-90 in the environment is from atmospheric nuclear testing that occurred between 1945 and 1980 when China conducted the last nuclear explosion in the air. During that time period 522 atomic and hydrogen bombs were set off in the atmosphere.[129] These tests injected 4.2 tonnes (4.6 tons) of strontium-90 into the global environment.[130] Because strontium-90 has a half-life of nearly 30 years, about one-third of that amount still remains; much of it has been washed into the sea, but some of it still remains in the food chain and is deposited in babies' teeth.

About 1 percent of the strontium-90 in the environment came from the Chernobyl nuclear accident. It is not as widely distributed as the fission products from atmospheric testing because the plume from the explosion and fire did not enter the upper atmosphere. But the strontium-90 signature from Chernobyl was detected in many areas far distant from the main plume that spread northwest toward Sweden.

It is not possible to determine the level of strontium-90 that is emitted from operating nuclear plants because it is either nonexistent or is so miniscule that it can't be detected as distinct from the amount released by nuclear testing and the Chernobyl explosion.[131] To top it all off, the levels of strontium-90 in baby teeth are not high enough to cause concern in the first place. Many studies have been conducted and they clearly indicate that there is no increase in cancer rates near nuclear plants.[132][133]

How Much Radiation Is Good for You?

Odd question, you might think, but not so odd once you know the facts. Antinuclear folks constantly repeat that any amount of radiation is bad for us. The "linear, no-threshold" model holds there is no safe dose of radiation. If this were true, we would have all been dead long ago. There are 60 naturally occurring radioactive substances in the air, earth, and water. We are exposed to these, along with radiation from the sun and the cosmic radiation from outside the solar system, every day of our lives. Radiation from natural sources is one of the driving forces of evolution,

129. L.A. Andryushin, N.P. Voloshin, R.I. Ilkaev, A.M. Matushchenko, L.D. Ryabev, V.G. Strukov, A.K. Chernyshev, and Yu.A. Yudin, "Catalog of Worldwide Nuclear Testing," Begell House, July 18, 1999, http://www.iss.niiit.ru/ksenia/catal_nt/4.htm#Table8
130. "History of Nuclear Weapons Testing," Greenpeace International, April 1996, http://archive.greenpeace.org/comms/nukes/ctbt/read9.html
131. "Fact Sheet on Radiation Monitoring at Nuclear Power Plants and the 'Tooth Fairy Issue,'" U.S. Nuclear Regulatory Commission, August 5, 2009, http://www.nrc.gov/reading-rm/doc-collections/fact-sheets/rad-monitoring-and-tooth-fairy.html
132. Seymour Jablon, MA; Zdenek Hrubec, ScD; John D. Boice, Jr, ScD, "Cancer in Populations Living Near Nuclear Facilities," Journal of the American Medical Association, March 20, 1991, http://jama.ama-assn.org/cgi/reprint/265/11/1403.pdf
133. "Backgrounder on the Three Mile Island Accident," U.S. Nuclear Regulatory Commission, August 11, 2009, http://www.nrc.gov/reading-rm/doc-collections/fact-sheets/3mile-isle.html

causing rare mutations that are usually neutral, sometimes negative, but occasionally beneficial.

Radiation is measured in millisieverts (mSv). The average person in the world receives a dose of 2.4 mSv of radiation per year from natural sources (referred to as background radiation).[134] Artificial sources, such as medical X-rays, smoke detectors, and residual nuclear weapons test fallout, can elevate the total exposure to about 3.6 mSv per year. The dose members of the American public receive from industry, including from the full life-cycle of nuclear power generation, nuclear medicine, and research where nuclear materials are used is 0.003 mSv per year. The full life-cycle of nuclear power generation is responsible for 15 percent of this small total dose from industry. The average dose to members of the public from nuclear power reactors themselves is 0.00045 mSv per year, about 1/10,000th the intensity of natural background radiation[135]

Some regions in Iran, Brazil, India, Australia, and China have very high background radiation. People in Ramsar, Iran, receive 260 mSv of background radiation per year due to naturally occurring radium, uranium, and thorium. This is several times greater than the maximum dose for nuclear workers recommended by the International Commission for Radiological Protection and 100 times the average worldwide. Yet there is no evidence of any ill effects on the populations living in very high background radiation environments. In fact the local people believe the radioactive hot springs in Ramsar promote healthier, longer lives. Many toxicologists and radiologists with PhDs agree with this assessment, that relatively low levels of radiation actually improve our ability to stave off disease and to heal from injury. This hypothesis is called "hormesis."[136]

There are three competing hypotheses regarding the health effects of low levels of radiation. The previously mentioned *linear no-threshold* model holds that any radiation above a zero dose is harmful. The *linear threshold* model asserts that there is a level below which no negative effect occurs, and above which a negative effect occurs. Finally the concept of *hormesis* theorizes that below a certain level radiation is beneficial, and then above that level it becomes progressively more harmful.

All organisms, including humans, have cellular repair mechanisms that respond to damage caused to DNA and other cellular components by toxic chemicals and radiation. Many radiologists believe low levels of toxic chemicals and radiation challenge the cellular repair mechanisms, conferring a degree of immunity to future damage, comparable to a vaccination.

---

134. "Background Radiation," Wikipedia, http://en.wikipedia.org/wiki/Background_radiation
135. Dr. Douglas Chambers, *Review of the Report, "Exposure to Radiation and Health Outcomes" June 2009 by Dr. Mark Lemstra; A Report Commissioned by the Canadian Centre for Policy Alternatives (Saskatchewan office) and the Saskatchewan Union of Nurses*, Canadian Nuclear Association, August 2009, http://cna.ca/english/pdf/studies/ReviewDrDouglasChambers09.pdf
136. Edward J. Calabrese, "Hormesis: A Revolution in Toxicology, Risk Assessment and Medicine," European Molecular Biology Organization, October 2004, http://www.ncbi.nlm.nih.gov/pmc/articles/PMC1299203/

It is clear to me that the linear no-threshold model is the least likely to be correct. Even if a near-zero dose of radiation causes damage, the body's repair mechanisms can fix the damage faster than it is occurring up to a certain point. In other words below a certain level there is no net damage. In summary, low levels of radiation are either not harmful or they are beneficial, while higher levels of radiation are clearly harmful.

It is difficult to prove experimentally which of these two models is closest to reality because the very low levels we are exposed to by background radiation make it impossible to discern any effect either way. So many other more important variables determine our health and well-being that it is impossible to discern whether low levels of radiation are slightly harmful, neutral, or beneficial. In any case it is clear the extremely low levels attributable to nuclear energy cause insignificant damage, if any. On the other hand it is possible that these low doses do have a significant beneficial effect.

Nuclear Terrorism?

In the aftermath of the September 11, 2001, attack on the World Trade Center, antinuclear groups latched onto the idea that nuclear plants are "sitting ducks for terrorists."[137] The fact that no nuclear plant has ever been targeted by terrorists is of no interest to Greenpeace and its allies who peddle sensationalism and fear as if such attacks were daily occurrences. There are much easier and more effective targets than nuclear plants: subways, government buildings, symbolic sites of power such as the World Trade Center, military installations, liquid natural gas plants, etc.

Having visited a number of nuclear plants and witnessed the security first-hand it is clear to me it would be suicide to try to get past the perimeter without permission. And as far as flying an aircraft into a reactor dome, engineers thought of that long before 9/11. The containment structures around the reactors were designed to withstand an impact from a falling aircraft, simply because of the possibility that a plane might fall out of the sky. If a terrorist did manage to drive an aircraft into a nuclear reactor, it would be a very bad day at the plant, but it would not breach the containment and would not release radiation into the environment.[138] Besides, it is virtually impossible to navigate an unauthorized large aircraft in American airspace in the post-9/11 world without it being

137. Keith Johnson, "Radford: New Greenpeace Boss on Climate Change, Coal, and Nuclear Power," *Wall Street Journal*, April 14, 2009,
http://blogs.wsj.com/environmentalcapital/2009/04/14/radford-new-greenpeace-boss-on-climate-change-coal-and-nuclear-power/
138. "Statement from Chairman Dale Klein on Commission's Affirmation of the Final DBT Rule," U.S. Nuclear Regulatory Commission, January 29, 2007, http://www.nrc.gov/reading-rm/doc-collections/news/2007/07-013.html

detected early on. The fact that no terrorist attack has been made on any nuclear plant might indicate terrorist groups are well aware of these facts.

Nuclear Weapons Proliferation?

Then there is the charge that nuclear power plants increase the risk of nuclear weapons proliferation. This is a more serious issue than safety or terrorism and deserves careful analysis. For many of us in the early years of the environmental movement our association of nuclear energy with nuclear weapons was the real deal-breaker. This was one of our biggest mistakes.

No nuclear weapon has been manufactured using the plutonium produced in a civilian power reactor. All the nuclear weapons states have dedicated military or research reactors for producing plutonium, which is extracted from used nuclear fuel. It is certainly possible to extract plutonium from the used fuel from civilian nuclear reactors. But the first question I have for people who insist civilian reactors increase the threat of proliferation is: If we shut down all every civilian power reactors, how would that convince the military to shut down its weapons-producing reactors? Aren't those the reactors we should be campaigning to shut down?

Another important point is that one does not need a nuclear power plant to build a nuclear weapon. In fact it is much easier to enrich uranium to weapons grade material with centrifuge technology than it is to extract plutonium from used nuclear fuel. The concern over Iran's nuclear program is primarily due to the fact that it has the centrifuges capable of enriching uranium to weapons-grade material. These same centrifuges can be used to produce the far less enriched uranium that fuels a nuclear reactor. This is why the strong international inspection program provided by the International Atomic Energy Agency is crucial.

But what about rogue states? you may ask. The answer is that shutting down all the nuclear plants in the world would not reduce the risk that deranged leaders or dictators might build nuclear weapons. The situation in North Korea, for example, can only be dealt with by political or possibly military means. Turning off a major portion of the world's cleanest electricity would be unlikely to dissuade Kim Jong-Il from building nuclear weapons and the means to deliver them.

Maybe the world would be a better place if nuclear weapons had not been invented. However, we will never know if this is so. While it may be possible to make nuclear weapons illegal, it is impossible to eliminate them. Therefore if good people give up nuclear weapons only evil people will acquire them. There are not many more fundamental dilemmas.

The above points make it clear that if civilian nuclear reactors pose a risk, it is a very small one and is by no means central to the challenge of preventing the further spread of nuclear weapons. Aside from these points, there is a more important general principle that should be considered.

Whether we like it or not, many of our most important tools and technologies can be used for destructive purposes. And many of our most useful and beneficial technologies were originally invented as weapons of war and only later adopted for nonmilitary means. It is likely that the club was invented before the hammer. Why would we outlaw the beneficial uses of a technology simply because it can also be used for destructive or evil purposes? Consider a few examples:

- Fire can be used to burn down a city and kill thousands of people. Should we ban fire for cooking and heating?
- Car bombs are made with fertilizer, diesel oil, and a car. Should we ban those three rather useful things?
- Guns can be used for hunting and for defending one's country or for committing genocide.
- Nuclear medicine is used to diagnose and treat millions of people every year, using radioactive isotopes that are produced in nuclear reactors. Should we ban nuclear reactors and nuclear medicine because nuclear technology can be used to make bombs?

What weapon has caused the most combat deaths in recent decades? Not guns, not car bombs, not cruise missiles, not nuclear weapons, but the simple machete, a big knife. Over a million people have died by the machete in the past 20 years, mainly in Africa, four times as many as in Hiroshima and Nagasaki combined. Yet the machete is the most important tool for millions of farmers in developing countries. They use it to clear land, cut firewood, and harvest their crops, which are all necessary activities.

You can bet the machete will not be banned anytime soon. But consider the fact that the machete used to harvest crops is exactly the same tool used to kill people. No modifications are required. But a nuclear power plant that is used to produce energy or medical isotopes is a completely different tool from a nuclear weapon. You can't drop a nuclear plant on a city.

Therefore I believe it is a general rule that we should not ban the beneficial uses of a particular technology just because that technology can be used for destructive purposes.

This harkens back to the earlier discussion about chlorine. While it is true that chlorine can be toxic and that it has been used to kill troops and civilians in war, it is also the most important element for public health and medicine. This recognition of a balanced, educated, and logical approach is a central theme on the path to becoming a sensible environmentalist.

Nuclear Waste: Fuel of the Future

For many people, nuclear waste is the key concern that leads them to reject nuclear energy as an option. This is partly because they fear radiation in the event of the escape of nuclear waste and partly because they are concerned about future generations' ability to manage nuclear waste. However, as we will see there is little reason to lose sleep over either worry. I'm not being flippant; it's just that the reality is so different from the popular perception that a little shock treatment is in order.

People in the nuclear industry, and those who understand the technical aspects of nuclear energy, prefer the term *used nuclear fuel* to *nuclear waste*. Antinuclear activists invariably refer to nuclear waste and they call facilities designed to store used nuclear fuel and other radioactive materials "nuclear waste dumps."

The fuel that originally goes into a typical nuclear reactor is pure uranium. During the nuclear reaction, part of the uranium is burned, splitting it in two and releasing vast amounts of energy, which is used to make steam to run turbines to produce electricity. The elements that result from splitting uranium are called "fission products." Uranium splits in many ways, so the fission products are a mixture of many different isotopes, some which decay in less than a microsecond and others that remain radioactive for a few centuries. Most of the used fuel is unburned uranium and another portion of it is uranium that has been converted, as a result of the nuclear reaction, into plutonium and other heavy elements, such as americium and californium.

Most of the fission products in the used fuel have no known useful purpose at present and can therefore be categorized as waste, although cesium-137 is used in medicine and uses for other fission products may eventually be found. The fission products include such isotopes as cesium-137, strontium-90 and iodine-131, which are biologically active and should not be ingested. They must be isolated from the environment until they decay into nonradioactive elements as they would otherwise pose serious problems to human health and the environment. Fortunately the longest lived fission products of concern decay into nonradioactive elements in about 300 years. This may seem like a long time, but in reality it is not difficult to design containers, and facilities in which to store those containers, that will be secure for much longer than 300 years.

The good news is that the majority of the used fuel, the uranium and plutonium in particular, can be recycled and made into new nuclear fuel. Used nuclear fuel contains at least 95 percent of the energy that was in the original fuel. In other words only about 5 percent of the energy is extracted from the nuclear fuel in its first cycle through the reactor. It makes no sense to call used fuel waste when 95 percent of it can be reused. Used nuclear fuel is one of our most important future energy resources.

And even if the original uranium was imported from another country, it is now a domestic energy resource, thus reducing concerns about energy security.

The technology for recycling used nuclear fuel was originally developed to extract the plutonium in the used fuel to make nuclear weapons. As mentioned earlier there are two main ways to make nuclear bombs: by enriching natural uranium to increase the level of uranium-235 to about 95 percent, or by extracting plutonium from used reactor fuel. The militaries of the nuclear weapons states were not interested in the other radioactive elements in the used fuel and during the Cold War these materials were disposed of in ways that today are totally unacceptable. It is similar to the manner in which toxic chemical wastes were simply buried or dumped prior to the advent of the environmental movement. This has resulted in a Cold War legacy of military nuclear waste that is being cleaned up at a cost of tens of billions of dollars.

In the same way nuclear fission, originally harnessed for weapons, is now used to make energy, recycling technology can be used for the peaceful purpose of producing even more energy rather than making bombs. Indeed, the trend is distinctly in this direction around the world, beating nuclear swords into nuclear plowshares.

When antinuclear folks tell us "nuclear waste will remain radioactive for millions of years" they are talking about the uranium, plutonium, and other heavy elements. But these can be burned as fuel and thus converted into fission products with much shorter lives. This is only one of the benefits of recycling used fuel. Another, of course, is the fact that the uranium that was mined in the first place can be recycled many times to produce over 100 times as much energy, if all the uranium-238 is burned. And not only are the fission products much shorter-lived than the uranium and plutonium, there is much less waste to dispose of because most of the used fuel has been recycled.

One of the principal mantras of the environmental movement is that we should "reduce, reuse, and recycle" the materials we employ to make goods and energy. The recycling and reuse of used nuclear fuel, and the reduction in the amount of waste fits squarely into this concept and should therefore be embraced by the movement as the correct approach to managing used nuclear fuel.

With conventional nuclear reactors we use less than 1 percent of the uranium that is mined from the ground. Natural uranium is 0.7 percent uranium-235, which is the *fissile* isotope (it is the only fissile isotope on the earth, without it there could be no nuclear energy). The balance of 99.3 percent is uranium-238, which is not fissile, but it is *fertile*. A fissile isotope is one that will support a chain reaction, and thus can be used as a nuclear fuel. A fertile isotope is one that can be converted into a fissile isotope in a nuclear reactor. For example, during a conventional reactor's operation, some of the uranium-238 is transmuted (converted) into plutonium-239, which is a fissile isotope and can be used as a fuel. Thorium is the other important fertile element that can be transmuted into a fissile isotope, in this case plutonium-233. There is about four times as much thorium in the earth's crust as there is uranium.

What this means is that we can eventually convert all the uranium-238 into plutonium and burn it as a fuel. Instead of using only 0.7 percent of natural uranium we can use 100 percent, increasing the energy potential by more than 100 times. In other words, 100 years of nuclear energy production can be turned into more than 10,000 years of energy production. It is somewhat akin to the biblical miracle of the loaves and fishes, according to which thousands of people were fed with five loaves of bread and two small fish. This is what is meant when nuclear energy is described as sustainable.

A number of countries are already recycling some of their used nuclear fuel. Of the 290,000 tonnes (319,700 tons) of used fuel produced during the past 50 years about 90,000 tonnes (99,200 tons) have already been recycled. France is in the forefront of this technology with a large recycling facility at Cap la Hague in Normandy, capable of recycling 1700 tonnes (1870 tons) per year.[139] Of France's 59 nuclear power stations, 22 have been modified to burn recycled fuel. Russia, the U.K., and India also have recycling facilities. Japan has recently completed a US$30 billion nuclear fuel fabrication and recycling facility at Rokkasho, north of Tokyo.[140] It is modeled on the French technology but with improvements that make it much less susceptible to the risk of proliferation. The United States had to approve the construction of the recycling plant in Japan because of treaties between the two countries regarding trade in nuclear materials.[141]

Recycling used nuclear fuel is a very complex subject and cannot be treated in depth here. For those who wish to dig deeper I suggest beginning with the World Nuclear Association's detailed explanation of the topic.[142]

It is ironic that while the United States is the largest producer of nuclear energy, with 104 of the world's 400 plus nuclear plants, it does not recycle any of its used nuclear fuel at this time. During the 1960s and 1970s three recycling plants were built to produce recycled fuel. One at West Valley, New York, operated successfully from 1966 to 1972. It was shut down when regulations were brought in that made it uneconomical. Another at Morris, Illinois, incorporated a new technology and did

139. "La Hague: Recycling Used Fuel," Areva, 2010,
http://www.lahague.areva-nc.com/scripts/areva-nc/publigen/content/templates/Show.asp?P=13&L=EN
140. "Japan's Nuclear Fuel Cycle Facilities," Japan's Nuclear Power Program,
http://www.japannuclear.com/nuclearpower/fuelcycle/facilities.html
141. "Nuclear Information, Comparison of the US-India and US-Japan Nuclear Cooperation (123) Agreements and Their Relationship with US Laws and International Frameworks," July 26, 2007, http://kakujoho.net/e/us_i_j.html
142. "Processing of Used Nuclear Fuel," World Nuclear Association, July 2010, http://www.world-nuclear.org/info/inf69.html

not perform satisfactorily. A third large plant was built at Barnwell, South Carolina, but never operated because the American government changed its policy in 1977 and ruled out all civilian recycling technology. Again ironically, the policy did not ban the military use of the technology to make weapons grade plutonium even though the ban on civilian recycling was rationalized in terms of preventing nuclear weapons proliferation. Thus ended U.S. attempts to enter the used fuel recycling business.

There is a common misconception that so-called nuclear waste is liable to leak out and contaminate the environment. As in *The Simpsons* cartoons, it is depicted as a yellowish-green corrosive liquid that roils around in its container trying to eat its way out. In fact used nuclear fuel takes the form of solid pellets that are not at all corrosive and are securely contained in steel and concrete casks built to last for hundreds of years.

The used nuclear fuel that is stored safely and securely at nuclear reactors around the world will certainly be recycled eventually. One of the reasons it is not all being recycled now is that new uranium is cheaper than recycled fuel. There is no panic to recycle the used fuel. It can be stored for decades or even centuries without difficulty before it is recycled.

In a typical reactor, one-third of the fuel is removed and fresh fuel added every two years. At the time of removal the used fuel is very radioactive and hot and must be cooled to prevent it from melting. This is done by placing it in a large pool of water adjacent to the reactor. Water is also a very good radiation shield. One can stand above the pool looking directly at the used fuel under six feet of water and not be exposed to harmful radiation. After five to ten years the fuel has cooled sufficiently and can be removed from the pool. At this time it can be placed in *dry casks*. (They are called dry casks because the fuel has been taken out of the water; really they are just casks made from concrete and steel.) These casks are designed to withstand the most severe imaginable impact by trains, planes, and large trucks.

Because the U.S. has not established either a recycling program or a long-term waste repository, all the used fuel is still stored at the nuclear reactor sites. At some reactors that have been operating for 30 to 40 years, the pools have become full and the older used fuel has been transferred to dry casks and stored on site on concrete pads with secure perimeters. The Nuclear Regulatory Commission has stated that the dry casks are capable of containing the used fuel for 120 years when stored outdoors.[143] This is certainly a very conservative estimate. And if the dry casks were in a climate-controlled building, they would be secure for 1000 years or longer.

All the used fuel produced in U.S. reactors over the past 50 years would fit on a football field stacked 22 feet high. If the used fuel were

143. "Safely Managing Used Nuclear Fuel," Nuclear Energy Institute, January 2009, http://www.nei.org/filefolder/Safely_Managing_Used_Nuclear_Fuel_0109.pdf

recycled, the fission products, the actual "waste," would cover a football field about nine inches in depth. We are certainly capable of securely storing this relatively small amount of material until it decays into nonradioactive elements. One hopes more people will come to understand we are not, and likely never will be, harmed by nuclear reactors or used nuclear fuel. And one further hopes the United States will join the other countries that are continuing to improve recycling technology and making use of this valuable source of future energy.

The fact that new uranium is less expensive than recycled used fuel has not stopped France, Japan, the U.K., or Russia from moving forward with recycling technology. One reason for this is that the nuclear industry in these countries is, or has traditionally been, state owned. State-owned corporations do not operate in the free market, as is largely the case in the U.S. If the French government wants to develop recycling technology, it simply makes the decision to do it and provides the necessary funds. In the U.S. the fact that it is less expensive to buy new uranium will cause the private companies that own nuclear plants to choose new uranium. Therefore the only way the American nuclear industry will consider investing in recycling is if the government provides sufficient incentives or funds to make it financially attractive.

There are two reasons for the U.S. government to create an environment that promotes recycling. First, unless you are engaged in developing the technology you can't be an effective part of the international dialogue about it, you can't work to improve the technology to make it more efficient, and you can't be as effective in improving security at an international level to prevent used fuel and its by-products from falling into the wrong hands.

Second, recycling used nuclear fuel is obviously the right thing to do in order to make use of the energy in it, to reduce the volume of waste and the time its takes to decay, and to live up to the principle of reuse, recycle, and reduce. In many cases it costs more to recycle glass and paper than it does to produce new glass and paper. But we recycle them anyway because this is a superior approach from the perspective of sustainability.

I do not propose that the U.S. enter into a crash program of recycling used fuel. France is not recycling all its used fuel, partly due to the higher cost, but it is recycling enough to create a viable industry. In the early years there were significant discharges of radiation to the environment from these recycling facilities. Through continual improvement this has been reduced to levels that are not significant from an environmental or health perspective. It would not have been possible to make such advances if there were no recycling plant to improve. Therefore it makes sense for the American government to develop a public-private partnership with the nuclear industry that results in the establishment of nuclear recycling, either as an advanced applied research project or as a commercial operation. As Canada has no recycling program it may be wise for it to join in a venture with the U.S.

The Next Generation of Nuclear Power

Research and development programs are under way in many countries to design and eventually build the next generation of nuclear reactors. Perhaps the two most important of these new designs are high-temperature gas-cooled reactors and fast neutron reactors, including those called breeder reactors.

Nearly all the world's conventional reactors are based on water-cooled low-temperature technology. These reactors are relatively inefficient at converting heat to electricity and they can't produce steam that is hot enough for most industrial processes. High-temperature gas-cooled reactors are much more efficient, produce high-temperature steam that can be used in place of steam produced by fossil fuels, and can produce hydrogen directly by splitting water through a thermo-chemical process. They will be capable of replacing fossil fuel energy in oil refineries, paper mills, chemical plants, and many other industries. They can also be used to desalinate water for domestic, irrigation, and industrial use. China, South Africa, and the United States are leading in this technology.[144]

Fast neutron reactors will be necessary to carry out the complete recycling of used nuclear fuel. Conventional reactors can be used for the first stages of recycling but cannot finish the job. Most importantly, fast reactors can burn a number of by-products from conventional reactors that conventional reactors cannot burn, thus making nuclear waste shorter lived and easier to handle. Fast reactors can also be used to desalinate water. A number of fast breeder reactors have been built and operated. The Russian BN-350 fast reactor ran from 1964 to 1999, producing 135 megawatts of electricity and 16 million gallons of water per day, which was used by people living in the town of Altau on the Caspian Sea. Fast reactors now operate in France, Japan, Russia, and India. Fast reactors are currently under construction in Russia and China and additional ones are being built in Japan and India. The United States operated a fast reactor at Hanford, Washington, from 1982 to 1993 when it was decommissioned. As a result the U.S. has fallen behind a number of other countries that use this technology.[145]

A breeder reactor is a type of fast neutron reactor that produces more fuel than it consumes. With this technology it is possible to burn all the uranium-238, thus extracting the maximum amount of energy from nu-

---

144. "Very High Temperature Reactor," Wikipedia, http://en.wikipedia.org/wiki/Very_high_temperature_reactor
145. "Fast-neutron Reactor," Wikipedia, http://en.wikipedia.org/wiki/Fast_neutron_reactor

clear fuel. This will ensure a supply of nuclear fuel that will last thousands of years.

Another interesting development is the renewed emphasis on small reactors, ranging in size from under 50 megawatts up to 300 megawatts, for electricity, hydrogen, industrial heat, and desalination. Small reactors are not new but in the past most of them were used in either research or military contexts. The reactors that power nuclear submarines, aircraft carriers, and icebreakers fall into this category. Small reactors are especially useful in remote areas off the electric grid and on islands, where the only alternative is often diesel generators.

In a remote area of Siberia there are four small reactors in four communities that produce steam for district heating and 11 megawatts of electricity each. They have performed well since 1976, at a much lower cost than fossil fuel alternatives in the Arctic region.

Russia is developing both 35-megawatt and 200-megawatt floating reactors on self-propelled barges to service remote industries, such as the oil and gas and mining industries, in Siberia. In addition, Argentina, Japan, South Korea, South Africa, and the United States are in the late stages of developing various types and configurations of small reactors.[146] There are 15 small reactor programs worldwide that are well advanced, including three in the US, four in Russia, two in China, and one each in Argentina and South Africa. In the future they will serve markets and industries that can't be served by large centralized reactors.

Swords to Plowshares

The proliferation of nuclear weapons represents one of the greatest threats to world peace and security. The situations in the Middle East and North Korea are extremely difficult with no obvious solution in sight. This problem will no doubt be with us for centuries to come. Even if a true world government is someday realized, society will always have to contend with rogue elements, tribal factions, and criminal activity. But as explained earlier, the threat of nuclear proliferation has very little to do with nuclear energy. It is a problem that must be dealt with separately and that will require hardball diplomacy and possibly force, one hopes with United Nations approval.

Meanwhile there are many positive activities and trends on the other side of the coin, which involve turning nuclear weapons programs and materials toward peaceful purposes. One of the first of these involved South Africa.

During the 1970s and 1980s, while the apartheid regime was still in power, South Africa mined uranium, enriched it, and produced six nucle-

---

146. "Small Nuclear Power Reactors," World Nuclear Association, July 2010, http://www.world-nuclear.org/info/inf33.html

ar warheads as a deterrent against invasion. As preparations were made in the early 1990s for the post-apartheid democratically elected government, these weapons were dismantled. South Africa had become the first (and only) nuclear weapons state to voluntarily give up nuclear arms.[147]

South Africa had already built two nuclear reactors near Capetown by 1985, both of which still operate today. They had nothing to do with the nuclear weapons program. When the nuclear bombs were dismantled, the highly enriched uranium was stockpiled to make isotopes for nuclear medicine. One of the most important medical isotopes, technetium-99m, is produced by bombarding enriched uranium with neutrons from a nuclear reactor, thus producing molybdenum-99, which has a half-life of 66 hours. The molybdenum is then delivered to hospitals around the world, where it then decays into technetium-99m, with a half-life of only six hours. Technetium is used to diagnose more than 20 million medical conditions every year and provides the best possible images of the brain, kidneys, liver, lungs, skeleton, blood, and tumors. Eighty-five percent of all nuclear diagnostic imaging is done with this isotope. South Africa is now one of the top producers of medical isotopes in the world.

Beginning with the first Strategic Arms Limitation Treaty between the United States and the Soviet Union in 1972, the number of nuclear weapons actively deployed in the world has been reduced from 65,000 to about 20,000, only about 8,000 of which remain in active operation.[148] In March 2010, the U.S. and Russia signed a deal to reduce each other's arsenals to 1550 warheads each.[149] While this is still more than enough to destroy our civilization, it is certainly a move in the right direction. And while these weapons may threaten our future, the uranium and plutonium from the thousands of dismantled warheads offers hope for the future of clean energy.

The major nuclear powers—the U.S., Russia, the U.K., and France—have a large surplus of plutonium and highly enriched uranium. All of this can eventually be used as nuclear fuel to produce energy. The supply is immense, especially when you take into account the much larger stockpiles of depleted uranium that resulted from the enrichment of uranium for bombs. The main use for depleted uranium is on armored vehicles and tanks, and for bullets and shells. It is harder than steel and heavier than lead, so it serves both those military purposes well. But wouldn't it be better to burn this uranium in fast reactors to power our world?

The most significant example of nuclear swords to plowshares today is the fact that 50 percent of American nuclear energy is fueled with uranium

---

147. David Albright, "South Africa's Nuclear Weapons Program," Institute for Science and International Security, March 14, 2001, http://web.mit.edu/ssp/seminars/wed_archives_01spring/albright.htm

148. "List of States with Nuclear Weapons," Wikipedia, http://en.wikipedia.org/wiki/List_of_states_with_nuclear_weapons

149. Michael Evans, "Obama and Medvedev Seal the Deal on Nuclear Arms by Phone," *Sunday Times*, March 27, 2010, http://www.timesonline.co.uk/tol/news/world/us_and_americas/article7078003.ece

from dismantled Russian warheads. Yes, 10 percent of all US electricity comes from bombs taken apart under disarmament agreements. In 1993 the U.S. and Russia signed a 20-year agreement for 454 tonnes (500 tons) of Russian highly enriched uranium (90+ percent U-235) to be down-blended to reactor grade uranium (4 to 5 percent U-235) and shipped to the U.S., where it would be used as nuclear fuel. As of June 2009, 367 tons of weapons grade uranium had been converted into 9,635 tonnes (10,621 tons) of reactor fuel. This is by far the largest effort to convert nuclear weapons to peaceful purposes.[150] Russia has announced that it will not renew the contract when it expires in 2013, presumably because it wants to use the fuel in the 50 new reactors it plans to build in the coming years.

I have told this story to at least 50 reporters, many of whom work for large newspapers, television networks, and magazines. Not one mention of this situation has been included in the many articles and TV pieces based on these interviews. I have searched the Internet for news stories and found only two mentions of the deal since it was signed in 1993. This more or less proves the adage, "good news is no news." What a shame.

If we add up all the uranium that can be mined from the earth's crust, all the thorium, which is at least four times as abundant as uranium, all the used nuclear fuel with more than 95 percent of the energy remaining, all the weapons grade uranium that is now in stockpiles, and all the depleted uranium from the production of both nuclear weapons and nuclear fuel, there is enough nuclear fuel for thousands of years. How about adding the highly enriched uranium that is still in active nuclear warheads? That may still be a dream, but we are now surely moving in that direction.

Following on the agreement between the United States and Russia to reduce their nuclear weapons arsenals, in April 2010 it was announced both countries would take 34 tons of plutonium out of their military stockpiles for use as nuclear fuel. The 68 tons of plutonium are enough for 17,000 nuclear warheads.[151] This is ample evidence that on balance we are moving toward more peace and less war.

A Nuclear Renaissance

The term *nuclear renaissance* did not come into general use until 2006. Now it pervades media reportage and public statements around the world. An Internet search produced more than 327,000 mentions of the term. Nuclear energy will likely be the most important energy technology for the next 100 years and beyond.

---

150. Matthew Bunn, "Reducing Excess Stockpiles: U.S.-Russian HEU Purchase Agreement," Nuclear Threat Initiative, March 5, 2003, http://nuclearthreatinitiative.org/e_research/cnwm/reducing/heudeal.asp
151. Mary Beth Sheridan, "U.S., Russia Reach Deal on Disposing of Plutonium from Nuclear Weapons," *Washington Post*, April 9, 2010, http://www.washingtonpost.com/wp-dyn/content/article/2010/04/08/AR2010040805405.html

At present there are more than 400 operating nuclear reactors in 30 countries and they provide 15 percent of the world's electricity. Fifty-six new reactors are under construction, mainly in Asia, where China has 21 and India and South Korea each have 5 reactors under construction. Russia is building 11 reactors and others are under way in Finland, Slovakia, Korea, Romania, Japan, Argentina, France, Bulgaria, and Iran. Canada has announced it will build between 4 and 8 new reactors in Ontario, which already produces 50 percent of its electricity with nuclear power. In all there are about 100 firm plans for new reactors beyond those already under construction and proposals for about 250 additional plants. As of late 2009, there were 30 plants in the planning stage in the United States, with 20 of those already in the process of obtaining licenses to build and operate through the Nuclear Regulatory Commission. Most of these are planned for existing nuclear sites, where public opinion strongly favors the new plants.

The number of operating reactors may well double in the next 30 to 40 years. This truly is a nuclear renaissance of global proportions. Unlike 30 years ago, there are no 10,000-strong marches or demonstrations against the proposed nuclear plants. Only a handful of diehard activists strenuously oppose the renewed commitment to nuclear energy. Most environmentalists are more strongly focused on preventing new fossil fuel plants from being built. Even though many of them publicly oppose nuclear energy they are quietly aware that the choice in many countries, in particular those with no additional hydroelectric potential, is between fossil fuel and nuclear power. Their lack of direct action against nuclear proposals speaks loudly that they would prefer nuclear to coal. This was not the case 30 years ago, long before climate change drifted to the top of environmentalists' agendas.

Perhaps the biggest boost to date for the nuclear renaissance in the U.S. came in President Barack Obama's February 2010 announcement of $8.3 billion in federal loan guarantees for the construction of two nuclear reactors in the state of Georgia.[152] He also announced that he intended to triple the total loan guarantee program from $18.5 billion to $54.5 billion.[153] In his speech the president stated, "On an issue that affects our economy, our security, and the future of our planet, we can't keep on being mired in the same old stale debates between the left and the right, between environmentalists and entrepreneurs."

His announcement represented a direct challenge to the antinuclear movement, most of whose members tend to support the Democratic

---

152. Lynn Sweet, "Obama Wants to Invest in Nuclear Energy: Transcript," *Chicago Sun-Times*, February 16, 2010, http://blogs.suntimes.com/sweet/2010/02/obama_wants_to_invest_in_nucle.html
153. Daniel Whitten and Hans Nichols, "Obama Said to Seek $54 Billion in Nuclear-Power Loans," Bloomberg Businessweek, January 29, 2010, http://www.businessweek.com/news/2010-01-29/obama-said-to-seek-54-billion-in-nuclear-power-loan-guarantees.html

Party, to get with the program and change their stance on nuclear power. President Obama has always made it clear he favors nuclear energy. After all, the 11 reactors in his home state of Illinois produce 50 percent of the state's electricity. And he knows a majority of Democrats in Congress also support nuclear energy, despite the fact that a vociferous minority in the party strongly opposes it. One hopes the president's announcement will put to rest any doubts about the United States' determination to join the nuclear renaissance.

Fossil Fuels

Early humans harnessed fire for heat and cooking more than 100,000 years ago. Eventually they learned to smelt copper and iron ores and to melt sand to make glass. For 100,000 years most of the fuel for these tasks was wood. While there are records of coal being used to smelt copper ore as early as 3,000 years ago in China, it was the invention of the steam engine by James Watt in 1775 that ushered in the era of widespread use of fossil fuels.

Fossil fuels were created from organic sediments in the sea and from plants on the land. Much of the oil (petroleum) and natural gas (methane) was produced from marine sediments, with plankton such as diatoms, which are tiny plants, contributing the bulk of the material. Coal was generated from swamp forests, where trees and other plants died and decomposed. These processes took millions of years as the organic remains became buried and subject to heat and pressure.

The fossil fuels have in common their chemical composition as hydrocarbons, essentially hydrogen and carbon. As you move from the lightest, natural gas, to the heaviest, coal, the carbon content increases and the hydrogen content decreases. When hydrocarbons burn, energy gets released from both the carbon and the hydrogen. This is why coal produces the most carbon dioxide and natural gas produces the least carbon dioxide per unit of energy generated.

Today coal, oil, and natural gas supply 86 percent of the world's primary energy. In the space of two centuries, with most of the growth in consumption occurring in the past 50 years, we have become utterly dependent on the unsustainable use of these fuels. Our future depends greatly on how we manage the remaining fossil fuels and how we eventually transition to other forms of energy as fossil fuels become depleted. There are fiercely competing theories about how we should go about this evolution.

It comes down to nothing less than the fundamental debate over how we should be organized as a society. On one side are the free-marketers, who believe the invisible hand will guide us collectively to solutions without the need for major state intervention. On the other side are the planners and socialists, who believe we must implement controls on the use of fossil (carbon) fuels by intervening in the market in such a way that individuals and organizations change their behavior and use less fossil fuels, even before they become depleted. This can be done with incentives, disincentives, or prohibitions. No wonder it seems impossible to come to consensus on the subject; our most critical energy resources and our most basic political divisions are wrapped up in one whopper of a philosophical disagreement.

The three main fossil fuels have basic chemistry in common, but they are very distinct from one another in their applications. Let's look at them individually:

Natural Gas

Natural gas is composed primarily of a single compound, methane, and is the simplest of the hydrocarbons, one carbon and four hydrogen atoms. It is generally found in the same regions, often in the same drill-hole, as petroleum. Even though it is a simple compound natural gas is an extremely versatile material. Aside from its use as an energy source for heating buildings, producing electricity, and powering industry, it is one of the main inputs into making vinyl (PVC). When converted to methanol it has myriad uses in chemistry and manufacturing, and it is the primary source for the production of hydrogen in industry.

Natural gas is the cleanest burning fossil fuel, both in terms of air pollution and greenhouse gas emissions. While the gas contains impurities such as sulfur and carbon monoxide when it is pumped from the earth, these are removed in refineries close to the wellhead before the gas is sent to market. Burning gas for heating and electricity production does produce considerable amounts of nitrogen oxides, a contributor to smog. Even this can be reduced substantially with pollution control technology.

North America consumes about 25 percent of global gas production. Until recently it was believed domestic production would continue to decline as North America had only about 5 percent of conventional global gas reserves. Plans were well under way to expand the ability to import liquid natural gas (LNG) from offshore. But only a few years ago a technology was developed that made it possible to extract natural gas from shale formations in Texas. More recently shale formations in Louisiana and Pennsylvania have been tapped. There are extensive deep shale formations across much of the U.S., and it is possible there will be an ample supply of gas well into the future. In 2008 the declining production trend in the U.S. was reversed with a 7 percent increase in production. Natural gas prices have fallen, making it more economic to use gas to produce electricity. The future of large-scale LNG imports is now not so certain. This highlights the fact that just when we think we are running out of a particular fossil fuel, new discoveries and advances in technology can change the picture, at least for the time being.

The technology whereby natural gas, and petroleum in some locations, is extracted from shale is known as "hydraulic fracturing", or simply "fracking". It is accomplished by using two techniques. First, it is now possible to drill down vertically a mile or more and then turn the drill horizontally and drill another mile or more. This is called directional drilling. Second comes the fracking where high-pressure water mixed with sand and a number of chemicals are injected into the shale formation, fracturing it and releasing the trapped gas or oil. All the shale deposits being worked are well below water tables used for domestic water consumption. This hasn't stopped activists from claiming that fracking is contaminating drinking water supplies. In the documentary "Gasland", producer Josh Fox contends that gas from a fracking well can be lit aflame from a water tap in a private home. He is taking advantage of the fact that in many parts of the world there is natural seepage of gas to the surface and that this can find its way into water wells. In the more recent documentary "FrackNation" produced by Phelim McAleer and Ann McElhinney, it is made abundantly clear that Josh Fox is a sensationalist with no regard for the facts about fracking. More that 35,000 gas and oil wells have been fracked during the past 40 years and there is zero evidence of contamination of water supplies. Yet massive opposition to the technology has emerged in Europe, making it virtually impossible to introduce the technology on the Continent or in Great Britain.

Fracking may eventually increase the available supply of oil and gas by many times the conventional reserves. Whereas only a few years ago there was a lot of talk about "peak oil" and dwindling natural gas supplies, it now appears that there will be oil and gas in abundance at least through this century, and likely beyond. Just one more example of how difficult it is to predict the future.

Petroleum

Commonly known as oil, petroleum provides nearly 35 percent of the world's energy, making it the most important energy source today. And yet the world's major oil companies—Exxon-Mobil, Shell, Chevron, and British Petroleum (BP) —are vilified as symbols of environmental destruction due to the greenhouse gas emissions associated with burning fossil fuels. They are characterized as holding the world hostage, making obscene profits, and refusing to embrace a politically correct energy policy that would favor renewable energy over fossil fuels. And yet they remain strongly focused on continuing to produce our most important energy resource; shouldn't they be cheered for this, even if oil does become much scarcer in the future due to no fault of their own?

The BP blowout in the Gulf of Mexico has made matters far worse and will be a major wake-up call for the entire offshore oil industry. And it highlights the extreme conditions oil companies now operate under, drilling in mile-deep waters and then drilling another four or five miles to get to the deposit. In North America, at least, the cheap oil is largely gone and drilling is required in ever more extreme and remote locations to keep up with the demand. And although we know the sea will eventually heal when the leak is stopped, in the meantime thousands of people's lives and livelihoods have been disrupted and the shoreline has been severely damaged. There is clearly a high price to pay for going further and further afield to drill for black gold.

It's true the political system needs its horses to flog, but surely oil companies have some cause to be proud that they produce over one-third of the world's energy. Take that energy away and try to come out of an economic recession. "Sorry, there is no gas for the cars this year."

We environmentalists need to get real in the sense of recognizing where we are now and not just where we think we should be. Getting from A to B is not a slam-dunk at the best of times. And sometimes idealism is just plain misguided. Sure the oil might run out sooner than later. And yes, we will need a strategy to move beyond oil at some point. So let's work together on that rather than continually looking for who's to blame. Again, it comes down to the reality that this debate cuts to the core of human needs. We want to survive and we have satisfied that instinct by continuing to produce what we use each day. Oil is more than one-third of the energy required to meet that need today. Rather than demonizing it we need to pay attention to the choices we have when it becomes scarcer.

At one time a lot of oil was burned to make electricity. This is no longer the case except in the major oil-producing regions. Oil has become the most important fuel for transportation and has nearly achieved a monopoly in this regard. From gasoline to diesel to aviation fuel to bunker oil for ships, oil is the source of fuel for travel by land, sea, and air. That's because it is a liquid as opposed to a gas like natural gas or a solid like coal. Even though, like liquids, gases can be moved through pipes into tanks, they have a much lower energy content than liquids, so you need a very large tank to travel a long distance. Liquid propane and liquid natural gas under pressure have not been able to compete with gasoline or diesel, which do not need to be pressurized. Solid fuels such as coal and wood are simply impractical for transportation unless they are converted into liquid fuels. As petroleum becomes more expensive due to scarcity and higher cost of production, coal-to-liquid fuel and cellulose-based liquid fuels will gradually play a greater role in transportation.

Advances in the efficiency of internal combustion engines and the use of catalytic converters have reduced air pollution from our cars by more than 90 percent in the past 30 years. But the number of cars has greatly increased and the public is even more concerned about the state of the environment than 30 years ago. We can all agree it would be desirable to reduce or eliminate air pollution from vehicles if it were cost-effective. For many years it was hoped hydrogen fuel cells would provide pollution-free transportation. It now seems there are too many technical obstacles to the production and delivery of hydrogen and that the cost of the fuel cells would be prohibitive. Most bets are now on advanced battery technology, with the plug-in hybrid the most likely successor to the conventional automobile. Initially this will come at an increased cost, but mass production and improvements in battery technology may offset this in the future.

Many analysts believe we are approaching "peak oil" when the ever-increasing rate of production will come to an end and begin to decline.[154] This would result in a sharp increase in the price of oil, which in turn would put downward pressure on demand as alternatives are adopted: smaller cars, plug-in hybrids, cellulose-based fuels, etc. But we have not yet reached peak oil and there are conflicting opinions about when it will occur. We do know that people in Europe and Japan, where fuel prices are about double North America's, tend to buy smaller cars with better fuel economy.

Cars produce about one-third of all the CO_2 emissions in the U.S. and similar but lower percentages in the other industrialized countries. Depending on how quickly plug-in hybrids are taken up, there is the potential for deep cuts in this major cause of both air pollution and CO_2 emissions.

The Canadian Oil Sands

There is a region about the size of Florida in northern Alberta where the soil is soaked in thick oil. Originally the area was called the tar sands, but it became known as the oil sands when commercial production of oil began in 1967 (there is actually no tar in the sand).[155] Today, many activists are working hard to rebrand the region as the tar sands, presumably because tar sounds worse than oil.

There are proven reserves of 1.7 trillion barrels of oil in the region, enough to supply Canada's needs at the present rate of consumption for 400 years. Most of the 1.4 million barrels of oil produced today is exported to the U.S. Canada supplies more oil to American markets than any other country, and the oil sands production is slated to double or triple in the coming years.

Some of the oil-soaked soil is at the surface, where it is mined in a

---

154. Brandon Robshaw, "Why Your World Is About to Get a Whole Lot Smaller, by Jeff Rubin," *Independent*, March 14, 2010, http://www.independent.co.uk/arts-entertainment/books/reviews/why-your-world--is-about-to-get-a-whole-lot-smaller-by-jeff-rubin-1919283.html
155. "Oil Sands," Wikipedia, http://en.wikipedia.org/wiki/Oil_sands

manner similar to open-caste coal mining. The vegetation is removed, the soil and sand are trucked to a plant where the oil is removed and the sand is returned to the site, eventually to be restored with native trees and shrubs. In some areas the oil lies well below the surface and here it is mined *in situ* (in place) by injecting hot water to release the oil from the sand. In the case of *in situ* mining there is minimal disturbance to the surface environment.

It has lately become fashionable among activists to attack the oil sands operations as an example of unacceptable environmental damage. In one incident, about 1600 ducks were killed when they landed in a settling pond. A great hue and cry went up, which occupied the airwaves for days, and cast the oil sands companies as criminals. While it is unfortunate that the ducks were killed, and certainly corrective action is necessary, it was never mentioned that Alberta produces 50 percent of all the waterfowl in North America or that tens of thousands of ducks are intentionally killed by hunters every year.

Greenpeace contends that the production of oil from the oil sands results in five times the emissions of greenhouse gas when compared to conventional oil.[156] But it is not including the burning of the oil in cars and other vehicles after it is produced. When the full life-cycle, or "wells-to-wheels," is calculated, oil from the oil sands emits between 18 percent higher and 8 percent lower greenhouse gases compared to other sources of crude oil.[157] Oil from the oil sands does not deserve to be called "dirty oil" anymore than any other source of oil. And a BP-style blowout like the one in the Gulf of Mexico can't occur on the land-based oil sands.

To put things into perspective, consider when a gas station spills oil or gasoline from a leaky underground tank. The site is declared "toxic real estate" and must be cleaned up, often at the cost of millions of dollars. The oil sands in Alberta are a massive area of toxic soils, and the companies that operate in the oil sands are removing oil from the soil, on a very grand scale, making a profit selling the oil as transportation fuel. Is it not a fact they are leaving the sand cleaner than when they found it? The oils sands represent a natural "oil spill" over 100,000 times larger than the largest human-caused spill. If it is desirable to clean up an oil spill in the sea or underground, surely it is acceptable to clean up the oil sands.

None of the above is meant to imply there aren't serious environmental issues involving oil. But I do find a degree of hypocrisy among activists who paint the oil companies as environmental criminals while they go about driving, flying, and otherwise enjoying the benefits of living in a society that depends on oil for over one-third of its energy.

---

156. "Questions and Answers about the Alberta Tar Sands," Greenpeace Canada, July 26, 2007,
http://www.greenpeace.org/canada/en/recent/tarsandsfaq/
157. "Greenhouse Gas Emissions and the Oil Sands," Government of Alberta, December 2009,
http://oilsands.alberta.ca/documents/GHG_oil_sands.pdf

Coal

Known as "King Coal" by its fans and as the dirtiest fuel on earth by its detractors, coal is the most abundant fossil fuel by far. Whereas natural gas and oil were formed mainly in marine sediments, coal was formed in vast forested swamps. Coal is derived from trees, peat moss, and other forms of vegetation that were preserved, then buried over the millennia and converted to coal under heat and pressure, a kind of natural charcoal production on a grand scale. Coal is king in many parts of the world, where it is mined to run electric plants, make steel, power industry, and converted into liquid fuels for transportation.

The United States has the world's largest reserves of coal, 25 percent of the world total at 247 billion tones. This is more than twice as much as China has, even though China produces two times more coal than the U.S. annually. Russia has the second largest reserves and is also a major exporter along with Australia and Indonesia. Between them China and the U.S., export less than 1 percent of their production, because they need nearly all of it for themselves.[158]

There have been major advances in reducing the air pollution caused by burning coal for electricity. But coal is still the worst polluter and it causes the most negative impact on human health of any fuel we burn. Presumably all the birds and animals that breathe the air pollution from coal plants are similarly affected. And if it concerns you, coal produces far more greenhouse gas per unit of energy produced than any other fuel. That is why, finally, many in the environmental movement make opposition to coal a higher priority than opposition to nuclear power. Unfortunately many also still remain opposed to both nuclear energy and hydroelectric power. But they may get it straight in the future as the futility of only championing wind and solar energy sinks in.

Coal provides 50 percent of the electricity in the United States. China derives 78 percent of its electricity from coal while India produces 69 percent of its electricity from coal. Australia produces 80 percent of its electricity from coal. At the extreme end, South Africa and Poland each depend on coal for 93 percent of their electricity. Many other countries, including Germany, Britain, Indonesia, and Ukraine depend on coal for a significant percentage of their electricity. In total, more than 40 percent of all the world's electricity is produced from coal. This cannot be changed overnight.

It is easy to become morally incensed by this and declare that it must end. Greenpeace has taken to blocking coal ships and its members chain themselves to the augers delivering coal to the furnaces of large coal-fired plants. They need to be reminded that there are hundreds of millions of

---

158. "Coal," Wikipedia, http://en.wikipedia.org/wiki/Coal (This website contains very good basic information about coal.)

CONFESSIONS OF A GREENPEACE DROPOUT

people whose existence depends on those ships and coal plants. A more constructive approach is required—one that recognizes the impossibility of replacing more than 60 percent of global energy now generated by fossil fuels with wind and solar power, one that recognizes the only technologies that can replace coal (and gas) in a big way are hydroelectric and nuclear energy.

The vast deposits of coal on this planet are capable of providing the feedstock for liquid fuels, plastics, chemicals, fertilizers, and other valuable products for thousands of years to come, but not if we burn them all in the next few hundred years. The huge potential for nuclear energy plus the renewable rainfall used for hydroelectric energy, where it is available, will also last for thousands of years. The answer is staring us in the face. Nuclear and hydro are a win-win-win solution for the environment (they eliminate air pollution), the economy (they provide reliable, low-cost electric power), and for society (they offer wealth without damage to health).

"Clean Coal"?

Billions of dollars are now earmarked for "clean coal" technology. The coal industry is spending millions on advertising to convince the public that clean coal is a reality, when in fact it remains a distant hope. The objective is to capture the CO_2 from the coal plant's exhaust gasses and to pump it underground into geological formations, where the CO_2 will be permanently stored. Governments are spending billions of dollars on research and pilot plants to demonstrate the feasibility of carbon capture and storage (CCS).

There are a number of significant obstacles to achieving widespread adoption of CCS technology:

- The volume of CO_2 exhausted for a large coal plant is huge. A 500-megawatt coal plant produces three million tons of CO_2 per year. There are about 600 coal plants in the U.S., even more in China, where there are plans to build 500 more in the next decade. Global CO_2 emissions from coal- and gas-fired power generation are about 12 billion tons per year, 25 percent of total CO_2 emissions. The prospect of pumping this amount of CO_2 into underground formations is simply not plausible.
- If the CCS technology can be developed, and if there are suitable geological formations under the thousands of existing coal plants, the cost of retrofitting each plant will likely be more than the cost of the original plant itself.
- CCS technology will be energy intensive; therefore it will use a significant percentage of the electricity generated by the plant, thus making the plant's electrical output more expensive and requiring

more electrical generating capacity to be built to satisfy the existing demand for power.

- Compared to nuclear, the cost of CCS technology may well make new nuclear plants look even better than they do at present. This would result in the cancellation of plans to build coal plants in favor of nuclear plants and the replacement of existing coal plants with nuclear plants when either the coal plants reach their end-of-service or when the cost of retrofitting them with CCS becomes prohibitively high.

The first integrated coal plant with CCS technology has been built in Germany by the electrical utility Vattenfall. At this writing the company has been unable to find a single suitable place to store the CO_2 underground. Communities are in open revolt, fearing the impact if the CO_2 were to escape. Ironically, Vattenfall finds itself in competition with natural gas importers who have been using underground formations to store their gas for many years. This practice has never been controversial even though natural gas is obviously much more of a potential hazard than CO_2.[159]

Another irony is the fact that the only viable CO_2 capture operations involve pumping CO_2 into oil fields to increase the recovery of petroleum.[160] In other words carbon is being pumped into the ground in order to extract more carbon-emitting fuels, a self-defeating situation.

A Path to Sustainable Energy

There are, of course, many complexities in seeking a path to a sustainable energy future. Each country and region has different energy resources and different energy requirements. But there are a few key policy directions that could take us toward sustainability if we could only break the lock that the solar promoters and their believers have on politicians and the public. Here are the priorities as I see them:

- Where there are suitable sites for hydroelectric development these should be developed as a first priority. Countries such as Brazil, China, Russia, Canada, India, the Congo, and Chile have substantial hydro potential and they should develop it as needed. This is renewable, clean, and often the lowest cost energy technology.
- The world should embrace the nuclear renaissance and build alliances between governments, businesses, universities, and research institutions so that hundreds of nuclear reactors can

---

159. Paul Voosen, "Frightened, Furious Neighbors Undermine German CO_2-Trapping Power Project," *New York Times*, April 7, 2010, http://www.nytimes.com/gwire/2010/04/07/07greenwire-frightened-furious-neighbors-undermine-german-35436.html
160. David Bielo, "Enhanced Oil Recovery: How to Make Money from Carbon Capture and Storage Today," *Scientific American*, April 9, 2009, http://www.scientificamerican.com/article.cfm?id=enhanced-oil-recovery

be constructed over the coming decades. Today, more than 400 reactors provide nearly 15 percent of the world's electricity and many of them are smaller than the new class of reactors. Therefore 800 reactors could supply at least 30 percent and 1600 reactors could supply 60 percent, not counting for growth in demand. Then let's aim for 2000 reactors by 2100, not quite five times as many as are operating today. Hydroelectric already accounts for 15 percent of global electricity and could hold that percentage if the available capacity were developed. With 75 percent clean and reliable energy, we would be on a path to sustainability.

- With increased nuclear and hydroelectric energy, we would have the clean energy to charge batteries at night in all-electric and plug-in hybrid passenger cars and small delivery vehicles. This would drastically reduce the use of petroleum for light transport.
- The use of biofuels, which in the future would be derived mainly from wood and woody materials, should be focused on heavy transport (buses, trucks, trains [trains that are not electrified], and aircraft), where batteries alone will not be sufficient.
- Clean nuclear and hydro energy could be used to power ground source (geothermal) heat pumps in most new buildings and retrofitted into many existing buildings. This would greatly reduce the amount of natural gas and other fossil fuels used to heat and cool buildings.
- Direct solar hot water heating, especially in the tropics, should become far more widespread, which would reduce natural gas consumption for this essential service.
- Continued improvements in energy efficiency will come as a matter of course as inventors and engineers work to get more from less, which is a natural part of human ingenuity and technology improvement. The green building movement, the rising cost of energy, and the increased demands of a growing and more affluent global society will all result in a trend toward improved conservation and efficient use of energy.
- Smaller contributions will continue to come from wind, deep geothermal, solar voltaic, and solar thermal electric. More research and development is needed to make these technologies more cost-effective, because they are not cost-effective at present. We should pursue other promising technologies, such as nuclear fusion, vigorously.

Energy policy has many other nuances, but these few directions, if pursued with political will, could reduce fossil fuel consumption by the 50 to 80 percent demanded by environmentalists and promised, without a technically feasible plan, by politicians around the world. I can only hope to live to see the day when the logic of this approach is more widely recognized.

Vinod Khosla was a cofounder of Sun Microsystems in Silicon Valley in 1980 and now heads Khosla Ventures, a company that invests in a wide range of clean tech startups. He is one of the most influential entrepreneurs in computer science and clean technology. In a 2008 interview he was asked, "What do you think is the single biggest failure of American environmental policy that we could actually do something about?"

His reply: "For every nuclear plant that environmentalists avoided, they ended up causing two coal plants to be built. That's the history of the last 20 years. Most new power plants in this country are coal, because the environmentalists opposed nuclear. They'd like to see wind and solar photovoltaics. Well, it doesn't work if it's 40 cents a kilowatt hour, and it doesn't work if you have to tell Pacific Gas and Electric's customers: 'We'll ship you power when the wind's blowing and the sun's shining, but otherwise, you gotta miss your favorite soap opera or NFL game.' That's just the reality, so you have to be pragmatic about this. What is the most cost-effective way to do it?"[161]

The past few years have seen dramatic changes in the energy world. Most people hear about all the wind turbines and solar energy panels being installed and because the idea is so popular many electrical utilities use images of these technologies in their promotions. Even businesses with no relation to energy are using windmills to advertise their products. It is becoming common to see a few windmills and solar panels prominently displayed in front of coal and nuclear plants. The utility people and the electrical system operators know how expensive the electricity from wind and solar really is. But in many cases they are required by law to produce wind and solar energy due to popular demand fueled by activists and promoters of wind and solar energy. Wind and solar energy have become synonymous with "green," even though solar is economically unsustainable and both wind and solar are intermittent.

The big change that's coming is the shift away from coal toward nuclear. This will happen in a big way in the U.S., where 50 percent of electricity is now produced by coal and where there is sufficient wealth to make the large capital investment needed to build new nuclear plants. It is already happening in China, where there are only 11 nuclear plants in operation today but 21 under construction and many more to come.

The coal industry needn't worry about being shut down overnight. Many countries will continue to use coal, in some cases a lot of coal, preferably with better pollution control. The thousands of coal plants that operate today were built to run for 40 to 50 years, so even if no more coal

161. Katie Fehrenbache, "Five Questions for Vinod Khosla, *Mendo Coast Current*, January 30, 2008, http://mendocoastcurrent.wordpress.com/2008/01/30/five-questions-for-vinod-khosla/

plants were built, which will not be the case, there will be a continuing demand for coal for at least the next 50 years.

The International Energy Agency (IEA), founded by 28 industrialized countries in 1974 during the oil crisis, predicts that without major policy changes the use of coal will increase by 53 percent by 2030.[162] Clearly such changes must be implemented if we are to avoid such a dramatic rise in consumption. We need a policy that increases the use of hydroelectric energy where possible, and one that supports an aggressive program of new nuclear power plant construction. This policy should also focus on converting cars and light trucks to battery and plug-in hybrid technology, and replacing fossil fuel with geothermal heat pumps in buildings. There are clear signs this is already under way.

One of the most important objectives for the future of energy is to connect to the grid the 1.6 billion people who have no electricity. In order for this to happen the people of sub-Saharan Africa and South Asia must become wealthier and better organized. The IEA predicts universal access to electricity will require $35 billion per year between now and 2030.[163] This seems like a lot of money, but it is about equal to the estimated $700 billion and counting spent on the Iraq War.[164]

The prospects for oil and gas are daunting, even in the short span of the next 20 years. The IEA predicts the demand for oil will increase by 24 percent by 2030 and more than half of this will have to come from as yet undiscovered oil fields. This makes it clear peak oil is not an unreasonable prediction, as we have no guarantee these new fields will be found. The demand for natural gas is forecast to increase by 42 percent, from 3 trillion cubic meters today to 4.2 trillion cubic meters by 2030. More than 60 percent of this demand must be filled by as yet undiscovered new wells. This would indicate that "peak gas" is just as likely as peak oil in the coming decades.[165]

The likely potential for a shortfall in oil and gas supplies underlines the importance of conserving coal for eventual conversion to liquid fuels for transportation and as chemical feedstock for plastics and other products now made from oil and gas. Again, an aggressive program of new nuclear construction will be the most important policy to assist in conserving coal and fossil fuels in general.

Smart meters, which allow time-of-use pricing for electricity, should become universal. This will allow utilities to charge more for electricity during peak loads and less when the demand is low. Note that smart meters

162. "World Energy Outlook 2009 Fact Sheet," International Energy Agency, ...
... http://www.worldenergyoutlook.org/docs/weo2009/fact_sheets_WEO_2009.pdf
163. Ibid.
164. Malou Innocent, "The Iraq War: Still a Massive Mistake," Cato Institute, April 5, 2010,
http://www.cato.org/pub_display.php?pub_id=11658
165. "World Energy Outlook 2009 Fact Sheet," International Energy Agency,
http://www.worldenergyoutlook.org/docs/weo2009/fact_sheets_WEO_2009.pdf

do not result in lower energy use. They simply encourage consumers to change the time of day when they use electrical appliances. Instead of turning on the dishwasher at 8 p.m. during peak demand, a timer on the dishwasher could start it at 3 a.m. when the demand for electricity is low. This is a win-win for the utility and the customer. The utility does not need to build as much energy capacity because the peak demand is lowered, the customer doesn't end up paying for additional plant capacity and gets a better price as a result of changing the time of consumption.

The price of gasoline and diesel oil in Europe is often more than double the price in North America, due entirely to a higher tax rate.[166] This has resulted in an automobile fleet that gets much better mileage without compromising utility. Granted there are not as many 350-horsepower cars in Europe, although they are available. It's just that the average consumer doesn't want to pay that much for fuel, so only wealthy people tend to buy luxury vehicles. But it is impossible to avoid the argument that such high taxes are punitive, excessive, and even undemocratic. On the other hand, how else is it possible to get otherwise sane people to realize they don't need 350 horsepower to get to work and back? In the U.S. and Canada the strategy is to legislate average fleet efficiency, with California, as usual, in the lead. America's love affair with the automobile does not pass easily as it seems every improvement in efficiency is matched by an increase in horsepower.

One approach to reducing fuel consumption in cars is referred to as a *tax shift*. This means increasing taxes on environmentally destructive practices while adopting a tax-neutral policy of reducing income tax by the same amount. Many European countries, such as Sweden in particular, have adopted this approach with considerable success in reducing fuel consumption, traffic congestion, and air pollution.[167]

I said at the beginning of the book that each of these issues could fill more than 20 books. Energy is no exception, so I will end this chapter simply by saying, "Buy a smaller, more fuel-efficient car, take mass transit when convenient, insulate your home, and put in a geothermal heat pump."

---

166. James Martin, "Gas Prices in Europe—European Gasoline and Diesel Prices," About.com, http://goeurope.about.com/od/transportation/a/gas_prices.htm
167. Lester R. Brown, "Lowering Income Taxes While Raising Pollution Taxes Reaps Great Returns," Earth Policy Institute, April 7, 2010, http://www.earthpolicy.org/index.php?/book_bytes/2010/pb4ch10_ss2

CHAPTER SIXTEEN
Food, Nutrition, and Genetic Science

Before the advent of agriculture humans were hunters and gatherers, who relied on nature to produce their food and fiber. It is generally accepted that agriculture first emerged in the Fertile Crescent of the Middle East about 10,000 years ago. There the ancestors of modern cattle, sheep, and goats were farmed and wheat, barley, oats, and flax were first cultivated, making it possible for humans to abandon a nomadic lifestyle and settle permanently in towns and cities. Eventually agriculture arose independently in other regions: in Asia, where it was based on chickens, pigs, and rice; in Central and South America, where it centered on corn, beans, peas, and potatoes; and in Sub-Saharan Africa, where it was based on millet and cassava.

Ever since farmers began to raise plants and animals for food, the most successful ones have cultivated seeds from the most desirable plants and have selectively bred the most desirable animals. As each of the many hundreds of species brought into cultivation and animal husbandry were adopted, a process of improving them began to better serve the needs of domestication and the human diet. The many qualities of domesticated plants and animals are called traits. Faster growth, sweeter flesh, disease-resistance, drought- tolerance, higher content of various nutritional ingredients, longer shelf-life, bigger fruit, more tender meat—these are examples of desirable traits in food. The desire and the competition to improve on the original wild species has been a principle driving force in the advancement of agriculture since it began 10,000 years ago.

During those 10,000 years, through selective breeding we have transformed hundreds of originally wild species into varieties that barely resemble the original wild strain. Today corn, or maize (*Zea mays*) is the most widely cultivated crop in the Americas. Yet scientists do not agree which species of wild grass was first cultivated and selectively bred into the many varieties of corn we have today.[168] The sweet corn we now take for granted as a summer treat is found nowhere in nature; it is purely a product of human engineering. This illustrates both the plasticity of genetic material and the ingenuity of farmers.[169]

Consider the *Brassicas*, also known as the cabbages. From a single species of wild ancestor, *Brassica oleracea*, 10 of the most important vegetables have been bred. Cabbage, kale, collard greens, Chinese broccoli (kai-lan), Brussels sprouts, kohlrabi, broccoli, broccoflower, broccoli romanesco, cauliflower, and wild broccoli are all derived from the same species. In addition, bok choy, Chinese cabbage, turnips, rutabaga, rapeseed (canola), mustard, radish, daikon (the most widely cultivated vegetable in Japan), horseradish, wasabi, arugula, and watercress have been bred from very closely related species in the same family of plants.[170]

All the varieties of cattle farmed today originated from their now extinct wild ancestors known as the aurochs (*Bos primigenius*). Over the years the descendents of the aurochs were also interbred with species of yaks and bison to form hybrids that today are entirely distinct from their progenitors.[171] Goats, sheep, pigs, horses, and other domesticated animals have similar histories.

There are 24 billion chickens in the world today, about four for every human on earth. Chickens outnumber any other species of bird. These have all descended from the wild bird, *Gallus gallus*, thought to have originated in northern Thailand. They too have been bred to grow faster, lay more eggs, and be thoroughly domesticated to serve the human need for food.

The species of fish and shellfish only recently brought into cultivation in marine aquaculture provide an interesting contrast to the plants, animals, and birds that have been farmed for thousands of years. The salmon, shrimp, tilapia, scallops, oysters, mussels, and other aquaculture species now farmed around the world are still very similar to their wild relatives. They have only been bred for a few generations. As time goes by and they

---

168. "Maize," Wikipedia, http://en.wikipedia.org/wiki/Maize
169. As an illustration of the plasticity of genetic material consider the dog. All 200-plus breeds from the Chihuahua to the Great Dane were bred from the grey wolf, *Canis lupis*. See: "Dog," Wikipedia, http://en.wikipedia.org/wiki/Dog
170. "Cruciferous Vegetables," Wikipedia, http://en.wikipedia.org/wiki/Cruciferous_vegetables
171. "Cattle," Wikipedia, http://en.wikipedia.org/wiki/Cattle

are selected for desirable traits, they too will become distinct from their origins, more suitable for domestication and providing superior nutrition.

Transformation of the Land

Since agriculture began, and in particular during the past few centuries as our population soared, farming has transformed more than one-third of the earth's land surface into landscapes that produce food.[172] About 12 percent is used for growing crops while the balance serves as pasture and grazing lands. Clearing native forests and other natural ecosystems for agricultural purposes has had a significant impact on the earth's environment, a more significant impact to date, perhaps, than all the CO_2 we have emitted over the past 100 years. The effect on biodiversity has been particularly severe. In the past, agricultural clearance was one of the primary causes of species extinction. For example, a number of species became extinct in the Western Australian Wheat Belt due to rapid and extensive clearing. It is hardly surprising that clearing and completely altering landscapes for the production of food would have a major impact on biodiversity. One of the most important elements of modern sustainable agriculture is the conservation of as many native species of plants and animals in the agricultural landscape as is reasonably possible. This never includes agricultural pests, however. Any farmer who is crazy enough to try to save the insects that are devouring his or her produce will not have the financing to plant another crop.

There are a few things about agriculture we must accept. Along with air and water it is the primary requirement for our survival. Rather than simply decrying the negative impacts of farming, a sensible environmentalist will recognize the significance of food to our survival. Even today millions of people don't have enough food, or enough of the foods that keep you healthy. Therefore the overall objective of sustainable agriculture should be to continue to feed the human population while at the same time working to reduce the negative impacts of farming. We must increase the production of food as the population grows, while at the same time developing techniques to minimize impacts on biodiversity, soil fertility, and water quality. This is one of our greatest challenges as agriculture by its very nature radically alters ecosystems. Simply put, we must learn to be better gardeners of this earth.

Intensive Agricultural Production

On April 30, 2002, I joined Nobel Peace Prize recipient Dr. Norman Borlaug, former U.S. senator George McGovern, former president of

---

172. "Earth's Land Resources," The Habitable Planet, http://www.learner.org/courses/envsci/unit/text.php?unit=7&secNum=2

Costa Rica Dr. Oscar Arias, Dr. James Lovelock, and others in signing a Declaration in Support of Protecting Nature with High-Yield Farming and Forestry.[173] The signing ceremony took place in Washington, D.C., at the Center for Global Food Issues and received extensive media coverage.

Our purpose was clear. We all wanted the world to know one of the best ways to protect nature is to employ modern intensive agricultural practices; these include the use of fertilizers, pesticides, GPS systems, and genetic science. This is not obvious to many people, who might feel the best way to protect nature would be to adopt organic farming and to reject synthetic chemicals and high technology. The problem with this approach is that it's simply not possible to grow as much food on an area of land with organic methods as it is with modern farming techniques. The more food we can produce on a given area of land, the less native forest must be cleared to grow it. One benefit of higher productivity is improved economic efficiency but from an environmental perspective the real benefit is that less land is converted from nature to food production.

Over the past 100 years, through advances in technology, chemistry, and genetics, we have learned to produce about five times as much food per unit of land. Imagine if we went back to the practices of 100 years ago; it simply wouldn't be possible to grow as much food as we do today because, even if we cultivated every suitable place on earth, there would not be five times as much land. But regardless, some people feel genuinely concerned about so-called chemical fertilizers and pesticides and genetic modification. Let's look at these things in more detail:

Fertilizer

Early agriculture was practiced on fertile lands. River deltas, flood plains, and former sea and lake bottoms are naturally rich in the nutrients plants require. It was soon discovered that applying animal manure and plant compost helped to increase crop productivity. Controlled irrigation was adopted early as a way of getting through dry periods and droughts. Over the centuries selective breeding improved crops and livestock by enhancing desirable traits. But it was not until the advent of the scientific revolution beginning in the 18th century that modern agriculture began to take shape.

One of the first major advances in increasing productivity in agriculture was the addition to soil of fertilizers other than farm manure and compost. Most people know that the three major nutrients used as fertilizers are nitrogen, phosphorus, and potassium; they are also called NPK, after their chemical symbols. Plants also require calcium, magnesium, and sulfur in relatively large amounts. The minor nutrients are the elements iron,

173. "Declaration in Support of Protecting Nature With High-yield Farming and Forestry," Center for Global Food Issues, http://www.highyieldconservation.org/declaration.html

CONFESSIONS OF A GREENPEACE DROPOUT

copper, manganese, boron, zinc, molybdenum, and chlorine. All of these are essential for healthy plant growth. Of course the elements carbon, hydrogen, and oxygen, which come from the air and water, are the most important building blocks for plants as they are the components of the carbohydrates: the sugars, starches, oils, and fats.[174] Because they are sourced directly from air and water, they are not normally considered fertilizers, but they are certainly essential nutrients. And we are beginning to recognize that in the context of rising CO_2 levels in the atmosphere, it is correct to characterize CO_2 as a fertilizer because higher CO_2 promotes faster plant growth. There is no question CO_2, and the carbon it contains, is the single most important nutrient for plants, and hence for life on earth.

The first industrial fertilizers consisted of seabird droppings called guano. These were mined on islands in the tropical regions, which contained huge deposits of guano. The largest deposits were found on islands off Peru and Chile, where the Guanay Cormorant and other birds roosted for hundreds of thousands of years. These deposits, which are really just another form of animal manure, were rich in nitrogen and phosphorus. They also had insecticidal and fungicidal properties when sprayed on a plant's leaves. Guano became a major commercial commodity during the 19th century but declined in importance when other sources of nitrogen and phosphorus became available. Guano is still mined in small quantities for use in organic farming.[175]

As an interesting aside, guano is also a source of saltpeter, or sodium nitrate, which is a key ingredient in explosives for warfare. This made the guano-rich islands off Peru and Chile into strategic assets, resulting in the War of the Pacific between the Peru-Bolivia alliance and Chile, which lasted from 1879 to 1883. To this day nitrogen fertilizers are one of the main ingredients, along with diesel fuel, used to make car bombs, roadside bombs, and suicide bombs; terrorists employ these bombs to further their evil work. This is but one of many examples of materials and technologies that can be used for both beneficial and destructive purposes.

One of the primary rules for "organic" farming is that no "synthetic" fertilizers or pesticides may be used. I have placed quotes around these words for good reason. The word organic, as it is used in organic farming, is not a scientific or technically meaningful term. In the context that organic farmers employ the word it is in fact a marketing term designed to sell products. The real definition of organic is both general (it has to do with living things) and specific (it has to do with compounds that contain carbon, as in *organic chemistry*) Because living things are based on carbon-containing compounds (chemicals), it follows that organic farming

174. "Plant Nutrient Needs," North Carolina State University, March 15, 1999,
http://www.ces.ncsu.edu/cumberland/fertpage/plantnutri.html
175. "Guano," Wikipedia, http://en.wikipedia.org/wiki/Guano

should follow suit. But this is not the case. Organic farmers are free to use such inorganic materials as copper sulfate, calcium hydroxide, ferric sulfate, and sulfur, even though they are not organic. They can also use ethylene, which although chemically organic, is a synthesized product of the petrochemical industry.[176] In fact the U.S. Department of Agriculture's National List of Prohibited and Allowed Substances for organic crop and livestock production includes a section titled Synthetic Substances Allowed for Organic Crop Production.[177] Among these are ethanol, isopropanol, calcium hypochlorite, chlorine dioxide, sodium hypochlorite, calcium polysulfide, copper hydroxide, copper oxide, copper oxychloride, chlorhexadine and iodine. Among the few synthetic substances not allowed are strychnine, lead, and arsenic, hardly the staple chemicals of modern nonorganic agriculture. So even though organic farmers claim to avoid synthetic chemicals, the list of the ones they can use is much longer than the ones they can't. They seem to arbitrarily decide which synthetic substances are acceptable even though they oppose synthetic substances in principle. And the fact that a certain chemical is *inorganic* rather than *organic* is not that important even though everything is supposed to be, well, "organic."

Organic growers reject "synthetic" nitrogen, phosphorus, and potassium,—the three most important soil nutrients—yet they are allowed to farm with synthetic micronutrients including: sulfates, carbonates, oxides, or silicates of zinc, copper, iron, manganese, molybdenum, selenium, and cobalt. One can only conclude that organic farming is a rather bizarre superstition.

Judging by the number of allowed synthetic substances containing chlorine, the so-called devil's element, you would think Greenpeace would blow the whistle on this situation, rather than badgering Apple and Hewlett-Packard about using vinyl insulation on the wires in their electronic devices.[178]

The Allowed Substances list also gives the green light to a number of pharmaceuticals that are used in raising organic livestock. These include butorphanol, described as a "morphinan-type synthetic opioid analgesic," in other words a synthetic painkiller that behaves like morphine and opium.[179] One wonders why they don't just use morphine and opium seeing as these are derived directly from plants and are therefore organic. Then there is flurosemide, an organochlorine chemical that prevents

---

176. "Pesticides Used in Organic Farming," European Crop Protection Association, March 23, 2009,
http://www.ecpa.be/en/newsroom/press-releases/_doc/18563/
177. "Synthetic Substances Allowed for Use in Organic Crop Production," vLex,
http://cfr.vlex.com/vid/205-601-synthetic-allowed-organic-crop-19902860
178. "Greenpeace Activists Paint 'HP US HQ Hazardous,'" CRN, July 29, 2009,
http://mobile.crn.com.au/Article.aspx?CIID=151426&type=News
179. "Butorphanol," Wikipedia, http://en.wikipedia.org/wiki/Butorphanol

racehorses from bleeding from the nose during races. I was not aware that there were organic racehorses.

Perhaps the most curious of all is the provision to allow the use of oxytocin, a mammalian hormone known in some circles as "the love hormone." Oxytocin is a peptide involved in regulating birth, breast milk production, and maternal behavior, as well as orgasm, anxiety, trust, and love. In livestock rearing oxytocin is used to induce labor when it does not come naturally in a timely fashion.[180] I had always imagined hormones were one class of substance that would be absolutely taboo in organic farming. Otherwise, why all the fuss about using another natural hormone, bovine growth hormone, in dairy cows?

In 1909 the German chemist Fritz Haber succeeded in combining nitrogen from the air with hydrogen to form ammonia. He did this by using heat and high pressure. The chemical company BASF purchased the technique. At BASF, it fell to Carl Bosch to scale Haber's lab work up to commercial production. By 1913 ammonia was being manufactured in commercial quantities for use as fertilizer, and then for explosives during World War I. The Haber-Bosch method is to this day one of the most important chemical processes ever devised. Fritz Haber received the Nobel Prize for his invention in 1918, as did Carl Bosch in 1930. Today more than 80 percent of the nearly 136 million tonnes (150 million tons) of ammonia produced annually is used to make fertilizer. The balance is used for cleaning agents, nitrogen chemistry, pollution control, refrigeration, and explosives. Manufacturing ammonia consumes more than 1 percent of global energy production.[181]

Nitrogen is naturally abundant, as it comprises 79 percent of the atmosphere. But plants cannot take up nitrogen directly as they can other nutrients. Nitrogen is essential for the production of proteins (muscle tissue, for example) and enzymes, the catalysts that make many chemical reactions in plants and animals possible. Enter one of the unsung heroes of living creation: the nitrogen-fixing bacteria. These microscopic wonders are capable of ingesting nitrogen directly from the air and synthesizing nitrogen compounds that can then be taken up and used by plants as a source of nitrogen. Some species of nitrogen-fixing bacteria dwell in the soil, where, as they live and die, they add nitrogen to the soil in a form that plants can take up and utilize. Other species have formed a symbiotic relationship with the roots of certain plants, in particular the pea family, also known as the legumes (*Fabacea spp.*).

The roots of these plants have specialized nodules, which are designed to provide a home for the nitrogen-fixing bacteria. There the bacteria produce nitrogen compounds, some of which are shared with the plant.

180. "Oxytocin," Wikipedia, http://en.wikipedia.org/wiki/Oxytocin
181. "Ammonia," Wikipedia, http://en.wikipedia.org/wiki/Ammonia

In turn the plant provides some of its sugars to the bacteria, which they use for energy. These plants are commonly called *nitrogen-fixers,* even though it is actually the bacteria that do the specialized work. Nitrogen fixers are capable of colonizing mineral soil when the organic layer has been washed away by flooding or burned off by fire. Nitrogen-fixers such as alfalfa, peas, lentils, and beans are often used as rotation crops partly because they replenish nitrogen in the soil.

Dr. Norman Borlaug is known as the father of the Green Revolution for his work in India and Pakistan in the 1960s, where he developed improved varieties of wheat, thus saving millions of people from starvation.[182] He estimates that the nitrogen fertilizer made from synthetic ammonia is responsible for the survival of nearly five billion of the seven billion people on earth today. In other words, without the nitrogen we harvest from the air there would only be enough natural nitrogen in soils, compost, and manure to feed about two billion people.[183] This is a sobering point. It highlights both the fact that it would not be possible to have a population of seven billion if Fritz Haber had not invented a way to make ammonia, and the fact that we now depend on this process. Extreme greens might argue the world would have been better off if there were only two billion people. They may have their opinion, but the fact is there *are* nearly seven billion of us and unless we wish to see a calamity like no other we must recognize the importance of the Haber-Bosch process for our continued survival.

For the life of me I do not understand how nitrogen harvested from the atmosphere can be characterized as "artificial" or "unnatural." The nitrogen in the atmosphere is entirely natural and not artificial in any way. It is true that through science we learned how to synthesize ammonia from the nitrogen in the air. But we also learned to produce (synthesize) steel by blending iron with other metals, yet organic farmers are happy to use a steel hoe for weeding their fields. One can only conclude the ban on "synthetic" nitrogen in organic farming is either a kind of superstition or an illogical rule based on faulty information about the origin of the nitrogen.

The story of phosphorus use as a fertilizer is not quite as fascinating as that of nitrogen. Phosphorus comes from phosphate rocks of sedimentary origin. These were laid down in ancient seas and are mined in a number of countries, chiefly the United States, China, and Morocco. Phosphorus is a constituent of DNA and the phospholipids, which form all cell membranes, and is thus central to the existence of life. Organic farmers use phosphate rock as a fertilizer, despite the fact that it is an inorganic mineral.

---

182. "Norman Borlaug," Wikipedia, http://en.wikipedia.org/wiki/Norman_Borlaug
183. Personal communication, April 2002.

CONFESSIONS OF A GREENPEACE DROPOUT

Potassium has a source that is similar to the source of phosphorus; it is mined from massive potash deposits that are also of sedimentary origin from ancient seas. The province of Saskatchewan in Canada produces nearly 25 percent of the world's potash from huge underground deposits. These were formed when the North American prairies were a great inland sea. Organic farmers use mined potash as a fertilizer even though it is an inorganic mineral, like phosphate rock.

It is time consumers recognized that the premium they pay for foods marked "organic" is not doing them any good from a nutritional standpoint, or any standpoint, for that matter. This was made clear in an independent 2009 study, funded by the UK Food Standards Agency and carried out by the London School of Hygiene and Tropical Medicine. It concluded, "There is currently no evidence to support the selection of organically over conventionally produced foods on the basis of nutritional superiority."[184] While organic farm groups routinely dispute this, they do not supply any evidence to back their claims.

My conclusion on the issue of fertilizer application is that the so-called synthetic nitrogen fertilizers are obtained from the atmosphere and are therefore perfectly natural, that "organic" growers actually use quite a number of inorganic and synthetic substances, and that eating foods labeled "organic" has no nutritional benefits. In addition, more land is required to grow the same amount of organic food as conventional food and therefore there is a serious environmental downside to these production methods.

Pesticides

In the same way that human health and longevity has been greatly improved by modern medicine, crop and livestock health has been greatly improved by the use of pesticides and through veterinary science. Indeed the use of medications in agriculture is at least as important as fertilizer and genetics, which in combination have increased yields up to five times during the past hundred years.

Most of us think nothing of taking medicine to cure an infection or a disease. We don't think of it as taking pesticides in relatively large doses, right into our bodies. Many human medicines are designed to kill pests, otherwise known as bacteria, parasites, and viruses, in our bodies. The term *pesticide* comes from pest, as in pestilence (the most famous of which was the Black Death, or Great Pestilence, which killed about one-quarter of the human population in the 14th century), and *cidium*, from the Latin

---

184. "Organic Food Not Nutritionally Better Than Conventionally-Produced Food, Review Of Literature Shows," *Science Daily*, July 30, 2009, http://www.sciencedaily.com/releases/2009/07/090729103728.htm

meaning "a killing." [185] [186] Pests, diseases, weeds, and vermin are all categories of biodiversity that can destroy our food and our health, and we'd rather they didn't exist.

The general term for a substance used to kill living things is *biocide*, the literal meaning of which is "to kill life," in other words, a poison. In medicine we use the term *antibiotic* (anti-life), which means exactly the same thing as biocide. Pesticides are used to kill living things that we judge as harmful. More specific terms for pesticides are: fungicide, herbicide, insecticide, rodenticide, algicide, germicide, and spermicide, depending on the category of living things one is trying to kill. The main reason chlorine is the most important element for human health is precisely because it is toxic to many of the pests and diseases that can harm us. It turns out that poisons, also known as medicines and pesticides, are essential for our survival.

Why is it that we generally wish to take pesticides (medicine) to cure disease yet many of us fear the slightest residue of pesticides on our food? Are the chemicals we use to kill crop pests and cure livestock more dangerous than the medicines we take? Is there any evidence that pesticide residues on food damage our health? The answer to the last two questions is no, therefore the answer to the first one is that the fear of agricultural pesticide residues is largely irrational. Of course, as with many medications, it is possible to overdose, but the amount of pesticide residues on our food is thousands of times lower than any amount that would harm us.

In the 1990s, the Cancer Research Institutes of the U.S. and Canada collaborated on a multi-year study of all scientific publications about the connection between cancer in humans and pesticide residues on food.[187] They could not find a single piece of evidence connecting the two. And yet they concluded 30 percent of human cancer is caused by tobacco consumption, from a perfectly natural plant, and 35 percent of cancers are caused by poor diet, mainly too much fat and cholesterol, which are also natural substances.

The concern that pesticide residues may do harm often causes parents to avoid or buy fewer fresh fruits and vegetables for themselves and their children. The authors of the article pointed out the irony of the fact that one of the best ways to stay healthy and prevent cancer is to eat lots of fresh fruits and vegetables. So, the people who listen to the scare campaigns about pesticide residues are liable to adopt eating habits that put them at higher risk of getting cancer than they would have been had they ignored the campaigners and eaten more fresh fruits and vegetables.

---

185. "Black Death," Wikipedia, http://en.wikipedia.org/wiki/Black_Death
186. "Pesticide," Online Etymology Dictionary, http://www.etymonline.com/index.php?term=pesticide
187. Len Ritter et al., "Report of a Panel on the Relationship between Public Exposure to Pesticides and Cancer," *Cancer* 80 (1997): 2019-33.

Dr. Bruce Ames received the U.S. National Medal of Science in 1998 for his lifelong research into the causes of cancer.[188] [189] He developed the Ames Test, which is used to determine the relative carcinogenicity of various chemicals. For much of his life he has worked to live down the legacy of this test. [190] What he found was that many otherwise harmless substances, if administered in huge doses, resulted in tumors and mutations in bacteria, rats, and mice. This led to the conclusion among many scientists and activists that these substances were therefore carcinogens and should be banned. They tended to forget the first rule of toxicology: the poison is in the dose.

Take simple table salt, sodium chloride, for example. It is essential for our health. It regulates the electrolyte balances in our bodies, and without it we would die. Yet it is possible to take too much salt and if you overdose on salt it can kill you. Many chemicals behave in a similar fashion. At low doses they are essential, beneficial, or harmless, while at higher and higher levels they become harmful and even fatal. It is a matter of degree.

For me, Dr. Ames's most interesting work involved comparing the relative carcinogenicity of a number of synthetic pesticides with a number of natural pesticides. Largely because plants can't run from danger or swat flies they produce natural pesticides to ward off predatory bacteria, insects, and fungi. The chemicals they produce are either toxic or extremely unpleasant to the pests that want to attack them.

Dr Ames administered large doses of a number of common synthetic pesticides and a similar number of natural pesticides extracted from plants. He found the synthetic and natural pesticides had virtually identical effects. At high doses about 50 percent of both the synthetic and natural pesticides produced tumors in white mice. He then calculated the doses of the synthetic and natural pesticides we would be exposed to by eating a typical diet of conventionally grown fruit and vegetables.

When synthetic pesticides are applied to crops there is a period of time required after the final application before the crop can be harvested and consumed. During this time the pesticide biodegrades so that at the time of harvest there is an undetectably low or negligible level of pesticide on the food. This is not the case for the natural pesticides, however. The plants keep producing these defensive chemicals right up until they are harvested. Dr. Ames estimated that when the food from these crops is consumed it contains about 10,000 times as much natural pesticide as synthetic pesticide residue. In other words, there is about 10,000 times as much risk of getting cancer from the natural pesticides as from the

188. "The President's National Medal of Science: Recipient Details," National Science Foundation, http://www.nsf.gov/od/nms/recip_details.cfm?recip_id=15
189. Virginia Postrel, "Of Mice and Men," Reason, November 1994, http://www.reason.com/news/show/32261.html
190. Gina Kolata, "Scientists Question Methods Used in Animal Cancer Tests," New York Times, August 31, 1990, http://www.nytimes.com/1990/08/31/us/scientists-question-methods-used-in-animal-cancer-tests.html

synthetic ones. And this risk is very close to zero in the first place. To quote Dr. Ames, "The effort to eliminate synthetic pesticides because of unsubstantiated fears about residues in food will make fruits and vegetables more expensive, decrease consumption, and thus increase cancer rates." [191]

For centuries farmers used nicotine from tobacco plants as a natural pesticide. Organic farmers continued to use nicotine to kill insect pests until very recently. Nicotine is one of the most poisonous examples of a natural pesticide and it has now been banned even for organic farming. Some synthetic pesticides developed in the 1950s and 1960s have also been banned, as they too are very poisonous compared with the synthetic pesticides in wide use today. The lesson is that it is not so much whether a chemical is natural or synthetic that determines the risk of using or ingesting it. It is the nature of the specific chemical, how much of it we are exposed to, and how it affects living tissues.

Everyone has heard of DDT, the insecticide that became the subject of controversy in the 1960s, partly due to Rachel Carson's influential book, *Silent Spring.*[192] Whereas DDT had originally been used to control mosquitoes and other insects that are responsible for the spread of typhus and malaria, after World War II it came into widespread use as a way to control insect pests in agriculture. As a result of the concern about DDT's impact on wildlife, many countries, beginning with Hungary in 1968, banned the chemical's use in agriculture. The U.S. Environmental Protection Agency banned DDT in 1972. Additional bans followed around the world. DDT was even discontinued for use in malaria control by the World Health Organization and USAID. This decision proved to carry a high cost in terms of human lives.

The movement against mass aerial spraying of DDT initially focused on the use of DDT to kill insect pests on farms. Euphemistically known as "crop dusting," in the 1950s and 1960s, the aerial spraying of food crops with insecticides and other pesticides became widespread. Some of these chemicals, including DDT, are known as *broad-spectrum* poisons. DDT, for example, is deadly to all insects, not just the target insects that prey on food crops. It addition, DDT does not break down or biodegrade quickly. And it tends to accumulate up the food chain. Such chemicals should be used sparingly, and only when there is no substitute that is more selective, breaks down quickly, and does not bio-accumulate.

Shortly after DDT was banned for use in farming, new chemicals were developed that were an improvement over the first wave of pesticides that came in after World War II. Today the chemicals used in agriculture are designed to be more selective. In our own gardens we might want to kill

191. Bruce N. Ames, "The Causes and Prevention of Cancer," National Institute of Environmental Health Sciences Center, March 15, 1997, http://users.rcn.com/jkimball.ma.ultranet/BiologyPages/A/Ames_Causes.html
192. Rachel Carson, *Silent Spring*, (Boston, Houghton Mifflin, 1962).

the aphids on our roses, but we might want the little ants that eat aphids to survive. If we get a huge nest of wasps in our eaves, we want to exterminate them, but we don't want to kill every insect in the yard. Most chemicals used in modern farming biodegrade quickly and do not accumulate up the food chain.

Here is a case where the logic of restricting, or in this case outright banning, the use of a chemical for farming had the effect of also banning it for a medical use, killing the mosquitoes that spread malaria and dengue fever. The medical use does not involve widespread aerial spraying over vast landscapes, only the occasional indoor spraying on the walls of huts and homes. It doesn't even involve killing all the mosquitoes. DDT is a very strong repellent, so spraying it in the home causes the mosquitoes to avoid coming into the house. The inhabitants avoid the bite and the infection, even though the mosquitoes may still be alive outside.

So even though DDT ended up being a story about chemicals and human health rather than farming practices and the environment, I will include its discussion here. There will be a chapter on chemicals further along.

There is no evidence that DDT is very toxic to humans. It was used to delouse tens of thousands of troops in wartime, and was sprayed on nearly every farm in the country with no clearly established effect on people's health. The Environmental Protection Agency classifies DDT as a "presumed carcinogen," which means it suspects DDT might be carcinogenic but doesn't have any proof. DDT was finally condemned due to the belief it caused thinning eggshells among wild birds of prey. Even this is contentious, as it was never actually proven, and the evidence was circumstantial. For an alternative view to the common belief that DDT is "one of the deadliest chemicals in existence" it is informative to read the JunkScience.com posting on the subject. [193]

By the 1960s, largely due to the use of DDT, malaria had been eliminated from most industrialized countries but was still rampant in many tropical regions, Africa and India in particular. When the use of DDT was either banned or discontinued due to the policies of aid agencies, malaria continued to take an average of more than a million lives per year, 85 percent of which were in sub-Saharan Africa. During the time it was banned as many as 50 million people died from malaria. The majority of malaria deaths are among young, elderly, and poor people, the most vulnerable members of society. By 2005 the outrage among health professionals, scientists, and humanitarians resulted in the formation of a campaign called "Kill Malarial Mosquitoes NOW!" which called for the reintroduction of DDT as an essential tool to eradicate malaria.

---

193. J. Gordon Edwards and Steven Malloy, " "100 Things You Should Know About DDT," JunkScience.com, http://www.junkscience.com/ddtfaq.html

Archbishop Desmond Tutu, a South African Nobel Prize recipient, soon joined the campaign and became its chief spokesperson. I was an early signatory and due to my past Greenpeace credentials was featured as a supporter of the campaign. [194]

During the years the WHO and USAID refused aid to countries that used DDT for malaria control, the rate of infection skyrocketed. The poorer countries relied on these aid agencies for health care and were therefore held hostage by the anti-DDT policy. Fortunately both South Africa and India had sufficient resources of their own and decided to reject outside aid and retain the right to use DDT. The success of their efforts at controlling the spread of malaria became one of the main beacons for the campaign to Kill Malarial Mosquitoes Now! [195] While malaria infections plummeted by 90 percent in South Africa, they remained very high just across the border in Mozambique, where DDT was not used. In September 2006 the World Health Organization and USAid announced they would reintroduce DDT as an essential tool to combat malaria. "The scientific and programmatic evidence clearly supports this reassessment. Indoor residual spraying is useful to quickly reduce the number of infections caused by malaria-carrying mosquitoes," said Dr Anarfi Asamoa-Baah, World Health Organization assistant director-general for HIV/AIDS, TB and malaria.[196]

The Stockholm Convention of the United Nations was finalized in Johannesburg in December 2000. Its aim is to eliminate persistent organic pollutants (POPs), many of which are chlorinated compounds. DDT was named to the high-priority list known as the "dirty dozen." Greenpeace and the WWF consistently opposed any use of DDT, even for malaria control, even though there is no evidence it causes harm when used in this context. In fact there is no conclusive evidence that DDT is harmful to humans even when one uses it indoors to kill mosquitoes at levels that are far higher than typical exposures. If it had not been for the intervention of sufficient African delegates, it is likely Greenpeace and its friends would have succeeded in having the Stockholm Convention ban DDT outright. Fortunately this didn't happen and when the Convention was ratified in Paris in 2004, it contained an exception for the use of DDT in fighting malaria.[197] Later in 2004, under great pressure from humanitarians and scientists, both Greenpeace and the WWF made statements that they now

---

194. Paul K. Driessen, "The Truth About Malaria and DDT," The Progressive Conservative, USA, July 17, 2006, http://www.proconservative.net/PCVol8Is129DriessenMalariaDDT.shtml
195. "WHO Follows SA Lead on DDT," SouthAfrica.info, September 20, 2006, http://www.southafrica.info/about/health/malaria-190906.htm
196. "Reversing Its Policy, UN Agency Promotes DDT to Combat the Scourge of Malaria," UN News Center, September 15, 2006, http://www.un.org/apps/news/story.asp?NewsID=19855&Cr=malaria&Cr1
197. "Stockholm Convention on Persistent Organic Pollutants," Secretariat of the Stockholm Convention, April 14, 2010, http://chm.pops.int

agreed DDT should be used to control malaria.[198] Following a de facto ban that spanned more than 30 years and caused great harm, concern for human health finally triumphed over a dogmatic belief.

And it turns out that right from the start, extremist interpretations of Rachel Carson's writings from the early 1960s were responsible for these millions of unnecessary deaths. On page 12 of *Silent Spring*, she states clearly, "It is not my contention that chemical insecticides should never be used." Rather she argued against their "indiscriminate" and "unchecked" use.[199] This was reasonable seeing that at the time thousands of tons of DDT were being aerially sprayed on millions of acres of farmland, with little regard for their impact on water, wildlife, or even non-target insects. It was not Rachel Carson who was unreasonable, but rather the extremists who used her writings to further a zero-tolerance agenda in their efforts to obtain political power on the back of what should have been a more sensible, balanced environmental and health agenda.

If you search the Internet for "Rachel Carson, malaria," you will find hundreds of recent websites accusing her of genocide and mass murder and comparing her to Hitler and Stalin. I'm thankful she is not alive to see this undeservedly harsh backlash. I hope her descendants and friends have thick skins.

Genetic Engineering

There is a lowly soil bacterium named *Bacillus thuringiensis* that produces a natural insecticide.[200] Bt, as it is commonly known, is particularly poisonous to the larvae (caterpillars) of moths and butterflies, which are common pests to a number of important agricultural crops. The European corn borer and the cotton bollworm can cause devastating losses for farmers around the world. This reduces both crop production and the prosperity of farmers and their families.

Since the 1920s Bt has been used to control a number of crop pests and has been particularly favored by organic farmers as it is considered a "natural" insecticide. Bt is commonly used as a spray, and thus affects the larvae of all moths and butterflies in the treated fields. In 1984 a Belgian plant breeding company became the first company to introduce a genetically engineered crop—a tobacco plant with the insecticide from Bt bacteria built into the DNA of the plant. Thus began one of the most important advances in the history of agriculture, the ability to move desirable traits from one species to another directly by transferring DNA. It's ironic

198. James Hoare, "Greenpeace, WWF Repudiate Anti-DDT Agenda," Heartland Institute, April 1, 2005, http://www.heartland.org/policybot/results/16803/Greenpeace_WWF_Repudiate_AntiDDT_Agenda.html
199. Rachel Carson, *Silent Spring*, (Boston, Houghton Mifflin, 1962). ,
200. "*Bacillus thuringiensis*," Wikipedia, http://en.wikipedia.org/wiki/Bacillus_thuringiensis

that the process started with a tobacco plant, one of the most damaging products of farming.

Genetic engineering (or genetic modification, often called GM, the products being genetically modified organisms, or GMOs) is an entirely organic procedure. In this sense it resembles conventional breeding as it does not require chemicals or radiation to produce changes in the DNA of the product. Genetic modification simply involves moving a small piece of organic DNA from one plant or animal to another. It is very precise in that the DNA that is moved is known to be responsible for expressing the desired trait in the species being modified.

Conventional breeding is a slow and imprecise process. It can take many generations and many failed efforts to finally develop an improved variety of food crop in this way. Some traits simply can't be developed through sexual reproduction. For many decades now, plant breeders have used a couple of shortcuts to develop new varieties without going though the laborious breeding procedure. These are referred to as *chemical mutagenesis* and *nuclear mutagenesis*. Both techniques are used to induce mutations in the DNA of crop plants in the hope of generating desirable traits. The vast majority of mutations are useless, detrimental, or even fatal. But on occasion a mutation occurs that improves some aspect of the plant's growth, productivity, resistance to disease, or other factors. It is very much a scattergun approach.

Chemical mutagenesis involves exposing seeds or other parts of a plant to a chemical known to cause mutations in the DNA.[201] The technique was developed in Russia and the U.K. in the 1940s and became popular in many countries, including Sweden and the United States. Many new seed varieties have been produced by this method and many are used in both conventional and organic farming.

Nuclear mutagenesis uses various forms of radiation, including X-rays, to induce mutations in the DNA. Typically the plants and their seeds are exposed to varying levels of radiation. Some receive a high enough dose that it kills most of the plants, others get such a low dose that very few plants are affected and in between, at a medium dose, some are damaged and others appear normal. At all levels from high to low doses, it is possible a mutation will occur that will make the plant better from an agricultural or nutritional point of view. It takes thousands, even millions of replications but when a desirable trait is generated it is like striking gold.

Interestingly, organic farmers are not prohibited from using seeds that are genetically modified through nuclear and chemical mutagenesis. These methods are clearly not organic in any way; they involve toxic chemicals and radiation. And yet organic farmers have universally

201. A. T. Natarajan, "Chemical Mutagenesis: From Plants to Humans," *Current Science* 89, no. 2 (25 July 2005), http://www.ias.ac.in/currsci/jul252005/312.pdf

rejected genetic modification that uses only the organic genes themselves, transferred from, say, a corn plant into a rice plant to give the rice the ability to produce beta-carotene, which is essential for good eyesight.

Instead, many organic growers have thrown their lot in with anti-GM activists, who claim there is something sinister about this important advance in crop improvement. The detractors dubbed genetically modified crops "Frankenstein foods" or simply "Frankenfoods." They also use the epithets "Killer Tomatoes" and "Terminator Seeds" to describe a technology that has yet to harm a single person or damage any aspect of the environment. This is classic propaganda. Note that all three of these terms have been borrowed from scary Hollywood movies: *Frankenstein*, *Revenge of the Killer Tomatoes*, and the classic *Terminator* series, which stars Arnold Schwarzenegger. These movies are fantasies, and the campaign of fear waged against genetic modification is equally based on fantasy rather than facts. The sense of fear is conjured by the associating scary ideas with genetic science, as if some monster is being created. Greenpeace and its allies have been at the forefront of this campaign of fear.

All the genetic modifications being developed around the world are aimed at improving our farms, food, and medicine. There are no evil scientists involved and the genetically modified crops are rigorously tested to ensure that they will not harm us. Every major academy of science supports genetic modification as a way to address malnutrition and a variety of environmental issues. Genetic modification is the only practical means to address many nutrient deficiencies, including vitamin A, vitamin E, iron and lysine (an amino acid).

The campaign against GM science is both intellectually and morally bankrupt. If it were not such a serious issue, one that means life or death for millions of people, the opposition to genetic engineering would be laughable. In reality it is enough to make one weep.

Despite its efforts, the anti-GM movement has not stopped the ever-growing acceptance of these new varieties of crops around the world. Genetically modified soybeans, corn, cotton, and canola (rapeseed) lead the trend, occupying the majority of the millions of acres of GM crops in 28 countries planted in 2012. Most of the traits in these new varieties are designed to combat insect pests, increase production, and reduce pesticide use. They have had strong support from the major seed companies partly because they represent huge volumes and therefore large markets. It has become very expensive to get new GM varieties approved, due mainly to the onerous amount of red tape involved. Every variety is treated as if it is a new pharmaceutical that could have unknown side effects on human health. There is no reason to believe, and no evidence in the facts to assume, that GM foods could be harmful. They are not new drugs; they are new foods. Well, they are the same old foods but with a little or a lot of improvement.

Unfortunately Greenpeace and its friends succeeded in getting a precautionary principle enshrined in the Cartagena Protocol, the international treaty that sets out the rules for adoption and trade in GM seeds. This has made it possible for activists to prevent many varieties of nutritionally improved crops from being planted, even when there is no evidence any harm could result. It will be some time before the international community wakes up and realizes the calamity that it has allowed to occur. But it will inevitably recognize that a great humanitarian error has been made in denying a cure for nutrient-deficiency-related disease in hundreds of millions of people.

One can predict with some certainty that the area planted in GM varieties will continue to increase. Many new traits, including nutritional improvements, drought tolerance, salt tolerance, enhanced nitrogen uptake, disease resistance, etc., have been developed in a number of crops, including beets, cassava, papaya, potatoes, eggplant, wheat, and rice. Most of these have yet to be introduced due to opposition from anti-GM campaigners. Countries once opposed to GM crops are gradually changing their positions and embracing them as a key part of agricultural policy. The benefits are so obvious when weighed against the nonexistent "risks" that anyone with a clear understanding of the precautionary approach would embrace the technology. While caution is always warranted when introducing new science, there is nothing in the evidence to justify the zero-tolerance policy adopted by Greenpeace and others.

In a May 2010 article in *Forbes* Magazine, Henry I. Miller does an excellent job of deconstructing a biased article in the *New York Times*. [202] A read of Miller's piece will give you an excellent example of how bad journalism can turn a positive story into a negative one, and by quoting sources in the zero-tolerance camp, the Times can make it appear that GM crops are a failure rather than the success they really are.[203]

The adoption of GM varieties has been an uphill battle on the part of farmers around the world. The anti-GM folks attempt to depict farmers as gullible dupes, who are forced by Monsanto and other "seed giants" to buy GM seeds, thus destroying their "traditional agricultural practices." This is nonsense of course. Farmers are free to buy seed from whomever they wish, as long as it is legal, and sometimes even when it isn't. If they wish, they can start their own seed company. In the name of "free choice," activists work to deny farmers the choice by campaigning to make GM illegal. They were particularly successful with this approach in Europe, where incidences of mad-cow disease and chemical contamination have sensitized the public to food scares. European agriculture is shaped more

202. Henry I. Miller, "All the News That Fits," Forbes, May 19, 2010,
http://www.forbes.com/2010/05/19/science-new-york-times-agriculture-opinions-columnists-henry-i-miller.html
203. Andrew Pollack, "Study Says Overuse Threatens Gains From Modified Crops," New York Times, April 13, 2010,
http://www.nytimes.com/2010/04/14/business/energy-environment/14crop.html

by social policy than by economic necessity. Farmers are paid not to grow food, as there is a regional surplus. Those who do grow food receive large subsidies. So European farmers do not have much incentive to improve their yields or profits.

The European Union (EU) established a de facto moratorium on GM crops in 1998, citing the precautionary principle and unspecified threats to human health and the environment. This caused many countries in Asia, Africa, and Latin America to place bans on growing GM crops for fear their food exports to Europe would be embargoed. In 2005 the EU lifted the moratorium, but many restrictions remain in place and a number of EU countries are defying the decision. The fear of GM crops in Europe, where there is a surplus of food, has serious impacts on developing countries, where food shortages and nutritional deficiencies are common. This is where the campaign against genetic modification has done real harm. Whereas the big money crops have been able to power through the pressure groups and adopt many improved varieties, the traits that would improve nutrition for hundreds of millions of people in the developing countries do not have as much economic muscle behind them.[204]

The most serious nutritional problems in the world stem from *micronutrient deficiencies*. Most people, unless they live in a zone of conflict or disaster, get enough calories (energy) from carbohydrates in the form of sugar, starch, and oils. They are not "starving," but rather they lack key minerals, vitamins, and amino acids. Among the main micronutrient deficiencies are iron (especially in women), vitamin A, vitamin E, and certain amino acids that make up proteins. Most of this deficiency occurs in the rice-eating cultures of Asia and Africa because rice has so few nutrients other than starch. The cultures that get their carbohydrates from wheat, potatoes, and corn rarely lack micronutrients because those crops are richer in vitamins and minerals.

The inhumanity of the anti-GM stance can be no better illustrated than with the example of Golden Rice. About two billion people eat rice as their primary supply of carbohydrates for energy. Most of these people are healthy because they can afford a variety of foods, including greens, fruits, and vegetables that provide them with the necessary vitamins, minerals, and protein. But the World Health Organization estimates that 124 million people suffer from a vitamin A deficiency and one to two million die each year from this deficiency. It is therefore almost as deadly as malaria. The deficiency results in 250,000 and 500,000 irreversible cases of blindness annually, mainly in children, half of whom die within a

---

204. Pamela C. Ronald and James E. McWilliams, "Genetically Engineered Distortions," *New York Times*, May 14, 2010, http://www.nytimes.com/2010/05/15/opinion/15ronald.html?partner=rss&emc=rss

year of becoming blind.[205] Most of these people live in urban slums where poverty restricts their diet to a daily ration of rice.

In 1992, as molecular biologists were beginning to succeed with recombinant DNA technology, which would eventually become known as genetic engineering,[206] [207] two humanitarian scientists set to work in Switzerland. Dr. Ingo Potrykus[208] of the Institute of Plant Sciences at the Swiss Federal Institute of Technology and Dr. Peter Beyer[209] of the University of Freiburg were aware of the tragedy of vitamin A deficiency. For eight years they worked in their labs to engineer a rice plant that would solve this problem. In 2000 they published an article in the journal *Science* that indicated they had created a variety of rice containing beta-carotene, the precursor to vitamin A.[210] They did this by inserting a gene from corn into the rice's DNA, the gene that gives corn its bright yellow color. The yellow color in daffodils, corn, and mangoes, and the orange color in carrots, yams, and pumpkins are caused by the presence of beta-carotene. The addition of beta-carotene to rice gives it a golden color and provides enough of the nutrient to prevent vitamin A deficiency and blindness.

Common white rice and Golden Rice

The invention of Golden Rice was hailed as a great breakthrough in the fight against malnutrition. *Time* magazine carried a cover photo of Dr. Potrykus posing beside Golden Rice plants with the headline, "This Rice Could Save a Million Kids a Year." The subheading carried the ominous warning: "But protestors believe such genetically modified foods are bad for us and our planet." Thus began the campaign, led by Greenpeace, to discredit both Golden Rice and its inventors. Greenpeace dubbed Golden Rice "fool's gold" and claimed you would have to eat nine kilos of it to get enough Vitamin A to prevent blindness.[211] This was a lie, of course, but it was picked up by media around the world and a negative tone was soon established. Dr. Potrykus found himself having to defend his invention against these phony accusations. Greenpeace threatened to "rip the rice from the ground" if anyone dared plant it. They claimed that Golden Rice was merely a front for multinationals like Monsanto who were using

---

205. J. H. Humphrey, K. P. West Jr, and A. Sommer, "Vitamin A Deficiency and Attributable Mortality Among Under-5-Year-Olds," *World Health Organization Bulletin* 70, no. 2, (1992), …
… http://whqlibdoc.who.int/bulletin/1992/Vol70-No2/bulletin_1992_70(2)_225-232.pdf
206. "Genetic Engineering," Wikipedia, http://en.wikipedia.org/wiki/Genetic_engineering
207. The term genetic engineering was first used by Jack Williamson in the science fiction novel Dragon's Island, published in 1952, two years before the discovery of DNA. See: "Jack Williamson," Wikipedia http://en.wikipedia.org/wiki/Jack_Williamson
208. "Prof Ingo Potrykus," goldenrice.org, http://www.goldenrice.org/Content1-Who/who_Ingo.html
209. "Prof Peter Beyer," goldenrice.org, http://www.goldenrice.org/Content1-Who/who_Peter.html
210. "Beta-Carotene," Wikipedia, http://en.wikipedia.org/wiki/Beta-Carotene
211. "Golden Rice: All Glitter, No Gold," Greenpeace International, March 15, 2005, http://www.greenpeace.org/international/news/failures-of-golden-rice

it to gain acceptance of their evil plot to control the seed industry. [212]

I met Dr. Potrykus at a conference in Helsinki shortly after he became embroiled in controversy. He was clearly distressed by the vehemence and ignorance of the anti-GM movement. An otherwise mild-mannered, typically tweedy research scientist had been turned into a radical activist himself. Greenpeace now claimed that Golden Rice was a "technical failure" and that it would be much more effective if people with a vitamin A deficiency were to take vitamin pills and create home gardens, where they could grow leafy vegetables that are rich in beta-carotene. From their plush international headquarters on the canals of Amsterdam, the Greenpeace campaigners ignore the fact that the reason people suffer from the deficiency is because they are too poor to afford pills or garden space. And Greenpeace offers no aid to these people from its bulging bank accounts. Dr. Potrykus was moved to state "If you plan to destroy test fields to prevent responsible testing and development of Golden Rice for humanitarian purposes, you will be accused of contributing to a crime against humanity. Your actions will be carefully registered and you will, hopefully, have the opportunity to defend your illegal and immoral actions in front of an international court."[213] I wholeheartedly agreed with him and seconded the motion.

Greenpeace has the nerve to resort to the "precautionary principle" to defend its zero-tolerance position on Golden Rice. Greenpeace says, "Golden Rice could breed with wild and weedy relatives to contaminate wild rice forever. If there were any problems the clock could not be turned back."[214] So Greenpeacers think that if a corn gene got into wild rice that would be worse than half a million blind children every year? What possible harm could rice plants cause with beta-carotene in them, a compound that occurs naturally in every green plant? All rice plants, including wild rice, contain beta-carotene, but it is in their leaves, where it provides no nutritional benefits . Carotenes are not only essential for eyesight in all animals, they are also one of the most important anti-oxidants in our diet. I challenge Greenpeace and the rest of the anti-GM movement to explain how beta-carotene or any other aspect of Golden Rice could have a negative impact on human health or the environment.

It is clear that Greenpeace's opposition to Golden Rice is a desperate attempt to justify its zero-tolerance approach to genetic modification.

---

212. Michael Fumento, "Golden Rice: A Golden Chance for the Underdeveloped World," *American Outlook*, July–August 2001, http://www.fumento.com/goldenrice.html

213. Ingo Potrykus, " 'Golden Rice and the Greenpeace Dilemma' Second Response to Greenpeace from Prof. Ingo Potrykus," February 15, 2001, http://www.biotech-info.net/2_IP_response.html

214. "Golden Rice: All Glitter, No Gold," Greenpeace International, March 15, 2005, http://www.greenpeace.org/international/news/failures-of-golden-rice

Greenpeace knows that if there is one good GM variety, there will be others. Then my old organization would need to have a rational discussion about the merits of each variety, like the rest of us mere mortals. Instead, it prefers to stand on high in judgment, even though it condemns millions to needless suffering and death. For this reason, on this subject, I condemn its actions. In Dr. Potrykus' own words:

> Golden Rice fulfils all the wishes the GMO opposition had earlier expressed in their criticism of the use of the technology, and it thus nullifies all the arguments against genetic engineering with plants in this specific example.

- Golden Rice has not been developed by and for industry.
- It fulfils an urgent need by complementing traditional interventions.
- It presents a sustainable, cost-free solution, not requiring other resources.
- It avoids the unfortunate negative side effects of the Green Revolution.
- Industry does not benefit from it.
- Those who benefit are the poor and disadvantaged.
- It is given free of charge and restrictions to subsistence farmers.
- It does not create any new dependencies.
- It will be grown without any additional inputs.
- It does not create advantages to rich landowners.
- It can be re-sown every year from the saved harvest.
- It does not reduce agricultural biodiversity.
- It does not affect natural biodiversity.
- There is, so far, no conceptual negative effect on the environment.
- There is, so far, no conceivable risk to consumer health.
- It was not possible to develop the trait using traditional methods.

Optimists might, therefore, have expected that the GMO opposition would welcome this case. As the contrary is the case, and the anti-GMO forces are doing everything to prevent Golden Rice reaching the subsistence farmer, we have learned that GMO opposition has a hidden, political agenda. It is not so much the concern about the environment, or the health of the consumer, or the help for the poor and disadvantaged. It is a radical fight against a technology merely for political success. This could be tolerated in rich countries where people lead a luxurious life, even without the technology. It cannot, however, be tolerated in poor countries, where the technology can make the difference between life and death, and health or severe illness. In fighting against Golden Rice reaching the poor in developing countries, GMO opposition has to be held responsible for the foreseeable unnecessary death and blindness of millions of poor every year.[215]

It soon became clear to Dr. Potrykus and his colleagues that it would not be easy to win approval for Golden Rice in the countries where vitamin A deficiency was most severe. The anti-GM movement had succeeded in erecting such a thicket of bureaucracy that it was impossible to gain approval even for field trials. They decided to form an organization, the Humanitarian Golden Rice Project, and to recruit support from key organizations. These include HarvestPlus (which in turn is funded by the Bill & Melinda Gates Foundation and the World Bank), the Swiss Development and Collaboration Agency, USAID, and the Syngenta Foundation, together with local research institutes and several nongovernmental organizations (NGOs), including the Rockefeller Foundation and the International Rice Research Institute (IRRI).[216]

The Project set out to obtain rights to the numerous patents involved in creating Golden Rice. It was decided that when the rice became available it would be given free to farmers in developing countries who earned less than US$10,000 per year. Then began the arduous work of steering the rice through the regulatory process in key countries. It was not until 2004 that the first field trial was conducted in Louisiana, which proved Golden Rice produced sufficient beta-carotene under farm conditions. Then in 2005, with the help of the Syngenta Foundation, a new variety of Golden Rice was produced that contained 23 times as much beta-carotene as the original strain. This, along with studies on human uptake of beta-carotene from Golden Rice, now provides proof Golden Rice will be effective in preventing vitamin A deficiency with a cup of rice per day.[217] Yet progress has been intolerably slow.

Despite their efforts it was not until 2008 that they received permission for field trials in the Philippines and Bangladesh.[218] As of this writing there are still no farmers growing Golden Rice in any country. Millions of people continue to suffer from a vitamin A deficiency for no good reason, and many of them die young and blind. If the World Health Organization's numbers are correct there have been four to eight million cases of childhood blindness since Golden Rice was invented.[219] When I left Greenpeace it was partly because I realized its members didn't really

215. Ingo Potrykus, "The Golden Rice 'Tale'," AgBioView, 2001 http://www.goldenrice.org/PDFs/The_GR_Tale.pdf (This account of the early development of Golden Rice by Dr. Potrykus is well worth reading. It is quite technical but provides a fascinating insight into the nature of scientific invention and the frustration of confronting irrational opposition.)
216. "Golden Rice Is Part of the Solution," goldenrice.org, http://www.goldenrice.org/
217. "Almost Everything You Wanted to Know About Golden Rice," goldenrice.com http://www.goldenrice.org/Content3-Why/why3_FAQ.html
(Here you will find the complete story of Golden Rice plus the answers to many questions about it)
218. "Golden Rice: First Field Tests in the Philippines," GMO Compass, April 19, 2008, http://www.gmo-compass.org/eng/news/358.golden_rice_first_field_tests_philippines.html
219. "Micronutrient Deficiencies: Vitamin A Deficiency," World Health Organization, 2010, http://www.who.int/nutrition/topics/vad/en/index.html

care about people. But I had no idea they could fall this low. I guess you *can* sink a rainbow.

But there is hope that by 2014 it will be possible to begin cultivating Golden Rice for public consumption. Surely it is inevitable that nutritional improvements such as this will eventually become accepted as conventional. Since Golden Rice was invented, scientists have developed many new varieties of GM crops with nutritional benefits : rice with a high iron content and enhanced vitamin E, tomatoes with increased anti-oxidants called anthocyanins, cassava with beta-carotene, carrots with twice the calcium. And there are many more to come. As Lawrence Kent, the senior program officer of agricultural development at the Bill & Melinda Gates Foundation stated, "We're hoping some initial successes are going to trigger additional interest, especially from national governments. If we can help get more nutrients into these staple foods, we really can help millions of people improve their lives."[220]

One of the main reasons for optimism about the future of GM foods is that farmers are demanding access to the seeds so they can benefit from increased yields and superior products. Contrary to the activist fabrication that GM seeds are being pushed down farmers' throats by greedy multinationals, it is the farmers themselves who are driving more and more countries to accept genetically modified crops. Typically, most politicians are afraid to buck the noisy, threatening rhetoric of the anti-GM crusaders. It has been left largely to the hard-working people of the land to fight for the right to plant genetically improved varieties.

The anti-GM campaigners shamelessly claim the farmers are on their side because they are victims, by virtue of their innocence and gullibility, of the multinational companies' diabolical plot to enslave them with "toxic" seeds. I suppose they can always find a few dissident farmers to support their cause, but there is no question the overwhelming majority of mainstream farmers support GM technology and the benefits it brings to them and their customers. The anti-GM forces have purposefully adopted a parasitic relationship with the world farming community. They are using farmers to gain sympathy from a largely urban support base that does not understand genetics and does not know what is going on out in the country. Dr. Ingo Potrykus is correct; they should stand trial for crimes against humanity.

The first field trial of insect-resistant cotton (Bt cotton) was conducted in the United States in 1990. By 1995 there were one million hectares (2.5 million acres) of GM cotton growing in the U.S., and today there are about four million hectares (10 million acres), or about 90 percent of the cotton grown in the country. American farmers are obviously free

---

220. Bob Grant, "Where's the Super Food?" Meridian Institute, September 22, 2009,
http://www.merid.org/NDN/more.php?id=2154

to buy cottonseed from whomever they wish. They have chosen to pay considerably more for Bt cottonseed over conventional varieties because reduced need for pesticides and increased yield more than make up for the increase in seed cost. In 1996 Australia followed the U.S. and approved GM cotton for planting. It achieved similar positive results. This early success did not pass unnoticed in the other major cotton-growing countries, including China, India, and Brazil.

China, which produces nearly one-third of the world's cotton, adopted GM cotton in 1997. Today 7.1 million Chinese farmers use genetically modified cottonseed as a result of which they get higher yields. This improves their standard of living. The Internet is loaded with misinformation about the failure of GM cotton in China. These stories are put out by Greenpeace and other anti-GM organizations that must rely on fabrications because there are no true examples of GM failure. China has become a leader in research and development of GM varieties. In 2002 it became the first country to establish plantations of GM trees (poplar).[221] In the U.S., the Department of Agriculture recently has given ArborGen approval to plant up to 250,000 GM trees in the American south-east.[222]

Farmers in India, the second largest cotton producer, didn't initially enjoy such a supportive government as their counterparts in China. GM crops were effectively banned in India due to anti-GM campaigns led by Vandana Shiva, a Western-educated feminist who claimed to be defending the "traditional agricultural practices" (read poverty and lack of education) of poor rural farmers. Then, in 2001, 10,000 hectares (25,000 acres) of GM cotton were secretly planted in the western-most state of Gujarat. By mid-summer, nearby farmers noted the GM cotton plants were healthy and green while the surrounding conventional cotton was brown and damaged by the usual plague of cotton bollworms. The state government became aware of the situation and announced the "illegal" GM cotton would be burned. This annoyed the farmers who organized and figuratively "marched on city hall with their pitchforks" to protest the planned burning. This resulted in the government changing its policy and approving GM cotton. It was first planted in 2002. By 2012 GM cotton was grown on 10.8 million hectares (26.7 million acres), where five million farmers chose to buy GM seeds, mainly from varieties developed in India. India's cotton production has more than doubled since GM cotton was introduced, and the country has gone from a cotton importing nation to a nation that exports about 20 percent of the total harvest. More than 70 million people are employed by this single crop. This amounts to nearly

---

221. "Cultivation of Bt Poplars in China: Seeing Once Is Better Than Studying a Thousand Times," *GMO Safety*, July 6, 2005, http://www.gmo-safety.eu/science/woody-plants/316.seeing-once-studying-thousand-times.html
222. "ArborGen Approved to Test GM Trees," *Environmental Leader*, June 10, 2010, http://www.environmentalleader.com/2010/06/10/arborgen-approved-to-test-gm-trees/

85 percent of the area of cotton under cultivation in India.[223] Clearly, the anti-GM movement's interpretation of this as a failure of GM technology or a refusal on the part of farmers to adopt these new varieties lacks credibility. Yet it doggedly continues to oppose these crops despite their popularity among the very farmers it claims to support against the "multinational" seed companies.

A similar situation emerged in the Philippines, where the government was afraid to give farmers permission to plant insect-resistant GM corn even though they wanted to do so to rid their crops of the devastation caused by the corn borer. In 2002 Greenpeace warned that planting "toxic" GM corn "would result in millions of dead bodies, sick children, cancer clusters and deformities."[224] They held a hunger strike for 29 days, finally calling it off on May 22, 2003, when it became clear that the government would allow farmers to plant GM corn because its top scientific advisors had recommended it do so. By 2009 400,000 hectares (one million acres) of land had been planted with GM corn.

In Brazil, Greenpeace succeeded in getting a judgment from a tribunal in 1999 to prevent the sale of GM soybeans. The government hesitated to step in, as it was typically sensitive to the high-profile attacks on GM foods. Meanwhile farmers in Argentina began to grow GM soybeans in 1996. By 1997 there were more than a million hectares (2.5 million acres) dedicated to producing these soybeans. As Brazil and Argentina share a common border it was not long before truckloads of GM soybean seeds were hauled from Argentina to Brazil, where farmers were eager to benefit from their higher yields. Thus began a long battle between farmers, Greenpeace and its allies, the courts and the government over the legality of GM crops.

In 2003 I traveled to Porto Alegre in southern Brazil, where I addressed a large group of soybean farmers at their union meeting. I encouraged them to continue to defy the edict against GM soy and to take their message directly to the government. Many members of the media attended the meeting and my presentation received extensive coverage. I like to think I had some small role to play in the fact that in 2004 the government of then president Lula de Silva finally lifted the ban. As of 2009 more than two-thirds of the Brazilian soybean area was planted with GM varieties. In Argentina, 95 percent of the soybean area is GM, while in the U.S. 85 percent is GM. Between them, the U.S., Brazil, and Argentina produce nearly 90 percent of the world's soybeans.

By the end of 2012 there were 25 countries growing GM crops on 170 million hectares (420 million acres), considerably more than the

223. "India's GM Cotton Plantation Seen Rising," Reuters, February 18, 2009,
http://in.reuters.com/article/topNews/idINIndia-38083820090218
224. Prakash Sadashivappa, "Bt Cotton in India: Development of Benefits and the Role of Government Seed Price Interventions," AbBioForum, 2009, http://www.agbioforum.org/v12n2/v12n2a03-sadashivappa.htm

total annual harvested cropland in the United States.[225] [226] This is an incredible accomplishment given that the first commercial GM crops were established only 15 years ago. There is every indication this trend will continue.[227] It is likely that long before the end of this century virtually every food crop will have one or more genetically modified traits built into it. GM technology is so powerful in its potential to improve growth, yield, efficiency, disease resistance, and nutrition that it almost certainly will become universally adopted around the world.

Why then do anti-GM forces continue to make a concerted effort to drown out this good news story with misinformation and propaganda? I believe it is because they do not care about human welfare or the environment for that matter, but are determined to strike a blow against the globalization of agriculture, multinational corporations, and capitalism in general. This campaign works for them because they are able to scare a large segment of the public who do not have an understanding of this relatively new science, which is both invisible and complicated. Despite the fact that there is not one iota of truth to their campaign of fear, they succeed with many people who are afraid of the unknown.

There is also a growing trend among environmental activists to take on campaigns they will never win in the foreseeable future. They will never stop the growth of GM technology; they will never stop nuclear energy or fossil fuel energy; they will never stop the sustainable management of forests for timber production; and they will never stop salmon aquaculture. This creates an opportunity for an endless campaign of propaganda, supporting an endless fundraising campaign to support even more propaganda. As a political strategy it is quite brilliant, except they didn't actually devise it themselves, it just happened that way. It happened that way because the campaigns they won are now over, and as they gradually abandoned science and logic in favor of zero-tolerance policies, they inevitably ended up with unwinnable campaigns. Unfortunately we will have to put up with these campaigns for a long, long time.

One very bright sign for the advancement of agriculture and the eradication of poverty, malnutrition, and disease in the developing countries is the emergence of the Bill and Melinda Gates Foundation on the international aid scene. With billions of dollars from Bill and Melinda Gates as well as from Warren Buffet, the foundation is bringing a new level of professionalism to the business of helping others. As a clear sign that the foundation is serious about bringing the most advanced agricultural

225. "Global Status of Commercialized Biotech/GM Crops: 2012." ISAAA, 2013, http://www.isaaa.org/resources/publications/briefs/44/executivesummary/default.asp

226. Marlow Vesterby, Kenneth S. Krupa, Ruben N. Lubowski, "Estimating U.S. Cropland Area," Amber Waves, July 2006, http://www.ers.usda.gov/Amberwaves/July06SpecialIssue/Indicators/BehindData.htm

227. Alexander J. Stein and Emilio Rodríguez-Cerezo, "The Global Pipeline of New GM Crops," JRC European Commission, 2009, http://ftp.jrc.es/EURdoc/report_GMOpipeline_online_preprint.pdf

practices to bear on the problems in Africa and other developing regions, it has hired Sam Dryden as head of agriculture development.[228] Mr. Dryden has a long career in genetic engineering and seed development. The company he developed, Emergent Genetics, was sold to Monsanto Co. in 2005. He serves on the U.S. board of the Global Crop Diversity Trust, which works to ensure crop diversity for food security. He also serves on the National Academies Roundtable on Science and Technology for Global Sustainability. His qualifications ensure that the foundation's work will make use of intensive agricultural practices and advances in genetic science, for the benefit of countries that do not yet share the benefits enjoyed by the developed countries. Three cheers for the Bill and Melinda Gates Foundation!

---

228. "Gates Foundation Names New Agricultural Director," Kristi Heim, *The Seattle Times*, January 8, 2010, http://seattletimes.nwsource.com/html/localnews/2010747556_gatesag09.html

Biodiversity, Endangered Species, and Extinction

The term *biodiversity* was first popularized by Edward O. Wilson in his book of the same title published in 1988.[229] The phrases *living nature* or *all of life* capture the meaning of this term. The emphasis on diversity highlights the number of distinct species of life. For example, arctic climates tend to have relatively low biodiversity while tropical climates have high biodiversity (because life thrives in warm climates more than in freezing ones). In any given ecosystem there tends to be a minority of species that are quite common and a majority of species that are comparatively uncommon. This gives rise to the bio-ditty, "Species here, species there; few abundant, many rare." You might get the impression that a species is *endangered* when it is normal for it to exist in low numbers in a particular ecosystem. These species tend to be more vulnerable to displacement or local extinction when circumstances change, that is, when new competing species evolve or invade, or when the climate changes more rapidly than usual.

In any given location there are often a number of species at the extreme extent of their geographical distribution. Every species has a preferred

---

229. Edward. O. Wilson, Harvard University, Editor, *Biodiversity* (Washington, D.C., National Academy of Sciences/Smithsonian Institution, 1988).

climate where it is most abundant. It will taper off in areas where it can't survive due to the climate or the presence of a species it can't compete with. At the fringes of their range these species become *endangered* because relatively small changes in climate and species composition could eliminate them from that region. When their elimination involves humans the word *extirpation* is used, as in the sentence "Grizzly bears have been extirpated from California." As a reminder of this extirpation, the grizzly remains prominently displayed on the state flag.

As the climate has constantly changed during the comings and goings of ice sheets, ice ages, greenhouse ages, and cataclysmic events of various types and proportions, species have migrated to more suitable climes or evolved to adapt to the change. When they fail to do so, they become extinct. To this extent extinction is an entirely natural phenomenon, as natural as the evolution of new species replacing the extinct ones.

Because humans are part of nature, one can argue that it is natural when we cause species to become extinct. But that doesn't mean it is a good or a positive thing to do. Most people feel happy that the smallpox virus is now extinct in nature; and there are many other species of vermin, parasites, and disease-causing bacteria and viruses that would not be missed if they happened to disappear—HIV-AIDS and malaria, for example. Yet most people do not want to be responsible for the extinction of anything cuddly or useful.

Until very recently humans were not concerned about the extinction of other species, even though we were clearly responsible for many of them. A few naturalists and philosophers lamented the passing of the dodo bird but most people thought, That's life. And the dodo birds fed a lot of sailors.

Beginning with the concern for preserving wilderness landscapes that emerged during Theodore Roosevelt's presidency and John Muir's founding of the Sierra Club, it became popular to care about the survival of species. The extinction of the passenger pigeon in the U.S. and Canada in the 1920s elevated this concern, and people started doing something about it. Starting around 1930, concern for species such as the California condor, wolves, birds of prey, whales, and large cats resulted in programs and policies to reverse trends toward extinction. Not all these species have been saved, but the record is a good one, proving we can prevent species from becoming extinct if we act to prevent it. There are grounds for considerable optimism that even as the human population grows larger, it will be possible to keep most of the other species that share this earth with us.

Search the Internet for "mass extinction" and you will find hundreds of websites devoted to the idea that we are in the midst of the Sixth Great Extinction, as humans drive more species into oblivion than at any other time since the era when dinosaurs disappeared. These websites contend that 50,000 species are going extinct each year and that half of all species on earth will be gone before the end of this century. This is not the result of an asteroid impact or massive volcanic eruptions; it is our doing, they claim. We humans are accused of driving the mass extinction. Here is a sample of the headlines on these web pages:[230]

- "Scientists Agree World Faces Mass Extinction" (CNN)
- "Quarter of Mammals 'Face Extinction'" (BBC)
- "Half of All Species May Be Extinct in Our Lifetime" (U.S. National Academy of Science)
- "Fastest Mass Extinction in Earth's History" (Worldwatch)
- "Headlong Drive to Mass Extinction" (Toronto *Globe and Mail*)
- "Wave of Extinctions Sweeping the Planet" (United Nations)
- "One Quarter of Primates Will be Extinct in 20 Years" (London *Times*, 2005)
- "One Third of Primates Face Extinction" (BBC, 2002)

So it must be true, an unassuming reader might think. No wonder some people don't want to have children, the planet is soon doomed and it won't be a good place to live anymore.

Note that some of these headlines are predictive in nature ("...May Be Extinct...") while others are written as if the extinction is already under way ("Wave of Extinctions Sweeping the Planet"). This is an important distinction, as we will see later when we consider the case of *National Geographic* magazine.

I began to study the mass extinction phenomenon after my trip to Nairobi in 1982. There I met the Kenyan conservationist Richard Leakey[231] and the British environmentalist Norman Myers.[232] Both had impeccable credentials and both feared we were causing a mass extinction of wild species. Norman Myers had become a kind of prophet of this belief and gave lectures about the coming collapse around the world. I listened carefully to both men when I met with them and over dinners, and I came away determined to get to the bottom of this subject.

Five major extinctions have occurred during the past 550 million years, since the time of the Cambrian explosion when large, multicellular life forms emerged.[233] These extinctions are clearly documented in the fossil record. During the three billion or so years before that time, when all life was microscopic, unicellular, and aquatic, there is not a sufficient fossil record to distinguish extinction events clearly.

230. David Ulansey, editor, "Mass Extinction Underway," The Current Mass Extinction, 2010, http://www.well.com/~davidu/extinction.html
231. "Richard Leakey," Wikipedia, http://en.wikipedia.org/wiki/Richard_Leakey
232. "Norman Myers, "Wikipedia, http://en.wikipedia.org/wiki/Norman_Myers
233. "The Cambrian Explosion," fossilmuseum.net, http://www.fossilmuseum.net/Paleobiology/CambrianExplosion.htm

The most devastating extinction known occurred 250 million years ago, marking the end of the Permian era.[234] By this time all the major forms of life that exist today had already developed. The major life forms are called phyla. All vertebrates, that is, animals with backbones, are grouped into the phylum Chordata. Other examples of phyla are mollusks (Mollusca), segmented worms (Annelida), arthropods such as insects and crabs (Arthropoda), corals (Cnidaria), and ferns (Pteridphyta). In the Permian extinction, about 90 percent of all marine species and 70 percent of terrestrial species were exterminated by what was likely either an asteroid impact, massive volcanic eruptions, or a combination of the two. Miraculously, after every major extinction event the number of living species recovered and became even more abundant than they were before the collapse. This is one of the great hallmarks of the evolution of life, particularly during the 560 million years since multicellular life forms developed. As a result, the biological diversity of living things is higher in our era than it has been at any time since life began.

The most recent mass extinction was what we call the dinosaur extinction, which occurred 65 million years ago, but it was much more than a dinosaur extinction. Tens of thousands of species of all life forms were lost in what many scientists believe was the aftermath of an asteroid impact between Florida and the Yucatan.[235] The environmental conditions necessary to cause such a vast extinction were extremely harsh. The sun was largely blocked by atmospheric dust and debris for years. Plant species died out for lack of light and the animals that depended on them died out with them. Nothing remotely resembling this is occurring today.

As with many catastrophe theories there is, however, a grain of truth to the current mass extinction theory. Humans are believed to have caused a number of extinctions, long before the modern era. This phenomenon began tens of thousands of years ago as we developed tools and weapons. In Australia, the extinction of most large mammals coincided with the arrival of humans about 50,000 years ago. Similarly, the arrival of humans in the New World (the Western Hemisphere) about 15,000 years ago is strongly correlated with the extinction of mammoths, mastodons, saber-toothed tigers, and many other large mammals that had evolved long before humans arrived on the scene. Interestingly, this pattern did not occur in sub-Saharan Africa, where our hominid ancestors evolved over millions of years and where the native wildlife had the opportunity to adapt to humans as they first threw rocks and then spears.

In more modern times, a considerable number of extinctions have occurred as a result of human activity. These fall into three categories:

---

234. "Permian-Triassic Extinction Event," Wikipedia, http://en.wikipedia.org/wiki/Permian-Triassic_extinction_event
235. "Cretaceous-Tertiary Extinction Event," http://en.wikipedia.org/wiki/Cretaceous-Tertiary_extinction_event

- *Overhunting and eradication.* In other words killing an entire species with clubs, spears, and guns. The dodo bird and the passenger pigeon were victims of overhunting for food; the Carolina parakeet, the only parrot that was native to North America, was eradicated by farmers because it ate their crops. The parakeets came in large flocks and as the farmer shot them one at a time the remaining birds circled around the growing heap of dead fellows until the last one was shot. Not a very good survival strategy in the face of a farmer with a gun. The evolution of human technology overwhelmed millions of years of parakeet evolution in a few decades. The species was pronounced extinct in 1939.[236]
- *Conversion of native forests and other ecosystems to vast areas of farmland.* About one-third of the original area of forest has been cleared and converted for agricultural use during the past 10,000 years. Most of this clearing has taken place in the past 200 years. Some species of plants, which can't easily migrate like birds and mammals, disappeared when their habitats were transformed to produce food for a growing human population.
- *The introduction of exotic species.* In particular, when Europeans colonized Australia, New Zealand, and many smaller islands in the Pacific and elsewhere, they brought with them rats, cats, foxes, snakes, and diseases not native to those places. Some species of native animals could not defend themselves from these new predators and diseases and were exterminated by them. This resulted in a pulse of extinctions as the most vulnerable native species succumbed.

There are well-documented lists of species that have become extinct due to these three human activities. The rate of extinction has slowed considerably in recent decades, partly because the most vulnerable species are already extinct, and partly because there are recovery programs in place to prevent currently endangered species from going extinct. But as the human population continues to grow there will be increasing pressure on vulnerable species.

Most overhunting for land animals and birds is now mainly an issue of illegal hunting and poaching. Tigers are poached for their hides, birds are taken for the pet trade and for their feathers, and rhinos are killed for the alleged aphrodisiacal power of their powdered horns. Ending these practices requires increased enforcement of hunting regulations and education about endangered species.

Overfishing of marine species is often done legally in international waters where there are no catch limits, or if there are limits, it may occur

---

236. "Carolina Parakeet," Wikipedia, http://en.wikipedia.org/wiki/Carolina_Parakeet

due to insufficient policing. While many fish species have been severely overfished, it is unlikely they could be driven to extinction, as it is virtually impossible to catch every last fish. Fish and other marine species are protected by the fact that they are underwater and much more difficult to detect than species that live on the land. Marine mammals are generally well protected, and even though Japan stubbornly insists on continuing to hunt whales in Antarctica, this will not lead to the extinction of any whale species.

One of the best examples of species loss due to clearing land for farming can be found in the Wheatbelt of Western Australia. The region around the city of Perth was extensively cleared over 100 years ago when there was little concern for endangered species or extinction, especially of plant species. Only about 5 percent of the original natural area remains today. There were many unique plants and animals in the region and they suffered from the combined impact of habitat loss and predatory species, which European settlers introduced. At least six species of mammals disappeared and many plant species are now critically endangered.[237] In recent decades a great effort has been made to prevent further extinctions by protecting the remaining natural areas and controlling introduced predators. These recovery programs have largely been successful, and they demonstrate that when we set our mind to it we can prevent extinction and even bring some species back to a healthy population size.[238]

The region of Brazil called the Cerrado is one of the most biodiverse areas on earth. It is largely savannah, open grasslands with large wooded areas. The region, which is three times the size of Texas, was once thought to be marginal or useless for agriculture due to nutritional deficiencies in the soil. Due to advances in agronomy, it has become one of the largest areas of agricultural expansion, allowing Brazil to surpass the United States in soybean production.

The Cerrado is home to 935 species of birds and nearly 300 species of mammals as well as more than 10,000 species of vascular plants. Some of these species, such as the Cerrado fox, jaguar, and maned wolf, are already listed as endangered. A wide range of environmental and conservation groups are focused on the Cerrado, working to prevent further clearing for agriculture. The state of Mato Grosso, which encompasses the largest part of the Cerrado, has established a number of large protected areas. The federal government has also intervened, creating protected areas and large reserves for the exclusive use of indigenous people, who tend not to clear land for farming. As a result, no "great extinction" will occur in the Cerrado.

---

237. "Biodiversity Assessment: Avon Wheatbelt," *Australian Natural Resources Atlas*, June 15, 2005, http://www.anra.gov.au/topics/vegetation/assessment/wa/ibra-aw-mammals-extinct.html
238. N. Carlile, D. Priddel, F Zino, C. Natividad, and D. B. Wingate, "Review of Successful Recovery Programs for Threatened Subtropical Petrels," *Marine Ornithology* 31 (2003): 185–192,. http://www.marineornithology.org/PDF/31_2/31_2_185-192.pdf

The Brazilian Cerrado will no doubt fare much better than the Australian Wheatbelt because the Cerrado is being developed in an era when concern for endangered species and extinction is almost universally shared. But both these examples highlight the fact that habitat loss caused by clearing land for farming is the biggest threat to biodiversity today. This is especially true in the tropical developing countries where populations are growing and biodiversity is highest.

There are a number of key elements that will prevent most endangered species from becoming extinct if they are adopted. First and foremost is the establishment of protected areas, some of which are large enough to provide sufficient habitat for large predators. The International Union for the Conservation of Nature and Natural Resources (IUCN) works to en-sure representative ecosystems are protected around the world, especially in "biodiversity hotspots," where large numbers of unique species live. Second, there must be proactive programs aimed at individual species in danger of becoming extinct. We now have a great deal of experience with species recovery programs and will no doubt get better as we learn more about what works and what doesn't. Third, we must recognize that intensive agricultural methods produce more food on less land, thereby reducing the amount of land cleared for farming. This means encour-aging the use of improved technology, chemistry, and genetics where this results in increased yields.

The threat of extinction from introduced species is not as great today as it was in the past, but there is still work to be done, such as eradicat-ing rats from islands that support nesting bird colonies. The main pulse of extinctions in modern times occurred as Europeans colonized islands, including the largest one, Australia. The most susceptible native species were wiped out early on and a vast majority of the ones surviving today will likely continue to meet the test of time. There are still active programs in Australia, New Zealand, Hawaii, and other islands to control or eradicate introduced predators and to protect native species from them.

Forestry and Biodiversity

It is most unfortunate that many leading environmental groups have purposely given the public the impression that forestry or "multinational forestry corporations," as they are fond of calling the industry, are respon-sible for the majority of deforestation and species extinction. This is one of the gravest mistakes of groups such as Greenpeace and the World Wildlife Fund. Everyone involved in the science of land use, biodiversity, and en-dangered species knows that clearing land for farming is the main cause of deforestation, and hence, along with hunting, one of the main threats of extinction.

When you think about it, it is clear the main purpose of forestry is to cause reforestation, the opposite of deforestation. The big environmental groups are likely aware that the UN Food and Agriculture Organization (FAO) publishes a lengthy document titled "State of the World's Forests" every two years. The FAO makes it abundantly clear that clearing land for agricultural purposes causes 95 percent of deforestation and yet Greenpeace and its friends, preying on the public's love of trees, paints the forest industry as the villain. It turns out deforestation is not an evil plot; it is what we do to grow our food and make room for our cities and towns. It is a basic part of our survival.

The 1992 UN Earth Summit in Rio de Janeiro produced agreements on two of the three key global environmental issues at that time. Consensus documents on climate change and biodiversity conservation have since led to international treaties on both these subjects. Yet agreement on forests eluded the delegates in Rio due to the conflict over whether the emphasis of an agreement should be the sustainable management of forested areas or on the preservation of forests. Those favoring sustainable forest management recognized the fact that wood is by far the most important source of renewable energy and renewable materials. Those who favor a preservationist approach are generally opposed to large-scale forestry and wish to see the majority of forests placed off-limits to commercial activity. The twain has yet to meet on this point as the debate continues, pitting forest companies and anti-forestry activists against each other as governments struggle to find compromise. At the meeting in Rio it was agreed that in order to continue discussions on forests they would create the UN Intergovernmental Panel on Forests.

In March 1996, the World Wide Fund for Nature (WWF) held a media conference in Geneva during the first meeting of the Intergovernmental Panel on Forests. They stated that 50,000 species now become extinct every year due to human activity, more than at any time since the dinosaurs became extinct 65 million years ago. Most significantly, WWF stated that the main cause of these extinctions is "commercial logging."[239] This was largely due, according to then WWF director general Claude Martin, to "massive deforestation in industrialized countries." The statements made at the media conference were broadcast on radio and television and published in newspapers around the world, giving millions of people the impression that forestry was the main cause of species extinction.

I have tried to determine the basis for this allegation, openly challenging the WWF to provide details of species extinctions caused by logging. It would appear there is no scientific evidence on which to base such a claim. WWF has provided no list of species, nor even one species, that have become extinct due to logging. In particular, the claim of "massive deforestation" in industrialized countries runs counter to information

239. "Wildlife Habitat at Risk," *Vancouver Province*, Associated Press Wire Story, March 12, 1996, p. A16

CONFESSIONS OF A GREENPEACE DROPOUT

provided by the FAO. According to the FAO, the area of forest in the industrialized world is actually growing by about 0.2% per year, due to the reforestation of land previously cleared for farming.[240]

In May 1996, I wrote to Prince Philip, the Duke of Edinburgh, in his capacity as President of WWF International. I said in part:

> Myself and many colleagues who specialize in forest science are distressed at recent statements made by WWF regarding the environmental impact of forestry. These statements indicate a break with WWF's strong tradition of basing their policies on science and reason. To the best of our knowledge, not a single species has become extinct in North America due to forestry.[241]

Prince Philip replied:

> I have to admit I did not see the draft of the statement that [WWF spokesperson] Jean-Paul Jeanrenaud was to make at the meeting of the Intergovernmental Panel on Forests in Geneva. The first two of his comments [50,000 species per year and the dinosaur comparison] are open to question, but they are not seriously relevant to the issue. However, I quite agree that his third statement [logging being the main cause of extinction] is certainly contentious and the points that you make are all good ones. All I can say is that he was probably thinking of tropical forests when he made the comment.[242]

Since this exchange of correspondence, WWF has changed the way it characterizes the impact of forestry in relation to species extinction. At their Forests for Life conference in San Francisco in May 1997, there was no mention of forestry being the main cause of species extinction. Instead, WWF unveiled a report stating, "three quarters of the continent's forest ecoregions are threatened with extinction, showing for the first time that it is not just individual species but entire ecosystems that are at risk in North America."[243] The word *extinction* normally means something has been completely eliminated. It is entirely beyond reason to suggest three quarters of the forested areas of North America will become extinct as WWF publicly proclaimed .

240. "Recent Trends and Current Status of Forest Resources," UN Food and Agriculture Organization, 1995, "http://www.fao.org/docrep/W4345E/w4345e03.htm#recent%20trends%20and%20current%20status%20of%20forest%20resources
241. Correspondence, Patrick Moore to HRH the Duke of Edinburgh, May 14, 1996, http://www.beattystreetpublishing.com/confessions/references/PMtoHRH
242. Correspondence, Prince Philip to Patrick Moore, May 27, 1996, http://www.beattystreetpublishing.com/confessions/references/HRHtoPM
243. Nigel Dudley, Don Gilmour, and Jean-Paul Jeanrenaud, *Forests for Life* (Gland, Switzerland: WWF and IUCN, 1997).

In August 1998, again using a United Nations forest conference as a platform, WWF held a media conference at which it declared that 8,753 species of trees—10 percent of the world's total—are "endangered with extinction."[244] This statement was based on a report titled "World List of Threatened Trees" produced by the World Conservation Monitoring Center with funding from the Dutch government. A reading of the report reveals that of the 8,753 tree species WWF declared "endangered with extinction," 6,969 are not classified as "endangered" but rather as "vulnerable," "lower risk," or "data deficient."[245]

Two days after the WWF press conference a feature story appeared in the largest British Columbia daily newspaper with the headline, "Three Trees Native to BC Face Extinction."[246] The three species were: a variety of mountain hemlock, whitebark pine, and western yew. None of these species is listed as endangered in the report. The mountain hemlock is listed as "data deficient," western yew as "lower risk," and whitebark pine as "vulnerable" due to an outbreak of fungus that is killing many of the trees in part of their natural range. In a subsequent newspaper article the chief forester for British Columbia stated, "The report doesn't define any of the B.C. species as in danger of extinction the way the news article noted. So to imply they are at risk of extinction is absolutely incorrect."[247] A spokesperson for WWF responded to the chief forester, stating, "Inevitably some flexibility slips in."[248] Indeed!

The inclusion of species such as the California redwood and the giant sequoia calls the credibility of the entire report into question. They are listed as "lower risk" and "vulnerable," respectively. It is hard to imagine how anyone could believe either the California redwood or the giant sequoia is at the slightest risk of becoming extinct. Redwood is prolific and flourishes in the coastal zone from southern Oregon to Big Sur, California. The giant sequoia is heavily protected throughout its natural range in the mountains of the Sierra Nevada, and is grown extensively on streets and in parks and gardens from southern California to northern Vancouver Island.

In June 1997, Greenpeace released a report at the United Nations Earth Summit 2 in New York predicting "mass extinctions" and the loss of 50 percent of plant and animal species in British Columbia under current land use policies.[249] Written by an environmental studies professor from the University of California, Santa Cruz, the report uses island biogeography

---

244. "10% of World's Tree Species Threatened with Extinction," WWF News Release, August 25, 1998,
http://wwf.panda.org/wwf_news/press_releases/?1846/10-OF-WORLDS-TREE-SPECIES-THREATENED-WITH-EXTINCTION
245. "The World List of Threatened Trees," World Conservation Monitoring Center, World Conservation Press, 1998,
http://www.unep-wcmc.org/resources/publications/otherpubs.htm
246. "Three Trees Native to BC Face Extinction," *Vancouver Sun*, August 27, 1998, p. A3.
247. "Official Denies Claim Trees Facing Extinction," Gordon Hamilton, *Vancouver Sun*, September 2, 1998, p. A3.
248. Ibid.
249. M.A. Sanjayan and M.E. Soulé., "Moving Beyond Brundtland: The Conservation Value of British Columbia's 12 Percent Protected Areas Strategy," Greenpeace, June 1997.

theory to support these claims. One of the theory's principles is that if an island in the sea is reduced to 10 percent of its original size it will only be capable of supporting 50 percent of the species supported by the larger island. The Greenpeace report concludes that if only 12 percent of British Columbia is totally protected as parks and wilderness areas, these will be the only "islands" of biodiversity (Since the Greenpeace report was first released, more than 14 percent of B.C. has been preserved as parks and protected areas). In other words, Greenpeace assumes the other 88 percent of the land will have zero value for biodiversity, as if it were all paved with asphalt. This is patently absurd as less than 5 percent of the province has been converted to settlement and farms; the remainder consists of managed native forest or wilderness, where there will always be high biodiversity values.

In March 2009, an agreement was finalized between environmental campaigners, the provincial government, First Nations, and forest companies to preserve one-third of what is now called The Great Bear Rainforest on the Central Coast of British Columbia. The agreement should be applauded because activists, industry, government, and First Nations were able to come together and build consensus around a seemingly intractable dispute. Yet the anti-forestry campaign that preceded the agreement and targeted B.C.'s forest product customers, particularly in the United States and Europe, was entirely unfair. That campaign was squarely based on allegations that "BC's coastal grizzlies will likely face extinction in the next four decades if logging operations continue to move north up the coast" and "142 stocks of salmon are now extinct" and logging is "a primary threat" to the remaining stocks.[250] Yet environmental campaigners failed to mention logging had been taking place on the Central Coast for more than 100 years. It is a fact that grizzly bear populations are classified as "viable" in areas where logging is the main industrial activity. It is only in areas of urban development and extensive cattle ranching that grizzly bears are threatened or extirpated.[251]

It is true that 142 stocks of the 9,663 known stocks of migratory salmon and trout in British Columbia and the Yukon are considered extinct. It is also true all but three of these stocks were either in the populated southwest corner of B.C. in and around Vancouver and Victoria or in the Columbia River watershed, where hydro dams were the cause of extinction.[252] Nearly half of them were in what is now Vancouver, where the former spawning creeks have been replaced with drainage pipes. Only one of the 142 extinct stocks is in the Central Coast and there is no evidence

---

250. "The Great Bear Rain forest," Greenpeace, June 1997, p. 21 and p. 8.

251. "Grizzly Bear," Les Gyug et al., Government of British Columbia, 2004, p.7, http://www.llbc.leg.bc.ca/public/pubdocs/bcdocs/370399/m_grizzlybear.pdf

252. T. L. Slaney et al., "Status of Anadromous Salmon and Trout in British Columbia and Yukon," *Fisheries*, 21, no. 10 (October 1996): 20-35.

to link that stock's demise with logging. Even the authors of the report conclude, "The largest proportion of the 142 extinctions we note resulted from urbanization and hydropower development."[253] An exhaustive review of the factors influencing declines of fish stocks in the Strait of Georgia concluded that the main causes are overfishing, climate change, and urban development.[254] The report did find that logging practices had contributed to habitat loss but concluded, "Now that logging standards are improved under the Forest Practices Code, it is unlikely that the type of logging-related habitat change documented...will be a continuing problem in the Strait of Georgia in particular, and for British Columbia generally."

Most recently, Greenpeace has waged successful international campaigns to damage the reputation of forestry practices in Canada's boreal forests. This has forced an industry agreement on a great swath of largely uninhabited forestland stretching across the continent from Alaska to the Canadian maritime provinces. Greenpeace has claimed species face extinction due to forest harvesting. People in far away places who have no idea of the vastness and wildness of the boreal forest can be forgiven for sending money to Greenpeace to "save the boreal."

The campaigns to link forestry with species extinction have been very successfully communicated through the media to the general public. The release of each report published by activists or announcements they make is carefully orchestrated to reach media outlets like the Associated Press, CNN, and the BBC and also widely distributed via blogs or other Internet resources. As a result members of the public, who often trust the major environmental groups, think species are going extinct by the thousands and that forestry is to blame.

Where did WWF and other environmental groups get the idea species were becoming extinct at the rate of 50,000 per year or 137 per day? It seems this estimate stems from the work of entomologist (insect specialist) Edward O. Wilson of Harvard University, who is widely cited as the expert on the subject.[255] Wilson's reasoning goes something like this:

Scientists have named and recorded about 1.7 million species. There are probably many more, particularly in tropical forests, that have not been discovered, possibly as many as 50 million in all. Forests are being cleared, mainly for agricultural purposes, and this is surely causing species to become extinct. Using the theory of island biogeography, in a computer model, as many as 50,000 species are calculated to be going extinct each year.

By choosing the number 50 million, Wilson and others are implying that 48.3 million of the species on earth are unknown and not named.

253. Ibid. p. 31.
254. D.A. Levy et al., "Strait of Georgia Fisheries Sustainability Review," Hatfield Consultants Ltd., West Vancouver, January 1996.
255. E. O. Wilson, The Diversity of Life (New York: W.W. Norton, 1992).

So if some of them became extinct, we would never know it happened because we didn't know they were there in the first place. This does not strike me as a good example of the scientific method but rather a good example of hocus-pocus. In addition, it is likely we do know 90 percent or more of the larger species (mammals, birds, reptiles, fish, etc.). It is likely there are many smaller species of insects, worms, and other invertebrates yet to be discovered, but I would hazard a guess that 50 million is wildly exaggerated.

This model also assumes that an island of forest surrounded by land disturbed by human activity is analogous to an island in the sea. Very few of the terrestrial species found on an island can live in seawater. Yet a large number of species found in a forest can survive in habitats such as second-growth forests, agricultural landscapes, and even urban areas.

The model is therefore flawed in two fundamental ways. First, it is impossible to verify that species we are not aware of have disappeared; under this model five million unknown species could go extinct and we would not have a clue that it occurred. Second, the model assumes the land surrounding intact forest areas has no habitat value for species living in that forest. And it is simply not believable that we have discovered less than four percent of the living species on earth.

Another problem with this theory is that the species are going extinct according to a computer model when there is little actual evidence of these hypothetical extinctions in the real world. WWF authors take the speculation a step further. Forestry occurs in areas where biodiversity is richest; they argue, therefore, that forestry must be the main cause of biodiversity loss. They fail to consider another possibility, *that the reason those areas where forestry occurs are so rich in biodiversity is because forestry causes less damage to biodiversity than other types of land use.*

It is true our species has caused the extinction of hundreds of other species. The causes of those extinctions have been clearly documented as previously mentioned: overhunting and eradication, clearing for farming, and introduced species of predators and disease. Forestry and forest management are decidedly not a cause of species extinction and yet anti-forestry groups have been willing to launch aggressive campaigns based on the myth that forestry is a primary cause of extinction. If I thought forestry were the main cause of extinction, I would be against it unless it could be changed to eliminate that problem. So I don't blame members of the public who oppose forestry if they are convinced it causes extinction. But I do blame the people who spread this misinformation under the guise of saving the environment. When the public is misinformed about such an important topic, it is unlikely to help find solutions to the real causes of extinction.

National Geographic Gone Bad

I had subscribed to *National Geographic* since my father first gave it to me as a gift when I was in school. I always looked forward to the latest issue, with all the wonders of the world between its covers. Over the past decade even this stalwart of objective science has fallen prey to the prophets of doom who believe a human-caused "mass extinction" is already under way.

The February 1999 special issue on "Biodiversity: The Fragile Web" contains a particularly unfortunate article titled "The Sixth Extinction."[256] The first two pages of the article feature a photo of the Australian scientist Dr. Tim Flannery looking over a collection of stuffed and pickled small mammals that are now extinct. The caption reads: "In the next century half of all species could be annihilated, as were these mammals seen in Tim Flannery's lab at the Australian Museum. Unlike the past five [extinctions], this mass extinction is being fueled by humans." To be sure, the article subsequently mentions that the Australian extinctions were caused by the introduction of cats and foxes when Europeans colonized the region more than 200 years ago. This resulted in the loss of about 35 animal species, mainly flightless birds and ground-dwelling marsupials that could not defend themselves against these new predators. [257] This is hardly a "mass extinction" and the cause was a one-time introduction of exotic species. The rate of extinction of Australian mammals has slowed considerably in recent decades, partly because the most vulnerable species are already extinct, and partly because people started to care about endangered species and began to work to prevent further extinctions. In Australia today programs exist to control wild cats and foxes, some of which have resulted in the recovery of native animal populations.

The use of the Australian example to justify claims we are experiencing a mass extinction is put into focus by Brian Groombridge, the editor of the International Union for the Conservation of Nature Red List of Threatened Species, when he states, "around 75 percent of recorded extinctions...have occurred on islands. Very few extinctions have been recorded in continental tropical forest habitat, where mass extinction events are predicted to be underway."[258] It is misleading to point to the specific and exceptional case of extinctions caused by the introduction of new species to islands as evidence of a worldwide mass extinction. The *National Geographic* article goes on to quote the biologist Stuart Pimm; "It's not just species on islands or in rain forests or just birds or big charismatic mammals. It's everything

---

256. Virginia Morell and Frans Lanting, "The Sixth Extinction," *National Geographic* 195, no. 2 (February 1999), 42–59, http://magma.nationalgeographic.com/media/ngm/9902/fngm/index.html

257. "Expert Panel Set to Discuss Australian Mammal Extinction Crisis," CSIRO, August 2009, http://www.csiro.au/multimedia/Australian-Mammal-Extinction-Crisis.html

258. B. Groombridge, ed., *1994 IUCN Red List of Threatened Animals* (Gland, Switzerland: IUCN, 1993).

and it's everywhere. It is a worldwide epidemic of extinctions." Yet nearly every example given in the article involves islands such as Australia and Tasmania, Mauritius, Easter Island, and the many islands of the South Pacific.

On pages 48 and 49 of this article a graph depicts the number of taxonomic families that have existed on Earth for the past 600 million years. In taxonomy a family is a large grouping of species, examples of which are the cat family, the weasel family, and the ape family, of which we are proud members. The taxonomic name of a species goes family, genus, species, as in *Ursidae* (bear family) *Ursus* (bear genus) *maritimus* (species), the polar bear. There are often many species in a genera and usually more than one genera in a family. No entire family of species has become extinct in the past 20 million years, never mind in the past 100 years. It is unlikely that any entire family has become extinct since the extinction of the dinosaurs 65 million years ago.

During the Permian extinction 250 million years ago, nearly half of all the taxonomic families of life, and about 80 percent of all species, became extinct. The graph shows that despite the five great extinctions that occurred during this period, the number of living families has risen steadily, from around 200 families 500 million years ago to more than 1,000 families today. This tendency to diversify over time is one of the major features of evolution. The line of the graph is a thick, solid one until it reaches the present day when it turns abruptly downward as if to indicate a loss of families due to the "mass extinction" now under way. But the line does not remain thick and solid; it turns fuzzy right at the point where it turns down. I wrote to *National Geographic* and asked, "Why does the line turn fuzzy? Is it because there are actually no known families that have become extinct in recent times? I do not know of any families of 'beetles, amphibians, birds and large mammals' that have become extinct as implied in the text."

The reply to my inquiry came from Robin Adler, one of the researchers who worked on the article. She thanked me for "sharing my thoughts on this complicated and controversial issue" but offered no answer to my question about the graph. Instead she asked me to "Rest assured that... the many members of our editorial team . . .worked closely with numerous experts in conservation biology, paleobiology, and related fields. The concept of a 'sixth extinction' is widely discussed and, for the most part, strongly supported by our consultants and other experts in these areas, although specific details such as the time frame in which it will occur and the number of species that will be affected continues to be debated."

The *National Geographic* article makes no mention that the "sixth extinction" is a controversial subject. It is presented as if it is a known fact in the article, whereas in her reply Ms. Adler refers to it as a "concept." Her reply indicates that the "mass extinction" will actually occur in the future ("the time frame in which it *will* occur" [emphasis added]). In other words there is no evidence that a mass extinction is occurring now, even though the article plainly implies that it is. Perhaps a better title would have been "No Mass Extinction Yet, Maybe Someday."

It is very frustrating when a trusted publication such as the *National Geographic* resorts to sensationalism, exaggeration, and misleading illustrations. One finds enough bad science and misinformation in the popular press as it is. One can only hope that the present tendency to ignore science and logic, rightly referred to as a "bad intellectual climate" by the environmental philosopher Henry H. Webster, will eventually come to an end.[259] As of this writing, it seems we will have to wait a while longer for the *National Geographic* to change its tune on this subject. Its website contains the following passage:

> Today, many scientists think the evidence indicates a **sixth mass extinction** is under way. The blame for this one, perhaps the fastest in Earth's history, falls firmly on the shoulders of humans. By the year 2100, human activities such as pollution, land clearing, and overfishing may have driven more than half of the world's marine and land species to extinction.[260]

It is ridiculous to suggest that extinctions are occurring more rapidly today than they did during the Permian or Cretaceous events when hundreds of thousands of species disappeared. Yet these pessimistic prophecies are popular with the environmental movement. Wouldn't it be better to have an environmental philosophy that looked for positive outcomes, especially where we could help out a bit?

Many references in the scientific literature and the media suggest human-caused climate change will drive a mass extinction event as the earth warms. This is despite the fact that most biodiversity can be found in the warmer tropical climates. A recent paper published in the journal *Science* makes the case that climate change is not a major driver of extinction but that hunting and land use change are the primary causes.[261] The lead author, Kathy Willis, states, "alarmist reports were leading to ill-founded biodiversity policies in government and some major conservation groups." She says climate change has become a buzz word that is taking priority while, in practice, changes in human use of land have a greater impact on the survival of species. The International Union for the Conservation

---

259. Henry H. Webster, "Some Sources of Persistent Error in Thinking About Resources," *Forestry Chronicle* 75, no. 1 (January/February 1999), 63-66.

260. "Mass Extinctions: What Causes Animal Die-Offs?" *National Geographic*, http://science.nationalgeographic.com/science/prehistoric-world/mass-extinction.html

261. K. J. Willis, and S. A. Bhagwat, "Biodiversity and Climate Change," *Science* 326, no. 5954 (November 6, 2009), 806-807, http://www.sciencemag.org/cgi/content/short/326/5954/806

of Nature, a leading authority on endangered species,[262] supports this conclusion.

In May 2010 *Science* Magazine, a publication of the American Association for the Advancement of Science (AAAS), published an article claiming that 20 percent of the world's lizards could become extinct by 2080 due to climate change.[263] "This rivals some of the greatest *extinctions* of any organisms in the geologic record," said the lead author, Barry Sinervo of the University of California-Santa Cruz.[264] At 200 sites in Mexico that were surveyed for 48 species of lizards, the researchers found that, "Since 1975, 12 percent of local populations have gone extinct." What this means is that they did not observe individuals of the 48 species at 12 percent of the sites where they were previously observed in 1975. It is reasonable to expect that on a given day in 2009 one might not see 100 percent of the lizard species that were observed on a given day in 1975 at all 200 sites. Yet each species that was not observed is declared extinct. But note that they say "local populations" have gone extinct, not that "species" have gone extinct. It is not correct to use the word extinction when a species is no longer present in a certain locale but still survives elsewhere. The correct word, as explained previously, is extirpation, which refers to the local loss of a species due to land use change, hunting, etc. The authors do not claim that a single species of Mexican lizard has gone extinct, only that they didn't observe any at certain locations.

From this dubious data the authors, using a computer model of course, predict that by 2080, 20 percent of lizard species worldwide will become extinct due to the warming climate. They conclude, "lizards have already crossed a threshold for extinctions caused by climate change." This is based on the assumption that lizards are getting too hot in the warmer springs, avoiding the sun by hiding under rocks, and therefore not eating enough and failing to reproduce. No evidence for this far-fetched story is presented in the "study." Yet because *Science* published the article the media carried the story far and wide, including the publications *Nature*, *Scientific American*, *Discover*, and *New Scientist*. The climate alarmists have captured *Science* and it seems they will publish any fabrication to push their agenda of imminent doom.

It is worth noting that most of the extinctions of large land animals caused by humans occurred thousands of years ago when there were no guns and when the human population was miniscule compared to today. It is also significant that even though our population has more than

---

262. Hannah Devlin, "Experts Say That Fears Surrounding Climate Change Are Overblown," *Sunday Times*, November 6, 2009, http://www.timesonline.co.uk/tol/news/science/article6905082.ece
263. Barry Sinervo et al., "Erosion of Lizard Diversity by Climate Change and Altered Thermal Niches," *Science* 328, no. 5980 (May 14, 2010): 894-899. , http://www.sciencemag.org/cgi/content/abstract/328/5980/894
264. Doyle Rice, "Lizards in Danger of Extinction, Study Finds," *USA Today*, May 14, 2010, http://www.usatoday.com/NEWS/usaedition/2010-05-14-lizards14_ST_U.htm?csp=34

tripled since the early part of the last century when we began to care about endangered species, the number of species going extinct has declined. Today thousands of programs are devoted to preventing the extinction of endangered species. They don't always succeed, often due to unrelenting poaching for hides, horns, and supposed aphrodisiacs. But many of these efforts have succeeded and as we gain more experience and as more people become involved there is still hope for many species that were driven to the brink of extinction. Certainly one of the most worthwhile endeavors for people who care about nature and biodiversity is to support species recovery programs.

To conclude, there is no real-world evidence that we are experiencing "mass extinction" today. The most effective way to prevent future extinctions is to set aside large wilderness areas and to include biodiversity conservation in land use planning for forestry and agriculture. Preventing illegal hunting and fishing will also be helpful.

CHAPTER EIGHTEEN

Chemicals Are Us

Among the most misunderstood and abused words in the English language is *chemical*. We are encouraged to avoid chemicals even though our food is made entirely of chemicals. Water is a chemical. Our medicines are all chemicals. Without chemicals there could be no life, never mind civilization. Obviously when the word chemical is used as if it is a bad thing we must be talking about something else.

Perhaps we mean *synthetic chemicals*, the ones made with chemistry by people in the chemical industry. But most of our medicines are synthetic and so is most of the vitamin C added to our fruit drinks. And the nitrogen fertilizer that keeps four billion of us alive is synthetic too; it is made from air and natural gas. Plastics are synthetic. Now I'm getting into controversial territory, as if plastics were wrong. Greenpeace's Pyramid of Plastics is essentially a priority hit-list to rid the earth of these very useful substances.[265] Nevertheless, only a real back-to-the caves type would not admit there are some very good and useful synthetic chemicals. As previously mentioned, organic farmers use a large number of them.

Then maybe we mean *toxic chemicals*. Okay, there are certainly lots of toxic chemicals, but most of them occur naturally. Snake venom is a good example. Many medicines are derived from natural chemicals that

---

265. "PVC Alternatives Database," Greenpeace Int., http://archive.greenpeace.org/toxics/pvcdatabase/bad.html

are toxic to bacteria. The smoke from natural forest fires is a pretty vile mix of chemicals, including dioxins. Many plants produce toxic chemicals to discourage animals from eating them. Most of us drive around with a tank full of gasoline or diesel, transformed by nature from ancient plants into chemicals you wouldn't want in your stomach or your eyes. So even if the word chemicals is used as code for poison, chemicals are certainly not all made by large chemical companies.

Many toxic chemicals that are produced by these companies are rather useful when properly employed. Ammonia, the building block for the nitrogen fertilizers so vital to our survival, is a very poisonous gas. Yet it is the second largest chemical by volume produced today. You wouldn't want sulfuric acid on your corn flakes, yet it is the chemical produced in the largest volume worldwide (165 million tonnes [182 million tons] annually). Like ammonia it is used to produce fertilizers along with hundreds of other useful products, including the acid in our car batteries. The chlorine added to our drinking water and used to disinfect our homes, hospitals, and workplaces is essential to control the spread of infection and disease. Yet chlorine is one of the most toxic substances if used improperly. And again there are our medicines, purposely designed to be toxic to the billions of bacteria aiming to kill us. If we were foolish enough to stop producing these important toxic chemicals, we would have a heavy price to pay in human lives.

Chemicals, otherwise known as molecules or compounds, are composed of elements, which form the basic building blocks of our universe.[266] Elements are the simplest substances in chemistry; chemistry is about how elements fit together to make molecules. The elements hydrogen and oxygen combine to make the molecule/chemical/compound water. Every substance in our world is either an element or a compound (combination of elements). So if chemical is just another word for molecule or compound, the stuff everything in the universe is made of, surely we should not use the word as if it were automatically negative.

Every element on earth can be found dissolved in water. Uranium, arsenic, lead, mercury, cadmium, chlorine; you name it and it can be detected, even if in minute quantities, in the water in rivers, lakes, and especially in oceans, where they tend to accumulate in seawater. You wouldn't want to drink a lot of seawater, as it is dehydrating due to the salts (chemicals) it contains, but if applied externally it has a healing quality as a mild antiseptic, because it contains chemicals that have antibacterial properties. One of the most important of those chemicals is sodium chloride, common table salt, and the most abundant molecule in the sea other than water. Sodium chloride is essential for life but is toxic at high concentrations.

---

266. "Periodic Table (large version)," Wikipedia, http://en.wikipedia.org/wiki/Periodic_table_(large_version)

If chemicals are so good, then why are the environmental movement, industry, and world governments so concerned about them? By far the most important reason is the issue of toxic waste. Many industrial processes produce by-products that are toxic but have no useful purpose. In the past it was the practice to emit many toxic wastes into the nearest ravine, creek, river, lake, or seashore, and, in the case of toxic waste in exhaust gases, into the air. This resulted in tremendous damage to aquatic life, to forests and wildlife, and to people who breathed the toxic air.

The development of regulations to prevent the release of toxic wastes into the environment, which began in the 1970s, was one of the environmental movement's first major achievements. Today most industrialized countries have largely eliminated the disposal of toxic wastes into water bodies. This has resulted in much improved health of freshwater ecosystems. Many developing countries, including China, Indonesia, and India, have not succeeded in reducing water pollution to acceptable levels. In numerous ways it is the wealthiest countries that are the cleanest. They can afford to clean the water after they make it dirty. As developing countries become wealthier, they too will choose to employ the technology that is needed to keep toxic waste out of their waterways.

Air pollution has also been reduced substantially, but here is where the most problems remain, in both industrialized and developing countries. In many developing countries, smoke from indoor cooking and heating has the biggest impact on public health. The World Health Organization (WHO) estimates 1.5 million people die each year from breathing indoor smoke from burning wood, dung, and other farm waste. Today this is the world's most serious health issue that stems from pollution.

By far the largest source of outdoor air pollution is caused by the combustion of fossil fuels. Energy generation and transportation are the two most significant causes of air pollution. Burning coal for electricity and burning petroleum products for transportation cause the most damage to public health and the environment. WHO estimates nearly one million people die from these and other fossil fuel emissions every year.[267]

Clearly the answer to indoor pollution lies in eliminating the poverty that results in such primitive cooking and heating methods. More efficient stoves with a means of exhausting the smoke outdoors would solve the problem, but this costs money these people don't have. The estimated 1.5 million people who die from breathing indoor air is of the same magnitude as the number who die every year from malaria. This is one of the many reasons it is obvious to me that the world's worst environmental problem is poverty.

The air pollution caused by burning fossil fuels for energy and

267. "Estimated Deaths and DALYs [Disability Adjusted Life Years]Attributable to Selected Environmental Risk Factors." World Health Organization, January 2007, http://www.who.int/quantifying_ehimpacts/countryprofilesebd.xls

transportation must also be addressed by changes in technology. In this case the industrialized countries can likely afford to make the necessary changes. Replacing coal plants with nuclear or hydroelectric energy is already affordable and feasible. Replacing fossil fuels in passenger cars and delivery vehicles with batteries may one day be more affordable than it is today.

Toxicology

Toxicology is the study of the adverse effects of chemicals on living organisms. It is concerned with the symptoms, mechanisms, treatments, and detection of poisoning of people and the environment. The most important truism in toxicology is "the poison is in the dose." This means there is a level of exposure below which there is no poisoning effect and therefore no harm. Therefore it is not sufficient to declare that a certain substance is "toxic" or "poisonous." Rather one needs to study the relationship between the dose received and the degree of toxicity.

Theoretically all substances are toxic at a sufficiently high dose. Even water will kill you if you take it into your lungs where it prevents the absorption of oxygen. As mentioned earlier, table salt is a required nutrient at low levels, does not cause harm at moderate levels, and is fatal at high levels. There are other chemicals such as ethanol that are not required nutrients but that still cause no harm at low or moderate levels but definitely cause harm or even death at high levels. Other substances, such as snake venom and chlorine gas, are extremely toxic and can kill you at quite low levels, yet even these are not harmful at very low doses. It is clear from this that a black-and-white approach to chemicals and toxicity has no place in a scientific discussion. Yet many activists, including my old friends in Greenpeace, tend to take a zero-tolerance approach to many issues involving chemicals. It is so much simpler to call for a ban on useful substances, thus avoiding the hard work of determining safe levels of a substance that can be toxic at high levels.

As discussed in the section on nuclear energy, the reason there is a level below which otherwise toxic chemicals cause no harm is because our bodies have a cellular repair mechanism. Most poisons harm us either by killing cells or by damaging key components in cells, such as DNA. Our cellular repair mechanisms are able to counteract the damage by continually repairing it as it occurs. As long as the body repairs itself faster than the damage occurs, there is no net damage. As soon as the toxic effects overwhelm the body's ability to keep up with repairs, we are being poisoned. Many scientists believe this principle also applies to the effects of nuclear radiation. For example, we can be exposed to solar radiation for a short time without harm. At a certain level of exposure the sun's radiation begins to damage our skin faster than it can repair itself and we develop a sunburn. If one were foolish enough to lie in the hot sun for eight hours without protection the result would be a long recovery in a hospital's intensive care burn unit.

One of the most impressive advances in modern science is the ability to detect substances at parts per billion and even at parts per trillion. The electron capture detector has made this possible. It is the most sensitive instrument for determining low levels of materials in the environment and in our bodies. It was invented in 1957 by James Lovelock, who also fathered the Gaia Hypothesis as we discussed. With this very simple instrument, we can detect minute traces of many natural and industrial chemicals. It was a great contribution to science but it also led to the idea that any substance measured in the body is a sign of pollution and toxic contamination. Of course the emphasis is always on "synthetic chemicals" rather than natural chemicals, once again inferring humans are the real problem. The class of chemicals known as dioxins, for example, are routinely produced in nature by forest fires and volcanoes. Human activities do produce some dioxins, but they have been drastically reduced, primarily due to more efficient incineration technology. Yet environmentalists routinely place all the emphasis on dioxins produced by industrial activity. And they do so very selectively at that.

Polyvinyl Chloride (PVC)

Earlier I told the story of my departure from Greenpeace and how its decision to adopt a policy to ban chlorine worldwide informed my decision to leave. This was a classic case of throwing the baby out with the bath water. Chlorine is the most important element for public health and medicine. It is also extremely toxic in its elemental form as a gas. But there are many chlorine compounds that are very useful and nontoxic. I've also mentioned PVC. I'd like to dig a little deeper into the activist campaign against vinyl, to show it up for the textbook case of misinformation-based environmentalism it is.

Vinyl is one of the most important materials in our society. Of the plastics, only polyethylene and polypropylene are produced in larger quantities. Whereas polyethylene and polypropylene are made entirely from petroleum, vinyl is produced by combining natural gas with chlorine derived from salt. This is why most of the vinyl production plants in North America are in Louisiana, where both materials exist in abundance. Vinyl has some important properties not found in other major plastics.

One of the most important of these properties is vinyl's fire resistance. While it is possible to burn vinyl, it will not burn on its own; if the source of a fire is removed then vinyl is self-extinguishing. This is why nearly all insulation on electrical wiring and most electrical conduit is made of vinyl.

This is required by building codes in most jurisdictions. In other words, vinyl is a material of choice in case of fire around electrical equipment.

Most vinyl is used to make rigid pipes for water, sewer, and drainage applications. It is far superior to concrete or steel pipes as it seldom breaks and does not corrode. Vinyl pipe that has been buried for 50 years shows no sign of corrosion or decay. It is likely it could remain in service for 500 years or more as long as it is protected from sunlight. The second major use for vinyl is in construction, for siding, roofing, flooring, wall coverings, decks, and railings. Vinyl can be impregnated with UV inhibitors that give it a 50-year-plus lifetime in direct sunlight in the desert. It is also very easy to add pigments to vinyl to create a complete range of colors. Unlike polyethylene and polypropylene, vinyl can be glued with solvents, making it very convenient to work with on job sites.

Whereas pure vinyl is rigid and somewhat brittle, it can be made to nearly any degree of softness by adding plasticizers, the most important of which are called phthalates (pronounced "thalates"). Soft vinyl is used to make a wide range of products, including toys, fabric for furniture, flooring, carpet backing, packaging, car interiors, kitchen utensils to name a few.

When Greenpeace first adopted the campaign to call PVC "the poison plastic" it focused on the creation of dioxins in the manufacture of the vinyl monomer that is the building block for the plastic polymer. While it is true that a very small amount of dioxin is produced in vinyl plants, less than one-half of 1 percent produced by human activity, the levels emitted are not considered harmful by the U.S. Environmental Protection Agency (EPA). In fact all the charges that PVC is "toxic" come from activist groups rather than environmental regulators. The activists' response to the EPA's evaluation is that it is "in the pocket of industry," a blatantly false assertion, but a last resort for people who have no real evidence of harm.

Most of the dioxin produced by humans comes from incineration, wood combustion, diesel trucks, oil-fired power plants, coal-fired industry, and cement kilns. The entire chemical industry does not even rate in the top 10.[268]

PVC itself is about as nontoxic as a substance can be. Exposure to PVC does not cause any harm. It is not possible to eat enough PVC to cause toxicity as it would pass through one's body undigested (I do not recommend you try this, however. PVC contains zero nutrition!). Faced with the fact that calling PVC "poison" was an outright lie, the anti-PVC movement eventually changed tactics. Instead of attacking vinyl itself, its crusaders turned to the many substances that are added to PVC to give it desirable characteristics. For years metals such as lead, cadmium, and tin

---

268. "The Inventory of Sources and Environmental Releases of Dioxin-Like Compounds in the United States: The Year 2000 Update," U.S. Environmental Protection Agency, March 2005,
http://www.epa.gov/ncea/pdfs/dioxin/2k-update/pdfs/Dioxin_Frontmatter.pdf

were added to PVC as stabilizers. This is changing as zero-tolerance policies for elements like lead have come into force. Again, this change has not been imposed by regulatory agencies but rather by politicians playing into activist agendas.

There is no evidence that lead added to PVC causes harmful exposure to lead, even though lead is toxic at relatively low levels. Nevertheless, the vinyl industry is moving away from lead and working to find suitable substitutes.

More recently PVC has been attacked because of the plasticizers used to make it soft. The little rubber ducky our kids use as a bath toy has become the symbol of "toxic PVC." Every statement by Greenpeace on the subject refers to PVC as "toxic PVC." There is a book titled *Slow Death by Rubber Duck*.[269] This is a classic case of a campaign based on misinformation (toxic PVC), promoted through the use of sensationalism ("one of the most toxic substances saturating our planet and its inhabitants")[270] and fear ("linked to cancer and kidney damage".[271] There's that word *linked* again.)

Our credit cards and bankcards and drivers' licenses are made of vinyl. We carry them around with us and handle them regularly. Are credit cards "linked" to cancer? How about that old collection of vinyl records? In truth there is no evidence vinyl is harming anyone. It's as trumped up as the killer sea lice story, but it seems to sell papers and attract funding, so why give up on a good thing?

For some years now activists have focused on children's toys, packaging, and the green building movement as arenas to push for a ban on vinyl. Preying on parents' concern for their children's welfare, a number of groups have claimed that phthalates in children's toys are a hazard. A number of key science and regulatory bodies have rejected this charge. In Europe the Scientific Committee on Toxicity, Ecotoxicity and the Environment concluded that DINP, one of the most common phthalates, "poses no risk to either human health or the environment from any current use."[272] Yet the political arm of the European Union chose to ban phthalates for "precautionary" reasons. The EPA determined exposure to phthalates was so low that it posed no danger to anyone, including infants. This did not stop politicians, former president George W. Bush among them, from banning phthalates in children's toys. It is so compelling for politicians to be seen to care about babies that they will ignore the best scientific advice and "do the right thing."

The campaign against vinyl as a packaging material has focused on big-box retailers like Wal-Mart and Staples. These big brands are very

269. Rick Smith and Bruce Laurie, *Slow Death by Rubber Duck: How the Toxic Chemistry of Everyday Life Affects Our Health*, (Berkeley, Counterpoint, 2009).
270. "Go PVC-Free," Greenpeace International, http://www.greenpeace.org/usa/campaigns/toxics/go-pvc-free
271. "Polyvinyl Chloride," Greenpeace International, http://www.greenpeace.org/international/campaigns/toxics/polyvinyl-chloride
272. "EU Risk Assessment," DINP Information Centre, http://www.dinp-facts.com/RA

sensitive about their reputations and are therefore easy targets for what I call "blackmail in the boardroom."

It's a simply formula. Activists threaten to besmirch the good name of the corporation if it doesn't cooperate. The management knows its job is to protect the company from public criticism. It is often possible to extract statements from the companies that indicate they are on the activists' side.

When pressed in this manner about its use of PVC for packaging, Wal-Mart announced it would phase out PVC packaging for its own brand-name products. This put wind into the sails of the anti-PVC movement who then used Wal-Mart's promise to pressure other retailers to do the same or more. Note Wal-Mart did not promise to eliminate PVC altogether from its stores. Surely Wal-Mart would want to get rid of all PVC if it were toxic and a poison. But as I told a Wal-Mart executive later, "Wal-Mart stores would look like mausoleums if you took all the vinyl products out." Not only are many of the items on sale made from PVC but the plumbing, wiring, and flooring all contain vinyl.

Just search the Internet for "Wal-Mart PVC" and you will see there is a mixture of articles reporting Wal-Mart has "banned PVC" on the one hand and on the other hand lots of other websites where Wal-Mart advertises bargain prices on merchandise made with PVC. But its token gesture to ban the use of PVC in certain packages gives the impression there is something wrong with vinyl and that the activists' cause is valid.

In its 2009 Global Sustainability Report Wal-Mart stated:

> "in 2007, we missed meeting our goal to eliminate PVC from our private-brand packaging. We made progress toward this goal by converting PVC clamshells to PET [Polyethylene-terephthalate] and either completely removing PVC windows in packaging or replacing the PVC windows with PET. While we continue to look for alternatives to PVC, we have been unable to find suitable replacements for PVC used in over-the-counter, tamper-evident bands, metal can sealants and meat wrapping, among others. Until we identify another material of equal performance, we will not eliminate PVC from certain items to ensure the safety of our customers."

So PVC is important for the safety of its customers but Wal-Mart continues to seek ways to eliminate it, not because there is anything wrong with vinyl but because the chain has been blackmailed into adopting a stupid policy. Hopefully Wal-Mart will eventually see the error of its ways.

The anti-vinyl lobby has worked very hard to give PVC a bad name in the green building movement. For years activists have tried to get the U.S. Green Building Council (USGBC) to adopt their anti-PVC agenda. At first they asked the Council to adopt a negative point for buildings that used

PVC in construction. As it would have been the only negative point in the entire rating system the Council eventually decided instead to award a point for "deselecting" vinyl. The USGBC is responsible for the LEED (Leadership in Energy and Environmental and Design) rating system for green buildings. LEED has many good attributes, but it also acts as a kind of Trojan horse to deliver key activist agendas into the green building movement. In particular it discriminates against wood and hydroelectric energy, the two most important sources of renewable materials and energy, respectively, and nuclear energy. The USGBC was founded by the Natural Resources Defense Council, a prominent Washington, D.C.-based organization composed largely of environmentalist lawyers, with the support of Greenpeace, WWF, etc. The LEED standard does not discriminate against steel or concrete, even though they require far more energy to produce, resulting in more air pollution than either wood or PVC.

Some manufacturers of vinyl have used the negative publicity generated by the smear campaign against vinyl as a marketing advantage. Some seem genuinely convinced there is something wrong with vinyl while others readily admit that they are playing off the anti-vinyl campaign. It's pretty cynical but it works with people who buy into the activists' misinformation and are therefore keen to avoid using vinyl, except of course for their credit cards. I attended the 2009 Green Building conference put on by the U.S. Homebuilders Association. Some manufacturers of vinyl flooring were also offering "PVC-free" flooring that looks a lot like vinyl flooring. It is obviously made with a different plastic or mix of plastics and it costs more than vinyl. It struck me as odd that the marketing strategy for this flooring product was all about what it *wasn't* made from. There was no indication of what it *was* made from, only that it was "PVC-free." Such are the distortions caused by fanatics who claim vinyl is killing us.

Under pressure to adopt an anti-PVC standard, the USGBC struck an expert panel in 2002 called the Technical and Scientific Advisory Committee (TSAC). In late 2004, after it had received hundreds of submissions and considered all the available evidence the committee's draft report concluded, "the available evidence does not support a conclusion that PVC is consistently worse than alternative materials on an environmental life-cycle and health basis."[273] In other words it is as good as the other materials. The committee added that, "such a simple credit could steer designers to use materials which performed worse over their life cycles." In other words a credit for deselecting vinyl might result in the choice of an alternative material that causes more damage to consumers'

---

273. Kara Altshuler et al., "Assessment of a Technical Basis for a PVC-Related Materials Credit in LEED," TSAC PVC Task Group, US Green Building Council, December 17, 2004, p. 10, https://www.usgbc.org/ShowFile.aspx?DocumentID=1287

health or the environment. Examples would include using steel pipe rather than PVC pipe, using tar and gravel roofing rather than PVC roofing, and using linoleum instead of PVC for flooring in health care facilities.

As a result of the TSAC recommendation, a splinter group called the Healthy Building Network (HBN) broke off from the USGBC to campaign against PVC in buildings. Obviously no amount of scientific study is good enough for zealots who don't want to give up a good fundraising campaign. Led by former Greenpeace activist Bill Walsh, the HBN works tirelessly to convince architects, builders, and the public that PVC is poisoning them and their clients. Of all the great ironies the HBC has placed a strong emphasis on health care facilities, claiming that the vinyl products used in building and operating hospitals and care facilities harm patients. The campaign has since broadened to include all of the halogens, which include fluorine, chlorine, bromine, and iodine and anything containing them.

The reason this is ironic is because fluorine, chlorine, bromine, and iodine are so important for public health and medicine. As mentioned earlier, chlorine is the most important disinfectant we have. Bleach is made with chlorine and chlorine is added to our drinking water to kill the bacteria that can kill us. Chlorine is the basis for many important medicines. Bromine is also used to make medicines and to make brominated pucks that prevent our swimming pools and spas from turning into cesspools. Fluorine is added to drinking water, or taken in the form of pills or drops to prevent tooth decay in children. I did not receive fluorine as a child and consequently had more than 30 cavities by the time I was 20. My two sons had fluoride drops and neither one had a single cavity before age 20. Iodine was once the most important antiseptic and it is an essential nutrient. That's why it is added to table salt in the same way vitamin C is added to apple juice. Iodine is essential for thyroid function and an iodine deficiency can result in slowed mental and physical development. So removing all halogens from health care would be a bit like removing most of the food from a restaurant.

The list of vinyl products used in health care facilities and products is impressive. It includes blood bags, intravenous tubing, antiseptic gloves and caps, catheters, goggles, oxygen delivery, thermal blankets, and dialysis equipment. Just as important are the materials used to build health care facilities. Vinyl flooring and wall coverings can be applied seamlessly and provide an easily disinfected surface. Vinyl wall coverings can be impregnated with anti-microbial compounds that kill bacteria. Vinyl windows are superior in terms of both energy efficiency and cleanliness. All in all the halogens make a greater contribution to the safety of health care and medical treatment than any other class of substances. And it is largely because they are toxic to bacteria and other disease agents and because products made from them are easy to disinfect.

The result of removing vinyl and other halogenated compounds from health care would be twofold. It would lead to increased health care costs and an increased risk of infection while in a health care facility. And this does not take into account the ridiculous notion that chlorine should be removed from water supplies and medicines. Vinyl is chosen for its many applications because it is the best product and it is cost-effective. I have provided comments to the USGBC on the subject of halogens in health care in which I have warned of the increased risks of "super-bugs" in health care facilities if vinyl is eliminated. It is a fact that two million people get infections annually in American hospitals, at least 100,000 die from these infections, and this adds $30 billion per year to health care costs.[274] Chlorine and the other halogens play an important role in reducing this toll. Campaigns to eliminate them are based on misinformation, sensation, and fear— the stock-in-trade of environmental extremists.

At this writing the USGBC, which is under constant pressure from anti-PVC activists, has introduced a Pilot Standard for the elimination of chlorine and other halogens from buildings. This is in complete violation of its own TSAC recommendations. But politics has trumped science at the USGBC and will infect the green building movement for years to come.

Bisphenol A (BPA)

Another chemical that has come into disrepute lately is bisphenol A, otherwise known as BPA. It is the building block of plastics known as polycarbonates. Activists claim it is a "gender-bender" that mimics the female hormone estrogen. To quote Margaret Wente, a noted Canadian journalist, "activists have warned that BPA in plastic water bottles is associated with cancer, diabetes, man-boobs, reduced sperm counts, shrunken testicles, early onset puberty and obesity."[275] She goes on to explain, "A mountain of evidence has been thoroughly evaluated by regulators, scientists and expert panels in Japan, Australia, the European Union, France, Germany, Switzerland, Denmark and Norway. None found any risk. The World Health Organization and the U.S. Food and Drug Administration have weighed in, too. All have rejected the environmentalists' claims." Yet a vocal and concerted effort continues to scare parents and the public into thinking they are being poisoned.

This time Canada was first out of the blocks. In 2008 it banned BPA in baby bottles. When announcing the ban, then environment minister John Baird stated, "Although our science tells us that exposure levels to newborns and infants are below the levels that cause effects, we believe

274. "Hospital Infection Control Saves Lives, Cuts Costs," *Medical News Today*, March 11, 2007, http://www.medicalnewstoday.com/articles/64886.php
275. Margaret Wente, "Does BPA Give You the Willies? It Shouldn't," *Globe and Mail*, November 9, 2009, http://www.beattystreetpublishing.com/confessions/references/does-bpa-give-you-the-willies

that the current safety margin needs to be higher. We have concluded that it is better to be safe than sorry." Just what is the basis for the "belief" that safety margins should be higher than "science tells us"? Maybe because we trust activists and politicians more than we trust scientists, especially toxicologists? Lord help us. I have saved my polycarbonate drinking bottle and will continue to use it knowing that it keeps my water clean and safe.

The alleged dangers of BPA have been written about in every Lifestyle section of every newspaper and magazine in the English language. But regulatory authorities don't usually get their information from Lifestyle sections; they're supposed to get it from scientists working in labs. At this writing neither the U.S. nor the U.K. has officially banned baby bottles that contain BPA. The U.K. Food Standards Agency recently stated, "The Food Standards Agency, working closely with the European Food Safety Authority (EFSA), and the European Commission have looked into the potential risks from BPA and found that exposure of UK consumers to BPA from all sources, including food contact materials, was well below levels considered harmful."[276]

The April 2010 issue of *Toxicological Sciences* reports on a study conducted by Dr. Earl Gray of the EPA on the effect of BPA on rats. He fed the rats up to 4,000 times the highest dose of BPA than the average human might be exposed to and found it had absolutely no adverse effects on the animals.[277] Professor Richard Sharpe of the Medical Research Council's Centre for Reproductive Biology in Edinburgh stated, "The results [of the study] are unequivocal and robust and are based on a valid and rational scientific foundation,".[278] (Sharpe is one of Britain's leading specialists in endocrine-disrupting chemicals in the environment.) It's time to dig your BPA water bottle back out.

Both phthalates and BPA are very useful substances. They have been thoroughly studied by many regulatory agencies and have been found to be harmless at typical levels of exposure. Yet a massive campaign is being waged against them in the media and more frequently in legislatures across the globe. The impetus for this can be traced to a combination of the media tending toward sensationalism and perpetuating conflict, activist groups perpetuating fear and therefore fundraising, activist scientists trying to make a name for themselves, and politicians wishing to look like they are saving babies from large corporations. This is not so much a conspiracy but rather a case of converging interests. Everyone benefits: more papers get sold, more funds are raised, more research grants handed out, and more politicians wear halos. Only the truth, the public,

276. "Plastics Industry Reassures on the Safety of Bisphenol-A (BPA)," British Plastics Federation, December 1, 2009, http://www.bpf.co.uk/Article/Detail.aspx?ArticleUid=97b49741-856b-4e4e-82c7-62f27ef2eb65
277. Steve Conner, "Scientists Declare War Over BPA," *Independent*, April 13, 2010, http://www.independent.co.uk/news/science/scientists-declare-war-over-bpa-1943087.html
278. Ibid.

and the economy lose out in this case of what one of my friends calls a classic clusterfuck.[279]

Brominated Flame Retardants

Another class of chemicals that have borne the brunt of activist wrath are the brominated flame retardants. They are added to a number of consumer items, including mattresses, upholstered furniture, infants' clothing, and electronics, including computers. In the event of a fire, these items do not ignite as quickly or burn as intensely as those that are not treated with a flame retardant. These retardants have saved many lives in house fires. In one dramatic incident an Air France passenger jet crash landed and burned to the ground. Yet every passenger escaped uninjured due to the fact that the upholstered seats did not catch fire quickly, leaving time for the evacuation. The seats had been treated with brominated flame retardants.

Once again we are dealing with a halogenated substance for which groups like Greenpeace have an automatic banning policy. But there is no evidence that brominated flame retardants cause any harm and there is ample evidence that people are being saved by them. It's not as if the very presence of bromine will give you cancer. I treat my spa with brominating tablets to keep it antiseptic, so I am essentially swimming in bromine. I know this is a lot better for me than the risk of infection from untreated water. I would suggest whatever risk is associated with the brominated flame retardants in our beds and computers it is worth taking to avoid immolation in our sleep or at our desk. Activists do not accept this common sense approach, rather they emphasize the (unknown) risk and ignore the known benefits of flame retardants. That is no way to interpret the precautionary approach.

Tobacco and Nicotine

It is a shame so much energy is wasted campaigning against substances that cause no harm while there are many chemicals that really do harm us. Tobacco and the nicotine it contains deserve more attention from activists who are concerned with human health. I was a heavy smoker for 15 years and it was a real struggle to quit. I haven't had a cigarette for more than 30 years and I know quitting was the best thing I ever did for my health. In a perfect world it is obvious tobacco would be banned like so many other harmful addictive substances. But that would just create another black market and the crime that goes with it. Surely there should be even more effort put into campaigns to convince young people not

---

279. "Clusterfuck," Wikipedia, http://en.wiktionary.org/wiki/clusterfuck

to start smoking and to help addicts kick the habit. If Greenpeace really cared about people's health, it would adopt an antismoking campaign and put some real effort into it. Greenpeacers say nothing about a substance we know causes 30 percent of all cancer, yet they spend millions on campaigns against substances for which there is no evidence of harm. And they spend millions more campaigning to stop the development of crop varieties that could save millions of lives. In fact the only time they express concern for people's health is when it furthers one of their misguided efforts to ban something useful.

Thalidomide

Chemicals are not simply good or bad. Take the example of thalidomide. It was prescribed for morning sickness in pregnant women in the U.K. and Canada in the late 1950s and early 1960s. The resulting birth defects were horrific and included missing and misshapen limbs. Up to 20,000 babies were born with serious defects. This was possibly the worst accident in the history of modern medicine and it resulted in many of the safeguards that are in place today to make sure such a thing never happens again. If there were a chemical you would think deserves an absolute ban from the face of the earth, thalidomide would be near the top of the list.

In 1964 Jacob Sheskin, a professor at Hadassah University Hospital in Jerusalem, discovered thalidomide could be used to treat leprosy, a disease that still occurs in a number of countries, including Brazil.[280] Thalidomide has been used successfully to fight leprosy in Brazil since 1965. In 1998 the U.S. Food and Drug Administration approved thalidomide for treatment of lesions caused by leprosy. Since then thalidomide has been found to be an effective treatment for multiple myeloma, a cancer of the white blood cells that typically kills two-thirds of the people who contract the disease.[281]

At present thalidomide is being investigated as a possible treatment for amyotrophic lateral sclerosis, aphthous ulcer, behcet's syndrome, brain cancer, breast cancer, cachexia, colorectal cancer, congestive heart failure, crohn's disease, diarrhea, fibrodysplasia ossificans progressiva, graft-versus-host disease, hematological malignancies, HIV infections, Hodgkin's disease, Kaposi's sarcoma, leprosy, leukemia, macular degeneration, malignant melanoma, mycobacterium avium complex infections, myelodysplastic syndromes, myelofibrosis, myeloid leukemia, non-Hodgkin's lymphoma, non-small cell lung cancer, ovarian cancer, pain, prostate cancer, prurigo nodularis, renal cancer, rheumatoid arthritis, small cell lung cancer, solid tumors, systemic lupus erythematosus, thyroid cancer, and tuberculosis.[282]

---

280. "Thalidomide," Wikipedia, http://en.wikipedia.org/wiki/Thalidomide
281. "Multiple Myeloma," Wikipedia, http://en.wikipedia.org/wiki/Multiple_myeloma
282. "Thalidomide"
http://bi.adisinsight.com/rdi/viewdocument.aspx?render=view&mode=remote&adnm=800004827&PushValidation=121745

Thalidomide is already recognized for a number of treatments but the list could grow much longer as a result of these investigations.

This long list stresses the fact that a chemical that has such deleterious effects in some circumstances can save lives in other circumstances. Today the rules that govern whether or not to prescribe thalidomide focus on preventing pregnant women from accessing the drug. And this brings us straight to a hard question: If it can be demonstrated that legalizing thalidomide to treat certain illnesses would save 100,000 lives per year but might also result in unauthorized access to the drug resulting in two children with birth defects, what choice would you make? The precautionary approach would clearly come down on the side of the 100,000 saved lives. But what politician could stand up to the charge that he or she was condemning a few people to lives of extreme disability by supporting a chemical that would save thousands from an early death?

The Dirty Dozen

The Stockholm Convention on Persistent Organic Pollutants (POPs) came into effect in 2004 when the minimum of 50 countries ratified it. With the notable exceptions of the United States, Russia, and Saudi Arabia, most countries have ratified the convention.

It is a United Nations treaty aimed at eliminating or reducing a number of chemicals that do not biodegrade quickly in the environment and are considered toxic to humans and wildlife. The 12 chemicals in the original list for discussion became known as the "Dirty Dozen." There are now 17 chemicals in the list, including DDT. Most of them are chlorinated or brominated pesticides that are used to control insects in agriculture and to control termites in order to protect wooden structures. Some of them are chemicals used in industry and still others are unintentional by-products of chemical manufacturing.

Most environmental groups, including Greenpeace and the Word Wildlife Fund, initially took the position that all POPs should be eliminated. But as the meetings progressed, it became clear that even some of the most toxic chemicals had uses that were considered sufficiently beneficial to adopt exemptions for certain purposes. Of the 17 POPs listed for elimination, 7 have been registered for exemptions. These include chlordane, which is used to control termites, dieldrin, which is used in agriculture as an insecticide, and DDT, which is used in the production of dicofol, used to control mites on fruit and vegetable crops. These exemptions were made because no other suitable chemical could be found to replace the ones in use. This highlights the fact that when one applies the precautionary approach in a balanced fashion, reasonable people will sometimes decide a toxic chemical is worth keeping in our arsenal for limited or restricted use.

In addition, DDT has a special exemption for use in controlling mosquitoes that carry malaria. Seventeen countries, mostly in Africa but also including China and India, have filed notice they intend to continue using DDT for this purpose.

I would certainly not argue in favor of toxic chemicals if there is no use for them or if suitable, less toxic, substitutes were available. But even then we should not just forget about them. As the cases of DDT and thalidomide demonstrate, certain uses of the chemicals may prove so valuable they should not be subjected to an outright ban.

A few generalities follow from the above discussion:

- All material things are made of elements and chemicals (molecules, compounds).
- No chemical is inherently evil.
- Some chemicals are extremely dangerous under certain circumstances.
- Many chemicals have both negative and positive attributes.
- In general, bans should be placed on the way a chemical is used, rather than on the chemical itself.
- If an otherwise toxic chemical has uses where the benefits far outweigh negative impacts, it should be used.
- There is no end to learning—continual advances in knowledge must be the goal of science and technology.

It is not possible to provide an exhaustive review of chemicals in a single chapter. But I hope these examples and principles have provided some new perspectives on the vast array of substances, both natural and synthetic, that make up ourselves and our world.

Population Is Us

Population is a very tricky subject. Many people believe we have a right, even a moral obligation, to go forth and multiply. Others complain there are far too many of us already and it would be a good thing if some calamity befell us, thinning the human herd. These opposing views are strongly linked to religious convictions on the one hand, and extreme antihuman sentiments on the other. What can a sensible environmentalist make of this chasm in philosophical outlook?

On the World Day of Peace in December 2008, Pope Benedict XVI pointed out poverty has been reduced as a percentage of the human population in recent years. "In other words, population is proving to be an asset, not a factor that contributes to poverty," the pope affirmed.[283] The only form of birth control tolerated by the Catholic Church is the very unreliable rhythm method. Modern contrivances such as condoms and birth control pills need not apply. Yet many Catholics, especially in the industrialized countries, choose to defy this edict and actively limit the size of their families, using modern birth control techniques.

On the other extreme, Paul Watson, the early Greenpeace activist who is now head of the Sea Shepherd Conservation Society, believes, "We need to radically and intelligently reduce human populations to fewer than one

---

283. John-Henry Westen and Kathleen Gilbert, "Pope Against Population Control," Catholic Online, December 13, 2008, http://www.catholic.org/international/international_story.php?id=31054

billion." He warns, "Curing a body of cancer requires radical and invasive therapy, and therefore, curing the biosphere of the human virus will also require a radical and invasive approach."[284] A little genocide anyone? It's only a virus. The pope looks pretty good by comparison.

In December 2009, the prominent Canadian journalist Diane Francis wrote an editorial in the *National Post* calling on the world to adopt China's "one-child policy." This policy punishes parents and their children if a mother has more than one child. It is credited for reducing population by 250 million during the past 30 years, but this is questioned, and can't be proven either way. The editorial received almost universal condemnation, clearly indicating that people in Canada and the U.S. do not believe in such intrusive state policies in matters of family planning.

By 2020 there will be 30 million more men than women in China. That's 30 million men with no chance of finding a partner of the opposite sex. This is largely due to the fact the Chinese prefer boys to girls, resulting in forced abortions and girl infanticide. In addition, many girl babies are adopted out illegally so that couples can avoid punishment for going over the one-child limit.[285] The United States government has stated this policy contravenes the Universal Declaration of Human Rights, and Amnesty International has also condemned the one-child policy.[286]

Too often, discussions about human population degenerate into political debates about race, class, gender, and left-right dogma. Fortunately there is a middle ground between unbridled procreation and a collective death wish. The trick is to get beyond knee-jerk discrimination and to objectively analyze what is going on in the real world. Let's forget about whether humans are good or bad for a moment and take a look at the current trends.

The Population Division of the United Nations Department of Economic and Social Affairs projects a global population of between 8 billion and 10.5 billion by 2050, up from the present population of about 7 billion.[287] Without exception, all the growth will occur in the developing countries while the developed countries will experience negative internal growth rates, only growing in population due to immigration from the developing countries. It is clear from this that wealth results in reduced population growth. Why is this the case when wealthier people can afford more children?

---

284. Paul Watson, "The Beginning of the End for Life As We Know It on Planet Earth? There Is a Biocentric Solution," Sea Shepherd Conservation Society, May 7 2007, http://www.sea-shepherd.com/news-and-media/editorial-070504-1.html
285. "One-Child Policy," Wikipedia, http://en.wikipedia.org/wiki/One-child_policy
286. "Amnesty International Shocked, Dismayed by U.S. Secretary Clinton's Comments That Human Rights Will Not Top Her China Agenda," Amnesty International USA, February 20, 2009,
http://www.amnestyusa.org/document.php?id=ENGUSA20090220001&lang=e
287. Leiwen Jiang, "Smaller Population Size in the New UN Population Projection Depends on Expanded Access to Family Planning" Population Action, March 16, 2009, http://www.populationaction.org/blog/2009/03/the-smaller-population-size-in.html

It turns out that one of the most important factors in determining average family size is the number of people employed in agriculture. In 1870 between 70 to 80 percent of the workforce in the United States was employed in agriculture. Today, due entirely to mechanization and intensive farming practices, only 2 to 3 percent of workers are required to grow food. And even with so few people involved, the United States has a surplus of food exports over imports of nearly $35 billion annually. Today, 70 percent of the workforce in India and 65 percent in China are engaged in food production. Imagine how many millions of people would be able to pursue productive careers in other sectors if only 2 to 3 percent were required for agriculture. The implications for population growth are also staggering.

People who live by subsistence farming tend to have large families because children are an asset when unskilled labor is required to work the land. When agriculture becomes mechanized, far fewer people are required to work on farms. In China alone, 300 million people will move from the country into cities in the next 10 years, largely due to mechanization. This will represent the largest migration of humans in history. And it will result in a dramatic decline in birth rates because families that move into urban areas tend to have fewer children. Children are a liability in cities, and their mothers become better educated, politically empowered, and more in control of their reproductive future, unlike their counterparts in subsistence farming, who are barefoot and pregnant most of their lives.

It is therefore of paramount importance that the mechanization of agriculture, employing all the advances in technology, chemistry and genetics, be encouraged throughout the developing world. In combination with improved education and literacy, electrification, refrigeration, health care, and clean water, the adoption of modern farming techniques will lead to a better life for billions of people who are now trapped in poverty. At the same time, it will result in reduced birth rates in the same way this has already occurred in the developed countries.

I can thank Stewart Brand, founder of the Whole Earth Catalogue and an elder of mine in the environmental movement, for helping to inform me on this subject. His book, *Whole Earth Discipline: An Ecopragmatist Manifesto*, elaborates on these and other issues.[288]

As mentioned previously, there is great hope in the initiatives of the Bill & Melinda Gates Foundation, with support from Warren Buffet and others. Their approach is to increase the professionalism of international aid efforts and to use the best science in health, agriculture, sanitation, and technology in general.

There is not a lot more that needs to be said on the subject of population; putting these principles into action is the real challenge. It is clear

---

288. Stewart Brand, *Whole Earth Discipline: An Ecopragmatist Manifesto* (New York: Viking, 2009).

that a sensible environmentalist would support the mechanization of agriculture and development of the necessary energy, technological, and biological resources to support it. There is no need to politicize the issue of population growth and there is no need for draconian measures such as China's punitive one-child policy. It is abundantly clear that population will sort itself out if we can only help developing nations to lift themselves out of poverty.

CHAPTER TWENTY
Sustainable Mining

"Sustainable mining": now there's a concept that seems to be a contradiction in terms. How can mining be sustainable when it is inevitable that every mine will eventually be exhausted and shut down? Let me take you through the logic.

But first, let's recognize that if it weren't for mining there would be no civilized world. Few people stop to realize that virtually all our built environment, our buildings, our transportation systems, and our communications hardware, are made from materials that were mined from the earth. Concrete, steel, glass, plastic, ceramics, silicon, and so many other materials are mined and then transformed into the infrastructure that makes cities, factories and farms a reality. And most of the energy that powers this material infrastructure is also mined; coal, oil, natural gas, and uranium all come from the earth's crust. Even our food and the wood we obtain from trees are ultimately derived from the soil. The only exceptions to this are hydroelectric energy from rainfall, and a bit of inefficient wind and solar energy from the air and sun. The history of mining is to a large extent the history of human civilization.[289]

So how can mining be sustainable? It can be sustainable by restoring the land to a healthy ecosystem after the mine closes and by leaving

---

289. Robert Raymond, *Out of the Fiery Furnace: The Impact of Metals on the History of Mankind*, (Penn State University Press, March 28, 2000)

surrounding communities with more wealth, education, health care, and infrastructure than they had before the mine went into production. In the mining industry this must be the objective of corporate social responsibility and the outcome of the successful ecological restoration of landscapes. I have seen it in practice with my own eyes around the world.

Interestingly, the environmental challenges faced by the mining industry are much less complicated than the social challenges. From an environmental perspective the two key issues are the management of water, to prevent pollution, and the ecological restoration of the disturbed lands (called reclamation in the mining industry). These are largely technical challenges involving engineering and biological solutions. The social challenges are not so simple. They involve community politics with all the competing interests that make communities politically volatile under the best of circumstances. Add the prospect of a gold mine, an iron mine, or a uranium mine to the normal affairs of a village in Africa, Asia, South America, Europe, or just about anywhere, and you have a lot of work to do.

Yet great progress has been made in recent years, in both the environmental and social spheres. Whereas previously it was the norm to leave abandoned mining sites without restoring the environment, it is now accepted practice to do so. It is not difficult to reshape the land, replace the soil, and plant native grasses, shrubs, and trees on the disturbed areas. In the oilsands of Alberta, for example, it has proven possible to re-create the boreal forest ecosystem in a short time after the disturbance of mining is completed. Sustainable mining means leaving sustainable landscapes behind that will remain healthy into the foreseeable future. This aspect of sustainable mining has been achieved around the world.

One of the best examples of ecological restoration of a heavily disturbed mining site is the Island Copper Mine on northern Vancouver Island that was the subject of my Ph.D. thesis in the early 1970s. After 24 years of operation and the extraction of $3 billion of copper, the open pit, which was adjacent to the sea, was more than 1200 feet (370meters) deep, making it the second lowest land in the world after the shores of the Dead Sea. This was the first large mining project in Canada that required a detailed restoration plan before the mine went into operation. When the ore body was exhausted the open pit was flooded with seawater and then isolated from the sea to create a maromictic lake, a lake with dense salt water below and a layer of fresh water from rainfall above. A maromictic lake never turns over, so the seawater remains there indefinitely. Acidic runoff from area around the lake is collected and piped into the deep waters where it is neutralized and where any metals are precipitated into the sediment below.

The entire area of disturbed land was planted with native trees (red alder) that fix nitrogen and will build a layer of rich soil on the bare mineral surface. Today the area that was disturbed is fast returning to a native forest ecosystem with a new lake where aquaculture projects are underway.

The social, and economic, side of sustainable mining is still a work in progress in many parts of the world but great advances have been made in recent years. It is now standard practice for international mining companies to engage with communities near a prospective mine site and to work towards a plan that satisfies the interests of local citizens. This includes investment in schools, hospitals, community centers, water and sewage systems, training programs, and micro-finance loans to local entrepreneurs. Mining projects can offer employment in both the construction and operational phases of development. It is fast becoming an essential part of sustainable mining to focus on the needs of nearby communities. The objective is to leave these communities with better living conditions and opportunities than they had before the mine was established. That is sustainable mining. It is a growing reality around the world and it should be encouraged, not met with the zero-tolerance attitude of Greenpeace today. How senseless is it to oppose all mining when it is the lifeblood of civilization?

CHAPTER TWENTY-ONE

Climate of Fear

If a man will begin with certainties, he shall end in doubts;
but if he will be content to begin with doubts he shall end
in certainties.
—Sir Francis Bacon

The global media tells us plainly and bluntly that the vast majority of the world's scientists believe we are headed for a climate catastrophe that will devastate human civilization and the environment. We have no choice but to act immediately to save ourselves from this apocalypse. The greatest threat is the CO_2 released from burning fossil fuels and cutting forests. Fossil fuel use must be cut by 80 percent or more, and we must stop cutting trees. How should we react to this warning?

The subject of climate change, also referred to as global warming, is perhaps the most complex scientific issue we have ever attempted to resolve. Hundreds, possibly thousands of factors influence the earth's climate, many in ways we do not fully understand. So, first, let us recognize that the science of climate is not settled. In fact, we are only beginning to understand how the earth's climate works.

It is not correct to use the terms *global warming* and *climate change* as if they were interchangeable. Global warming is a very specific term meaning exactly what it says, that the average temperature of the earth is increasing over time. Climate change is a much more general term that includes many factors. For one thing the climate is always changing, whereas it is not always getting warmer. The old maxim "the only constant is change" fits perfectly here. And as the belief in human-caused global warming has come into doubt the term climate change has been adopted as a substitute, even though it means something completely different.

It is one thing to claim increases in CO_2 cause global warming and quite another to claim increases in CO_2 cause:

- Higher temperatures
- Lower temperatures
- More snow and blizzards
- Drought, fire, and floods
- Rising sea levels
- Disappearing glaciers
- Loss of sea ice at the poles
- Species extinction
- More and stronger storms
- More storm damage
- More volcanic eruptions
- Dying forests
- Death of coral reefs and shellfish
- Shutting down the Gulf Stream
- Fatal heat waves
- More heat-related illness and disease
- Crop failure and food shortages
- Millions of climate change refugees
- Increased cancer, cardiovascular disease, mental illness, and respiratory disease[290]
- And, a devastating effect on the quality of French wines[291]

The science of climatology is only a few decades old. It is not a single science but rather an interdisciplinary cluster of sciences. These include meteorology (the study of weather), atmospheric chemistry, astrophysics and cosmic rays, geology and other earth sciences, oceanography, carbon cycling through all living species, soil science, geology, climate history through the millennia, ice ages and greenhouse ages, study of the sun, knowledge of earth wobbles, magnetic fields and orbital variations, etc. All of these disciplines are interrelated in complex, dynamic patterns that cannot be reduced to a simple equation. That is why climatologists have built very complicated computer models in the hope of predicting future climatic conditions.

A "climate change community" has evolved over the past 30 years consisting of widely divergent groups with sharply differing opinions. The most prominent and formally structured group is the United Nations Intergovernmental Panel on Climate Change (IPCC) and the scientists,

290. "A Human Health Perspective on Climate Change," National Institute of Environmental Health Sciences, April 2010, http://www.niehs.nih.gov/health/docs/climatereport2010.pdf
291. "Impact of Climate Change on Wine in France," Greenpeace International, September 2009, http://www.greenpeace.org/raw/content/international/press/reports/impacts-of-climate-change-on-w.pdf

scholars, activists, and politicians who associate themselves with this organization. The IPCC was created in 1988 as a partnership between the World Meteorological Organization and the United Nations Environment Program, put simply, meteorologists and environmentalists. Members of this group generally believe humans are causing global warming, that we are changing the climate, and this will generally be negative for civilization and the environment. They claim to represent an "overwhelming consensus among climate scientists."[292]

The IPCC is rather insular, believing its members are the only true climate scientists and that those who disagree with them are either some other kind of scientists, or not really scientists at all. Thus there is a self-defined overwhelming, even unanimous, consensus because they don't recognize the legitimacy of those who disagree with them. In 2007 the IPCC published its *Fourth Assessment Report*, which stated, "Most of the observed increase in global average temperatures since the mid-20th century is very likely due to the observed increase in anthropogenic (human-caused) greenhouse gas concentrations."[293]

At the other end of this spectrum there is a considerable contingent of scientists and scholars, largely schooled in the earth and astronomical sciences, who believe climate is largely influenced by natural forces and cycles. They were not organized into an official body until 2007 when the Nongovernmental International Panel on Climate Change (NIPCC) was formed in Vienna. Led by atmospheric scientist Dr. Fred Singer, the NIPCC published "Climate Change Reconsidered," a comprehensive scientific critique of the IPCC's findings, in 2009.[294] This report was signed by more than 31,000 American scientists and concluded, "there is no convincing scientific evidence that human release of carbon dioxide, methane, or other greenhouse gases is causing or will, in the foreseeable future, cause catastrophic heating of the Earth's atmosphere and disruption of the Earth's climate."[295] Clearly there is no overwhelming consensus among scientists on the subject of climate.[296] In my opinion the believers and the skeptics of human-caused, catastrophic climate change can be roughly divided between those who see history in very recent terms (years to thousands of years) and those who see history in the long term (thousands to hundreds of millions of years). Both meteorologists and environmentalists tend to think about weather and climate in

292. "Statistical Analysis of Consensus," realclimate.org, December 16, 2004,
http://www.realclimate.org/index.php/archives/2004/12/a-statistical-analysis-of-the-consensus/
293. "Summary for Policymakers," *Fourth Assessment Report*, Intergovernmental Panel on Climate Change, 2007, p. 3,
http://www.ipcc.ch/pdf/assessment-report/ar4/wg1/ar4-wg1-spm.pdf
294. Craig Idso and S. Fred Singer, "Climate Change Reconsidered," Nongovernmental International Panel on Climate Change,
2009. http://www.heartland.org/publications/NIPCC%20report/PDFs/NIPCC%20Final.pdf
295. "Climate Change Reconsidered," Center for the Study of Carbon Dioxide and Global Change," 2009, www.nipccreport.org/
296. "More Than 700 International Scientists Dissent Over Man-Made Global Warming Claims: Scientists Continue to Debunk
'Consensus' in 2008 & 2009," U.S. Senate Minority Report, March 16, 2009,
http://epw.senate.gov/public/index.cfm?FuseAction=Files.View&FileStore_id=83947f5d-d84a-4a84-ad5d-6e2d71db52d9

terms of recent human history. Geologists, evolutionary biologists, and astrophysicists tend to think of climate in the context of the 3.5 billion-year history of life and the 4.6 billion-year history of the Earth.

The various camps have invented some names for each other and for themselves. Pretty much everyone involved thinks they are "climate scientists." But people who are convinced we are the main cause of climate change have been dubbed "true believers" and "warmists," highlighting what are seen to be religious and ideological orientations, respectively. People who are undecided, critical, or questioning are called "skeptics." The skeptics are happy with this description as it indicates they have an open mind and as scientists they believe they have a duty to challenge unproven hypotheses. The true believers use the word skeptic as a slur, as in "unbelievers," as if it is unacceptable to question their beliefs. Then there are the "climate deniers," or "denialists," terms invented by the true believers, and characterized by skeptics as associating them with Holocaust deniers. Much of this is just name-calling, but it is useful in the sense that it defines the battleground.

Over the years the media have largely ignored the scientists and organizations that remain skeptical of human-caused global warming and climate change. The public has been inundated with alarmist headlines about catastrophic climate change and many governments have bought into the belief there is a global emergency that must be addressed quickly and decisively. As with fear of chemicals, fear of climate change results in a convergence of interests among activists seeking funding, scientists applying for grants, the media selling advertising, businesses promoting themselves as green, and politicians looking for votes. It may not be a conspiracy, but it is a very powerful alignment that is mutually reinforcing.

In 2007 the IPCC and one of its main champions, Al Gore, were awarded the Nobel Peace Prize for alerting the world to the dire threat of human-caused climate change. One would imagine the public would strongly support this alarmist position, having been exposed to such one-sided media coverage and the news of prestigious awards. Amazingly this is not the case, even in countries such as the United States and England, where the official government positions are sharply accepting of catastrophic human-caused warming.

A Pew Foundation poll conducted in October 2009 found only 36 percent of the general public in the United States believes humans are the cause of global warming, whereas 33 percent does not believe the earth is warming and 16 percent believe the earth is warming but that it is due to natural causes. Public opinion was sharply divided along partisan lines: 50 percent of Democrats believe global warming is caused by humans, while 33 percent of independents, and only 18 percent of Republicans agree with this. The trend since 2007 is decidedly downwards with about

10 percent fewer people believing in human-caused global warming in all categories.

Another Pew Foundation poll taken in May 2010 asked Americans to rank priorities for Congress. It found only 32 percent think it is very important for Congress to address climate change in the coming months, including 47 percent of Democrats, 29 percent of independents, and 17 percent of Republicans.[297]

The partisan spread mirrors the poll on belief in human-caused climate change almost perfectly. This is a strong indication that the reason a majority is not concerned about climate change legislation is because it doesn't believe in human-caused climate change in the first place.

A poll taken by Ipsos Mori in June 2008 found 60 percent of Britons believed, "many scientific experts still question if humans are contributing to climate change."[298] Clearly a majority of the British public does not believe there is a scientific certainty on the subject.

A more recent British poll in February 2010, again taken by Ipsos Mori, showed that only 17 percent of Britons put climate change in their top three most important issues facing them and their families.[299]

In one of the most surprising surveys taken, 121 U.S. television weather presenters, all members of the American Meteorological Society, were asked their opinions on climate change in April 2010. Ninety-four percent of those surveyed were accredited meteorologists. When asked about the UN's Intergovernmental Panel on Climate Change's statement, "Most of the warming since 1950 is very likely human-induced," a full 50 percent either disagreed or strongly disagreed. Twenty-five percent were neutral and only 24 percent said they agreed or strongly agreed.[300]

In April 2013 a US Department of Agriculture-funded survey of US Midwest corn farmer's beliefs in climate change was published. 18,800 farmers with an income of US$100,000 or more were polled, of whom 26 percent responded (4,778). Only 8 percent of these farmers, who spend their lives in the weather and the climate, agreed with the statement, "Climate change is occurring and it is caused mostly by human activities." In other words, 92 percent of corn farmers do not believe humans are the main cause of climate change. I say give them all honorary doctorates of science.

297. "Public's Priorities, Financial Regs: Congress's Job Rating—13%," Pew Research Center for People and the Press, May 18, 2010, http://people-press.org/report/615/
298. "Scientists Exaggerate Climate-Change Fears, Majority of Britons Believe," Mail Online, June 22, 2008, http://www.dailymail.co.uk/news/article-1028425/Scientists-exaggerate-climate-change-fears-majority-Britons-believe.html
299. "Climate Change Omnibus: Great Britain," Ipsos Mori, February 24, 2010, http://www.ipsos-mori.com/researchpublications/researcharchive/poll.aspx?oltemId=2552
300. Edward Maibach et al., "A National Survey of Television Meteorologists About Climate Change: Preliminary Findings," George Mason University Center for Climate Change Communication, March 29, 2010, http://www.climatechangecommunication.org/images/files/TV_Meteorologists_Survey_Findings_(March_2010).pdf

Why is there such a high degree of skepticism among professionals and the public when the mainstream media is so biased toward the IPCC view? It would appear they are reading about skeptical opinions on the Internet, blogs in particular, and talking to one another about the subject in an open-minded manner. Obviously most weather presenters are acutely interested in and aware of the fine points of the debate. The fact they disagree with the IPCC "consensus" by two-to-one speaks volumes about where these weather professionals find credibility on the subject of global warming.

Climate science is a classic case of the necessity to distinguish between historical and present facts on the one hand, and predictions of the future on the other. There are a number of things we can say with relative certainty:

- During the past 500 million years, since modern life forms emerged, the earth's climate has been warmer than it is today most of the time. During these "Greenhouse Ages" the earth's temperature averaged around 22 to 25 degrees Celsius (72 to 77 Fahrenheit).[301] All the land was either tropical or subtropical and the world was generally wetter. The sea level was much higher than today and life flourished on land and in the oceans. These warm periods were punctuated by three Ice Ages during which large ice sheets formed at the poles and in mountainous areas, effectively eliminating most plants and animals in those regions.

- The two Ice Ages that preceded the current one occurred between 460 and 430 million years ago and between 360 and 260 million year ago. From 260 million years ago until quite recently, a Greenhouse Age existed for about 250 million years. Ice started to accumulate in Antarctica beginning 20 million years ago and eventually the current Ice Age, known as the Pleistocene, began in earnest about 2.5 million years ago.[302] *The Pleistocene, which we are still in today and during which our species evolved to its current state, accounts for only 0.07 percent of the history of life on earth.*

- During the coldest periods of the Pleistocene Ice Age the average temperature of the earth was around 12 degrees Celsius (54 degrees Fahrenheit) and there were large ice sheets on both poles. Before the recent retreat of the glaciers, beginning 18,000 years ago, the ice extended below the U.S./Canada border, over all of Scandinavia, much of northern Europe, and well into northern Russia. The sea was about 122 meters (400 feet) lower than it is today, having risen steadily since then and continuing to do so today.[303] In recent times the sea has risen about 20 centimeters (8 inches) per century. The

301. Christopher R. Scotese, "Climate History," Paleomar Project, April 20, 2002, http://www.scotese.com/climate.htm
302. "Ice Age" Wikipedia, http://en.wikipedia.org/wiki/Ice_age
303. "Sea Level," Wikipedia, http://en.wikipedia.org/wiki/Sea_level

cause of sea level rise is a combination of melting glaciers (ice on land) and rising ocean temperature, as water expands when it gets warmer.

- The earth's climate underwent a general warming trend beginning with the end of the last major glaciation, about 18,000 years ago. This has not been an even warming, as there have been many fluctuations along the way. For example, during the Holocene Thermal Maximum between 9000 and 4000 years ago it was warmer than it is today by as much as 3 degrees Celsius (5.4 degrees Fahrenheit).[304] During this time the present-day Sahara Desert was covered with lakes and vegetation, clearly indicating there was much more rainfall there than today.[305] We know for a fact this was not caused by humans. Many scientists believe it was caused by variations in the earth's orbit around the sun.

- This historical record highlights the importance of analyzing the starting point and end point of temperature measurements when explaining trends, both up and down. It is warmer today than it was 18,000 years ago. But it is cooler today than it was 5,000 years ago during the Holocene Thermal Optimum. So it could be said we have been in a cooling trend for the past 5000 years even though it is warmer now than it was when the glaciation ended. I will try not to "trick" the reader by cherry-picking timelines that support a particular bias.

- Today the average temperature of the earth is about 14.5 degrees Celsius (58 degrees Fahrenheit), decidedly closer to the Ice Age level than the Greenhouse Age level and only 2.5 degrees above the temperature at the height of the last major glaciation. The fact is we are still in the Pleistocene Ice Age and it is possible another major glaciation may occur sometime in the next 10,000 years, but that is a prediction, not a fact.

- Carbon Dioxide (CO_2) is a greenhouse gas in that it tends to heat the atmosphere and thus raise the temperature of the earth. But water vapor is by far the most important greenhouse gas, contributing at least two thirds of the "greenhouse effect." CO_2 and other minor gases, such as methane and nitrous oxide, make up the other third of the greenhouse effect.[306] It is not possible to prove the exact ratios among the various greenhouse gases as they interact in complex ways.

304. Chris Caseldine et al., "Holocene Thermal Maximum up to 3oC Warmer Than Today, *Quaternary Science Reviews* 25, no. 17-18 (September 2006): 2025-2446.

305. "Earth's Climatic History: The Last 10,000 Years," *CO₂ Science*, http://www.co2science.org/subject/other/clim_hist_tenthousand.php

306. J. T. Kiehl and Kevin E. Trenberth, "Earth's Annual Global Mean Energy Budget," *Bulletin of the American Meteorological Society* 78, no. 2 (February 1997): 197-208, www.atmo.arizona.edu/students/courselinks/spring04/atmo451b/pdf/RadiationBudget.pdf

In particular, the balance between water vapor and clouds (made up of condensed water vapor) is impossible to predict accurately.[307]

- We know global levels of CO_2 in the atmosphere have risen steadily from 315 parts per million (ppm) to nearly 390 ppm since scientists began taking regular measurements at Mauna Loa on the big island of Hawaii in 1958.[308] This is a very short time compared to the 3.5 billion years of life on earth. Many scientists assume that human emissions of CO_2 from burning fossil fuels are the main cause of this increase. Some scientists question this assumption. It is a fact that CO_2 levels were much higher than they are today during previous eras. This will be discussed in detail later.

- The average temperature of the earth has fluctuated during the past 100 years, sometimes cooling, sometimes warming, and in balance has increased somewhat, especially during the periods from 1910 to 1940 and from 1980 to 1998. Since 1998 there has been no further warming and apparently a slight cooling. There is a lot of controversy around the accuracy of these trends. In particular there is a concern that many of the weather stations used to determine the global average were originally in the countryside but over the years have been swallowed up by expanding urban development. The "urban heat island effect" refers to the fact that concrete and heat from buildings results in an increase in temperature in urban areas compared to the surrounding countryside,[309] thus the possibility exists that the results have been skewed.

In November 2009 the release of thousands of emails, leaked or hacked, from the Climatic Research Unit of the University of East Anglia in the U.K. shocked the climate change community. It was quite clear from a number of email exchanges that the scientists with this most important source of information had been manipulating data, withholding data, and conspiring to discredit other scientists who did not share their certainty that humans were the main cause of climate change. These revelations were quickly dubbed "Climategate" and have since been hotly debated in climate change circles.[310] [311] [312] It is very difficult to find

---

307. "Forecast: Water and Global Warming," ESPERE, http://www.espere.net/Unitedkingdom/water/uk_forecast.html

308. R. F. Keeling et al., "Atmospheric CO_2 Values (ppmv) Derived from In Situ Air Samples Collected at Mauna Loa, Hawaii, USA," Scripps Institute of Oceanography, September 2009, http://cdiac.ornl.gov/ftp/trends/co2/maunaloa.co2

309. "Surfacestations Project Reaches 82% of the Network Surveyed," surfacestations.org, July 16, 2009, http://www.surfacestations.org/

310. "The Tip of the Climate Change Iceberg," Wall Street Journal, December 8, 2009, http://online.wsj.com/article/SB10001424052748704342404574576683216723794.html

311. James Delingpole, "Climategate: The Final Nail in the Coffin of 'Anthropogenic Global Warming'?" Telegraph, November 20, 2009, http://blogs.telegraph.co.uk/news/jamesdelingpole/100017393/climategate-the-final-nail-in-the-coffin-of-anthropogenic-global-warming/

312. Andrew C. Revkin, "Hacked E-Mail Is New Fodder for Climate Dispute," New York Times, November 20, 2009, http://www.nytimes.com/2009/11/21/science/earth/21climate.html

a balanced account of this scandal. Commentary is divided sharply, with believers claiming that while the scientists involved behaved badly, this does not change the fact that the science is clear that humans are causing warming, while skeptics claim the revelations demonstrate the books have been cooked, placing the entire hypothesis of global warming in doubt.

In December 2009, after months of promotion and hype, the Copenhagen conference on climate change ended in disaster for the true believers. The delegates at the largest international meeting in history failed to reach a single binding decision to control CO_2 emissions. There does not seem to be any conceivable strategy to achieve international agreement on this subject. The United States will not sign a deal that does not include China, India, Brazil, and the other developing countries. The developing countries will not agree to reduce or restrict their CO_2 emissions so long as the U.S. and other industrialized countries have far higher emissions on a per capita basis. Whereas the U.S. emits nearly 20 tonnes (22 tons) of CO_2 per person, China emits 4.6 tonnes (5.1 tons) and India emits 1.2 tonnes (1.3 tons). There is no possibility this impasse will be resolved in the near future. The U.S. will not agree to reduce its emissions to a lower level while the developing countries increase theirs. The developing countries will not agree to a system in which the U.S. and other industrialized countries are allowed even higher per capita emissions. Despite this obvious impasse, the delegates continue to meet regularly, thousands of people jetting to desirable locations like Bali, Montreal, and Rio de Janeiro at public expense, with no possibility of ever reaching agreement.

We can be fairly certain of the facts listed above, with the qualifications given. While this is very interesting, it is not the known facts but rather the unanswered questions that are most intriguing. Climate change cannot be defined by a single question. It is much like peeling back the layers of an onion, beginning with the science, leading to possible environmental impacts, followed by potential economic and social impacts, and concluding with policy options. Among these questions are:

- Is CO_2, the main cause of global warming, either natural or human-caused?
- Are human-caused CO_2 emissions the principal cause of recent global warming?
- Is the recent warming trend fundamentally different from previous warming and cooling trends?
- If warming continues at the rate experienced in the 20th century into the 21st century will this be positive or negative for human civilization and the environment?
- Is the melting of glaciers and polar ice really a threat to the future of human civilization?

- Will increased CO_2 result in "acidification" of the oceans and kill all the coral reefs and shellfish?
- Is it possible for humans to halt global warming and to control the earth's climate?
- Which would cost more to the economy, an 80 percent reduction in fossil fuel use or adaptation to a warmer world?
- Could the United States and China ever agree to a common policy on reducing CO_2 emissions?
- Is the effort to conclude a binding agreement to control CO_2 emissions among all nations futile?

These are just some of the many questions we must answer if we are to make intelligent choices about the direction public policy should take on the subject of climate change.

Before going into more detail I will clarify two key points. First, the fact that both CO_2 and temperature are increasing at the same time does not prove one is causing the other. It may be that increased CO_2 is causing some or most of the increased temperature. It may also be that increased temperature causes an increase in atmospheric CO_2. Or it may be they are both caused by some other common factor, or it may be just coincidental they are both rising together and they have nothing to do with one another. Correlation does not prove causation. In order to demonstrate one thing causes another, we need among other things, to be able to replicate the same cause-effect sequence over and over again. This is not possible with the earth's climate as we are not in control of all (or any of) the factors that might influence climate. Now, if we had a record of CO_2 and temperature going back many millions of years and it showed that increased temperature always followed increased CO_2, we would be a long way toward proving the point. As we shall see later, the historical record is not so clear on the relationship between CO_2 and temperature.

Second, it is often assumed that the interests of humans and the interests of the environment are one and the same. This may be the case for some factors, such as rainfall, but for others it simply does not apply. Take sea level rise, for example. If the sea level rises relatively rapidly, it will damage a great deal of human infrastructure and a great deal of work and expense will be required either to protect or to replace farms, buildings, wharfs, roadways, etc. But fish and other marine creatures will be perfectly happy with the rising sea level and most land animals will not find it difficult to move a few feet higher. A 1.5 meter (5-foot rise) in sea level may inundate Bangladesh, turning much of it into a salt marsh and displacing millions of people. This would be devastating for humans, but from an environmental perspective there is nothing wrong with a salt marsh. From an ecological point of view, a natural salt marsh represents an improvement over intensive agriculture with monocultures of nonnative food crops. Fortunately, no credible scientist believes the sea level will rise anywhere near 1.5 meters in the next century.

A Longer View

Our lifetimes are so short compared to the billions of years of life's history on earth that we tend to dwell on the very recent past when considering historical information. Nearly all the discussion of climate change is in the context of the past 100 years, or occasionally the past 1000 years, even though the earth's climate has changed constantly for billions of years. Let's take a look at the history of climate change in this larger context, in particular the past 500 million years since modern life forms evolved.

Temperature

The earth's average temperature has fluctuated widely over the past one billion years (see Figure 1). It is interesting to note that during the Cambrian Period, when most of the modern life forms emerged, the climate was much warmer than it is today, averaging 25 degrees Celsius (77 degrees Fahrenheit). Only at three other times during the past billion years has the temperature been as cold as or colder than it is today. The age of the dinosaurs, the Jurassic and Cretaceous Periods, experienced a warm climate with a moderate cooling spell in the late Jurassic. Following the dinosaur extinction the climate remained warm for 10 million years, spiking to 27 degrees Celsius (80 degrees Fahrenheit), followed by a gradual decline that eventually led to the Pleistocene Ice Age. As the graph below indicates, it is colder today than it has been throughout most of the past billion years.

Humans generally prefer warmer climates to colder ones. When I mention that the global climate was much warmer before this present Ice Age, people often say something like, "But humans were not even around five million years ago, certainly not 50 or 500 million years ago. We have not evolved in a warmer world and will not be able to cope with global warming." The fact is we did evolve in a "warmer world." The human species originated in the tropical regions of Africa, where it was warm even during past glaciations nearer the poles. Humans are a tropical species that has adapted to colder climates as a result of harnessing fire, making clothing, and building shelters. Before these advances occurred, humans could not live outside the tropics. It may come as a surprise to most that a naked human in the outdoors with no fire will die of hypothermia if the temperature goes below 21 degrees Celsius (70 degrees Fahrenheit). Yet as long as we have food, water, and shade we can survive in the hottest climates on earth without fire, clothing, or shelter.[313] The Australian Aborigines survived in

---

313. Claude A. Piantadosi, *The Biology of Human Survival: Life and Death in Extreme Environments*

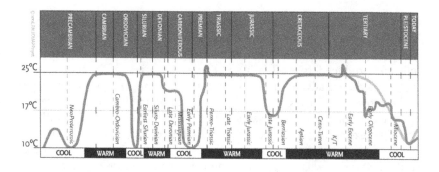

Figure 1. Graph showing global average temperature during the past billion years.[314]

temperatures of over 45 degrees Celsius (113 degrees Fahrenheit) without air conditioning for 50,000 years.

The fact that humans are essentially a tropical species explains why even today there are no permanent residents of Antarctica and only four million people living in the Arctic (0.06 percent of the global population). Most of the Arctic population is engaged in resource extraction and would not choose to live there otherwise. Historically, the very small populations of indigenous people in the Arctic managed to eke out a living by inhabiting ice-shelters, getting food from marine mammals and oil from marine mammals for heating and light. They used sled dogs for transport and protection from polar bears. There is a good reason why there are more than 18 million people in Sao Paulo, Brazil, only 4,429 residents in Barrow, Alaska,[315] and 3,451 inhabitants of Inuvik, Northwest Territory.[316]

Why are there 300 million people in the United States and only 30 million in Canada, which is larger geographically? One word answers this question: cold. About 80 percent of Canadians live within 100 miles of the U.S. border, as it is warmer there (although not by much in many regions) than it is in 90 percent of Canada, which is frozen solid for six or more months of the year.

So clearly, on the basis of temperature alone, it would be fine for humans if the entire earth were tropical and subtropical as it was for millions of years during the Greenhouse Ages. It would also be fine for the vast majority of species in the world today, most of which live in tropical and subtropical regions. But this would not be the case for some other species that have evolved specifically to be able to survive in cold climates.

The polar bear did not exist until the Pleistocene Ice Age froze the Arctic and created the conditions for adaptation to a world of ice. Polar

(Oxford: Oxford University Press, 2003).

314. Global Temperature Curve by C.R. Scotese, PALEOMAP Project, http://www.scotese.com/climate.htm

315. "City of Barrow – Farthest North American City," http://www.cityofbarrow.org/

316. "Inuvik," http://www.inuvik.ca/tourism/faq.html

bears are not really a distinct species; they are a variety of the European brown bear, known as the grizzly bear in North America. They are so closely related genetically that brown bears and polar bears can mate successfully and produce fertile offspring.[317] The white variety of the brown bear evolved as the ice advanced, the white color providing a good camouflage in the snow. Once bears could walk out to sea on the ice floes, it became feasible to hunt seals. It is possible that if the world warmed substantially over the next hundreds of years that the white variety of the brown bear would become reduced in numbers or even die out. This would simply be the reverse of what happened when the world became colder. Some varieties of life that exist today are only here because the world turned colder a few million years ago, following a warmer period that lasted for over 200 million years. If the climate were to return to a Greenhouse Age those varieties might not survive. Many more species would benefit from a warmer world, the human species among them.

The polar bear did not evolve as a separate variety of brown bear until about 150,000 years ago, during the glaciation previous to the most recent one.[318] [319] This is a very recent adaptation to an extreme climatic condition that caused much of the Arctic Ocean to freeze over for most of the past 2.5 million years. The polar bear did manage to survive through the interglacial period that preceded the one we are in now even though the earth's average temperature was higher during that interglacial than it is today.[320] So as long as the temperature does not rise more than about 5 degrees Celsius (9 degrees Fahrenheit) above the present level, polar bears will likely survive. But that is a prediction, not a fact.

To listen to climate activists and the media, you would think the polar bear population is already in a steep decline. A little investigation reveals there are actually more polar bears today than there were just 30 years ago. Most subpopulations are either stable or growing. And the main cause of polar bear deaths today is legally sanctioned trophy hunting, not climate change. Of an estimated population of 20,000 to 25,000 bears, more than 700 are shot every year by trophy hunters and native Inuit. One hundred and nine are killed in the Baffin Bay region of Canada alone. And yet activist groups like the World Wildlife Fund use the polar bear as a poster child for global warming, incorrectly alleging that they are being wiped out by climate change.

The population of polar bears was estimated at 6000 in 1960. In 1973 an International Agreement between Canada, the United States, Norway,

---

317. Katherine Hamon, "Climate Change Likely Caused Polar Bear to Evolve Quickly," *Scientific American*, March 1, 2010, http://www.scientificamerican.com/article.cfm?id=polar-bear-genome-climate
318. "Polar Bear" Wikipedia, http://en.wikipedia.org/wiki/Polar_bear
319. Katherine Hamon, "Climate Change Likely Caused Polar Bear to Evolve Quickly," *Scientific American*, March 1, 2010, http://www.scientificamerican.com/article.cfm?id=polar-bear-genome-climate
320. "Interglacial," Wikipedia, http://en.wikipedia.org/wiki/Interglacial

Russia, and Greenland ended unrestricted hunting and introduced quotas. Since then only native people have been allowed to hunt polar bears, although in Canada the native Inuit often act as guides for non-native hunters. As a result of this restriction on hunting, the population has rebounded to its present level of 20,000 to 25,000. The International Union for the Conservation of Natural Resources Polar Bear Specialist Group reports that of 18 subpopulations of bears, two are increasing, five are stable, five are declining, while for six subpopulations, mainly those in Russia, there is insufficient data.[321] There is no reliable evidence that any bear populations are declining due to climate change and all such claims rely on speculation; they are predictions based on conjecture rather than actual scientific studies.

At the other end of the world in Antarctica, numerous species of penguins have evolved over the past 20 million years so that they can live in ice-bound environments. There are also many species of penguins that live in places where there is no ice, such as in Australia, South Africa, Tierra del Fuego, and the Galapagos Islands. It took 20 million years for the Antarctic ice sheet to grow to the extent it has been for the past 2.5 million years, during the Pleistocene Age. Antarctica differs significantly from the Arctic in that most of the ice is on land and at higher elevation. It is very unlikely Antarctica will become ice-free in the near future. It took millions of years for the present ice sheet to develop. In all likelihood the penguins will be able to breathe easily for thousands, possibly millions of years.

Coming closer to the present day, there is good historical evidence that it was warmer than it is today during the days of the Roman Empire 2000 years ago and during the Medieval Warming Period 1,000 years ago.[322] [323] We know that during the Medieval Warming Period, the Norse (Vikings) colonized Iceland, Greenland, and Newfoundland. The settlements in Newfoundland and Greenland were then abandoned during the Little Ice Age that lasted from about 1500 to the early 1800s.[324] The Thames River in England froze over regularly during the cold winters of the Little Ice Age. The Thames last froze over in 1814.[325] Since then the climate has been in a gradual warming trend. Given that there were very low levels of CO_2 emissions from human activity in those times, it is not possible that humans caused the Medieval Warming Period or the Little Ice Age. Natural factors had to be instrumental in those changes in climate.

---

321. "Summary of Polar Pear Population status per 2010," IUCN Polar Bear Specialist Group, http://pbsg.npolar.no/en/status/status-table.html

322. "Roman Warm Period (Europe – Mediterranean) – Summary," CO_2 Science, http://www.co2science.org/subject/r/summaries/rwpeuropemed.php

323. "Medieval Warm Period Project," CO_2 Science, http://www.co2science.org/data/mwp/mwpp.php

324. "20th Century Climate Not So Hot," Harvard Smithsonian Center for Astrophysics, March 31, 2003, http://www.cfa.harvard.edu/news/archive/pr0310.html

325. "The Frozen Thames in London: An Introduction," History and Traditions of England, January 10, 2010, http://www.webhistoryofengland.com/?p=613

Speaking of natural factors, it is clear the climate changes over the past billions of years were not caused by our activities. So how credible is it to claim we have just recently become the main cause of climate change? It's not as if the natural factors that have been causing the climate to change over the millennia have suddenly disappeared and now we are the only significant agent of change. Clearly the natural factors are still at work, even if our population explosion and increasing CO_2 emissions now play a role in climate change. So the real question is, are human impacts overwhelming the natural factors or are they only a minor player in the big picture? We do not know the definitive answer to that question.

Let's go back to the IPCC's *Fourth Assessment Report* in 2007, which stated: "*Most* of the observed increase in global average temperatures *since the mid-20th century* is *very likely* due to the observed increase in anthropogenic (human-caused) greenhouse gas concentrations"[my emphasis]. The first word, *most*, in common usage means more than 50 percent and less than 100 percent, i.e., more than half but not all. That's a pretty big spread, so clearly IPCC members don't have a very precise estimate of how much of the warming they think we are causing. If they are that uncertain, how do they know it's not 25 percent, or 5 percent? They restrict the human influence to "since the mid-20th century," implying humans were not responsible for climate change until about 60 years ago. So the logical question is, What was responsible for the significant climate changes before 60 years ago, the warming between 1910 and 1940, for example? The most problematic term in their statement is "very likely," which certainly provides no indication of scientific proof. The IPCC claims that "very likely" means "greater than 90 percent probability."[326] But the figure 90 is not the result of any calculation or statistical analysis. The footnote entry for the term "very likely" explains, "in this Summary for Policymakers, the following terms have been used to indicate the assessed likelihood, *using expert judgement,* [my emphasis] of an outcome or a result: *Virtually certain* > 99% probability of occurrence, *Extremely likely* > 95%, *Very likely* > 90%, *Likely* > 66%, *More likely than not* > 50%, *Unlikely* < 33%, *Very unlikely* < 10%, *Extremely unlikely* < 5%."[327] One expects "judgments" from judges and opinionated journalists. Scientists are expected to provide calculations and observable evidence. I'm not convinced by this loose use of words and numbers.

According to the official records of surface temperatures, 1998 was the warmest year in the past 150 years. Since then the average global temperature remained relatively flat down, completely contrary to the

---

326. "Summary for Policymakers," Intergovernmental Panel on Climate Change, 2007, p. 3
http://www.ipcc.ch/pdf/assessment-report/ar4/wg1/ar4-wg1-spm.pdf
327. Ibid.

predictions of the IPCC, and in spite of steadily growing CO_2 emissions from countries around the world. This drop in temperature is now attributed to natural factors, something that was downplayed in previous predictions. Mojib Latif, a prominent German meteorologist and oceanographer, explains it this way, "So I really believe in Global Warming. Okay. However, you know, we have to accept that there are these natural fluctuations, and therefore, the temperature may not show additional warming temporarily."[328] The question is, How long is temporarily? At this writing the global temperature has not increased during the past 16 years. The assertion that it will resume warming at some time in the future is a prediction, not a fact. And even if warming does resume, it is possible that this may be due to natural factors. *It is not logical to believe that natural factors are only responsible for cooling and not for warming.*

The situation is complicated further by the revelations of "Climategate" in November 2009, which clearly showed that many of the most influential climate scientists associated with the IPCC have been manipulating data, withholding data, and conspiring to discredit other scientists who do not share their certainty that we are the main cause of global warming.[329] It has also been well documented that the NASA Goddard Institute for Space Science, which is responsible for one of the primary temperature records, has dropped a large number of weather stations, mainly in colder regions, thus likely making it seem warming is occurring even though this may not be the case.[330] The situation is in such a state of flux that it may be several years before an objective process is in place to sort out what is believable and what is not.

Leading up to the 15th Conference of the Parties in the Framework Convention on Climate Change in Copenhagen in December 2009, the IPCC, the European Union, and many other participants warned we must keep global temperatures from rising more than 2 degrees Celsius (3.6 degrees Fahrenheit) or we will face climate catastrophe.[331] Yet the global temperature has been 6 to 8 degrees Celsius (11 to 14 degrees Fahrenheit) warmer than it is today through most of the past 500 million years. It seems clear that the real "climate catastrophes" are the major glaciations that occurred during the Ice Ages, not the warm Greenhouse Ages when life flourished from pole to pole.

328. "Scientist Explains Earth's Warming Plateau," National Public Radio, November 22, 2009
http://www.npr.org/templates/story/story.php?storyId=120668812&ft=1&f=1007
329. James Delingpole, "Climategate: The Final Nail in the Coffin of 'Anthropogenic Global Warming'?" *Telegraph*, November 20, 2009, http://blogs.telegraph.co.uk/news/jamesdelingpole/100017393/climategate-the-final-nail-in-the-coffin-of- ...
... anthropogenic-global-warming/
330. Joseph D'Aleo and Anthony Watts, "Surface Temperature Records: Policy-Driven Deception?" Science & Public Policy Institute, June 2, 2010, http://scienceandpublicpolicy.org/images/stories/papers/originals/surface_temp.pdf
331. James Murray, "IPCC Chief Warns Even Two Degree Rise Spells 'Bad News'," businessgreen.com, March 10, 2009, http://www.businessgreen.com/business-green/news/2238184/ipcc-chief-warns-two-degree

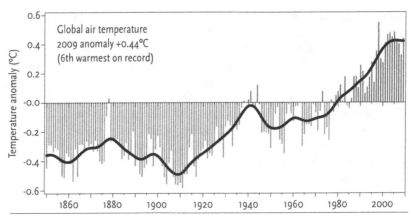

Figure 2. Global temperature trends 1860–2008 according to Phil Jones of the Climatic Research Unit in the U.K.

The graph on this page, Figure 2, is a record of global temperatures from 1850 to 2008, as prepared by the Climatic Research Unit at the University of East Anglia in the U.K.[332] It was authored by Phil Jones, who was at the centre of the "Climategate" scandal. As previously mentioned, the emails he and his colleagues exchanged indicated they withheld data, manipulated data, and attempted to discredit other scientists who held contrary views. Jones was suspended from his post in November 2009, pending an inquiry into the scandal. Therefore the data this graph is based on are not necessarily credible; they need to be rigorously re-examined.[333] But the graph does provide a useful tool for examining a couple of points about recent temperature trends.

The graph indicates global temperature has risen by about 0.8 degrees Celsius (1.4 degrees Fahrenheit) over the past 150 years. But about half of this warming occurred from 1910 to 1940, before the huge increase in CO_2 emissions from fossil fuel that began after the Second World War. What caused this increase? We simply don't know. Then there was a period of cooling from 1940 to 1980, just as CO_2 emissions started to increase dramatically. In the mid-1970s, mainstream magazines and newspapers, including *Time*, *Newsweek*, and the *New York Times*, published articles on the possibility of a coming cold period, perhaps another Ice Age.[334] [335] These articles were based on interviews with scientists at the National Academy of Sciences and NASA, among others. Prominent supporters of

332. Phil Jones, "Global Temperature Record," Climatic Research Unit, March 2010, http://www.cru.uea.ac.uk/cru/info/warming/
333. Joseph D'Aleo and Anthony Watts, "Surface Temperature Records: Policy-Driven Deception?" Science & Public Policy Institute, June 2, 2010, http://scienceandpublicpolicy.org/images/stories/papers/originals/surface_temp.pdf
334. Mauritzio Marabito, "Same Fears: Different Name?" *Spiked*, December 10, 2009, http://www.spiked-online.com/index.php/site/article/7817/
335. Robert Bradley Jr, "The Global Cooling Scare Revisited ('Ice Age' Holdren Had Plenty of Company)," Master Resource, September 26, 2009, http://www.masterresource.org/2009/09/the-global-cooling-scare-revisited/

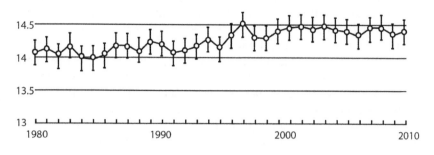

the global cooling theory included present-day global warming supporters such as John Holdren, the Obama administration's science czar[337] and the late Stephen Schneider, a former leading member of the IPCC.[338]

In 1980, global temperatures began a 20-year rise, according to the now questionable records used by the IPCC for its predictions of climate disaster. This is the only period in the 3.5 billion years of life on earth in which the IPCC attributes climate change to human activity. Since 1998 there has been no further increase in global temperature, even according to the IPCC sources. How does one 20-year period of rising temperatures out of the past 150 years prove we are the main cause of global warming?

The alarmists declare that the present warming trend is "unprecedented" because it is happening on a scale of centuries whereas past warming trends have been much slower, giving species time to adapt. This is shown to be false even during the past century. The IPCC does not contend that humans caused the warming from 1910 to 1940; therefore it must have been a natural warming trend. But the warming from 1910 to 1940 was just as large (0.4 degrees Celsius or 0.7 degrees Fahrenheit) and just as rapid over time as the supposed human-caused warming from 1975 to 2000. How can scientists who claim to be on the cutting edge of human knowledge miss this point?

It is a testament to the fickleness of trends in science, public policy, and media communications that such certainty about human-caused climate change came about. That era finally seems to have ended now that more attention is being paid to the proposition that we really don't have all the answers. One hopes this will usher in a more sensible conversation about climate change and a more balanced approach to climate change policy.

336. http://www.thegwpf.org/temperature-standstill-continues-2012-scrapes-top-ten/hadcrut3-2/
337. "John Holdren in 1771: 'New Ice Age Likely'," Zomblog, September 16, 2009, http://www.zombietime.com/zomblog/?p=873
338. John L. Daly, "Stephen Schneider: Greenhouse Superstar," August 2008, http://www.john-daly.com/schneidr.htm

In early 2013 there were three independent announcements by lead-ing believers in human-caused catastrophic climate change that con-firmed the standstill in global temperature. James Hansen, Director of the NASA Goddard Institute for Space Studies and senior science advisor to Al Gore, stated "The 5-year running mean of global temperature has been flat for the past decade." In January 2013 The UK Met Office and the Climatic Research Unit of the University of East Anglia released the data for December in their Hadcrut3 and Hadcrut4 global temperature datasets. The data clearly shows that there has been no increase in global temperature for 16 years, since 1997. In an interview with The Australian in February 2013, Rajenda Pachauri, the chair of the Intergovernmental Panel on Climate Change, acknowledged the reality of the post-1997 standstill in global average temperatures.

Carbon Dioxide

The trains carrying coal to power plants are death trains.
Coal-fired power plants are factories of death.
—James Hansen, director, NASA Goddard Institute for Space Studies, science advisor to former vice president Al Gore

The entire global warming hypothesis rests on one belief—human emis-sions of CO_2 are causing rapid global warming that will result in a "catas-trophe" if we don't cut emissions drastically, beginning now. Let's look at the history, chemistry, and biology of this much-maligned molecule.

Carbon dioxide (CO_2) and carbon are probably the most talked about substances in the world today. We hear the term "carbon footprint" every day and fossil fuels are now routinely described as "carbon-based energy." True believers speak of CO_2 as if it is the greatest threat we have ever faced. Perhaps our CO_2 emissions will have some negative effects. But in my view CO_2 is one of the most positive chemicals in our world. How can I justify this statement given that the US Environmental Protection Agency has declared CO_2 and other greenhouse gases are "pollutants" that are dangerous to human health and the environment?[339]

What about the undisputed fact that CO_2 is the most important food for all life on earth? Every green plant needs CO_2 in order to produce sugars that are the primary energy source for every plant and animal. To be fair, water is also essential to living things, as are nitrogen, potassium, phosphorus, and many other minor elements. But CO_2 is the most im-portant food, as all life on earth is carbon-based, and the carbon comes from CO_2 in the atmosphere. Without CO_2 life on this planet would not exist. How important is that?

---

339. "Endangerment and Cause or Contribute Findings for Greenhouse Gases under Section 202(a) of the Clean Air Act," U.S. Environmental Protection Agency, December 7, 2009, http://www.epa.gov/climatechange/endangerment.html

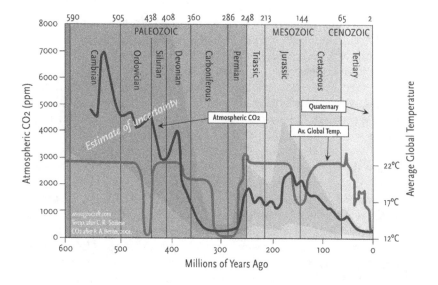

Figure 4. This graph shows global levels of CO2 and the global temperature for the past 600 million years. The correlation between the two parameters is mixed at best, with an Ice Age during a period of high CO2 levels and Greenhouse Ages during a period of relatively low CO2 levels.340

When President Obama appointed Lisa Jackson as head of the EPA, she promised to "ensure EPA's efforts to address the environmental crises of today are rooted in three fundamental values: science-based policies and programs, adherence to the rule of law, and overwhelming transparency." During the EPA's deliberations on the "endangerment" ruling for CO_2, one of its top economic policy experts, Alan Carlin, a 35-year veteran of the agency, presented a 98-page analysis concluding that the science behind man-made global warming is inconclusive at best and that the agency should re-examine its findings. His analysis noted that global temperatures were on a downward trend. It pointed out problems with climate models. It highlighted new research about climate change that contradicts apocalyptic scenarios. "We believe our concerns and reservations are sufficiently important to warrant a serious review of the science by EPA," the report read.

In response to the report Carlin's boss, Al McGartland, emailed him, forbidding him from engaging in "any direct communication" with anyone outside his office about his analysis. In a follow-up email, McGartland wrote, "With the endangerment finding nearly final, you need to move on to other issues and subjects. I don't want you to spend any additional EPA

340. Monte Hieb, "Climate and the Carboniferous Period," Plant Fossils of West Virginia, March 21, 2009, http://www.geocraft.com/WVFossils/Carboniferous_climate.html

time on climate change. No papers, no research, etc, at least until we see what EPA is going to do with Climate."[341] These emails were leaked. So much for transparency, and so much for science.

There is an interesting parallel here with the issue of chlorine, a chemical described by Greenpeace as the "devil's element." There are some chlorine-based chemicals that are very toxic and should be tightly controlled and even banned in certain contexts. But as discussed earlier, chlorine is the most important element for public health and medicine, just as carbon is the most important element for life. And yet Greenpeace and its allies give the impression these two building blocks of nature are essentially evil. It is time to bring some balance into this discussion.

Al Gore is fond of reminding us that there is more CO_2 in the atmosphere today than there has been for the past 400,000 years.[342] He may be correct, although some scientists dispute this.[343] But 400,000 years is a blink of an eye in geological history. It is also true to state that CO_2 levels in the atmosphere have rarely been as low as they are today over the entire 3.5 billion years of life on earth, and particularly during the past 500 million years since modern life forms evolved. Figure 4 (previous page) shows the historic levels of CO_2 as well as the global temperature, going back 600 million years

Note the graph shows CO_2 was at least 3000 ppm, and likely around 7000 ppm, at the time of the Cambrian Period, a Greenhouse Age when modern life forms first evolved. This is nearly 20 times the CO_2 concentration today. The Ice Age that peaked 450 million years ago occurred when CO_2 was about 4000 ppm, more than 10 times its present level. If both warm and cold climates can develop when there is far more CO_2 in the atmosphere than today, how can we be certain that CO_2 is determining the climate now?

The graph does show a limited correlation between temperature and CO_2 during the late Carboniferous, and a very weak correlation from then until today. It is true that the most recent Ice Age corresponds with a relatively low CO_2 level in the atmosphere. None of this is intended to make the argument that CO_2 does not influence climate. I am no denier. We know that CO_2 is a greenhouse gas and that it plays a role in warming the earth. The real questions are: How much of a role? and If warming is caused by our CO_2 emissions, does this really harm people and the planet?

Coming closer to the present, one of the best sets of data comes from ice cores at the Russian Vostok station in Antarctica. These cores give

341. Kimberley A. Strassel, "The EPA Silences a Climate Skeptic," *Wall Street Journal*, July 3, 2009, http://online.wsj.com/article/SB124657655235589119.html
342. Dave McArthur, "The Inconvenient Truth About *An Inconvenient Truth*," *Scoop*, July 26, 2006, http://www.scoop.co.nz/stories/HL0607/S00400.htm
343. Ernst-Georg Beck, "180 Years of Atmospheric CO_2 Gas Analysis by Chemical Methods," *Energy and Environment*, 18, no. 2 (2007), http://icecap.us/images/uploads/EE_18-2_Beck.pdf

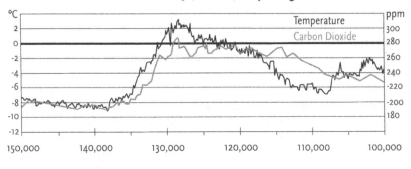

Vostok Ice Cores 150,00 - 100,000 years ago

Figure 5. Graph showing temperature and CO_2 levels from 150,000 to 100,000 years ago. Note that temperature rises ahead of a rise in CO_2.

us a picture of both temperature and atmospheric CO_2 levels going back 420,000 years. Al Gore uses this information in his film *An Inconvenient Truth* to assert that it provides evidence that increased CO_2 causes an increase in temperature. Closer examination of the data shows that it is the other way around.[344] Through most of this period it is temperature that leads CO_2 as shown for the period 150,000 to 100,000 years ago in Figure 5. When temperature goes up, CO_2 follows and when temperature goes down, CO_2 follows it down.

This does not prove that increases in temperature cause increases in CO_2, it may be that some other common factor is behind both trends. But it most certainly does not indicate rising CO_2 levels cause increases in temperature. It may be that CO_2 causes a tendency for higher temperatures but that this is masked by other, more influential factors such as water vapor, the earth's orbit and wobbles, etc.

The April 2008 edition of *Discover* magazine contains a full-page article about plants, written by Jocelyn Rice, titled, "Leaves at Work." The article begins with this passage, "In the era of global warming, leaves may display an unexpected dark side. As CO_2 concentrations rise, plants can become full. As a result, their stomata—the tiny holes that collect the CO_2...will squeeze shut. When the stomata close, plants not only take less CO_2 from the air but also draw less water from the ground, resulting in a run of water into rivers. The *stomata effect* [my emphasis] has been responsible for the 3 percent increase in river runoff seen over the past century."[345] At this point my BS meter came on. There is no possibility anyone has a data set that could determine a 3 percent increase in global

344. Joanne Nova, "Carbon Follows Temperature in the Vostok Ice Cores," JoNova, 2008–2010, http://joannenova.com.au/global-warming/ice-core-graph/

345. Jocelyn Rice, "Leaves at Work," *Discover* magazine, April 2008, p. 17 http://www.beattystreetpublishing.com/confessions/references/stomata-effect

river runoff in the past 100 years. The U.K.'s Hadley Centre for Climate Prediction and Research was given as the source of this information. A thorough review of the Hadley Centre website turned up nothing on the subject.[346]

The story goes on to predict that, given present trends in CO_2 emissions, "runoff within the next 100 years could increase by as much as 24 percent above pre-industrial levels... in regions already hit hard by flooding, the stomata effect could make matters much worse." The Great Flood will return and inundate the earth due to trillions of tiny stomata shutting their doors in the face of too much CO_2!

I also knew immediately that the entire article was bogus because I am familiar with the fact that greenhouse growers purposely divert the CO_2-rich exhaust gases from their wood or gas heaters into their greenhouses in order to greatly increase the CO_2 level for the plants they are growing. I searched the Internet using the phrase "optimum CO_2 level for plant growth." All I needed were the first few results to see plants grow best at a CO_2 concentration of around 1500 ppm, which boosts plant yield by 25 to 65 percent.[347] The present CO_2 level in the global atmosphere is about 390 ppm. In other words, the trees and other plants that grow around the world would benefit from a level of CO_2 about four times higher than it is today. There is solid evidence that trees are already showing increased growth rates due to rising CO_2 levels.[348]

Greenhouse growers are able to obtain growth rates that are 40 to 50 percent higher than the rates plants grow under in today's atmospheric conditions. This makes sense when you consider that CO_2 levels were generally much higher during the time when plant life was evolving than they are today. The fact is, at today's historically low CO_2 concentrations, all the plants on earth are CO_2-deprived. Those plants are starving out there!

Yet believers in catastrophic climate change will not abide by this clear evidence. In May 2010 Science magazine published an article titled, "Carbon Dioxide Enrichment Inhibits Nitrate Assimilation in Wheat and Arabidopsis."[349] The article implied that increased CO_2 levels in the atmosphere might inhibit the uptake of nitrogen. The popular press interpreted this as evidence that increased CO_2 might not result in increased growth rates, as has been conclusively demonstrated in hundreds of lab and field experiments.[350] This is why greenhouse growers purposely inject CO_2 into their greenhouses. Typically, the *Vancouver Sun* ran with the headline,

346. "Met Office Hadley Centre," Met Office, http://www.metoffice.gov.uk/climatechange/science/hadleycentre/

347. "Indoor Growing: Using CO_2," Planet Natural, http://www.planetnatural.com/site/xdpy/kb/implementing-co2.html

348. "Forest are Growing Faster, Climate Change Appears to be Driving Accelerated Growth," Smithsonian Environmental Research Center, February 1, 2010, http://sercblog.si.edu/?p=466

349. Arnold J. Bloom, "Carbon Dioxide Enrichment Inhibits Nitrate Assimilation in Wheat and Arabidopsis," Science 328, no. 5980 (May 14, 2010): 899-903, http://www.sciencemag.org/cgi/content/abstract/328/5980/899

350. "Plant Growth Database," CO_2 Science, http://www.co2science.org/data/plant_growth/plantgrowth.php

"Rising Carbon Dioxide Levels May Hinder Crop Growth: Greenhouse Gas Is Not Beneficial to Plants, As Once Thought."[351] The Science article was clever enough not to suggest that CO_2 would "hinder" plant growth, or even to question the proven fact that CO_2 increases plant growth. But by raising a side issue of nitrogen uptake it encouraged the media to make sensationalist claims, apparently debunking the fact that doubling, tripling, or even quadrupling CO_2 results in increased growth, regardless of some point about nitrogen.

It may turn out to be a very good thing that humans discovered fossil fuels and started burning them for energy. By the beginning of the Industrial Revolution CO_2 levels had gradually diminished to about 280 ppm. If this trend, which had been in effect for many millions of years, had continued at the same rate it would have eventually threatened plant life at a global level. At a level of 150 ppm, plants stop growing altogether. If humans had not appeared on the scene, it is possible that the declining trend in CO_2 levels that began 150 million years ago would have continued. If it had continued at the same rate, about 115 ppm per million years, it would have been a little over one million years until plants stopped growing and died. And that would be the end of that!

This is perhaps my most heretical thought: that our CO_2 emissions may be largely beneficial, possibly making the coldest places on earth more habitable and definitely increasing yields of food crops, energy crops, and forests around the entire world. Earlier I referred to my meeting with James Lovelock, the father of the Gaia Hypothesis and one of the world's leading atmospheric scientists. I found it strange he was so pessimistic about the future, and cast our species as a kind of rogue element in the scheme of life.

Whereas the Gaia Hypothesis proposes that all life on earth acts in concert to control the chemistry of the atmosphere in order to make it more suitable for life, Lovelock believes human-caused CO_2 emissions are the enemy of Gaia. But surely humans are as much a part of Gaia as any other species, past or present? How could we know we are the enemy of Gaia rather than an agent of Gaia, as one would expect if "all life is acting in concert"? In other words, is it not plausible that Gaia is using us to pump some of the trillions of tons of carbon, which have been locked in the earth's crust over the past billions of years, back into the atmosphere? Perhaps Gaia would like to avoid another major glaciation, and more importantly avoid the end of nearly all life on earth due to a lack of CO_2. One thing I know for sure is we should be a lot more worried the climate will cool by 2 or 3 degrees Celsius than we should be about it warming by 2

351. Amina Khan, "Rising Greenhouse Gas Levels May Hinder Crop Growth," *Vancouver Sun*, May 15, 2010,
http://www.vancouversun.com/health/Rising+carbon+dioxide+levels+hinder+crop+growth/3031640/story.html#ixzzOoFzR7jth

or 3 degrees Celsius. Cooling would definitely threaten our food supply; warming would almost certainly enhance it.

I'm not saying I buy into the entire Gaia Hypothesis hook, line, and sinker. I find some aspects of it very compelling, but it might be a bit of a stretch to believe all life is acting in harmony, like on the planet Pandora in the movie *Avatar*. But that's not my point. What bothers me is the tendency to see all human behavior as negative. Lovelock and his followers seem to need a narrative that supports the idea of original sin, that we have been thrown out of the Garden of Eden, or is it the Garden of Gaia?

The Hockey Stick

No discussion of climate change would be complete without mention of the infamous hockey stick graph of global temperature. The graph, said to depict Northern Hemisphere temperatures over the past 1,000 years, was created by Michael Mann of Pennsylvania State University and his colleagues. It shows a very even temperature until the modern age when there is a steep rise.[352] The surprise for many scientists was that the graph implied the Medieval Warm Period and the Little Ice Age did not exist and that the only significant change in temperature during the past 1000 years was a precipitous rise during the past century. The graph was very controversial in climate science circles. Despite the sharp debate, it was showcased in the 2001 and 2004 reports of the IPCC. [353]

Two Canadians, Steve McIntyre, a retired mining engineer, and Ross McKitrick, an economist, became concerned that the data used to create the hockey stick graph were not objective and the statistical analysis used was not legitimate. They asked Mann and others to provide them with the original data and the statistical methods used to arrive at the hockey stick graph. Mann and his colleagues at the Climatic Research Unit (CRU) at the University of East Anglia refused repeated requests to supply the data. The effort to obtain the data went on for 10 years as the researchers even refused requests under Freedom of Information Act rules. It was not until the release of thousands of emails from the CRU that it became clear information was being withheld illegally and there was a conspiracy of sorts to manipulate the data and discredit opposing opinions.

In 2003 McIntyre and McKitrick published a critique of the hockey stick graph in *Energy & Environment* in which they contended that Mann's paper contained, "collation errors, unjustifiable truncation or

352. Michael E. Mann et al., "Global-Scale Temperature Patterns and Climate Forcing Over the Past Six Centuries," *Nature* 392 (April 23, 1998). http://www.junkscience.com/MSU_Temps/PDF/mann1998.pdf
353. Suzanne Goldenberg, "'Hockey Stick' Graph Creator Michael Mann Cleared of Academic Misconduct," *Guardian*, February 3, 2010, http://www.guardian.co.uk/environment/2010/feb/03/climate-scientist-michael-mann

extrapolation of source data, obsolete data, geographical location errors, incorrect calculation of principal components and other quality control defects."[354] As a result of this and other critiques the IPCC did not use the hockey stick graph again in its 2007 report. The continuing debate over this graph highlights the absence of a consensus on the temperature record, never mind whether or not humans are responsible for climate change.

What's So Good About Glaciers, Anyway?

Much has been made of the fact that many glaciers around the world have been retreating in recent years. By many accounts we should be viewing this with alarm. The potential loss of glaciers is portrayed as an ecological catastrophe, as if it were equivalent to a species becoming extinct. In its June 2007 issue the *National Geographic* magazine reported that a certain Peruvian glacier was in a "death spiral," as if it were a living thing.[355] What should we make of this hysterical reaction to melting ice?

It is important to recognize that glaciers have been retreating for about 18,000 years, since the height of the last glaciation. It has not been a steady retreat as there have been times, such as during the Little Ice Age, when the glaciers advanced. But there is no doubt that in balance there has been a major retreat and it appears to be continuing today.

The retreat of the glaciers is largely a result of the climate becoming warmer. It brings us back to the question of whether humans are responsible for the warming or if it is just a continuation of the trend that began 18,000 years ago. Either way, we then must ask whether, in balance, this is a good thing or a bad thing. We know the climate was warmer than it is today during most of the past 500 million years, and that life flourished during these times. We also know there is very little life on, in, or under a glacier. Glaciers are essentially dead zones, proof that ice is the enemy of life.

When a glacier retreats up the valley it carved, the bedrock and gravels are exposed to light and air. Seeds find their way there, on the wind and in bird droppings, and can germinate and grow. Before long the lifeless barrens become a newly developing ecosystem full of lichens, mosses, ferns, flowering plants, and eventually, trees. Isn't it fairly obvious that this is a better environmental condition than a huge blob of frozen water that kills everything beneath it? Glaciers certainly are photogenic, but as we dis-

---

354. Stephen McIntyre and Ross McKitrick, "Corrections to the Mann et al. (1998) Proxy Data Base and Northern Hemispheric Average Temperature Series," *Energy & Environment* 14, no. 6 (2003): 751-771,
http://www.uoguelph.ca/~rmckitri/research/MM03.pdf
355. Tim Appenzeller, "The Big Thaw," *National Geographic*, June 2007,
http://ngm.nationalgeographic.com/2007/06/big-thaw/big-thaw-text

cussed in the chapter on forests, you can't judge the health of an ecosystem by the fact that it looks pretty. Sand dunes make for nice scenery too, but they aren't very welcome when they bury a town and kill all the crops.

Much attention has been focused on the Greenland ice cap, virtually one big glacier with many arms to the sea. During the warming that occurred in the 1980s and 1990s it was reported that the Greenland ice cap was melting rapidly. Al Gore predicted the sea might rise by 20 feet in the next century, apparently assuming the entire ice cap might melt in 100 years.[356] This is a physical impossibility. The high elevation and extreme low temperatures dictate that it would take at least thousands of years for the glaciers of Greenland to disappear.

More recently the focus has been on the Himalayan glaciers, the largest ice cap outside the Polar Regions. The story of what has become "Glaciergate" helps to illustrate the present very confused state of climate science and of how important glaciers are, or are not. The 2007 report of the IPCC, its fourth report, stated Himalayan glaciers may be completely gone by 2035, less than 25 years from now.[357][358] The report warned, "if the present rate continues, the likelihood of them disappearing by the year 2035 and perhaps sooner is very high if the Earth keeps warming at the current rate." It was not until the lead-up to the 2009 Kyoto Protocol meeting in Copenhagen that scientists began to question this assertion. The Ministry of the Environment in India published a paper rejecting the 2035 prediction, stating that it would be hundreds of years before the glaciers melted, even if the present warming trend continued.[359] This caused the chairman of the IPCC, Dr. Rajendra Pachauri, who happens to be Indian, to denounce the Environment Ministry's report as "voodoo science."[360]

It was not until after the Copenhagen conference that the IPCC published an admission of error. They stated, "In drafting the paragraph in question, the clear and well-established standards of evidence, required by the IPCC procedures, were not applied properly."[361] Yet Dr. Pachauri refused to apologize for calling the Environment Ministry's report "voodoo science."[362] It was revealed that the 2035 date was based

356. Jeffrey Masters, "Al Gore's *An Inconvenient Truth*," Weather Underground, http://www.wunderground.com/education/gore.asp
357. "The Himalayan Glaciers," Intergovernmental Panel on Climate Change, 2007,
http://www.ipcc.ch/publications_and_data/ar4/wg2/en/ch10s10-6-2.html
358. "IPCC Slips on the Ice with Statement About Himalayan Glaciers," climatesciencewatch.org, January 19, 2010,
http://www.climatesciencewatch.org/index.php/csw/details/ipcc_slips_on_the_ice/
359. V. K. Raina, "Himalayan Glaciers," Science & Public Policy Institute, November 12, 2009,
http://scienceandpublicpolicy.org/reprint/himalayan_review_of_glacial_studies.html
360. "Pachauri Calls Indian Govt. Report on Melting Himalayan Glaciers as 'Voodoo Science,'" *Thaindian News*, January 9, 2010,
http://www.thaindian.com/newsportal/health/pachauri-calls-indian-govt-report-on-melting-himalayan-glaciers-as-voodoo-science_100301232.html
361. "Worldwide Glacier Melt a Real Concern; Himalaya Controversy Leaves Questions About IPCC Leadership, climatescience-watch.org, January 21, 2010, http://www.climatesciencewatch.org/index.php/csw/details/glacier-melt-ipcc-controversy/
362. "Pachauri Won't Apologies [sic.], Admits IPCC's Credibility Damaged," *India Post*, February 3, 2010,
http://www.indiapost.com/international-news/6964-Pachauri-wont-apologies-admits-IPCCs-credibility-damaged.html

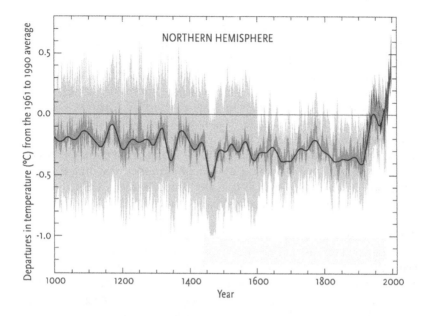

Figure 6. The Michael Mann Hockey Stick Graph as it appeared in the 2001 Assessment Report of the Intergovernmental Panel on Climate Change. 363

on an interview by *New Scientist* magazine of a single Indian scientist, who subsequently admitted his statement was "speculative."[364] The *New Scientist* article was then referred to in a 2005 WWF report on glaciers, which was cited as the only reference in support of the 2035 date.[365]

This has caused something of a crisis of credibility for the IPCC, which had insisted all its predictions were based on peer-reviewed science. As it turns out, the most credible scientists who specialize in the subject of Himalayan glaciers believe it would take at least 300 years for them to melt completely, even if it continues to get warmer. Other indefensible statements in the IPCC report then emerged regarding the disappearance of the Amazon rain forest[366] and the collapse of agricultural production in Africa.[367]

363. "Working Group I: The Scientific Basis," Intergovernmental Panel on Climate Change, 2001,
http://www.ipcc.ch/ipccreports/tar/wg1/005.htm
364. Fred Pearce, Debate Heats Up Over IPCC Melting Glaciers Claim, *New Scientist*, January 11, 2010,
http://www.newscientist.com/article/dn18363-debate-heats-up-over-ipcc-melting-glaciers-claim.html
365. Jonathan Leake and Chris Hastings, "World Misled Over Himalayan Glacier Meltdown," *Sunday Times*, January 17, 2010,
http://www.timesonline.co.uk/tol/news/environment/article6991177.ece
366. Christopher Booker, "Amazongate: New Evidence of the IPCC's Failures," *Telegraph*, January 30, 2010,
http://www.telegraph.co.uk/comment/columnists/christopherbooker/7113582/Amazongate-new-evidence-of-the-IPCCs-failures.html
367. Lawrence Solomon, "Climategate Is One of Many Known IPCC Failings," *Financial Post*, February 26, 2010,
http://network.nationalpost.com/np/blogs/fpcomment/archive/2010/02/06/392245.aspx

Perhaps the most bizarre case of logical disconnect in the climate change hysteria involves the predictions of disaster if the Himalayan glaciers continue to melt. Lester Brown, president of the Earth Policy Institute, predicts that if this happens there will be mass starvation in Asia.[368] The theory goes like this: the meltwater from the glaciers is essential for irrigation of food crops throughout much of Asia. The Ganges, Indus, Mekong, Yellow, Yangtze, and many other rivers flow from the Himalayas, providing water for over one-third of the human population. If these glaciers were to melt completely, there would be no more meltwater for irrigation, and so food production would plummet, resulting in mass starvation. This seems plausible to many people and has been repeated countless times in the media as another "catastrophic" aspect of climate change.

After hearing Lester Brown speak at length about this doomsday scenario, it dawned on me that his thesis was illogical. On the one hand he is saying the meltwater (from the melting glaciers) is essential for food production, and on the other hand he insists that we must try to stop the glaciers from melting so they will not disappear. Obviously if the glaciers stop melting, there will be no more meltwater from them. So my questions for Lester Brown, and the IPCC, are, Are you saying you want the glaciers to stop melting? Then where would the irrigation water come from? I might add, How about if the glaciers started growing again, reducing water flows even further, perhaps advancing on the towns where the food is grown?

It has since been revealed that only 3 to 4 percent of the water flowing into the Ganges River is glacial meltwater. Ninety-six percent of the river flow is from snow that fell in the previous winter and melted in the summer, and from rainfall during monsoons.[369] Therefore the people will not likely starve if the glaciers melt completely. A warmer world with higher CO_2 concentrations, and likely more precipitation, will allow expansion of agricultural land and will result in faster-growing, more productive crops. Forests and crops will grow where now there is only a sheet of ice. I say let the glaciers melt.

Arctic and Antarctic Sea Ice

The Arctic and Antarctic regions are polar opposites in more ways than one. Whereas the Arctic is mainly an ocean surrounded by continents, the Antarctic is a large continent, almost centered on the South Pole, surrounded by seas. The Antarctic is colder than the Arctic largely due

---

368. Lester R. Brown, "Melting Mountain Glaciers Will Shrink Grain Harvests in China and India," Earth Policy Institute, March 20, 2008, http://www.earthpolicy.org/index.php?/plan_b_updates/2008/update71
369. Palava Bagla, "No Sign of Himalayan Meltdown, Indian Report Finds," Observatory, November 15, 2009, http://www.thegwpf.org/the-observatory/91-no-sign-of-himalayan-meltdown-indian-report-finds.html

to its high elevation.[370] The Antarctic ice sheet began to form 20 million years ago and has been a permanent fixture since then, advancing and retreating with the pulses of glaciation over the past 2.5 million years during the Pleistocene Ice Age. The Arctic was largely ice-free until the onset of the Pleistocene and since then has had varying degrees of ice cover as glacial periods have waxed and waned.

Much has been made recently of the fact that the extent of summer sea ice in the Arctic has shrunk substantially. In September of 2007, typically the low month after summer melting, there was about three million square kilometers of ice cover, about two million less than the average since records were first made. Many pundits immediately predicted that the Arctic would be ice-free in the summer within 20 to 30 years, and that this would be our fault entirely. The fact that the area of ice recovered by about one million square kilometers in 2008 and again in 2009 didn't dampen the shrillness of their predictions. In September of 2012 the extent if ice cover again reached a record low, but winter ice cover continued to remain relatively steady, close to the average since measurements began.

Our knowledge of the extent of sea ice in the Arctic and Antarctic began in 1979, the first year satellites were used to photograph the Polar Regions on a continual basis. Before 1979 it is not possible to reconstruct the comings and goings of sea ice, as unlike glaciers, sea ice leaves no trace when it melts. There is an implicit assumption among the true believers that the reduction in sea ice observed in 2007 and 2012 is unique in the historical record and that we are now on a one-way trip to an ice-free Arctic Sea (see Figure 7 on next page). Putting aside the fact that mariners consider an ice-free sea a good thing, it is not possible to conclude a long-term trend in the extent of Arctic sea ice from 30 years of satellite observation.

Between 1903 and 1905 the Norwegian Raold Amundsen became the first person to navigate the Northwest Passage in a 47-ton sailing ship equipped with a small gasoline motor.[371] We do not know the extent of ice over the entire Arctic at that time but the fact that a small boat could sail through the passage indicates the present era was not the only time the area of ice was reduced.

Between 1940 and 1944, years before we had any idea of the extent of sea ice during the summers and winters, a small Canadian trawler name the *St. Roch* navigated the Northwest Passage twice, from west to east and from east to west.[372] [373] It was not an icebreaker and it had only a 150-horsepower diesel engine and sails. From 1910 to 1940 there was a well-documented rise in the average global temperature of nearly half

370. "Antarctic Climate," Wikipedia, http://en.wikipedia.org/wiki/Antarctica#Climate
371. "Roald Amundsen," Wikipedia, http://en.wikipedia.org/wiki/Roald_Amundsen
372. Noel Sheppard, "Reports of Record Arctic Ice Melt Disgracefully Ignore History," NewsBusters, September 9, 2007, http://newsbusters.org/blogs/noel-sheppard/2007/09/09/reports-record-arctic-ice-melt-disgracefully-ignore-history
373. "Second Through the Passage, First West to East," Athropolis, http://www.athropolis.com/arctic-facts/fact-st-roch.htm

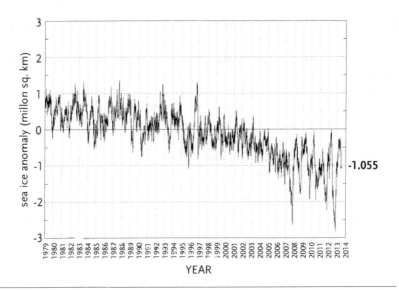

Figure 7. *Northern Hemisphere Sea Ice Anomaly (1979–2008 mean).* The extent of sea ice in the Arctic showed a clear downward trend from 1995 to 2007. Since 2007 it has recovered by about one-third over the lowest area. Only time will tell what the trend will be in the coming decades.

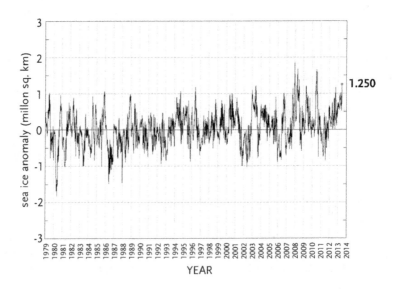

Figure 8. *Southern Hemisphere Sea Ice Anomaly (1979–2008 mean).* Graph showing the deviance from the 1979 to 2008 average extent of sea ice in the Antarctic. The winter of 2007 saw the greatest extent of Antarctic sea ice since measurements were first taken, coincident with the least extent in the Arctic. Whereas the extent of Arctic sea ice has shown a recent downward trend, the extent of Antarctic sea ice has shown an upward trend.

CONFESSIONS OF A GREENPEACE DROPOUT

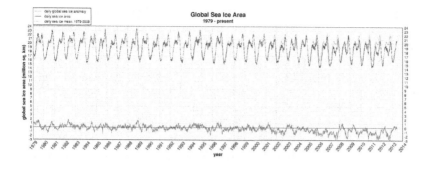

Figure 9. Global sea ice level, 1979 to present. The top line shows the total sea ice cover for the Arctic and the Antarctic. The bottom line shows the divergence from the mean of Arctic and Antarctic sea ice cover. As you can see, there is no significant trend when Arctic and Antarctic sea ice areas are added together.

a degree Celsius. There is every possibility that Arctic ice was as reduced when the *St. Roch* sailed through the passage as it has been in recent years. We will never know.

While all the media's and activist's attention has been on Arctic sea ice, the Antarctic has been playing out its own history in a very different way. The winter sea ice around Antarctica has grown above the average from 1979 to 2008 (See Figure 8). This has proven problematic for believers as it indicates Antarctica is cooling, contrary to what they have been led to believe by predictions based on computer models. In December 2008 *Nature* published an article claiming the Antarctic was warming.[374] Many climate activists, including Al Gore, seized on this article to bolster their belief in human-caused warming.[375] It turned out that the *Nature* article had been largely based on a computer model rather than real measurements of temperature. This represented another turning point in the questioning of the science used to claim humans were definitely causing the earth to warm up.[376]

In 2009 the U.S. Geological Survey (USGS) published a paper in which it reported sea ice had retreated in one part of the Antarctic Peninsula.[377] The paper made it clear that ice was growing in other parts of Antarctica and it was not clear whether the total amount of ice on and around the continent was shrinking or growing. In Greenpeace-like fashion the USGS then issued a media release claiming the sea ice was "disappearing" in Antarctica and that sea level rise was imminent.[378] News services

374. Eric J. Steig et al., "Warming of the Antarctic Ice-Sheet Surface Since the 1957 International Geophysical Year," *Nature* 457 (22 January 2009): 459–462, http://www.nature.com/nature/journal/v457/n7228/abs/nature07669.html

375. Al Gore, "The Antarctic Is Warming," February 5, 2009, http://blog.algore.com/2009/02/the_antarctic_is_warming.html

376. Christopher Booker, "Despite the Hot Air the Antarctic Is Not Warming Up," *Telegraph*, January 24, 2009, ...

... http://www.telegraph.co.uk/comment/columnists/christopherbooker/4332784/Despite-the-hot-air-the-Antarctic-is-not-warming-up.html

377. Ferrigno, J.G, Coastal-Change and Glaciological Map of the Palmer Land Area, Antarctica: 1947–2009,"
U.S. Geological Survey, 2009, http://pubs.usgs.gov/imap/i-2600-c/

378. "Ice Shelves Disappearing on Antarctic Peninsula: Glacier Retreat and Sea Level Rise Are Possible Consequences," U.S. Geological Survey Newsroom, February 22, 2010, http://www.usgs.gov/newsroom/article.asp?ID=2409&from=rss_home

picked up this story, which gave the impression Antarctica was melting away. Perhaps the USGS scientists feel the need to sensationalize their otherwise good research in order to get more funding. I don't know, but it certainly misleads the public about what is really happening down there.

The University of Illinois' website, *The Cryosphere Today*, contains the entire record of sea ice since 1979.[379] (The Cryosphere is the area of the earth covered with ice.) Figure 9 (on previous page) shows the global sea ice cover, adding together the Arctic and the Antarctic, from 1979 until the present.[380] This is our total knowledge of the history of sea ice cover on planet Earth. There is no obvious trend up or down because increased ice cover in the Antarctic offsets most of the reduced ice cover in the Arctic. So even the very short record we do have for global sea ice cover provides no evidence of rapid global warming.

Coral Reefs, Shellfish, and "Ocean Acidification"

It has been widely reported in the media, based on a few scientific papers, that the increasing levels of CO_2 in the atmosphere will result in "ocean acidification," threatening coral reefs and all marine shellfish with extinction within 20 years.[381] The story goes like this: The oceans absorb about 25 percent of the CO_2 we emit into the atmosphere each year. The higher the CO_2 content of the atmosphere, the more CO_2 will be absorbed by the oceans. When CO_2 is dissolved in water, some of it is converted into carbonic acid that has a weak acidic effect. If the sea becomes more acidic, it will dissolve the calcium carbonate that is the main constituent of coral and the shells of clams, shrimp, crabs, etc. It is one more doomsday scenario, predicting the seas will "degrade into a useless tidal desert,"[382]

In his latest book, *Eaarth: Making a Life on a Tough New Planet*, Bill McKibben claims, "Already the ocean is more acid than anytime in the last 800,000 years, and at current rates by 2050 it will be more corrosive than anytime in the past 20 million years." In typical hyperbolic fashion, McKibben, the author of the well-know essay, "The End of Nature," uses the words *acid* and *corrosive* as if the ocean will burn off your skin and flesh to the bone if you dare swim in it in 2050. This is just plain fear-mongering.

Results of research published in the journal *Science* by M.R. Palmer et al., indicate that over the past 15 million years, "All five samples record surface seawater pH values that are within the range observed in the oceans today, and they all show a decrease in the calculated pH with depth that

379. "The Cryosphere Today," Polar Research Group, University of Illinois, http://arctic.atmos.uiuc.edu/cryosphere/
380. "Global Sea Ice Area: 1979 to Present," Polar Research Group, University of Illinois, http://arctic.atmos.uiuc.edu/cryosphere/IMAGES/global.daily.ice.area.withtrend.jpg
381. Frank Pope, "Great Barrier Reef Will Be Gone in 20 Years, Says Charlie Veron," *Sunday Times*, July 7, 2009, http://www.timesonline.co.uk/tol/news/environment/article6652866.ece
382. Richard Girling, "The Toxic Sea," *Sunday Times*, March 8, 2009, http://www.timesonline.co.uk/tol/news/environment/article5853261.ece#cid=OTC-RSS&attr=3392178

is similar to that observed in the present-day equatorial Pacific." The five samples recorded pH values for 85,000 years ago and for 2.5, 6.4, 12.1, and 15.7 million years ago.[383]

First, one should point out that the ocean is not acidic, it has a pH of 8.1, which is alkaline, the opposite of acidic. A pH of 7 is neutral, below 7 is acidic, above 7 is alkaline. Researchers have reported in scientific journals that the pH of the seas has gone down by 0.075 over the past 250 years, "Between 1751 and 1994 surface ocean pH is estimated to have decreased from approximately 8.179 to 8.104 (a change of −0.075)."[384] One has to wonder how the pH of the ocean was measured to an accuracy of three decimal places in 1751 when the concept of pH was not introduced until 1909.[385]

It turns out that just as with climate science in general, these predictions are based on computer models. But oceans are not simple systems whose components can just be plugged into a computer. First, there is the complex mix of elements and salts dissolved in the sea. Every element on Earth is present in seawater and these elements interact in complex ways. Then there is the biological factor, tens of thousands of species that are consuming and excreting every day. The salt content of seawater gives the oceans a very large buffering capacity against change in pH. Small additions of acidic and alkaline substances can easily alter the pH of freshwater, whereas seawater can neutralize large additions of acidic and alkaline substances.

One of the most important biological phenomena in the sea is the combining of calcium, carbon, and oxygen to form calcium carbonate, $CaCO_3$, the primary constituent of corals and shells, including the skeletons of microscopic plankton. The formation of calcium carbonate is called calcification. All of the vast chalk, limestone, and marble deposits in the earth's crust are composed of calcium carbonate, which was created and deposited by marine organisms over millions of years. The carbon in calcium carbonate is derived from CO_2 dissolved in seawater. One might therefore imagine that an increase in CO_2 in seawater would enhance calcification rather than destroy it. It turns out this is precisely the case.

As is the case with terrestrial plants, it has been thoroughly demonstrated that increased CO_2 concentration in the sea results in higher rates of photosynthesis and faster growth. Photosynthesis has the effect of increasing the pH of the water, making it more alkaline, counteracting any minor acidic effect of the CO_2 itself.[386] The owners of saltwater aquariums

383. M. R. Palmer et al., "Reconstructing Past Ocean pH-Depth Profiles," Science 282, no. 5393 (November 20, 1998): 1468–1471, http://www.scienceonline.org/cgi/content/short/282/5393/1468 (Register with Science to see full article free-of-charge)
384. James C. Orr et al., "Anthropogenic Ocean Acidification Over the Twenty-First Century and Its Impact on Calcifying Organisms," Nature 437 (September 29, 2005): 681–686, http://www.ipsl.jussieu.fr/~jomce/acidification/paper/Orr_OnlineNature04095.pdf
385. "pH," Wikipedia, http://en.wikipedia.org/wiki/PH
386. "Acid Test: The Global Challenge of Ocean Acidification—A New Propaganda Film by The National Resources Defense Council

often add CO_2 to the water in order to increase photosynthesis and calcification, a practice that is similar to greenhouse growers adding CO_2 to the air in their greenhouses to promote the faster growth of plants. The vast bulk of scientific literature indicates increased CO_2 in the ocean will actually result in increased growth and calcification, as opposed to the catastrophe scenario pushed by the NRDC, Greenpeace, and many other activist organizations.[387][388]

A long list of scientific publications that support the view that increased CO_2 in seawater results in increased calcification can be found on the CO_2 Science website.[389] A paper by Atkinson et al., published in the journal *Coral Reefs*, states that their finding "seems to contradict conclusions ... that high CO_2 may inhibit calcification."[390]

"Ocean acidification" is a perfect example of a contrived catastrophe scenario. The average person does not have a grasp of the complexities of marine chemistry and biology. The activists simply coin a new, scary term like "acidification" and then effectively extort money from people who are concerned for the future. And all this emphasis on the dangers of CO_2 tends to divert people from thinking about the real dangers to coral reefs like destructive fishing methods and pollution from sewage.

Our little house by the Sea of Cortez in Cabo Pulmo in southern Baja, Mexico, looks out over a National Marine Park that contains the only large coral reef on the west coast of the Americas. Pulmo Reef is a popular dive site, known for its rich abundance of reef fish, many of which school in the thousands. It was after a dive on the reef during our first visit to Cabo Pulmo in 1999 that Eileen and I decided to make a base there. Since then we have dived and snorkeled on the reef many times each year.

In September of 2002 a tropical storm brought torrential rains that dumped over 20 inches of rainfall in a 24-hour period. It must have been a once in a 100-year event as the flooding was the worst the locals could remember. A lens of freshwater about 20 feet deep spread out over the reef as a result of the runoff from the mountains. This killed all the coral, as coral cannot live in freshwater. Only the corals below the 20-foot depth of the freshwater layer survived.

Fails the Acid Test," Science & Public Policy Institute, January 5, 2010,
http://scienceandpublicpolicy.org/images/stories/papers/originals/acid_test.pdf
387. "Ocean Acidification: The Other CO_2 Problem," Natural Resources Defense Council, September 17, 2009,
http://www.nrdc.org/oceans/acidification/default.asp
388. "Putting a Stop to the Arctic Meltdown," Greenpeace International, January 26, 2010,
http://www.greenpeace.org/international/news/hands-off-the-arctic-260110
389. "CO_2, Global Warming and *Coral Reefs*: Prospects for the Future," CO_2 *Science*,
http://www.co2science.org/education/reports/corals/part2ref.php
390. Atkinson, M.J., Carlson, B.A. and Crow, G.L. 1995, "Coral Growth in High-Nutrient, Low-pH Seawater: A Case Study of Corals Cultured at the Waikiki Aquarium, Honolulu, Hawaii," *Coral Reefs* 14, no. 4, pp. 215-223,
http://www.springerlink.com/content/g2554037454q13wp/

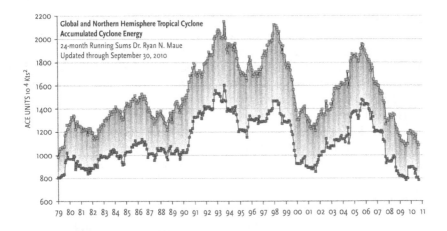

Figure 10. Global and Northern Hemisphere tropical cyclone energy 1979 to 2010. Since the peak during the 1990s, the frequency and intensity of tropical cyclones has diminished considerably.[391]

For a few years after the event virtually no living coral could be seen in the shallower waters. The reef turned white and became covered in green algae, which in turn resulted in an explosion of sea urchins where there had been very few before. By 2006 the reef began to recover noticeably with nodules of new coral becoming established. Coral polyps from the deeper regions of the reef were recolonizing the shallow waters. The sea urchins died out and fish returned in greater abundance. Today the reef is in full recovery as the coral is now growing substantially each year. It may take another 20 years or more to recover completely, and will only do so if there is not another torrential rainstorm.

I imagine some people who believe we are causing catastrophic climate change would suggest we were responsible for the torrential rains that killed part of the reef. I don't believe we can be so certain, especially as such events have been occurring since long before humans began emitting billions of tons of CO_2 each year. And regardless of the storm's cause, it is comforting to know that the reef can recover despite the dire predictions of the early death of coral reefs worldwide.

Storms, Hurricanes, and Severe Weather Events

Everyone likes to talk about the weather and climate activists are no exception. In the aftermath of Hurricane Katrina in 2005, which caused so much devastation to New Orleans and the surrounding regions, Al Gore

391. Ryan Maue, "Ryan N. Maue's 2010 Global Tropical Cyclone Activity Update," Florida State University, http://www.coaps.fsu.edu/~maue/tropical/

gave a rousing speech in which he predicted hurricanes would continue to become more frequent and more severe as global warming intensified.[392] Since that speech the intensity of global hurricanes has diminished by about half from the peak years of 1993 and 1998. Still, on the cover of his 2009 book, *Our Choice: A Plan to Solve the Climate Crisis*, Al Gore had four fake hurricanes airbrushed onto a photo of the earth from space.[393] [394] He continues to push the fear of hurricanes when it has become clear there is no longer any basis for such concern. In fact, scientists at the U.S. National Hurricane Center predict that global warming will result in not more but fewer hurricanes.[395] Al Gore must be aware of this.

Sea Level Rise

There is conclusive proof that increased CO_2 levels will be good for plants both on the land and in the sea. If increased CO_2 does make the world warmer, it will almost certainly make it wetter, which will also be good for plants and most animals, including us. Then what is so bad about global warming anyway, whether it is natural or caused by humans? The prospect that sea levels will rise in a warmer world is the main drawback as this would threaten the infrastructure we have built in low-lying coastal areas.

The seal level has fluctuated a great deal during the Pleistocene, as ice sheets have advanced and retreated and as temperatures have risen and fallen. At the height of the last glaciation, which ended 18,000 years ago, the sea was about 120 meters (nearly 400 feet) lower than it is today (See Figure 11). There was relatively rapid glacial melting and subsequent sea level rise between 15,000 and 6000 years ago as large, lower elevation ice sheets melted and disappeared. During the past 6000 years, the rise has been slower but steady. In recent times the sea level has risen by about 20 centimeters (8 inches) per century.[396]

Clearly human activity was not responsible for the end of the last glaciation, subsequent warming, and the retreat of the world's glaciers during the past 18,000 years. To date we have no indication that the rate of sea level rise is increasing, whether by natural causes or by our impact on climate. Many predictions of future sea level rise have been based on computer models. In its 2007 report the IPCC predicted sea level would rise between 18 and 59 centimeters (7 to 23 inches) during the

392. Al Gore, "On Katrina, Global Warming," Common Dreams, December 12, 2005,
http://www.commondreams.org/views05/0912-32.htm
393. Al Gore, *Our Choice: A Plan to Solve the Climate Crisis*, (Rodale Press, November 2009). http://ourchoicethebook.com/
394. Noel Sheppard, "Al Gore Photoshops Hurricanes Into New Book's Cover," Newsbusters, November 19, 2009,
http://newsbusters.org/blogs/noel-sheppard/2009/11/19/al-gore-photoshops-hurricanes-new-books-cover?page=1
395. Jonathan Leake, "UN's Climate Link to Hurricanes in Doubt," *Sunday Times*, February 28, 2010,
http://www.timesonline.co.uk/tol/news/environment/article7044158.ece
396. "Current Sea Level Rise," Wikipedia, http://en.wikipedia.org/wiki/Current_sea_level_rise

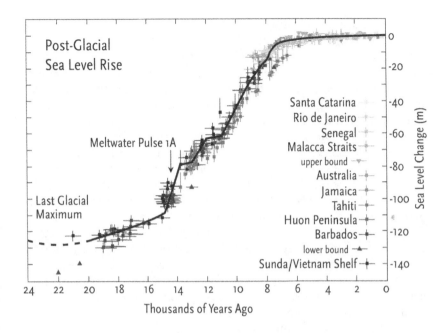

Figure 11. Graph showing that sea level was 120 meters (nearly 400 feet) lower at the height of the last glaciation.[397]

next century. The low end is entirely reasonable as this is about equal to the present rate. The high end is three times the present rate and would require a considerable amount of warming during this century. As yet there has been no warming in this century and sea level rise has not been increasing.

If the sea were to rise nearly two feet as the IPCC suggests in its extreme case, there would be disruptions to infrastructure and related activities. While natural ecosystems would adapt with little difficulty, coastal infrastructure would definitely be impacted negatively, especially our wharfs, buildings, farms, and industries. It wouldn't matter whether or not the sea level rise was due to natural or human causes.

The 120-meter (400-foot) sea level rise during the past 18,000 years did not damage the environment and was not a significant factor in human survival. We have managed to cope with the 20-centimeter (8-inch) rise over the past century. But we have built vastly more coastal infrastructure over the past century than we have in all of human history, and we will continue to do so during the next century.

What should we do about this? Is it wise to assume we are the cause of sea level rise and then to end the activities we think are responsible? Or

397. "Post-Glacial Sea Level," Wikipedia, http://en.wikipedia.org/wiki/File:Post-Glacial_Sea_Level.png"

would it make more sense to plan for a sea level rise of, say, 30 centimeters (12 inches) over the next century. If we are not the cause of sea level rise, which I believe is likely, then there is not much we can do to stop it anyway. If we plan for continued sea level rise at 50 percent above the present rate, we could avoid all or most damage by thinking ahead. We could build the dykes a little higher, not develop suburbs in areas that are susceptible to sea level rise, and generally plan our infrastructure to withstand sea level rise. How could that cause more negative impacts than an 80 percent or larger reduction in fossil fuel use worldwide in the next decade?

I repeat my assertion that we should make an effort to reduce our reliance on fossil fuels and switch to alternatives where this is technologically feasible and reasonably cost-effective. But anything approaching an 80 percent reduction in fossil fuel use over the next decade or two would do more to destroy our civilization than any plausible impact of climate change, even if we were responsible for it. Yet that is what many climate activists, including Greenpeace and Al Gore, are calling for. I believe there are more practical and logical steps that can be taken to find a balance between our environmental, social, and economic priorities. I believe it would be possible to reduce fossil fuel use by 80 percent over the next 50 to 75 years, but we must consider the economic and social cost of doing so.

Pacific Islands and Sea Level Rise

Climate change activists have made great fanfare about the possibility that many island states, such as the Marshall Islands, Kiribati, Tuvalu, and the Maldives, will be inundated and disappear due to rising sea levels caused by human-induced climate change.[398] The government of the Maldives has made the case that rich, carbon-emitting industrial nations should provide financial compensation for the loss of their countries. None of the projections of sinking island states has taken into account the fact that most of them are built on coral reefs and atolls and that coral reefs are alive. A recent survey of 27 Pacific Islands, comparing aerial photographs from up to 61 years ago with current photographs, demonstrated that 23 islands maintained the same land area or increased in size, while only four islands suffered a net loss in size. [399] [400] During this period there was

398. "Sea Level Rise Will Claim Island States." Seaweb, Vol. 15, no. 7 (April 6, 2010),
http://www.seaweb.org/news/ou15_7.php#sealevel
399. "Tuvalu and Many Other South Pacific Islands are Not Sinking, claims they are Due to Global Warming Driven Sea Level Rise are Opportunistic," Watts Up With That, Anthony Watts, June 2, 2010,
http://wattsupwiththat.com/2010/06/02/tuvalu-and-many-other-south-pacific-islands-are-not-sinking-claims-they-are-due-to-global-warming-driven-sea-level-rise-are-opportunistic/
400. "Pacific Islands 'Growing not Shrinking' Due to Climate Change," Paul Chapman, the Telegraph, June 3, 2010,
http://www.telegraph.co.uk/news/worldnews/australiaandthepacific/tuvalu/7799503/Pacific-islands-growing-not-shrinking-due-to-climate-change.html

a rise in sea level of 2 mm per year. This indicates that the coral is able to grow as fast or faster than the rising sea, and that coral islands grow as a result of coral breaking off and forming reefs that in turn catch more coral and grow in size. Many of the coral islands in the tropics have existed for thousands of years, while during that time the sea has risen by hundreds of feet. It is therefore likely that yet another doomsday scenario regarding the impact of climate change is wildly overblown and may actually have no impact even if the sea does continue to rise.

The "Trick" to "Hide the Decline"

The most quoted email among the thousands released from the Climatic Research Unit, which led to the "Climategate" crisis, was one from the CRU's head, Phil Jones, referring to "Mike's *Nature* trick...to hide the decline."[401][402] Mike is Michael Mann, the creator of the infamous and, to many, discredited hockey stick graph. *Nature* is the science journal that shows a marked bias in support of human-caused climate change. The "trick" was to discard tree-ring data that did not fit the true believer's bias, data that showed a drop in temperature in recent decades. These climate scientists clearly colluded to hide the data that showed the decline and to substitute data that indicated unprecedented warming over the past 50 years.

In response to the "Climategate" emails the U.K. House of Commons Science and Technology Committee held hearings to determine if Phil Jones and his staff at the Climatic Research Unit had done anything untoward. They concluded that "trick" and "hide the decline" were "colloquial terms used in private emails and the balance of evidence is that they were not part of a systematic attempt to mislead."[403][404] This is an obvious whitewash, because whether or not they are colloquial terms, "trick" means "trick" and "hide the decline" means "hide the decline." The committee did not provide an explanation of what it thought the terms meant in a "colloquial" context. It is amazing what deceptions can be perpetrated in broad daylight by people in responsible positions.

Another "independent inquiry" conducted by the University of East Anglia, where the Climatic Research Unit is housed, and supported by the Royal Society, concluded with the statement, "We saw no evidence of

401. Steve McIntyre, "IPCC and the 'Trick'," climateaudit.org, December 10, 2009,
http://climateaudit.org/2009/12/10/ipcc-and-the-trick/
402. Terry Hurlbut, "Context for 'Hide the Decline' Discovered," examiner.com, December 10, 2009,
http://www.examiner.com/x-28973-Essex-County-Conservative-Examiner~y2009m12d10-Context-for-hide-the-decline-discovered
403. "The Disclosure of Climate Data From the Climatic Research Unit at the University of East Anglia," Science and Technology Committee, U.K. Government, March 31, 2010, http://www.parliament.uk/parliamentary_committees/science_technology/s_t_cru_inquiry.cfm
404. "British Parliamentary Inquiry Clears 'Climategate' Scientists," Environmental News Service, March 31, 2010,
http://www.ens-newswire.com/ens/mar2010/2010-03-31-02.html

any deliberate scientific malpractice in any of the work of the Climatic Research Unit."[405] The inquiry was headed by Lord Oxburgh, who has deep personal and financial interests in climate policy. He is the chair of a multinational wind energy company and the chair of the Carbon Capture and Storage Association.[406] Missing from the inquiry's report is the fact that the inquiry did not examine the "Climategate" emails or consider evidence from anyone other than the CRU staff. In this report the "trick" "to hide the decline" was not even mentioned; never mind the many other indications of impropriety that were contained in the emails.[407] Phil Jones himself clearly requested that his colleagues delete previous emails containing damaging information.[408]

The Enigmatic Dr. Lovelock

James Lovelock is one of the most insightful and at the same time most enigmatic of scientists. He is certainly one of the leading experts on atmospheric chemistry. Earlier passages in this book have shown Lovelock to be profoundly pessimistic about the future of civilization and the earth's environment. In an interview in 2006, he stated, "We have given Gaia a fever and soon her condition will worsen to a state like a coma...Before this century is over, billions of us will die, and the few breeding pairs of people that survive will be in the Arctic where the climate remains tolerable... a broken rabble led by brutal war lords".[409] [410] Nice visuals! Cue James Cameron! I feel a Hollywood blockbuster coming on. Yet recently, in the wake of the "Climategate" scandal and the failure of the Copenhagen climate summit, Lovelock has had some change of heart.

Speaking at the London Science Museum in March 2010 Lovelock said, "It is worth thinking that what we are doing in creating all these carbon emissions, far from being something frightful, is stopping the onset of a new ice age.... If we hadn't appeared on the earth, it would be due to go through another ice age and we can look at our part as holding that up. I hate all this business about feeling guilty about what we're doing." This sounds surprisingly like the line of thinking I challenged him with

405. "Report of the International Panel Set Up by the University of East Anglia to Examine the Research of the Climatic Research Unit," University of East Anglia, April 12, 2010, http://www.uea.ac.uk/mac/comm/media/press/CRUstatements/SAP
406. Lawrence Solomon, "Climate-Change Partisans Find Mere Sins of Omission," National Post, April 16, 2010, http://network.nationalpost.com/NP/blogs/fullcomment/archive/2010/04/15/lawrence-solomon-climategate-scientists-we-re-not-guilty.aspx
407. James Delingpole, "Climategate: the Final Nail in the Coffin of 'Anthropogenic Global Warming'?" Telegraph, November 20, 2009, http://blogs.telegraph.co.uk/news/jamesdelingpole/100017393/climategate-the-final-nail-in-the-coffin-of-anthropogenic-global-warming/
408. Bishop Hill, "Climate Cuttings 33," November 20, 2009, http://bishophill.squarespace.com/blog/2009/11/20/climate-cuttings-33.html
409. Michael McCarthy, "Environment in Crisis: 'We Are Past the Point of No Return'," Independent, January 16, 2006, http://www.independent.co.uk/environment/environment-in-crisis-we-are-past-the-point-of-no-return-523192.html
410. James Lovelock, "The Earth Is About to Catch a Morbid Fever That May Last as Long as 100,000 Years," Independent, January 16, 2006, http://www.independent.co.uk/opinion/commentators/james-lovelock-the-earth-is-about-to-catch-a-morbid-fever-that-may-last-as-long-as-100000-years-523161.html

during my visit to his home in 2002. His other colleagues have undoubtedly raised similar points, that there is a possibility we are a positive force rather than an entirely negative one.

It is clear Lovelock was rattled by the revelations in the thousands of leaked emails from the Climatic Research Unit. During his first interview after the "Climategate" scandal he stated, "Fudging the data in any way whatsoever is quite literally a sin against the holy ghost of science. I'm not religious, but I put it that way because I feel so strongly. It's the one thing you do not ever do." And he was surprisingly warm toward skeptics, allowing, "What I like about skeptics is that in good science you need critics that make you think: 'Crumbs, have I made a mistake here?' If you don't have that continuously, you really are up the creek...If you make a [computer] model, after a while you get suckered into it. You begin to forget that it's a model and think of it as the real world."[411]

Some of his recent statements are chilling. Lovelock contends that, "We need a more authoritative world...even the best democracies agree that when a major war approaches, democracy must be put on hold for the time being. I have a feeling that climate change may be an issue as severe as a war. It may be necessary to put democracy on hold for a while."[412] If we are indeed preventing a new ice age, then why is it like a war, and why must we suspend democracy? Perhaps Lovelock just can't make up his mind which it is, catastrophe or salvation. In any case he provides good reason why brilliant scientists who have been cloistered in labs and research institutes most of their lives should not be running the government.

Conclusion

Beginning in the 1980s a widespread alarmist view has developed regarding future climate change. The United Nations, most national academies of science, the majority of political parties, the mainstream media, many scientists, and virtually all environmental activist groups have come to believe that if human emissions of CO_2 continue at present levels the global temperature will soar, resulting in untold destruction to civilization and the environment. This has caused many countries to consider, and even to adopt, policies to reduce fossil use to levels that could cripple their economies.[413]

As of 2013 it has become clear that the global temperature stopped rising 16 years ago, after a 20-year period of increasing temperature. This is despite the fact that CO_2 emissions have continued to rise at an increasing

411. Leo Hickman, "James Lovelock: 'Fudging Data Is a Sin Against Science'," *Guardian*, March 29, 2010, http://www.guardian.co.uk/environment/2010/mar/29/james-lovelock
412. Ibid.
413. "New Energy for America," Organizing for America, http://my.barackobama.com/page/content/newenergy_more

rate. No scientist professes to know why global warming has stopped, but many continue to believe humans are driving a "climate catastrophe." Experts and opinion leaders who have publicly bought into the climate crisis hypothesis are obviously reluctant to change their views. They can't do so without losing face, having invested their reputations in such a high-profile issue. There is a sense that the true believers have become the real deniers.[414]

Considering that the increase in temperature has stopped for the time being, and noting the three issues of the "Climategate" scandal, the collapse of the Copenhagen conference, and the errors in the 2007 IPCC report, it seems clear that the foundation of climate change alarmism has been shaken. Many top scientists have made public statements to distance themselves from the supposed prevailing view.[415] [416] [417] One of the most influential skeptical voices is that of physicist Freeman Dyson, considered one the world's most brilliant thinkers by many of his peers.[418] A feature article that made his views on climate clear appeared in the *New York Times Magazine* in March 2009 and turned a lot of heads.[419] He said, "The climate-studies people who work with models always tend to overestimate their models," and "They come to believe models are real and forget they are only models." He explained, "Most of the evolution of life occurred on a planet substantially warmer than it is now, and substantially richer in carbon dioxide." Dyson referred to Al Gore as climate change's "chief propagandist," and as someone who preaches "lousy science, distracting public attention from more serious and more immediate dangers to the planet."

While the author of this article politely derided Dyson's point of view, there was no doubt about where one of the great thinkers of our time stands on the subject. I think one Freeman Dyson is worth 10,000 true believers who mimic one another, falsely claiming that there is an "overwhelming consensus" and extolling, "the vast body of evidence showing the world is warming because of man-made greenhouse gas emissions" without providing any details of the "vast body of evidence."

In recent months a number of mainstream media outlets, including many British and American newspapers, have abandoned their strong biases and are now publishing articles that are balanced and even skeptical of human-caused warming. The collapse of the "overwhelming

414. "In Denial: The Meltdown of the Climate Campaign," Steven F. Hayward, *The Weekly Standard*, March 15, 2010, http://www.weeklystandard.com/articles/denial
415. "The Deniers," Wikipedia, http://en.wikipedia.org/wiki/The_Deniers:_The_world-renowned_scientists_who_stood_up_against_global_warming_hysteria,_political_persecution,_and_fraud
416. Marc Morano, "Scientists Write Open Letter to Congress," ClimateDepot, July 1, 2009, http://climatedepot.com/a/1745/Scientists-Write-Open-Letter-to-Congress-You-Are-Being-Deceived-About-Global-Warming-Earth-has-been-cooling-for-ten-years
417. Neil Reynolds, "Please Remain Calm: The Earth Will Heal Itself," *Globe and Mail*, July 19, 2010, http://www.theglobeandmail.com/news/opinions/please-remain-calm-the-earth-will-heal-itself/article1642767/
418. "Freeman Dyson," Wikipedia, http://en.wikipedia.org/wiki/Freeman_Dyson
419. Nicholas Dawidoff, "The Civil Heretic," *New York Times*, March 25, 2009, http://www.nytimes.com/2009/03/29/magazine/29Dyson-t.html

consensus" is good news for everyone who believes this topic should be discussed openly and objectively. There is a breath of fresh air in the climate change debate.

There is much work to do in trying to validate or reject the assertions of the major players in climate science. They include the Climatic Research Unit of the University of East Anglia, the U.S. National Oceanic and Atmospheric Administration, the Goddard Institute of Space Science of the U.S. National Aeronautics and Space Agency (NASA), and the Intergovernmental Panel on Climate Change. All these top agencies are implicated in the "Climategate" scandal and are being investigated by various authorities. The U.K. Institute of Physics' submission to the Parliamentary Committee investigating the leaked emails from the Climatic Research Unit made these observations:[420]

1. The Institute is concerned that, unless the disclosed e-mails are proved to be forgeries or adaptations, worrying implications arise for the integrity of scientific research in this field and for the credibility of the scientific method as practised in this context.

2. The CRU e-mails as published on the Internet provide prima facie [at first sight] evidence of determined and coordinated refusals to comply with honourable scientific traditions and freedom of information law. The principle that scientists should be willing to expose their ideas and results to independent testing and replication by others, which requires the open exchange of data, procedures and materials, is vital. The lack of compliance has been confirmed by the findings of the Information Commissioner. This extends well beyond the CRU itself – most of the e-mails were exchanged with researchers in a number of other international institutions who are also involved in the formulation of the IPCC's conclusions on climate change.

3. It is important to recognize that there are two completely different categories of data set that are involved in the CRU e-mail exchanges:
   - those compiled from direct instrumental measurements of land and ocean surface temperatures such as the CRU, GISS and NOAA data sets; and
   - historic temperature reconstructions from measurements of 'proxies', for example, tree-rings.

4. The second category relating to proxy reconstructions are the basis for the conclusion that 20th century warming is unprecedented.

---

420. Steve McIntyre, "Institute of Physics Submission," *Climate Audit*, February 26, 2010, http://climateaudit.org/2010/02/26/institute-of-physics-submission/

Published reconstructions may represent only a part of the raw data available and may be sensitive to the choices made and the statistical techniques used. Different choices, omissions or statistical processes may lead to different conclusions. This possibility was evidently the reason behind some of the [rejected] requests for further information.

5. The e-mails reveal doubts as to the reliability of some of the re-constructions and raise questions as to the way in which they have been represented; for example, the apparent suppression, in graphics widely used by the IPCC, of proxy results for recent dec-ades that do not agree with contemporary instrumental temper-ature measurements.

The Institute of Physics has no reason to exaggerate or to hold any bias. The Institute makes it clear that the information provided by the Climatic Research Unit may not be credible or trustworthy. Clearly it will be some time before the "science is settled."

On May 29, 2010, Britain's top science body, the Royal Society, an-nounced it would review its literature on climate change in order to reflect the skeptical view. The Royal Society stated, "Any public perception that science is somehow fully settled is wholly incorrect—there is always room for new observations, theories, measurements." Along with the change of tone by the London Science Museum this marks a sharp turning point, from certainty and "overwhelming consensus," to a balanced dialogue on the subject. One can only hope that other major science bodies will adopt the same policy.

At this writing the developments in the climate change debate are changing faster than the climate itself. The public is becoming more skep-tical by the day, while the believers work doubly hard to shore up their position, assuring us warming will eventually return in earnest. This may be, but it is not happening now, and even If warming does recur in future, that by itself won't prove that we are the main cause. I remain open to new information and continue to follow the discussion on a daily basis.

Some readers will argue that I have only presented the skeptical side of the debate. This is only because the historical evidence, what has actually occurred, does not support the idea that we are the primary cause of global warming, never mind that its impacts will be "catastrophic." All the pre-dictions based on computer models in this world can't change history or manufacture the future. For that we must patiently wait. Meanwhile we should embark on the path toward a future that focuses on sustainable energy as outlined in Chapter 15. We could gradually reduce our over-whelming reliance on fossil fuels and replace some of them with cleaner, sustainable energy sources. This will satisfy many agendas, including the agenda of the believers in human-caused climate change.

CHAPTER TWENTY-TWO:

Charting a Sensible Course to a Sustainable Future

Having grown up around boats and as I still spend quite a bit of time at sea, I have always been attracted to nautical expressions as metaphors for the greater human enterprise. Stay the course, steady as she goes, all hands on deck, alter course, full speed ahead—damn the torpedoes. As crew members of this mighty galleon called planet earth, we all have a duty to help chart a course to a sustainable future. But there is discord among the ranks, right up to the senior officers on the bridge. The breakdown of the Copenhagen climate negotiations in December 2009 indicates how divergent the visions for our future have become. Since then Canada has quit the Kyoto Protocol and the United States, Japan, Russia, and France have indicated they will not sign a second round of Kyoto scheduled for 2015. We have struck a large reef, so we must have been off course.

My friend Dave Hatherton's late father told him, "The best thing about falling down is getting back up again." I don't believe we need to go back to square one, but we certainly do need to rethink how we could get back on a sensible tack. I suggest setting the following course:

We should recognize that the liberal democratic form of governance is the right model for balancing individual rights and social responsibility. There is no place for dictatorship, totalitarianism, or fundamentalism of the Taliban variety in a sustainable world. As Winston Churchill said, "democracy is the worst form of government, except for all the others." Those countries that enjoy freedom of expression, assembly, religion, and individual rights should increase their efforts to defeat, peacefully if possible, the kind of repression and corruption that exists in so many countries, including Zimbabwe, North Korea, Saudi Arabia, and Iran.

Our public policies on everything from agriculture to zebra conservation should be based on science and logic. The hysteria that has crept into and taken over the environmental movement must be replaced by a commitment to a more logical approach that balances human needs with environmental values. Some species will be reduced or perhaps even lost in the evolution of life during this era of increasing human dominance. At the same time we should do what we can to protect areas of wilderness and the species that depend on them. But humans should not play second fiddle to other species except where a majority consciously chooses to do so. And we should not choose to do so on the basis that we are somehow inferior to other species.

Perhaps the greatest flaw in the more extreme environmental rhetoric is the tendency to characterize humans as a disease on the earth. This, in combination with doomsday predictions, causes people, especially young people, to give up hope for the future. Nothing could undermine more our prospects for finding solutions to environmental problems. We need bright young citizens with hope for the future, citizens who can apply their intelligence to solving problems and who can reject policies based on faulty logic and bad science.

In the introduction I outlined the positions that I would argue over the course of this book. As I repeat them here, I hope you will consider them again and determine if you now have some new perspectives on these important issues:

- We should be growing more trees and using more wood, not cutting fewer trees and using less wood as Greenpeace and its allies contend. Wood is the most important renewable material *and* energy resource.
- Those countries that have reserves of potential hydroelectric energy should build the dams required to deliver that energy. There is nothing wrong with creating more lakes in this world.
- Nuclear energy is essential for our future energy supply, especially if we wish to reduce our reliance on fossil fuels. It has proven to be clean safe, reliable, and cost-effective
- Geothermal heat pumps, which too few people know about, are far more important and cost-effective than either solar panels or windmills as a source of renewable energy. They should be required in all new buildings unless there is a good reason to use some other technology for heating, cooling, and making hot water.

- The most effective way to reduce our dependence on fossil fuels is to encourage the development of technologies that require less or no fossil fuels to operate. Electric cars, heat pumps, nuclear and hydro-electric energy, and biofuels are the answer, not cumbersome regulatory systems that stifle economic activity.
- Genetic science, including genetic engineering, will improve nutrition and end malnutrition, improve crop yields, reduce the environmental impact of farming, and make people and the environment healthier.
- Many activist campaigns designed to make us fear useful chemicals are based on misinformation and unwarranted fear.
- Aquaculture, including salmon and shrimp farming, will be one of our most important future sources of healthy food. It will also take pressure off depleted wild fish stocks and will employ millions of people productively.
- There is no cause for alarm about climate change. The climate is always changing. Some of the proposed "solutions" would be far worse than any imaginable consequence of global warming, which will likely be mostly positive. Cooling is what we should fear.
- Poverty is the worst environmental problem. Wealth and urbanization will stabilize the human population. Agriculture should be mechanized throughout the developing world. Disease and malnutrition can be largely eliminated by the application of modern technology. Health care, sanitation, literacy, and electrification should be provided to everyone.
- No whale or dolphin should be killed or captured anywhere, ever. This is one of my few religious beliefs. They are the only species on earth whose brains are larger than ours and it is impossible to kill or capture them humanely. Anyone who needs proof of this should view the 2009 Oscar-winning documentary *The Cove*, an exposé of the Japanese capture and slaughter of dolphins.

For me, the most gratifying result of the 15 years I spent with Greenpeace is that many whale species are now recovering around the world. It is disturbing that a few countries— namely, Japan, Iceland and Norway— continue to kill whales in violation of the moratorium established in 1981. I hope this will someday end and that these gentle creatures will once again live without fear of humans, as they did for 60 million years before we began to hunt them.

I encourage you to take the helm and in your own way help chart a course for a sustainable future, for the benefit of the environment and all the thousands of species, including our own, that live on this beautiful planet.

Index

Asamoa-Baah, Dr Anarfi 286
Asia 8, 57, 192, 230, 259, 271, 273, 291, 340, 370
Associated Press 308, 312
Association, American Heart 156, 157
Atlantic 18, 103, 104, 133, 143, 144, 146, 147, 156,
160, 161, 164, 185
Atomic Energy Commission 48
Australia 96, 110, 120, 121, 127, 143, 189, 192,
199, 228, 246, 266, 297, 304, 305, 306,
307, 314, 315, 329, 355
Avatar 9, 366

B

Bacon, Sir Francis 342
Bailey, Michael 94
Baird, John 329
Ballem, Peter 84, 86, 97, 98, 99, 100, 101, 106,
108
Barack Obama 117, 209, 259
Bardot, Brigitte 85, 86, 88
Bay, Hartley 92
BBC 34, 303, 312
BC Carbon Project 171, 177
BC Hazardous Waste Commission 180
B.C. Round Table on the Environment and the
Economy 163, 171, 177
BC Salmon Farmers Association 173
Belarus 236, 237
Belle Isle 74, 75, 77, 84, 86, 87
Bering Sea 47, 132
Bertrand Russell 41
beta-carotene 289, 292, 293, 295, 296
Beyer, Dr. Peter 292
Big Sur 310
Bikini atoll 48
Bill and Melinda Gates Foundation 299, 300
Binational Softwood Lumber Council 201
biocide 282
biodiversity 6, 8, 11, 15, 147, 174, 175, 187, 192,
193, 275, 282, 294, 301, 307, 308, 311,
313, 316, 318
biofuels 10, 17, 36, 210, 269, 389
Birmingham, Dave 50, 51
bisphenol A 329
Bisphenol A 329
Black Death 281, 282
Blanc Sablon 84, 85, 87, 88
blue whale 64
Blue whales 64
Bob Peart 165
Boeing 226
Bohlen, Jim 5, 50, 51
Bohlen, Marie 46, 53, 55
Bombardier 226
Bomb, The Population 56, 57
Bonneville Power Authority 225
Borgese, Elizabeth Mann 132

A

abalone 1, 159, 160
Adler, Robin 315
Africa 8, 57, 90, 188, 189, 205, 209, 225, 243,
249, 255, 256, 257, 266, 271, 273, 285,
286, 291, 300, 304, 334, 340, 352, 355,
369
agriculture 6, 8, 11, 15, 16, 25, 28, 44, 126, 147,
188, 189, 273, 274, 275, 276, 278, 281,
284, 287, 290, 299, 300, 306, 318, 333,
337, 338, 351, 388
Akutan 2, 49, 50
Albany 96
Alert Bay 52
Alzheimer 41, 144
Amchitka Island 48
American Association for the Advancement of
Science 317
American Tree Farmers 198
Ames, Dr. Bruce 283
Ames Test 283
Ammonia 279, 320
Amnesty International 336
Amundsen, Raold 371
anchovies 152, 153, 159
Anglia, University of East 349, 358, 366, 381, 385
Antarctic 355, 370, 371, 372, 373, 374
Antarctica 64, 90, 306, 347, 353, 355, 362, 371,
373, 374
aquaculture 6, 132, 133, 134, 143, 144, 148, 149,
151, 152, 153, 156, 157, 159, 160, 165,
274, 299
Arctic 229, 256, 353, 354, 355, 370, 371, 372, 373,
374, 376, 382
Argentina 173, 256, 259, 298
Arias, Dr. Oscar 276

Borlaug, Dr. Norman 57, 275, 280
Bowerman, Steve 100
Brand, Stewart 9, 208, 337
Brazil 125, 189, 197, 226, 227, 246, 268, 297,
298, 306, 332, 350, 353
Brent Spar 185
British Columbia 5, 2, 22, 43, 44, 47, 49, 92, 106,
108, 113, 114, 138, 143, 144, 146, 148,
149, 158, 163, 164, 165, 171, 175, 176, 181,
200, 201, 214, 227, 310, 311, 312
British Columbia Science Council 171
British Petroleum 238, 262
Broughton Archipelago 148, 149, 151
Brown, Lester 370
Brozek, Mirko 85
Brundtland Report 13, 164
B.T. San Diego 114, 115
Bulgaria 259
Burson-Marsteller 172, 173, 181
Bush, George W. 325

C

Cabo Pulmo 214, 376
cadmium 142, 199, 320, 324
California 16, 17, 43, 53, 63, 67, 68, 70, 78, 80,
94, 103, 106, 114, 129, 132, 158, 160, 191,
207, 211, 219, 221, 272, 302, 310, 317
California gray whale 63
California redwood 310
Cambrian explosion 303
Cameron, James 9, 382
Campbell, Gordon 200
Campbell, Tom 95
Canada 2, 2, 43, 44, 46, 48, 51, 61, 72, 73, 74,
100, 101, 105, 108, 109, 110, 113, 114, 116,
117, 120, 125, 126, 129, 130, 132, 133, 143,
151, 157, 161, 163, 164, 165, 166, 172, 174,
181, 182, 189, 190, 200, 201, 226, 227,
231, 232, 233, 242, 255, 259, 264, 265,
268, 272, 281, 282, 302, 312, 329, 332,
336, 340, 347, 353, 354, 355, 387
Canadian Standards Association 198
Canadian Wood Council 201
Candu 237
canthaxanthin 154, 159
Cap la Hague 252
carbon 36, 141, 145, 170, 171, 177, 187, 190, 195,
196, 197, 236, 260, 261, 267, 268, 277,
343, 344, 360, 362, 365, 375, 380, 382,
384
carbon dioxide 36, 170, 171, 187, 197, 260, 344,
384
Carl Bosch 279
Carlin, Alan 361
carotenoids 153, 154
Carson, Rachel 284, 287
Cartagena Protocol 290

Cartwright 99, 100
Castle, Jon 136
Caston, Phil 97, 102
Cat's Meow 130, 131
causation 20, 351
Center for Global Food Issues 276
Central Coast 49, 311
Cerrado 306, 307
Certification 198
cesium-137 47, 236, 250
Chechik, Michael 120
chemical mutagenesis 288
chemicals 5, 10, 11, 20, 26, 30, 56, 139, 141, 142,
153, 154, 155, 203, 244, 246, 267, 276,
277, 278, 282, 283, 284, 285, 288, 319,
320, 321, 322, 323, 330, 331, 333, 334, 345,
360, 362, 389
Chernobyl 208, 236, 237, 238, 239, 245
Chernobyl Forum 237
Chile 143, 158, 189, 268, 277
Chilliwack 46
China 8, 47, 48, 53, 133, 189, 197, 205, 212, 219,
226, 227, 228, 235, 238, 245, 246, 255,
256, 259, 260, 266, 267, 268, 270, 280,
297, 321, 334, 336, 337, 338, 350, 351, 370
Chinook 135
chlorine 5, 6, 25, 31, 127, 139, 140, 141, 142, 249,
277, 278, 282, 320, 322, 323, 328, 329,
362
Churchill, Winston 177, 388
CIA 48, 94
Circle, The Closing 56
Circumpolar Conservation Union 156
clearcut 39, 40, 192, 193, 194
Cliena 37
climate change 10, 11, 14, 20, 21, 22, 32, 33, 34,
36, 113, 170, 178, 195, 196, 197, 202,
203, 204, 207, 228, 233, 259, 308, 312,
316, 317, 342, 343, 345, 346, 349, 350,
351, 352, 354, 355, 356, 359, 361, 362,
364, 366, 367, 370, 377, 380, 381, 383,
384, 385, 386, 389
Climategate 349, 357, 358, 369, 381, 382, 383,
384, 385
Climatic Research Unit 349, 358, 366, 381, 382,
383, 385, 386
CNN 34, 72, 303, 312
CO2 36, 170, 195, 196, 203, 204, 208, 224, 227,
228, 232, 264, 267, 268, 275, 277, 342,
343, 348, 349, 350, 351, 355, 356, 357,
358, 360, 361, 362, 363, 364, 365, 375,
376, 383
CO2 Science 348, 355, 364, 376
coal 18, 33, 145, 205, 208, 210, 219, 220, 221, 223,
224, 226, 227, 228, 233, 238, 247, 259,
260, 263, 265, 266, 267, 268, 270, 271,
321, 324, 360
Coastal Alliance for Aquaculture Reform 144
Coldfish Lake 108

Cold War 5, 47, 51, 80, 235, 237, 251
Collingwood, Reg 119
Columbia River 78, 226, 311
Commoner, Barry 56
Connaghan, Chuck 165
Connecticut Kleen Energy 238
consensus 4, 122, 128, 138, 163, 165, 166, 167,
168, 169, 177, 261, 311, 344, 347, 367,
384, 385, 386
Copenhagen 350, 357, 368, 382, 384, 387
Copernicus 21, 25
Copper River 156
coral reefs 343, 351, 374, 376, 377, 380
Cormack, John 47, 49, 50, 51, 67, 93
Cornerbrook 102
correlation 20, 22, 361, 362
Correlation 20, 351
Crichton, Michael 28, 34
Cronkite, Walter 50
CRU 366, 381, 382, 385
Cryosphere 374
CSA 198
Cuellar, Xavier Perez de 137

D

Darnell, Bill 49, 50, 51
David and Lucile Packard Foundation 158
David Suzuki Foundation 144, 158
DDT 284, 285, 286, 287, 333, 334
Decker, Emily and Nate 74
Decker, Nate 74
Decker's Boarding House 74
Declaration in Support of Protecting Nature 276
deforestation 8, 15, 188, 189, 190, 191, 192, 193,
194, 196, 307, 308
Deforestation 191
Denmark 110, 147, 329
Department of Fisheries and Oceans 130, 149, 151
devil's element 5, 6, 25, 141, 278, 362
dioxin 5, 139, 140, 324
dirty dozen 286
Discover 317, 363
Dominique Prieur 137
Doney, Lee 163, 165
Don't Make a Wave Committee 2, 46, 51
Drake, Judy 119
Dr. Potrykus 292, 293, 294, 295
Dr. Truth 4
Dryden, Sam 300
Dudley, Nigel 181
Dulles, John Foster 234
Dungeness crab 162
Dyson, Freeman 384

E

Earth Policy Institute 272, 370
Easton, Fred 71, 83, 118, 130
ecological succession 194
ecology 1, 2, 4, 5, 6, 34, 43, 44, 45, 52, 53, 54, 67,
109, 175, 180, 183, 192, 193, 194
Edison, Thomas 63, 225
Ehrlich, Paul 56, 57
Eisenhower, Dwight D. 234
electrical grid 211, 212
Electric cars 10, 389
Embraer 226
Environmental Protection Agency, 157, 324, 360
EPA 324, 325, 330, 361, 362
Europe 6, 55, 62, 88, 89, 97, 103, 104, 105, 107,
108, 125, 135, 147, 181, 189, 192, 201,
219, 222, 227, 230, 237, 262, 264, 272,
290, 291, 311, 325, 340, 347, 355
European corn borer 287
European Food Safety Authority 330
European Photovoltaic Industry Association 219
extinction 3, 22, 32, 34, 61, 62, 63, 64, 127, 142,
148, 149, 275, 301, 302, 303, 304, 305,
306, 307, 308, 309, 310, 311, 312, 313,
314, 315, 316, 317, 318, 343, 352, 374
Exxon Valdez 93

F

Farmers, American Tree 198
farming 6, 7, 8, 10, 17, 127, 132, 133, 134, 135, 143,
144, 145, 147, 148, 149, 150, 151, 155, 157,
158, 159, 160, 161, 164, 173, 176, 189,
190, 193, 238, 275, 276, 277, 278, 279,
280, 284, 285, 288, 296, 306, 307, 309,
313, 337, 389
feed-in-tariff 220, 221, 223
fertilizer 132, 145, 249, 277, 279, 280, 281, 319
Figueiredo, Trevor 5, 181
Finland 232, 259
fin whale 64
Firnung, Bernd 75
fission products 236, 237, 244, 245, 250, 251, 254
Flannery, Dr. Tim 314
Flipper 65
food 3, 6, 7, 8, 10, 11, 14, 15, 17, 20, 27, 29, 35,
36, 38, 43, 47, 48, 56, 57, 62, 63, 77, 80,
83, 87, 95, 108, 121, 125, 127, 128, 130,
132, 134, 141, 143, 144, 145, 146, 152, 153,
154, 158, 161, 176, 184, 188, 189, 190,
191, 204, 213, 245, 273, 274, 275, 276,
281, 282, 283, 284, 285, 288, 289, 290,
291, 299, 300, 305, 307, 308, 319, 328,
330, 337, 343, 352, 353, 360, 365, 366,
370, 389
Ford Foundation 43
Forest Action Network 184

Forest Alliance of B.C. 171
ForestEthics 195, 196
Forest Practices Code 174, 175, 312
forestry 7, 15, 19, 41, 43, 60, 93, 126, 127, 165, 171,
    172, 173, 174, 175, 176, 177, 178, 181, 182,
    183, 184, 189, 190, 191, 192, 193, 194,
    195, 196, 197, 198, 199, 238, 307, 308,
    309, 311, 312, 313, 318
Forestry 43, 176, 177, 178, 179, 180, 190, 196,
    198, 276, 307, 313, 316
Forest Stewardship Council 198
Forgacs, Dr. Otto 171
Fowler, Ron 59
France 2, 3, 28, 47, 48, 53, 54, 55, 56, 57, 58, 76,
    88, 107, 108, 135, 136, 137, 221, 223, 224,
    227, 232, 233, 234, 252, 254, 255, 257,
    259, 329, 331, 343
Francis, Diane 336
Frankenfoods 25, 289
Friends of the Earth 88, 110, 126, 208
Fullerton, Arnie 180

G

Gaia Hypothesis 202, 203, 323, 365, 366
Galato River 135
Gallon, Gary 67, 125
Ganges River 370
Gannon, Bill 105
Garcia, Jerry 94, 95
Gates, Dr. David 43
Geldof, Bob 209
Genetic Science 7, 273
George, Russ 132
geothermal 17, 36, 206, 207, 211, 228, 229, 230,
    231, 232, 233, 269, 271, 272
geothermal heat pump 211, 229, 230, 231, 232
Germany 27, 88, 119, 139, 172, 181, 185, 219, 220,
    221, 223, 232, 266, 268, 329
Getting to Yes 165
Ghostbusters 14
giant sequoia 310
Gibbons, David 100, 101, 109, 116, 183
global warming 10, 33, 34, 35, 36, 203, 208, 342,
    343, 344, 345, 346, 347, 350, 351, 352,
    354, 357, 359, 360, 361, 363, 378, 384,
    386, 389
Global Warming 21, 170, 344, 349, 357, 376, 378,
    380, 382
GM cotton 296, 297
Goddard Institute of Space Science 385
Goklany, Indur 30
Goklany, Indur M. 30
Golden Rice 291, 292, 293, 294, 295, 296
Golden Rice Project 295
Goodall, Chris 209
Good Morning America 103

Gore, Al 345, 360, 361, 363, 368, 373, 377, 378,
    380, 384
Grateful Dead 94
Great Bear Rainforest 311
Great Britain 2, 55, 346
Green Building Council 198, 199, 326, 327
Greenland 133, 147, 355, 368
Greenland ice cap 368
Greenpeace 2, 5, 6, 7, 1, 2, 3, 4, 5, 6, 9, 11, 19, 25,
    28, 29, 30, 31, 32, 34, 49, 50, 51, 52, 53,
    54, 55, 56, 57, 58, 59, 60, 65, 68, 70, 71,
    72, 73, 74, 76, 79, 82, 84, 85, 86, 87,
    89, 90, 91, 92, 93, 95, 97, 98, 100, 103,
    104, 105, 106, 107, 108, 109, 110, 111,
    112, 113, 117, 119, 120, 123, 124, 126, 128,
    130, 131, 132, 134, 135, 137, 138, 139, 140,
    141, 142, 143, 144, 165, 171, 172, 173, 174,
    176, 180, 181, 182, 184, 185, 186, 195,
    196, 199, 200, 202, 207, 208, 217, 218,
    219, 226, 237, 242, 243, 245, 247, 265,
    266, 278, 286, 287, 289, 290, 292, 293,
    294, 295, 297, 298, 307, 308, 310, 311,
    312, 319, 322, 323, 324, 325, 327, 328, 331,
    332, 333, 335, 341, 343, 362, 373, 376, 380,
    388, 389
Greenpeace America 106
Greenpeace Canada 109, 110, 113, 117, 265
Greenpeace Foundation 2, 89, 90, 105, 106,
    107, 109
Greenpeace France 107
Green Revolution 57, 280, 294
Greenspirit Strategies Ltd. 181
Gregory, Mel 92, 94, 130
Griffith, Melanie 97
Groombridge, Brian 314
Gudmundsson, Magnus 98
Gulf of St. Lawrence 124

H

Haber-Bosch method 279
Haber, Fritz 279, 280
Hadley Centre for Climate Prediction and Re-
    search 364
Hansen, James 360
Harrison, Hank 72
Harvard University 301, 312
HarvestPlus 295
Hatherton, Dave 387
Hatherton, David 5
Hawaii 67, 81, 82, 83, 90, 93, 95, 103, 131, 307,
    349, 376
Hazardous Waste 180
Health Canada 157
Healthy Building Network 328
Hedren, Tippi 97
Heron, Matt 79, 82
Himalayan glaciers 368, 369, 370

Hiroshima 47, 55, 118, 119, 233, 234, 249
Hiroshima Memorial Peace Museum 234
Hockey Stick 366, 369
Holdren, John 359
Holling, C.S. (Buzz) 44
Holling, Dr. Buzz (C.S.) 5
Holocene Thermal Maximum 348
Holt, Sidney 134
Hope, Brad and June 143
hormesis 246
Horne, Anne-Marie 57, 69
Humanitarian Golden Rice Project, 295
Hume, Mark 151
Hummel, Monte 181
Hunter, Bob 5, 50, 51, 52, 53, 60, 65, 67, 69, 70,
        71, 73, 74, 75, 76, 77, 82, 85, 87, 89, 92,
        103, 108, 109, 111, 141, 182, 183
Hurricane Katrina 377
Husband, Vicky 165
hydroelectric energy 9, 10, 17, 19, 206, 210, 224,
        225, 228, 267, 269, 271, 322, 327, 339,
        388, 389
hydrogen 2, 46, 47, 48, 49, 82, 116, 145, 180,
        208, 245, 255, 256, 260, 261, 264, 277,
        279, 320
hydrogen bomb 2, 46, 47, 48, 49, 116, 180

I

India 8, 57, 125, 189, 197, 205, 246, 252, 255, 259,
        266, 268, 280, 285, 286, 297, 298, 321,
        334, 337, 350, 368, 370
individual tradable quotas 161
Indonesia 189, 197, 266, 321
Institute for Agriculture and Trade Policy 161
Intergovernmental Panel on Climate Change
        170, 195, 196, 343, 344, 346, 356, 368,
        369, 385
Intergovernmental Panel on Forests 308, 309
International Atomic Energy Agency 237, 248
International Commission for Radiological
        Protection 246
International Rice Research Institute 295
International Union for the Conservation of
        Nature and Natural Resources 307
Inuit 62, 124, 354, 355
iodine-131 47, 236, 250
IPCC 195, 196, 197, 343, 344, 345, 347, 356, 357,
        359, 366, 367, 368, 369, 370, 378, 379,
        381, 384, 385
Ipsos Mori 346
Itaipu dam 227
IUCN 307, 309, 314, 355

J

Jackson, Lisa 361

James Bay 77, 78, 79, 80, 81, 83, 91, 93, 94, 95,
        102, 226
James Bay hydro 226
Japan 47, 48, 130, 133, 159, 161, 189, 219, 234,
        252, 254, 255, 256, 259, 264, 274, 306,
        329, 389
Jeanrenaud, Jean-Paul 309
Jeffords, Jim 97
Jocelyn Rice 363
Johnston, Dan 174
Jones, Phil 358, 381, 382
Jonestown 79, 105
Jong-Il, Kim 248
Jr, Robert Kennedy 33, 34, 35
Jr., Robert Kennedy 32
Jurassic Age 62

K

Kaga, Marilyn 82
Kakadu 120
Kamchatka 132
Keddy, Caroline 80, 94
Keep It in the Ground 120
Kent, Lawrence 296
Keziere, Bob 50, 60
Keziere, Robert 49, 50, 51, 52
Khosla, Vinod 270
Kill Malarial Mosquitoes Now! 286
Kimmins, Hamish 45, 178
King, Dr. Martin Luther 43
Kitimat 92, 93, 113, 114, 118
Kohl, Helmut 185
Korea 48, 248, 256, 259, 388
Korotva 91
Korotva, Captain 80
Korotva, George 71, 90
Krause, Vivian 158
Kroesa, Renate 139, 142
Kwakiutl 37, 39, 52, 68, 104
Kyoto Protocol 195, 196, 207, 368
Kyuquot Fisherman's Co-op 41

L

LaLonde, Brice 88
Latvia 227
Law of the Sea 67, 132
Leadership in Energy and Environmental Design)
        198
Leakey, Richard 303
LEED 198, 199, 327
Le Monde 56
Leo Ryan 79, 94, 97, 98, 105
Les Amis de la Terre 88
Levuka 122
Lillehammer 199

Limited Test Ban Treaty 48
Lindbergh, Charles A. 29
Little Ice Age 355, 366, 367
London Dumping Convention 104
London School of Hygiene and Tropical Medicine
     281
London Science Museum 382, 386
Lovelock 383
Lovelock, James 202, 207, 208, 276, 323, 365,
     382, 383
Lovelock, Jim 203, 204
Lynas, Mark 209

M

MacMillan Bloedel 170, 182
Mafart, Alain 137
Major, John 185
malaria 284, 285, 286, 287, 291, 302, 321, 334
Mallard, Derrick 67
Malthus 57
Mann, Michael 366, 369, 381
Marining, Rod 53, 92
Martin, Claude 308
Martin, Pamela Sue 97
Mauna Loa 349
Mavinda Guest House 122
May, Tom and Linda 143
McDonald, Ross 180
McGartland, Al 361
McGovern, George 275
McIntyre, Steve 366, 381, 385
McKibben, Bill 374
McKitrick, Ross 366, 367
McTaggart, David 55, 57, 68, 103, 105, 107, 109,
     113, 119, 131, 134, 136, 140, 142
Meander 92, 118
Medieval Warm Period 355
Mediterranean diet 159
Metcalfe, Ben 5, 49, 50, 53, 54, 55
Metcalfe, Dorothy 53, 55
Mexico 47, 60, 123, 132, 214, 238, 263, 265, 317,
     376
Miller, Henry I. 290
Milner, Anton 219
mind bomb 65, 67
mining 28, 29, 44, 45, 113, 120, 126, 127, 168,
     169, 238, 256, 265, 339, 340, 341, 366
minke 62, 64
Mitchell, Joni 46
molybdenum-99 257
monoculture 192
Monsanto 290, 292, 300
Montefiore, Hugh 208
Moore, Bill 39, 40, 61
Moore, Eileen 5, 59, 60, 61, 67, 71, 74, 75, 76, 83,
     88, 99, 102, 103, 106, 107, 110, 120, 121,
     123, 135, 173, 183, 184, 214, 376

Moranis, Rick 14
Morton, Alexandra 151
Mowat, Farley 9
Muir, John 302
Muldaur, Maria 95
Munro, Jack 171, 172, 173, 181, 182
Murkowski, Frank 155
Murkowski, Lisa 155
Mururoa Atoll 53, 54
M.V. Peacock 102
Myers, Norman 303

N

Nagasaki 47, 118, 119, 233, 249
Nairobi 3, 13, 125, 126, 128, 163, 303
NASA 357, 358, 360, 385
National Aeronautics and Space Agency 385
National Geographic 73, 303, 314, 315, 316, 367
National Oceanic and Atmospheric Administra-
     tion 160, 385
natural gas 33, 205, 208, 210, 223, 227, 228, 238,
     247, 260, 261, 263, 266, 268, 269, 271,
     319, 323
Natural Resources Defense Council 33, 327, 376
Nature 30, 40, 276, 307, 308, 314, 317, 366, 373,
     374, 375, 381
Nawiliwili 81
Netscape News 155
Newborn, Susi 104
New Democratic Party 174, 177
Newman, Dr. Murray 61
Newman, Paul 209
New Scientist 317, 369
New York Times 21, 155, 268, 283, 290, 291, 349,
     358, 384
New Zealand 2, 28, 53, 54, 55, 57, 61, 105, 110,
     117, 135, 136, 137, 139, 143, 185, 189, 207,
     211, 305, 307
Niagara Falls 225
Nixon, President 2, 51
Nongovernmental International Panel on Climate
     Change 344
Norsal 114, 116
North, Art 134
North Sea 111, 185, 186
Northwest Passage 371
Norway 13, 63, 67, 98, 103, 133, 143, 146, 147, 185,
     199, 232, 329, 354, 389
Notre Dame Cathedral 56
Nuclear 9, 48, 53, 202, 206, 208, 209, 210, 233,
     235, 236, 237, 238, 244, 245, 246, 247,
     248, 249, 252, 253, 255, 256, 257, 258,
     259, 267, 388
nuclear energy 7, 9, 18, 19, 25, 113, 120, 127, 141,
     197, 202, 203, 204, 206, 207, 208, 209,
     211, 221, 224, 227, 228, 233, 234, 235,
     237, 238, 239, 244, 247, 248, 250, 251,

252, 256, 257, 259, 260, 266, 267, 299, 322, 327
Nuclear energy 9, 206, 210, 233, 258, 388
Nuclear mutagenesis 288
Nuclear Renaissance 258
Nulabar Desert 96

O

Obama, Barack 117
Ocean Acidification 374, 375, 376
Ohana Kai 93, 94, 95
Oil Sands 264, 265
oil tankers 113
Olympic 114, 199, 200, 201
Olympic Games 199
omega-3 144, 152, 153, 156, 158, 161
omega-3 oils 144, 153, 161
Oregon 310
organic farming 276, 277, 278, 279, 280, 284, 288
Our Common Future 13, 14, 163, 164
Ovalau Club 122

P

Pachauri, Dr. Rajendra 368
Pacific Gas and Electric 270
Pacific Islands 380
Pacific Salmon 44, 45, 133
Palmer, M.R. 374
Parana River 227
Paris Match 87
Partial Nuclear Test Ban Treaty 53
Paul Horn 62
PBDEs 154, 155
PCBs 154, 155, 156
Pedder Bay 130
PEFC 198
Permian era 304
Peru 31, 153, 277
pesticide 7, 281, 282, 283, 284, 289
pesticides 93, 179, 276, 277, 281, 282, 283, 284, 297, 333
petroleum 63, 185, 210, 261, 262, 263, 268, 269, 321, 323
Pew Charitable Trust 155
Philippines 233, 295, 298
Phil Oakes 46
phthalates 20, 324, 325, 330
Phyllis Cormack 47, 50, 51, 66, 67, 68, 79, 81
Pilgrim, Doug 75
Pimm, Stuart 314
Pleistocene Ice Age 347, 348, 352, 353, 371
plutonium 48, 248, 250, 251, 252, 253, 257, 258
plutonium-233 252
plutonium-239 252

Poland 227, 266
polyethylene 323, 324
polypropylene 323, 324
polyvinyl chloride 19, 140
Polyvinyl Chloride 323, 325
Potrykus, Dr. 292, 293
Potrykus, Dr. Ingo 292
precautionary approach 30, 31, 290, 331, 333
Precautionary Principle 29, 30
Prince Philip 309
Prince Philip, the Duke of Edinburgh 309
Princess Patricia 92
Principles of Sustainable Forestry 178, 179, 180
Programme for the Endorsement of Forest Certification 198
Project Cannikin 48
Prudhoe Bay 113
Puget Sound 114, 156
PVC 19, 25, 127, 135, 140, 141, 199, 261, 319, 323, 324, 325, 326, 327, 328, 329
Pyramid of Plastics 319

Q

Quatsino 37, 44, 134, 143, 163
Quatsino Seafarms 134, 143, 163
Queen Charlotte Islands 48

R

Race Rocks 130, 131
radiation 18, 169, 206, 236, 237, 244, 245, 246, 247, 250, 253, 254, 288, 322
Radiation and Public Health Project 244
Rainbow Warrior 104, 111, 112, 113, 123, 124, 131, 132, 135, 136, 137, 185
Rainforest Action Network 7, 172, 176
Ranger Mine 120
Ray Smith 170
RBMK reactor 236, 237
recycling used nuclear fuel 251, 254
reforestation 8, 15, 40, 178, 179, 189, 193, 308, 309
Rémi Parmentier 107
Renewable Portfolio Standards 222, 226
rice 16, 17, 28, 30, 57, 273, 289, 290, 291, 292, 293, 295, 296
Rockefeller Foundation 295
Rokkasho 252
Romania 259
Ron Precious 70, 75, 120
Roosevelt, Theodore 302
Round Table 163, 167, 168, 169, 171, 173, 177
Royal Society 209, 381, 386
Rupert Inlet 44, 45

Russia 48, 70, 94, 119, 132, 133, 161, 234, 236,
        237, 238, 252, 254, 255, 256, 257, 258,
        259, 266, 268, 288, 333, 347, 355

S

sablefish 160
Sacramento Valley 16, 17
salmon 7, 10, 18, 37, 41, 92, 133, 134, 135, 138, 143,
        144, 145, 146, 147, 148, 149, 150, 151, 152,
        153, 154, 155, 156, 157, 158, 159, 161, 162,
        164, 173, 190, 274, 299, 311, 389
Sawyer, Steve 136
Schleede, Glen 225
Schneider, Stephen 359
Schwarzenegger, Arnold 289
science 4, 5, 7, 10, 11, 13, 20, 21, 22, 23, 25, 26,
        28, 31, 33, 43, 44, 45, 110, 133, 140, 141,
        142, 150, 166, 183, 189, 193, 194, 197,
        203, 209, 228, 270, 276, 280, 281, 289,
        290, 292, 297, 299, 300, 307, 309, 314,
        316, 317, 323, 325, 329, 330, 334, 337, 343,
        347, 349, 350, 359, 360, 361, 362, 364,
        366, 368, 369, 373, 375, 381, 383, 384,
        385, 386, 388, 389
Scientific American 268, 317, 354
Scotland 34, 143, 146, 147
Seabright, Judge Gordon 101
Sealand of the Pacific 130, 131
Seal Protection Regulations 75, 101
Sea of Cortez 376
Sea Shepherd Conservation Society 90, 335, 336
Seattle Post-Intelligencer 161
SFI 198
Sheskin 332
Sheskin, Jacob 332
Shiva, Vandana 297
Shumagin Islands 50
Sierra Club, 165, 172, 176, 302
Silva, Lula de 298
silvicultural 179
silviculture 6, 189
Simmons, Terry 5, 50, 51
Sinervo, Barry 317
Singer, Dr. Fred 344
Sisiutl 52, 68, 104
Sixth Great Extinction 302
Skana 61, 62, 129
Slovakia 259
Slow Death by Rubber Duck 325
Smith, Lord Chris 208
Society Promoting Environmental Conserva-
        tion 67
solar energy 17, 28, 197, 207, 209, 210, 211, 212,
        219, 220, 221, 222, 223, 225, 228, 229,
        230, 266, 270
South America 192, 273, 340
South Park 90

Soviet Union 2, 46, 47, 51, 117, 236, 237, 257
Spaceship Earth 128
Spatsizi 108, 113, 119
Spong 91
Spong, Dr. Paul 59, 60, 61, 65, 67, 68, 77, 83,
        90, 129
Spong, Paul 60, 61, 65, 67, 68, 77, 83, 90, 129
spruce budworm 93
St. Anthony 74, 77, 84, 97, 100
Stockholm 3, 55, 56, 57, 125, 164, 286, 333
Stockholm Convention 286, 333
stomata effect 363, 364
Stowe, Dorothy 46
Stowe, Irving 46
Strait of Georgia 312
Strait of Juan de Fuca 114
Straits of Belle Isle 86
Strangway, David 164
Strategic Arms Limitation Treaty 257
St. Roch 371, 373
strontium-90 47, 236, 244, 245, 250
Strontium-90 47
sustainability 9, 10, 15, 17, 18, 28, 127, 128, 163,
        164, 165, 166, 174, 177, 181, 190, 215,
        220, 233, 254, 268, 269
Sustainability 9, 13, 18, 128, 182, 199, 200, 300,
        312, 326
Sustainable Forestry Committee 177
Sustainable Forestry Initiative 198
Sustainable mining 339, 340
Suzuki, David 144, 156, 158
Sweden 55, 227, 228, 231, 232, 236, 245, 272, 288
Swiss Development and Collaboration Agency
        295
Syndrome, The China 235
Syngenta Foundation 295

T

tailings disposal 127
Taunt, Bob 79, 94, 97, 99, 102, 103
Taylor, James 46
Taylor, Jim 103
Taylor, Peter 134
technetium 257
Tennessee Valley Authority 225
Testa, Chicco 208
Tevlin, Tom 5, 181
thalidomide 332, 333, 334
Thalidomide 332, 333
thorium 18, 211, 246, 252, 258
Thorium 252
Three Gorges Dam 226
Three Mile Island 208, 235, 236, 237, 245
Thurston, Dr. Lyle 60
Tilapia 160
tin 142, 199, 200, 324
Tindale, Stephen 208

tobacco 282, 284, 287, 288, 331
Tooth-Fairy Project 244
Toronto Star 156
Trudeau, Pierre 130
Tussman, David 73, 77, 106, 107
Tutu, Archbishop Desmond 286

U

U.K. 104, 172, 181, 201, 220, 252, 254, 257, 288,
    330, 332, 349, 358, 364, 381, 385
UK Food Standards Agency 281
U.K. Institute of Physics 385
U.K. Mariners Union 104
Ukraine 236, 237, 266
Union for the Conservation of Nature and Natural
    Resources 307
United Nations 1, 3, 56, 125, 132, 137, 163, 164,
    237, 256, 286, 303, 310, 333, 336, 343,
    383
United Nations Department of Economic and
    Social Affairs 336
United Nations Environment Program 125
United States 2, 16, 44, 46, 47, 51, 55, 73, 114, 117,
    129, 143, 201, 209, 221, 238, 252, 254,
    255, 256, 257, 258, 259, 260, 266, 280,
    288, 296, 306, 311, 324, 333, 336, 337,
    345, 350, 351, 353, 354
Universal Declaration of Human Rights 336
University of British Columbia 5, 2, 22, 43, 44,
    106, 164
University of East Anglia 349, 358, 366, 381,
    382, 385
UN World Commission on Environment and
    Development 13
Uranium 18, 169, 210, 250, 320
uranium-235 210, 251
uranium-238 210, 251, 252, 255
U.S. 2, 46, 47, 48, 49, 50, 51, 53, 57, 73, 80, 81,
    90, 94, 97, 105, 106, 108, 110, 114, 116,
    117, 119, 132, 133, 137, 155, 157, 158, 160,
    161, 172, 189, 190, 198, 206, 209, 219,
    221, 222, 225, 226, 227, 228, 231, 232,
    233, 234, 235, 238, 245, 247, 253, 254,
    255, 257, 258, 259, 261, 264, 266, 267,
    270, 272, 275, 278, 282, 283, 284, 296,
    297, 298, 299, 300, 302, 303, 324, 326,
    327, 329, 330, 332, 336, 344, 346, 347,
    350, 353, 360, 373, 378, 385
USAID 284, 286, 295
U.S. Bureau of Labor 238
U.S. Coast Guard 2, 49, 81, 114, 116
U.S. Council on Science and Nutrition 157
used nuclear fuel 203, 248, 250, 251, 252, 253,
    254, 255, 258
U.S. Food and Drug Administration 157, 329, 332
USGBC 198, 199, 326, 327, 328, 329
U.S. Geological Survey 373

U.S. Green Building Council 198, 326
U.S. Homebuilders Association 327
U.S. National Hurricane Center 378
U.S. Nuclear Regulatory Commission 235, 245,
    247
USS Ranger 117
Utah Mining and Smelting 44

V

Valhalla Wilderness Society 175
Vancouver 2, 37, 42, 43, 44, 46, 48, 51, 52, 53, 54,
    55, 57, 59, 60, 61, 65, 67, 68, 70, 71, 74,
    78, 88, 90, 91, 92, 93, 94, 105, 106, 107,
    108, 109, 110, 112, 113, 114, 117, 118, 121,
    125, 129, 130, 132, 158, 180, 181, 182, 183,
    200, 201, 203, 235, 308, 310, 311, 312,
    364, 365
Vancouver Aquarium Society 130
Vancouver Island 37, 44, 52, 114, 130, 203, 310
Vancouver Sun 2, 52, 65, 93, 310, 364, 365
Van der Ven, Monique 97
Vattenfall 268
Vega 55, 57, 66, 68, 69
Vermont Yankee 244
Victoria 130, 311
Vietnam War 43, 44, 46, 51, 54, 139, 235
Vinod Khosla 270
vinyl 19, 20, 127, 140, 199, 261, 278, 323, 324,
    325, 326, 327, 328, 329
VI, Pope Paul 56
vitamin 154, 289, 291, 292, 293, 295, 296, 319,
    328
vitamin A 289, 291, 292, 293, 295
vitamin C 154, 319, 328
vitamin E 289, 291, 296
Vostok station 362

W

Wallace, Jack 75
Wal-Mart 325, 326
Walters, Carl 151
Ward, Barbara 128
War in the Woods 171, 172
Warren Buffet 299, 337
Warriors of the Rainbow 52, 53, 89
Washington University 43
Watson, Paul 69, 70, 75, 76, 77, 82, 83, 84, 86,
    87, 90, 97, 335, 336
Wattenburg, Dr. Bill 73
Watt, James 260
Webster, Henry H. 316
Weyler, Rex 68, 69, 70, 78, 82, 83, 94, 96, 98,
    105, 109, 114, 115, 116, 183, 202
whale 1, 10, 52, 56, 60, 61, 62, 63, 64, 65, 67, 69,
    70, 71, 73, 77, 79, 80, 81, 90, 91, 93, 94,

95, 96, 107, 123, 124, 126, 129, 130, 131,
    142, 154, 155, 306, 389
Whole Earth Catalogue 9, 208, 337
Wildroot 59
Willis, Kathy 316
Wilson, Edward O. 301, 312
wind energy 33, 34, 206, 209, 212, 219, 223, 224,
    225, 382
Winter Harbour 37, 38, 41, 42, 44, 60, 61, 66, 67,
    68, 103, 133, 134, 135, 164, 183, 213, 214
Wood Works! 201
World Conservation Monitoring Center 310
World Health Organization 18, 157, 237, 284,
    286, 291, 292, 295, 321, 329
World Trade Center 247
World War II 40, 47, 234, 284
World Wide Fund for Nature (WWF) 181, 286,
    287, 308, 309, 310, 312, 313, 327, 369
World Wildlife Fund 28, 103, 110, 176, 181, 191,
    307, 354
Woznow, Ron 180
Wright, Jim 108

X

XVI, Pope Benedict 335

Y

Yucatan 62, 304
Yukon 311

Z

Zimmerman, Adam 181, 182

CPSIA information can be obtained
at www.ICGtesting.com
Printed in the USA
BVHW081921100719

553093BV00001B/31/P

9 780986 480829